HOMEGROWN REVOLUTIONARIES
AN AMERICAN MILITIA READER

Edited by D. J. Mulloy

D1419815

ARTHUR MILLER CENTRE FOR AMERICAN STUDIES

Homegrown Revolutionaries
An American Militia Reader
Edited by D. J. Mulloy

First Published by EAS Publishing in 1999
in conjunction with the Arthur Miller Centre for American Studies,
University of East Anglia, Norwich, NR4 7TJ

ISBN: 1-902913-02-7

Production: Julia Bell
Typesetting: Julian p Jackson
Copy editing: Emma Hargrave/Kate Sillence
Cover Illustration & Design: Steve Appleton for Sub-G

Printed by Biddles Ltd.

If we dismiss . . . ideas because they seem irrational to us, we may be depriving ourselves of valuable insights into society.

Christopher Hill, *The World Turned Upside Down*

For my parents, my brother, and Pamela;
and in memory of Josephine Dawson.

Acknowledgments

Much of the research for this book took place during a visit to the Wilcox Collection of Contemporary Political Movements at the University of Kansas in 1998. My thanks to the British Association for American Studies, the Arthur Miller Centre for American Studies at the University of East Anglia, and the Gilchrist Educational Trust for the grants which made that trip possible. I also wish to thank the Wilcox Collection's founder, Laird Wilcox, and the staff in the Kenneth Spencer Research Library, particularly, Rebecca Schulte, Lin Frederickson, Bryan Culip, Deborah Dandridge, Kristen Eshelman, Jennifer Evenson, Mary Hawkins, and Nancy Hollingsworth for making the time I spent in Lawrence such a rewarding and enjoyable experience.

I am extremely grateful to all the contributors to this volume for their permission to reproduce the material included herein. Needless to say the book would not have been possible without them.

Many other people also provided me with assistance during the writing of this book – thank you, Tom and Jo Dawson, Dr. Eric Homberger, Dr. Simon Middleton, Jason Mulloy, David Neiwert, Professor Glenn Reynolds, Nigel Woodcock, Dr. John Zvesper, and particularly Professor Christopher Bigsby, Dr. Richard Crockatt, and Dr. Martin Durham who read early drafts of the manuscript and offered suggestions for its improvement. My thanks as well to Julia Albert, Steve Appleton, Bill Bigge, Emma Hargrave, Kate Sillence, Paul Thompson, Alex Wade and especially to Julia Bell and Julian p Jackson for all their hard work in designing, preparing and checking the book.

Most of all I would like to thank my parents for their unstinting support, and my wife, Pamela, who listened to my ideas before anyone else and read all of the early drafts. Pamela's love, support and encouragement have made this book a reality.

CONTENTS

MILITIA TEXTS

INTRODUCTION

On April 19 1995 a massive bomb exploded outside the Alfred P. Murrah Federal Building in Oklahoma City. One hundred and sixty eight people, including nineteen children, were killed in the blast, and over 500 were injured in what was the worst act of domestic terrorism in American history. The bombing cast a spotlight on to a new, and until then a relatively unknown, political movement in the United States: the militia movement.[1] The issues raised by the emergence of armed civilian militias in America during the 1990s are the subject of this book. It examines the reasons for their formation, their principal beliefs, their claims to legal and constitutional legitimacy, and their roots in American history. It considers the response to their emergence from within the mainstream of American society, and the controversies in which the militias have become embroiled. Principally composed of primary documents – interviews, pamphlets, articles, essays, congressional testimony, presidential statements, press accounts and monitoring agency reports – the aim of the book is to allow the various participants in these controversies to speak, in the main, for themselves.

*

A Short History of the American Far Right

Although the militias are a relatively recent phenomenon, there is nothing new about the existence of right-wing extremism in American life. From the anti-Masonic movement of the 1820s and 1830s, through the anti-Catholic, anti-immigrant Know Nothings of the mid-nineteenth century (so-called because of their habit, when asked about their activities, of replying 'I know nothing'); the Ku Klux Klan of the 1920s; Father Charles Coughlin's National Union of Social Justice in the 1930s; the anti-Communism of McCarthyism in the 1950s and the John Birch Society of the 1960s, such extremism has always been present in one form or another.[2] David Bennett, in his comprehensive study of the Far Right in American history, *The Party of Fear*, argues that what unites these movements are their efforts 'to combat people and ideas that were seen as alien threats to a cherished but embattled American "way of life"'. They belong, he says, to a 'nativist tradition' in American history which regards America as a 'promised land' in need of 'protectors to preserve its promise for future generations'.[3]

Such beliefs, of course, are hardly remarkable. America is commonly regarded as a 'promised land', and this raises an important question: How exactly do we define extremism? What is it that distinguishes the extremist from the mainstream political actor? For Bennett, the men and women who joined groups such as the Ku Klux Klan or the John Birch Society 'became extremists when they violated democratic procedures and moved outside the norms of democratic society'.[4] In these commonly accepted terms, extremism is therefore seen as a matter of methods, tactics, or style. It is the manner of their politics, rather than the content of their programmes or their beliefs as such, which marks out the extremist. As Laird Wilcox puts it, 'It is not the position they take, but *how* they take it that matters.'[5]

Richard Hofstadter, in his hugely influential 1963 essay, 'The Paranoid Style in American Politics', argued that 'heated exaggeration, suspiciousness and conspiratorial fantasy' are the chief characteristics of how extremists view the world. 'The distinguishing thing about the paranoid style', he wrote:

> is not that its exponents see conspiracies or plots here and there in history, but that they regard a 'vast' or 'gigantic' conspiracy as *the motive force* in historical events. History *is* a conspiracy, set in motion by demonic forces of almost transcendent power, and what is felt to be needed to defeat it is not the usual methods of political give-and-take, but an all-out crusade.[6]

Although it is possible to see the militias as the latest manifestation of 'the paranoid style' in American politics,[7] or as 'the party of fear . . . in a new guise' – a guise in which fear of the federal government has replaced the fear of 'alien threats' to the American way of life in the post-cold war world[8] – there are also more immediate precursors to the militia movement. These include paramilitary-style groups from the 1960s, like William Potter Gale's California Rangers and Robert DePugh's Minutemen and, more recently, those associated with the Posse Comitatus and the Aryan Nations such as the Christian Patriots Defense League, the Covenant, the Sword and the Arm of the Lord, and the Order. Indeed, for some observers, the militia movement is best regarded as the Far Right of the 1970s and 1980s 'repackaged' for the 1990s.[9]

John George and Laird Wilcox point out, however, that none of the paramilitary groups from the 1970s and 1980s were 'as open, as up front with their ideas, or as apparently popular as the current militia movement'.[10] This is an important point because similarity is not sameness, and we must be alert to questions of difference and specificity if the Far Right in America is not to be treated as a monolithic and homogeneous entity. As Leonard Weinberg reminds us, the 'outstanding organizational attribute of the American radical right is its fragmentation'.[11] There is a huge range of groups operating on America's current right-wing fringe including constitutionalists, sovereign citizens, tax protesters, radical anti-abortion activists, Common Law advocates, Second Amendment advocates, militia members, Christian Identity believers, Klan members and neo-Nazis.[12] They are not all the same. They do not all believe the same things or act in the same way. Equally, we should be cautious about viewing extremists *only* in relation to other extremists. If we are to understand groups like the militias, we must be mindful both of the specific factors that have led to their existence and of their relationship with more general trends and developments in American society.

A Diverse and Decentralized Movement

The militia movement began to appear in America in early 1994. However, as will be seen, the idea of forming citizens' militias had already existed within the Far Right for some time,[13] and a Second Amendment group called the American Militia Organization had existed in the 1970s.[14] It is important to note at the outset, though, that what has emerged is not a 'movement' in the conventional sense. There are no national leaders directing militia affairs, nor even a national organization to which all militias belong. Rather, the militia movement is best understood as a diverse, decentralized and, to a large extent, localized collection of groups and individuals with certain shared concerns. These concerns centre around three key themes. First, a strong belief in the Second Amendment and the right of the people to bear arms against the state.[15] Second, considerable distrust of the federal government which, it is felt, has become increasingly intrusive, has overstepped its constitutional boundaries and is attacking personal freedoms and liberties.[16] And third, a fear that the American nation itself is under threat from an international conspiracy that is attempting to institute a 'New World Order'.[17]

The diversity of the militia movement is one of its most interesting features. Militia groups range from the extremely open to the intensely secretive. Some are predominantly paramilitary in nature, others little more than constitutional discussion groups. Most militia members are law abiding citizens, although a small, but significant, number are criminals and terrorists. Some militias are composed of racists, others welcome blacks, Latinos and other members of minority groups. And while some militias are essentially survivalist and have withdrawn from the world and its vices, others have embraced modernity and all the profits to be made from it. Classifying the movement becomes even more complicated when what the Southern Poverty Law Center's Klanwatch programme calls 'militia support groups' are included. These are groups such as the American Freedom Network, Police Against the New World Order or the Outpost of Freedom, which 'promote the formation of militias or provide information and materials to them' but which are not actually 'full-fledged militias' – although, of course, they may evolve into one.[18]

In their book, *American Extremists*, John George and Laird Wilcox suggest that if a group of militia members were selected at random, 'five categories' would be represented in the following order of frequency:

> 1. People generally conservative in outlook, although not very ideological, who are worried about what they see as a repressive government imposing all manner of strictures on them from unfair taxes to gun control.
>
> 2. Would-be adventurers – generally nonideological weekend-warrior types who like to wear camouflage and play soldier in the woods. They watch movies with western and military themes and like to hunt and fish.
>
> 3. Libertarian conservatives who accept some government on the local or state level, but who oppose federal regulations of almost all kinds.

4. Anarcho-libertarians who consider virtually all government as repressive and overbearing. They refer to themselves as 'freemen' or 'sovereigns.'

5. Hard-core extremists who harbor an obsessive conviction that the United States, indeed the world, is in the grip of an all-powerful conspiracy.[19]

As a result of this structural and ideological diversity, gauging the exact size of the militia movement is very difficult. Estimates of the number of militia members, for example, range from 7,000 to 300,000, but when militia 'supporters' or 'potential supporters' are included the figure rises to somewhere between 5 and 12 million.[20] Given that new groups are formed and others disappear almost on a daily basis, and that anyone with a fax or a modem can claim to have formed a militia, the problems for those monitoring the movement are considerable. The government is not allowed to keep track of political groups unless there is evidence that they are engaging in criminal activities and the militias themselves obviously have a vested interest in overstating their own significance. Militia leaders in Texas, Michigan and Montana, for example, have claimed, respectively, 100,000, 15,000 and 10,000 members.[21]

Militia groups can be found throughout America but they have their strongest presence in the western United States. The Anti-Defamation League's 1995 Report, *Beyond the Bombing*, found them to be most active in Montana, Texas, California, and Michigan, followed by Idaho, Arizona, Missouri, Colorado and Florida.[22] They also tend to be located in rural areas and small towns rather than in large cities. Unsurprisingly, those values most strongly associated with 'the West' – self-sufficiency, independence, and a common-sense practicality among them – find frequent expression within the movement and seem to inform militia members' hostile attitudes to the government 'back East'.[23] Indeed, for many militia members government is not only metaphorically 'remote', it is also physically remote. This remoteness causes difficulties for local law enforcement agencies which can find themselves outnumbered and with insufficient resources when they have to deal with problems caused by the militias and related groups.[24]

A striking feature of the militia movement, and one which has been instrumental to its growth, is its use of 'alternative' forms of media such as the Internet, computer bulletin boards, fax networks and short-wave radio. Kenneth Stern, of the American Jewish Committee, argues that the instant communication offered by the Internet in particular has 'more than made up for' the militias' 'lack of an organized center' and has allowed them 'to expand faster' than any comparative group in American history.[25] The ease and speed with which information can pass over the Internet causes considerable concern to those in mainstream America. Plans for making bombs and even biological weapons are said to be widely available, and the Internet's anonymity is seen as fuelling the conspiracism of the militias.[26] For the militias, however, access to such new technologies has allowed them to circumvent the 'biased' mainstream media, and enabled them to 'convey truth to the American people'. Such technologies are seen as vital tools for recruitment and funding.[27] They have also enabled the militias to spread their ideas worldwide. There are militias in Australia and Canada, and it has been suggested that the Far Right in Europe has adopted the idea of 'leaderless resistance' through the Internet.[28]

One of the most controversial aspects of the militia movement's emergence is the extent of its connections with the racist and anti-Semitic Right in America. Monitoring agencies and law enforcement agencies have expressed concern that members of Christian Identity groups, such as the Posse Comitatus and the Aryan Nations, have infiltrated the militias in order 'to present a "patriotic" face to the public and the media' and to exploit the recruiting potential of issues such as gun control.[29] The June 1995 issue of Klanwatch's *Intelligence Report* stated that, of the 224 militia and militia support groups its Militia Task Force had so far identified, forty-five had 'ties to neo-Nazi and other white supremacist organizations'.[30] The militias' proclivity for conspiracy theories are a further cause for concern. The Anti-Defamation League, for example, argues that, 'History has shown that . . . obsessive conspiracy mongering often ultimately fingers Jews or other minorities as scapegoats for the nation's ills.'[31]

Such charges are greatly resented by militia members, who see themselves as the target of a deliberate campaign of demonization.[32] Yet, as some of the militia texts in this volume show, militia members are aware of the need to avoid being *seen* to be white supremacists, or racists. Whether this is because they genuinely do not hold such beliefs, or whether they recognize the need to conceal them is in many cases difficult to determine.[33] The same can be said about the militias' embrace of the Tenth Amendment and their advocacy of 'states' rights'.[34] On the one hand, these beliefs can be seen as a genuine desire for the decentralization of political power and consequent localized government. On the other hand, groups like the Coalition for Human Dignity, the Anti-Defamation League and the American Jewish Committee are suspicious, because these beliefs are historically regarded as providing a 'cover for bigotry'.[35]

There is also concern that even without a deliberate and well co-ordinated plan by racists to exploit the militias, the ideological, organizational and personal links that exist within the world of the Far Right in America, and particularly within the world of the 'Patriot movement', place 'ordinary' militia members at risk of being drawn towards the more hardcore extremist element. Ken Toole of the Montana Human Rights Network has likened this process to a 'funnel moving through space':

> At the front end, it's picking up lots and lots of people by hitting on issues that have wide appeal, like gun control and environmental restrictions, which enrage many people here in the West. Then you go a little bit further into the funnel, and it's about ideology, about the oppressiveness of the federal government. Then further in you get the belief systems. The conspiracy. The Illuminati. The Freemasons. Then it's about the anti-Semitic conspiracy. Finally at the narrowest end of the funnel, you've drawn in the hard core, where you get someone like Tim McVeigh popping out.

The worry for Toole and others who monitor the Far Right in America is the 'bigger the front end of the funnel is, the bigger the number that get to the core'.[36]

Gun Control, Ruby Ridge and Waco

The reasons for the formation of the militias are manifold – as are the reasons why individuals make the decision to join such groups. In the broadest terms, as the documents in this volume show, the militias' emergence is connected to a sense that the United States is a nation in decline: politically, economically, morally and even spiritually. However, it is also widely agreed that the appearance and growth of the militia movement during the early 1990s has to be understood in relation to three specific events: the 'siege' of Randy Weaver and his family at Ruby Ridge, Idaho, in August 1992; the disastrous 'assault' on the Branch Davidian sect of David Koresh at Mount Carmel in Waco, Texas, in April 1993; and the successful passage, in the same year, of a piece of gun control legislation known as the Brady Bill.

The Brady Bill

The Brady Bill was signed into law by President Clinton on November 30 1993. Named after Ronald Reagan's press secretary, Jim Brady, who had been paralyzed in John Hinkley's attempted assassination of Reagan in 1981, the legislation was the culmination of a long and fiercely contested political battle which reflected the contentious nature of the gun control debate in America. The major effect of the law was to institute a five-day waiting period for handgun purchases. This was to enable law enforcement officials to conduct a check on the criminal record of the prospective buyer and to provide a 'cooling-off' period to prevent such guns being bought in the heat of anger or passion. The Brady Bill was followed by provisions in the Violent Crime Control Act of 1994 that banned the sale or use of nineteen types of semi-automatic assault weapons and placed a ten-bullet limit on gun clips. To many observers, particularly those outside the US, such measures might appear relatively minor. Militia members and other pro-gun advocates saw them as an attack on their fundamental constitutional right 'to keep and bear arms', and as harbingers of more restrictions to come.[37]

Ruby Ridge

Randy Weaver was a 'white separatist' who lived with his wife, children and a family friend, Kevin Harris, in an isolated cabin high on Ruby Ridge in the Selkirk Mountains of northern Idaho.[38] He was arrested in January 1991 for selling two illegally sawn-off shotguns to an undercover informant of the Bureau of Alcohol, Tobacco and Firearms (BATF/ATF) but he failed to appear for his February trial. Instead he retreated to his cabin and publicly announced that he would never surrender to the authorities. On August 21 1992, six camouflaged and heavily armed members of the US Marshals Service entered Weaver's land to continue their surveillance of the property and its inhabitants. During their reconnaissance one of the Marshals disturbed the family's hunting dogs. Weaver's fourteen-year-old son, Sam, together with Harris, went to investigate the dogs' barking. They arrived on the scene just as one of the dogs was being shot. A gun battle ensued. Sam was wounded in the arm and then fatally shot in the back and Marshal William F. Degan was shot and killed by Harris.

The FBI sent in its élite Hostage Rescue Team to take command of the resulting stand-off, as hundreds of agents from the FBI, BATF, US Marshals Service, the Idaho State Police and the National Guard surrounded Weaver's cabin. Helicopters and armoured personnel carriers were also brought in. The following day, as he attempted to open the door to the shack where his son's body lay, Weaver was shot and wounded by an FBI 'sharpshooter'. Weaver's wife, Vicki, who stood watching from the cabin door with her ten-month-old daughter in her arms, was then shot and killed by a bullet to the head. The eleven day 'siege' came to an end when Colonel Bo Gritz, a retired Special Forces Officer, and a leading figure in the Patriot movement, together with Jack McLamb, persuaded Weaver to surrender.

Harris and Weaver stood trial in April 1993 for the murder of Marshal Degan and other charges including conspiracy to subvert the United States' government. The jury acquitted Harris on all counts and Weaver was convicted only on two minor charges of failing to appear for his original trial and for committing an offence while on release from a federal magistrate. The jury found that Weaver had been entrapped by the BATF on the original shotgun charge. During the trial the judge accused the FBI of having shown 'a callous disregard for the rights of the defendants and the interests of justice', and subsequent investigations revealed that it had altered its own rules of engagement during the stand-off to allow agents to 'shoot to kill' any armed adult who was outside the cabin, regardless of whether any federal agents' lives were in danger. In August 1995, Weaver's family received $3.1 million in settlement of a civil damages claim they had brought against the federal government.

Some direct connections can be made between the events at Ruby Ridge and the formation of the militia movement. For example, before John Trochmann created the Militia of Montana he was the co-chairman of the United Citizens for Justice (UCJ), a Weaver support group which had been formed during the siege, and he used an UCJ mailing list to promote his new organization.[39] Much has also been made of a meeting, known as 'Rocky Mountain Rendezvous', which took place in Estes Park in Colorado, two months after the end of the siege. Called by Pete Peters, a Christian Identity minister, in protest at the government's handling of events, the meeting was attended by over 150 Far Right activists.[40] Its significance is twofold. First, during the three-day meeting Larry Pratt of Gun Owners of America is said to have advocated the formation of 'unorganized militias'. Second, the meeting endorsed the concept of 'leaderless resistance', an organizational strategy that would subsequently become a notable feature of some militia groups.[41]

However, important as these connections are, it is the symbolic significance of what happened to Randy Weaver and his family which is of greater importance. Ruby Ridge is seen to provide a clear example of oppressive government agencies at work. Not only did the government appear to have employed excessive force, but it seemed to be persecuting Weaver for his unorthodox religious and political beliefs as a 'white separatist' and as a Christian Identity adherent. The huge, high-tech, military-style operation mounted against Weaver, which included round-the-clock, movement-activated video camera surveillance and photo reconnaissance 'fly-overs' by F4 Air Force jets seemed out of all proportion to the relatively minor charges Weaver faced.[42] And it has been alleged that the whole operation was a vendetta on the part of the BATF following Weaver's refusal to act as an informer against the Aryan Nations based at nearby Hayden Lake. Weaver is seen as a man who just wanted to be left alone, who had moved to Idaho to 'home school' his children without interference from the state, but whom the government was determined to persecute.

The events at Waco, Texas, in the spring of 1993 seemed to confirm all the fears and concerns associated with what happened Ruby Ridge. They did so on a much greater scale, with even more tragic consequences.

Waco

About 130 members of the Branch Davidians, an offshoot of the Seventh Day Adventist Church, lived at Mount Carmel in 1993.[43] The 370 acre site was located approximately two and a half miles from Waco itself and had been the headquarters of the Davidians since 1935. The Davidians' leader, David Koresh, was under investigation by the BATF for illegal firearms possession. On February 28 1993, in an attempt to serve an arrest and search warrant on Koresh, over seventy BATF agents, some in camouflage gear and wearing ski-masks, and accompanied by three Texas Air National Guard helicopters, converged on the Mount Carmel complex. As the agents entered the property shots were fired. It is unclear whether it was the Davidians or the federal agents who fired first, but in the ensuing battle four BATF agents and six Davidians were killed.

Over 700 officers from various agencies, including the Waco police, the Texas Rangers, the BATF, the Texas National Guard, and the US Army then surrounded the property, under the overall control – as at Ruby Ridge – of the FBI's Hostage Rescue Team. The siege lasted fifty-one days. It came to an end on April 19 1993 when M60 tanks, modified for demolition duty with battering rams, began punching holes in the walls of the buildings to inject CS gas, in the hope of 'flushing' the Davidians out. Over 300 canisters of this tear gas were pumped into the complex for over four hours as the whole operation was broadcast live on television. A fire erupted in which seventy-four men, women and children were killed. It is disputed whether it was the CS gas that started the fire, or whether it was deliberately started from the inside as part of a suicide pact.[44]

In 1994 eleven survivors stood trial in San Antonio for conspiracy to murder federal agents and other lesser offences. Five were convicted of voluntary manslaughter, two were convicted of weapons charges (one for possession of a hand grenade and the other for the unregistered possession of a machine gun), and four were acquitted of all charges. The Treasury and Justice Departments, responsible respectively for the BATF and the FBI, both subsequently issued reports. The Justice report cleared the FBI of any blame attaching to the deaths at Waco, but the Treasury report found 'disturbing evidence of flawed decision making, inadequate intelligence gathering, miscommunication, supervisory failures and deliberately misleading post raid statements . . . by certain ATF supervisors'. It was also critical of the FBI's handling of events.[45]

The government did not come out of the affair well. As at Ruby Ridge, the sheer scale of the operation raised questions as to the nature of the policing tactics employed; and the original justifications for the raid proved to be largely spurious and have not withstood critical examination. There was no drug-making laboratory at the site; allegations of child abuse, which reportedly swayed Attorney General Janet Reno to authorize the use of tear gas, could not be supported; and far from 'stockpiling' weapons for a confrontation with the government, Koresh appeared to be trading them as part of a legitimate business. Though it is denied by the BATF, the real motivation for the initial high-profile raid seems to have been congressional budget hearings scheduled for March 10 1993. The Agency had been under threat since the Reagan administration threatened to disband it during the 1980s; it apparently needed a high-profile 'success' to improve its chances in the hearings. There is, of course, some irony in the fact that the Agency, which for the militias, and many others, has come to symbolize intrusive, regulatory government, was itself a target of those who wished to cut back on 'big government'.[46]

It is worth pointing out that militia members find events at Ruby Ridge and Waco significant, not because they are supporters of the Branch Davidians or Christian Identity adherents. Rather the significance is, in both cases, that these groups appeared to have been targeted by government agencies because of their minority views. If the government was prepared to violate the rights of these groups, so the militias' reasoning goes, what of those of other 'minorities'? Where would it all end? Who would be next? Michigan Militia member Bob Clarke's feelings are typical in this respect:

> First the feds put that Reverend Moon character in jail for tax evasion, I thought that was a great idea. Then they went after that guy from India with all those limousines in Oregon, which was OK with me too. But I started getting worried when I learned about what happened to Randy Weaver. When the FBI killed all those people in Waco, I asked myself who they were going to come for next, the Baptists?[47]

From the Margins to the Mainstream

Paramilitarism, anti-statism and paranoia are not the sole preserve of those on the margins of American life. Increasingly they are to be found within the political and cultural mainstream. It would be a mistake to ignore these factors when considering the emergence of the militia movement in America during the 1990s.

James William Gibson traces the development of a 'New War' paramilitary culture in America from the late 1960s to the early 1990s in his book *Warrior Dreams*. He sees the 'vast proliferation of warrior fantasies' in this period (evident, for example, in everything from the 'Rambo' films and the popular literature of Tom Clancy, to the foreign policy strategies of the Reagan and Bush administrations in Nicaragua, Grenada and Panama) as an attempt to reaffirm America's national identity in the wake of its defeat in Vietnam and the social, cultural and economic upheavals of the 1960s and 1970s; that is, 'to reverse the previous 20 years of American history and take back all the symbolic territory that had been lost'.[48] Michael Sherry largely agrees with Gibson's thesis but argues that the appeal of paramilitarism must also be seen in relation to the ending of the cold war. The removal of communism as a unifying 'external enemy' has led many Americans, he says, 'to reconceive war in a fundamental fashion – as something waged within America rather than as an international struggle'. Readily finding this attitude in an American political discourse that declares 'war' on drugs or crime, Sherry sees the paramilitarism of urban gangs and right-wing 'lunatic fringe' groups as just 'a more striking example' of the inward shift he identifies.[49]

America, in the post-Vietnam, post-Watergate era, has also witnessed a considerable increase in the amount of mistrust and hostility directed towards the institutions of the state. A succession of individuals, groups, and movements, including the New Left, neo-conservative intellectuals, libertarians, the New Right, and the Religious Right, have attacked the effectiveness, the efficiency, the morality and even the legitimacy of the federal government.[50] During the 1980s, Ronald Reagan promised to get government 'off the backs' of the American people, and his campaign was taken up again by the Republican Party in the 1990s under the congressional leadership of Newt Gingrich. Gingrich's 'Contract with America' promised, in an 'era of official evasion and posturing', to 'restore the bonds of trust between the people and their elected representatives', and to bring an end to government which was 'too big, too intrusive, and too easy with the public's money'.[51] In the November 1994 elections the Republicans won control of the House of Representatives for the first time in forty years and of the Senate for only the fourth time since the Second World War, a result described by Congressmen Phil Gram as 'not just as an anti-Clinton vote' but 'an anti-government vote'.[52] For many observers it was hardly surprising that groups like the militias had begun to form in such a political climate. As David Plotke commented in the summer 1995 issue of *Dissent*:

> After the bombing of the federal building in Oklahoma City, extremist anti-statism has been discovered by the national media. It deserves attention. But the paramilitary groups [connected with the bombing] represent the fringe of a broad popular mood that has flourished in the United States over the last two and a half decades. . . . Before the Contract [with America] a large and sympathetic audience existed for political attacks on the federal government.[53]

Opinion poll evidence highlights the extent to which the American people have grown increasingly distrustful of the state. According to the research of Daniel Yankelovich, in 1964 76 per cent of Americans answered 'always' or 'most of the time' to the question, 'How much of the time can you trust the government to do what's right?' By 1984 the figure was 44 per cent and in 1994, just as the militias were beginning to form, the figure reached 19 per cent, a 'new all time low'.[54] Unsurprisingly, over the same period there has also been a marked decline in the number of citizens who participate in the electoral process. Of the 196 million Americans eligible to vote in 1996, over 100 million did not.[55]

In addition to feelings of mistrust and apathy, Michael Kelly argues that increasingly, Americans are taking a paranoid view of their political leaders and institutions. 'In its extreme form, paranoia is still the province of minority movements', he writes,

> but the ethos of minority movements – antiestablishmentarian protest, the politics of rage – has become so deeply ingrained in the larger political culture that the paranoid style has become the cohering idea of a broad coalition plurality that draws adherents from every point on the political spectrum – a coalition of fusion paranoia . . . [T]he paranoid view of government and of government's allies has become received wisdom for many millions of Americans.[56]

Kelly uses the term 'fusion paranoia' to describe this hostility towards government because although it 'draws from, and plays to, the left and right, it rejects that bipolar model for a more primal polarity' of 'Us versus Them'. In this construct, 'the Us are the American people and the Them are the people who control the people – an élite comprising the forces of the state, the money-political-legal class, and the producers of news and entertainment in the mass media'. Kelly explains how an 'array of related beliefs' follow from this 'fundamental assumption':

> that the governing élite tells lies as a matter of course; that it is controlled by people acting in concert against the common good and at the bidding of powerful interests working behind the scenes; and that it routinely commits acts of appaling treachery.[57]

Examples of 'fusion paranoia' include, says Kelly, the widespread belief among African-Americans that the government 'intentionally spreads narcotics into black communities'; the presidential campaigns of Ross Perot in 1992 – 'the first fusion paranoia candidate for the Presidency' – and Pat Buchanan in 1996; the bestselling success of Pat Robertson's book *The New World Order*; and the array of conspiratorial misdeeds – murder and drug-running included among them – which are routinely laid at the door of both the current incumbent of the White House, Bill Clinton, and his predecessor, George Bush.[58]

American popular culture has also witnessed a huge outpouring of films and television programmes that depict the corruption, conspiracies and cover-ups apparently found at the highest levels of the United States' government in recent years. In *Shadow Conspiracy* (George P. Cosmatos, 1996) the 'president' is the subject of an assassination plot concocted by his White House Chief of Staff and various Pentagon generals. In *Murder at 1600* (Dwight Little, 1997) he is blackmailed by his National Security Advisor, while in *Absolute Power* (Clint Eastwood, 1996) an adulterous head of state played by Gene Hackman covers up a murder committed by his Secret Servicemen. Secret and malevolent government agencies are also seen in such films as *Conspiracy Theory* (Richard Donner, 1997) and *Enemy of the State* (Tony Scott, 1998), and in television programmes like *Dark Skies* and, of course, the *X-Files*.

Interestingly, the militias themselves have appeared in two episodes of the *X-Files*. In 'Tunguska' Special Agent 'Fox' Mulder is given an anonymous warning about a 'right-wing militia group', which is planning 'the next Oklahoma City', and in 'The Pine Bluff Variant' he undertakes a 'deep cover assignment' to prevent a militia group's use of a mysterious bioweapon. The fictitious militia members in these episodes are portrayed as racists, criminals and terrorists, but, ironically, 'real life' militia members might take some comfort in the fact that in both cases the greater enemy is shown to be the federal government. In 'Tunguska' Mulder and Scully learn that the government has been covering up its knowledge of how a Soviet-made 'black cancer' was used by Saddam Hussein during the Gulf War. In 'The Pine Bluff Variant' they discover that the government has been operating its own secret bioweapons programme against the interests of the American people.[59]

*

The militia movement is a new political movement, and the documents collected in this book trace it through the early stages of its development, from 1994 to 1999. For much of this period, millions of Americans, not just those who joined militias, saw the United States as a nation in decline. *The State of Disunion* survey in 1996, for example, reported that half the population felt this way, with a further one in five believing the US was in 'strong decline'.[60] It will be interesting to see how the militia movement develops over the next few years. On the one hand, the American economy is booming again, but, on the other, in the wake of the recent spate of shootings in the US including those at Littleton, Colorado, Atlanta, Georgia and at a Jewish community centre in Los Angeles, California, calls for stricter gun control are becoming ever more vociferous.[61] For different reasons both are factors that could have a profound impact on the future of the American militias.

Notes

1. The two men subsequently convicted of the bombing, Timothy McVeigh and Terry Nichols, were initially thought to be militia members, and although one of the most intensive FBI investigations since the assassination of John F. Kennedy found no evidence linking the bombing to the activities of any militia group, the association between Oklahoma City and the militia movement remains strong in the public mind.

2. See, for example, Daniel Bell (ed.), *The Radical Right* (New York, Doubleday & Co., 1963); Richard Hofstadter, *The Paranoid Style in American Politics and Other Essays* (London, Jonathan Cape, 1966); Seymour Martin Lipset and Earl Raab, *The Politics of Unreason: Right-Wing Extremism in America, 1790–1970* (London, Heinemann, 1971); David Bennett, *The Party of Fear: The American Far Right from Nativism to the Militia Movement* (New York, Vintage Books, 1995); Lyman Tower Sargent, *Extremism in America: A Reader* (New York, New York University Press, 1995); John George and Laird Wilcox, *American Extremists: Militias, Supremacists, Klansmen, Communists and Others* (Amherst, New York, Prometheus Books, 1996).

3. Bennett, *Fear*, 3.

4. Ibid.

5. George and Wilcox, *Extremists*, 56. See also Lipset and Raab, *Unreason*, 5; Michi Ebta, 'Right-Wing Extremism: In Search of a Definition,' in Aurel Braun et al. (ed.) *The Extreme Right: Freedom and Security At Risk* (Boulder, Colorado, Westview Press, 1997), 12–35; and the views of the Montana Human Rights Network and the Anti-Defamation League in this volume at pages 135–137 and 141–143.

6. Hofstadter, *Paranoid*, 29.

7. On the application of the 'paranoid style' to the militia movement see, for example, *Time*, 'Enemies of the State,' (May 8, 1995), 22–31; *Newsweek*, 'The View from the Far Right,' (May 1, 1995), 28–30; Marc Cooper, 'Montana's Mother of All Militias,' *The Nation*, (May 22, 1995), 714–721; Kenneth S. Stern, *A Force Upon the Plain: The American Militia Movement and the Politics of Hate* (Norman, University of Oklahoma Press, 1997) 141; Daniel Pipes and Jerrold M. Post, *Conspiracy: How the Paranoid Style Flourishes and Where it Comes From* (New York, The Free Press, 1997); and Robert S. Robins, *Political Paranoia: The Psychopolitics of Hatred* (New Haven, Yale University Press, 1997). In this volume see the extract from the Anti-Defamation League's Report *Vigilante Justice: Militias and 'Common Law Courts' Wage War Against the Government* (1997) at pages 242–245.

8. Bennett, *Fear*, xi, 469. As will be seen, however, a profound fear of 'alien threats' is also prevalent within the militia movement, particularly in relation to the United Nations.

9. See, for example, James Ridgeway and Leonard Zeskind, 'Revolution U.S.A,' *Village Voice*, (May 2, 1995), 23–26; Morris Dees and James Corcoran, *Gathering Storm: America's Militia Threat* (New York, Harper Perennial, 1996), 4; and in this volume see the extract from Klanwatch's June 1995 *Intelligence Report*, 'Contemporary Militia Movement More Than 30 Years in the Making,' at pages 239–241.

On the paramilitary Right of the 1970s and 1980s see, for example, Kevin Flynn and Gary Gerhardt, *The Silent Brotherhood* (New York, The Free Press, 1989); James Corcoran, *Bitter Harvest: The Birth of Paramilitary Terrorism in the Heartland* (New York, Penguin, 1990, 1995); James Coates, *Armed and Dangerous: The Rise of the Survivalist Right* (New York, Hill and Wang, 1987, 1995); George and Wilcox, *Extremists*, 340–349.

10. George and Wilcox, *Extremists*, 249.

11. Leonard Weinberg, 'The American Radical Right in Comparative Perspective,' in Peter H. Merkl and Leonard Weinberg (eds.), *The Revival of Right-Wing Extremism in the*

Nineties (London, Frank Cass & Co. Ltd, 1997), 248.

12. See, for example, the Montana Human Rights Network's report 'A Season of Discontent' at pages 133–134 in this volume. Collectively, these groups are said to form the 'Patriot movement' in the United States.

13. I am referring here, of course, to the idea of 'private' militias being established by individual citizens, not to the historical and legal institution of the militia based on universal military service as provided for by the Constitution and currently defined in the *United States Code*. Title 10, Chapter 13, Section 311 of the *United States Code* reads:

> (a) The militia of the United States consists of all able-bodied males at least 17 years of age, and . . . under 45 years of age who are, or have made a declaration of intention to become citizens of the United States and of female citizens of the United States who are commissioned officers of the National Guard.

> (b) The classes of the militia are–
> (1) The organized militia, which consists of the National Guard and the Naval Militia; and
> (2) the unorganized militia, which consists of the members of the militia who are not members of the National Guard or the Naval Militia.

The militia was a significant military and political institution in America until the early twentieth century. Militias played important roles in the War of 1812, the Mexican-American War, the Civil War, and the Spanish-American War, for example, as well as being involved in the preservation of 'internal order' through the suppression of slave uprisings, and the policing of labour disputes and other civil disturbances. Disputes between the states and the federal government over the mobilization, training and equipping of the militias, coupled with the need for a more professional army able to fight overseas, led to the creation of the National Guard through a series of legislative enactments beginning with the Dick Act of 1903. The National Guard now performs most of the tasks previously carried out by the militias.

See on this, for example, Lawrence Delbert Cress, *Citizens in Arms* (Chapel Hill, University of North Carolina Press, 1982); John K. Mahon, *History of the Militia and the National Guard* (New York, Macmillan, 1983); Alan Hirsh, 'The Militia Clauses of the Constitution and the National Guard,' *Cincinnati Law Review* (Vol. 56, Part 3, 1988), 919–969; Keith A. Ehrman and Dennis A. Hennigan, 'The Second Amendment in the Twentieth Century: Have You Seen Your Militia Lately?' *University of Dayton Law Review* (Vol 15, No. 1, Fall 1989), 5–57; and Brannon P. Denning and Glenn Harlan Reynolds, 'It Takes a Militia: A Communitarian Case for Compulsory Arms Bearing,' *William & Mary Bill of Rights Journal* (Vol. 5, Issue 1, Winter 1996), 185–214. On reviving the concept of the universal militia see Gary Hart, *The Minutemen: Restoring an Army of the People* (New York, The Free Press, 1998).

14. An American Militia Organization pamphlet is reproduced in Sargent, *Extremism*, 360–366.

15. The Second Amendment reads: 'A well-regulated Militia being necessary to the security of a free State, the right of the people to keep and bear Arms shall not be infringed.' The correct interpretation of these words is a recurring theme throughout this volume.

16. The militias do not regard themselves as 'extremists'; they see themselves as the *defenders* of the American Constitution and of the 'original' republic established by the nation's Founding Fathers. See, for example, the interview with the Missouri 51st Militia in this volume, especially pages 50–51 and 57–59 and 'The American Founding' section at pages 365–376. On the difficulties of defining republicanism, and for a discussion of its

importance in recent American historiography, see Daniel T. Rodgers, 'Republicanism: The Career of a Concept,' *The Journal of American History* (Vol. 79, No. 1, June 1992), 11–38.

17. See the 'Conspiracies and the New World Order' section of this volume at pages 423–446.

18. 'Over 200 Militias and Support Groups Operate Nationwide,' Klanwatch *Intelligence Report* (June 1995/#78) 2. Examples of the views of the group Police Against the New World Order can be found at pages 358–360, 404–408 and 426–434. For criticism of the concept of 'militia support groups' see Laird Wilcox in this volume at pages 292–293.

19. George and Wilcox, *Extremists*, 249.

20. John George and Laird Wilcox suggest the figure 7,000, the Anti-Defamation League thought 15,000 in a 1995 report, researchers Chip Berlet and Matthew Lyons estimated militia membership as being between 10,000 and 40,000, for Marc Cooper it was closer to 100,000, and Glenn Reynolds noted reports of up to 300,000. Morris Dees, Richard Abanes and *Time* magazine are among those supportive of the 5 to 12 million figure for the broader outline of the movement. George and Wilcox, *Extremists*, 260; ADL, *Beyond*, 1 (in this volume at page 235); Cooper, *The Nation*, 714; Glenn Reynolds, 'Up in Arms about a Revolting Movement,' *The Chicago Tribune* (January 30, 1995), 11 (in this volume at page 157); Dees, *Storm*, 32; Richard Abanes, *American Militias: Rebellion, Racism & Religion* (Downers Grove, Illinois, InterVarsity Press, 1996), 2; *Time*, Enemies, 25.

21. Quoted in George and Wilcox, *Extremists*, 256.

22. ADL, *Beyond*, 6–35.

23. See, for example, the views of the Missouri 51st Militia on this at pages 69–70 of this volume, and Norman Olson at page 190.

24. See, for example, the views of local law enforcement officials in this volume at pages 219–231. The search for Eric Rudolph, the anti-abortion activist charged with bombing abortion clinics in Alabama and Georgia, as well as the bombing of the Atlanta Olympics, has shown some of the problems that the law enforcement agencies can encounter. In an article for *The New Yorker* Tony Horwitz reports on how the people who inhabit the area of the Appalachian Mountains, where Rudolph is believed to be hiding, are so hostile to the agencies of the state that they have turned Rudolph into a folk hero. Tony Horwitz, 'Run, Rudolph, Run,' *The New Yorker*, (March 15, 1999) 46–52.

The adverse impact of the militia movement on 'grassroots democracy' in the United States is a concern of monitoring agencies such as the American Jewish Committee and the Montana Human Rights Network. See, for example the extract from their report, 'What to Do When the Militia Comes to Town,' at pages 271–277 of this volume.

25. Stern, *Force*, 228.

26. See, for example, President Clinton on the 'dark underside' of the technological revolution in this volume at page 174.

27. See, for example, Norman Olson's testimony to Congress reproduced at page 197 of this volume.

28. See, for example, Stern, *Force*, 241–244. On the wider relationship between the Far Right in Europe and the US see Leonard Weinberg 'On Responding to Right-Wing Terrorism,' *Terrorism and Political Violence* (Vol. 8, No. 1, Spring 1996), 80–92, especially 85–90.

The strategy of 'leaderless resistance' calls, Morris Dees explains, for organizing groups on the basis of 'autonomous cells, comprised of no more than eight to ten members'. Because these cells are 'organized around ideology not leaders' their infiltration by law enforcement agencies is made more difficult. The idea is said to have been originated by an Aryan Nation's leader, Louis Beam. Dees, *Storm*, 66.

29. 'Racist Extremists Exploit Nationwide Militia Movement,' Klanwatch *Intelligence Report* (December 1994/#76) 1, 4, reproduced in this volume at pages 147–148.

Adherents of the theology of Christian Identity believe that white 'Aryans' are the direct descendants of the 'lost tribes' of Israel, while Jews are children of Satan, and blacks and other minorities are 'mud people'. For further information see Michael Burkun, *Religion and the Racist Right: The Origins of the Christian Identity Movement* (Chapel Hill, The University of North Carolina Press, 1994).

30. Klanwatch, *Intelligence Report*, (June 1995/#78), 1.

31. The ADL, *Vigilante Justice*, (1997), 22–24. Extracts from this report are reproduced in this volume at pages 242–250.

32. See the 'Militia is not an Ugly Word' section of this volume at pages 357–364.

33. See, for example, the 'Recruitment, Organization and Structure' section of this volume at pages 333–355.

34. The Tenth Amendment reads: 'The powers not delegated to the United States by the Constitution, nor prohibited by it to the States, are reserved to the States respectively, or to the people.' For the importance of states' rights to the militias see the interview with the Missouri 51st Militia at pages 57–58 of this volume, and the documents contained in 'The American Founding' section at pages 365–376.

35. Stern, *Force*, 219. See also the Coalition of Human Dignity, 'The American Militia Movement,' (1995), 4.

36. Quoted in Stern, *Force*, 107. See also the extract from the Montana Human Rights Network's report 'A Season of Discontent' in this volume at pages 137–140.

37. Gun control is obviously one of the most contentious issues in American politics, raising questions of public health, crime prevention, constitutional rights and civil liberties, as well as the identity of the nation itself. On the militias' fear of gun control see the 'Gun Ownership and the Disarming of America' section in this volume at pages 391–408.

38. Various accounts of the events at Ruby Ridge are available. See, for example, Stern, Force, 19–42; Dees, *Storm*, 11–68; James A. Aho, *This Thing of Darkness: A Sociology of the Enemy* (Seattle, University of Washington Press, 1994), 50–67; David Kopel and Paul H. Blackman, *No More Wacos: What's Wrong With Federal Law Enforcement and How to Fix it* (Amherst, Prometheus Books, 1997), 32-39; Alan W. Bock, *Ambush At Ruby Ridge: How Government Agents Set Randy Weaver Up and Took His Family Down* (Irvine Press, Dickens Press, 1995); and Randy Weaver et al., *The Federal Siege at Ruby Ridge: In Our Own Words* (Mass Market Paperback, 1998).

39. Stern, *Force*, 41; Dees, *Storm*, 81; and see the extract from the Montana Human Rights Network's report, 'A Season of Discontent' in this volume at pages 139–140.

40. See, for example Dees, *Storm*, 50–69 and Joel Dyer, *Harvest of Rage: Why Oklahoma City is Only the Beginning* (Boulder, Colorado, Westview Press, 1997), 81–84.

41. For monitoring agencies' concerns about the strategy of leaderless resistance see pages 253–254 in this volume. On the militias adoption and advocacy of it, see pages 341 and 351–352.

42. The scale of the surveillance directed at Weaver is described by James Aho as 'historically unprecedented'. *Darkness*, 59.

43. On the events at Waco, see Stern, *Force*, 58–64; Dees, *Storm*, 70–80; Kopel and Blackman, *Wacos*; Dick J. Reavis, *The Ashes Of Waco: An Investigation* (New York, Simon & Schuster, 1995); James Tarbor and Eugene Gallacher, *Why Waco?: Cults and the Battle for Religious Freedom in America* (Berkley, University of California Press, 1995); James R. Lewis (ed.), *From The Ashes: Making Sense of Waco* (Lanham, Maryland, Rowman & Littlefield, 1994); Stuart A. Wright (ed.), *Armageddon in Waco: Critical Perspectives on the Branch Davidian Conflict* (Chicago, University of Chicago Press, 1995).

44. As this book was being prepared Attorney General Janet Reno announced that she was reopening the inquiry into the events at Waco. This was after the FBI admitted that its agents had used potentially incendiary CS gas cartridges in the final hours of the siege.

However, the FBI still denies causing the fire. See 'FBI in Dock for Role in Waco Inferno,' *The Guardian* (August 27, 1999), 13.

45. Quoted in *The New Republic*, 'Not So Wacko,'(May 15, 1995), 18.

46. On these and the host of other issues raised by the events at Waco, see the collected essays in Lewis, *Making Sense*, and Wright, *Armageddon*.

47. Quoted in Mack Tanner, 'Extreme Prejudice: How the Media Misrepresent the Militia Movement,' *Reason* (July, 1995), 44.

48. James William Gibson, *Warrior Dreams: Violence and Manhood in Post Vietnam America* (New York, Hill & Wang, 1994), 14.

On the application of Gibson's thesis to the militia movement see, for example, Peter Doskoch, 'The Mind of the Militias,' *Psychology Today* (July/August, 1995), 13; Garry Wills, 'The New Revolutionaries,' *The New York Review of Books* (August 10, 1995), 50–51; and Stephen Scheinberg, 'Right-Wing Extremism in the United States,' in Braul et al. (ed.), *Extreme*, 62–63. For criticisms of such an approach see Bennett, *Fear*, 468.

49. Michael Sherry, *In the Shadow of War: The United States Since the 1930s* (New Haven, Yale University Press, 1995), 453.

On the impact of the ending of the cold war on the militias see also Bennett, *Fear*, 469–475; Gavin Esler, *The United States of Anger: The People and the American Dream* (London, Penguin, 1998), 15; and Stern, *Force*, 99. While there is some truth to this connection, the documents in this book show that fear of Communism has not disappeared completely from the minds of militia members. It is still expressed, although to a large extent it has became associated with the United Nations and the plans of the so-called 'Global Elitists' for a New World Order.

On the importance of having 'enemies' for purposes of social cohesion see James Aho's *This Thing of Darkness*. Culturally, the militias have, in Communism's absence, found themselves portrayed as a new enemy (see the end of this section).

50. See, for example, E. J. Dionne, Jr, *Why Americans Hate Politics* (New York, Simon & Shuster, 1991) and William H. Chafe, *The Unfinished Journey: America Since World War II* (New York, Oxford University Press, 1995), 431–469.

51. Quoted in David Plotke, 'Against Government: The Contract with America,' *Dissent* (Summer, 1995), 350.

52. Quoted in *Time*, 'Loud and Clear,' (November 11, 1994), 30.

53. Plotke, *Dissent*, 352. On the question of the relationship between the Republican Party and the militia movement see also Albert R. Hunt, 'Stop Encouraging the Crazies,' *The Wall Street Journal*, (April 27, 1995), A15; Stern, *Force*, 217–218; and Dees, *Storm*, 111–136.

54. Quoted in Seymour Martin Lipset, *American Exceptionalism: A Double-Edged Sword* (New York, W. W. Norton & Co., 1996), 282.

55. Quoted in Esler, *Anger*, 209. See also Chafe, *Unfinished*, 458-459.

56. Michael Kelly, 'The Road To Paranoia,' *The New Yorker* (June 19, 1995), 63.

57. Ibid, 62.

58. Ibid, 64–65. At the same time, of course, many within the Clinton White House believe that 'a vast right-wing conspiracy' exists to remove the President from office. On the widespread existence of conspiracy theories in modern American politics see also Pipes, *Paranoid*, 1–19 and Esler, *Anger*, 232–248.

59. The militias have also been quickly absorbed by the larger popular culture, whether as figures of fun to be ridiculed in television programmes such as *King of the Hill*, *South Park*, and *Cybill*, or as multi-purpose 'bad guys' in films including *Face/Off* (John Woo, 1997), *Mad City* (Costa Gravas, 1998), *Mercury Rising* (Harold Becker, 1998), and *Arlington Road* (Mark Pellington, 1998).

Interestingly, themes of global conspiracy, the right to bear arms, and anti-government posturing have become prominent features of rap music and hip-hop culture during the 1990s. Indeed, the idea of citizens' militias have been positively cited by rap groups such as Spearhead on their 1997 LP *Chocolate Supa Highway* (Capitol Records) and Gang Starr on their 1998 LP *Moment of Truth* (Noo Trybe), and the usefulness of gun ownership as both a political weapon and a means of self-defence has been promoted by various artists including Public Enemy, Ice Cube, Ice-T, Wu-Tang Clan, Method Man, Killarmy, and The Firm. For further information regarding forms of resistance in rap politics see Tricia Rose, *Black Noise: Rap Music and Black Culture in Contemporary America* (London, Wesleyan University Press, 1994), especially 99–145.

60. Quoted in Esler, *Anger*, 13. Conducted by Gallup for the University of Virginia Post-Modernity Project, Esler describes *The State of Disunion Survey* as 'one of the most detailed and rich studies of its type conducted during the 1990s'.

61. See, for example, 'The Massacre That Challenges America's Love Affair with the Gun,' *The Guardian* (April 22, 1999), 1–3; 'The Atlanta Massacre,' *Time* (August 9, 1999), 20–32; and 'US Nazis Find Their Latest Hero,' *The Observer* (August 15, 1999), 20.

INTERVIEW

The Missouri 51st Militia

INTERVIEW WITH THE
MISSOURI 51st MILITIA

On the afternoon of Sunday March 22 1998 in Kansas City, Missouri, I met with eight members of the Missouri 51st Militia: Jim McKinzey; his brother, Mike McKinzey; Bill Bingham and his wife Joanne Bingham; Jim Johnston; Jackie Wittig; Rick Hawkins and Kay Sheil. A transcript of the interview which took place that afternoon is reproduced below.

The Missouri 51st Militia was formed by Jim McKinzey, Mike McKinzey, Chuck Wittig and Bob Gurski in the summer of 1994. The four men were friends and members of a number of Second Amendment groups in the Kansas City area – including the National Rifle Association, Gun Owners of America, the Western Missouri Shooters Alliance and Jews for the Preservation of Firearms Ownership – when they decided to form a militia. Naming their new organization for the fifty-one days of the 'siege' of the Branch Davidians in Waco, Texas, which had ended on April 19 1994, the Missouri 51st Militia held its first public meeting at a library in Kansas City in January 1995. Three hundred people attended this meeting and seventy members were sworn in. The group currently claims approximately 100 active members.

The Missouri 51st Militia is organized around a military structure, which its Commander, Jim McKinzey, a former military man (like his brother Mike and Chuck Wittig) compares to 'the Red Cross or the Salvation Army'. The reason for this, according to McKinzey, is simply that such a structure 'works'. Monthly meetings are held for the 51st's staff members who are given titles such as Colonel, Major, Captain and Sergeant. However, for Kay Sheil, the 51st's Special Operations Officer, 'rank isn't very important except if an emergency should arise and then it is needed to dispense reliable information to our members and others'. The 51st portrays itself as a organization of locally based political activists who, in addition to campaigning and lobbying for gun rights, have organized and equipped a portable kitchen to feed local people in case of an emergency, are capable of sandbagging their section of the Missouri River in the event of flooding, and who have also raised funds for such 'worthy causes' as the 'legal defense fund' of Larry Gates, a local man who was charged with weapons offences following his attempt to apprehend two murder suspects. Its members regularly attend the region's gun shows where they supply information on Second Amendment issues and sell Missouri 51st Militia merchandise including mugs, caps, videos, T-shirts and their monthly newsletter, *Necessary Force*.

It is important to point out that this interview is with one particular militia group and its members. As such, it cannot claim to represent the views of the militia movement as a whole, or even those of a 'typical' militia (assuming, of course, that such a group can be found, and there is not enough research available at present to indicate what such a group would look like or how it would operate). Nor, as the interview demonstrates, does the Missouri 51st Militia regard itself in this way. On the contrary, in many respects it sees itself as 'atypical'; as a group which is 'lead[ing] the curve' of the militia movement's development; as providing an example, in terms of its composition, organization and activities, which other militias should follow. Many of the issues that concern and motivate the Missouri 51st Militia, however, are exactly the same as those that concern and motivate other militia groups around the United States. These issues include the extent of Americans' Second Amendment rights and gun control; fears over the increasing powers of the federal government and the dangers of 'big government'; states' rights; concern with the apparent militarization of American law enforcement; and the events which took place at Ruby Ridge and Waco.

What this interview provides is an extensive and detailed illustration of how one particular militia understands and articulates these concerns. Sometimes the 51st's views are clearly in accord with those of the wider militia movement (as with their articulation of the importance of the Second Amendment), and at other times they appear to run counter to the more usually expressed militia views (as with their attitude towards the United Nations).

During the course of the interview one of the 51st's members, Kay Sheil, told me that she thought it was important for those who studied the militias 'to find out just who we are and what we do for a living because we're pretty ordinary middle-class people'. She is right, of course. It *is* important. It is too easy to categorize and dismiss people who join 'extremist groups' as 'nuts' or 'weirdos', to see them only as exemplars of extremism and to forget that they are also 'pretty ordinary people' with families and jobs and their own individual stories to tell; as people with interests and concerns outside their membership of a particular political group. But, it was their membership of that group that had led me to them in the first place. I was interested in them as members of the militia movement. I wanted to understand what it was that had made them want to join a militia and what they hoped to achieve through their membership. As interesting and informative as an account of each of their life stories would no doubt be, I knew that I did not have time during the interview to listen to these stories in detail, and that I would only be able to reproduce them in the briefest form (each person's story could be a book in its own right). In order to deal with these problems, I wrote to each participant after the interview asking them to tell me more about themselves and how they had become involved with the militia movement. My intention was to provide a short biographical sketch of each participant to accompany the text of the interview itself. I hoped that such a sketch would provide some suggestion, however sparse, of the events, people and places that had been important to these militia members; that it might at least partially indicate why they thought of themselves as being 'pretty ordinary'. These biographical sketches precede the interview below.

In addition, I have tried to present the interview in such a way that the reader can get a sense of the eight people who were there, of how they spoke, of what their personal preoccupations and individual concerns were, and of how they related not only to me but also to each other during the course of the afternoon we spent together. The interview is therefore organized chronologically, as it occurred, rather than broken down into thematic sections. If this sometimes leads to apparent digressions or repetitions, it has the advantage, I think, of giving more of a sense of the dynamics of the conversation, and of how particular concerns and issues kept appearing again and again, working themselves back into the conversation. Initially I had approached the interview with specific questions in mind, questions that covered areas of particular interest to me. It soon became clear, however, that a rigidly structured 'question and answer' session was simply not workable with eight people in the room at once, and so although the interview began with some of these questions it soon widened, taking me into areas of discussion that I had not necessarily anticipated. Sometimes a question I asked would not get an immediate or direct response and an answer would come later or in a more oblique manner. I did not try to rein in and control these responses, but let the conversation take us where it would, except where I considered that a particular area of discussion was exhausted or was taking us too far away from the main issues at hand. For the most part, I have endeavoured to let these militia members speak for themselves.

However, despite my efforts to preserve both the individual voices of the participants and the rhythm of the conversation as a whole it is not possible to present the conversation exactly as it occurred. I have removed the pauses, repetitions, and momentary losses of thought, which are a normal part of everyday speech, in order to make the interview more comprehensible as written text. I have also removed many of my own interventions in the conversation, whether these were promptings to continue, acknowledgments of understanding or questions of clarification, so as not to interrupt the flow of the written text too much.

These are the militia members I interviewed and this is what we discussed.

Bill and Joanne Bingham

Bill Bingham was born in August 1929 in New York State. His father was a member of the 121st Cavalry Unit of the New York National Guard. Bill recalls how he and his mother would watch it parade, 'looking proud and serious', every holiday and how they never missed seeing the Cavalry Circus with its 'rough-riders doing all kinds of mounted tricks and comedy routines'.

As a child, Bill says that he 'rode every chance' he got, and when he wasn't riding he 'was climbing'. His father taught him to shoot 'at an early age' and he became 'a pretty fair shot' with both pistol and rifle. 'Much better', he says, than he is now.

When he was sixteen, Bill joined the New York State Guard (formed after the National Guard was mobilized during the Second World War), and marched in the parades he had watched as a child. During national holidays he also worked on 'various firing squad ceremonies' for chapters of the

Erecting a Radio Tower 1996

38

American Legion and Veterans of Foreign Wars. He says he was better at being 'in the Guard' with its close order drills, rifle ranges and two weeks of camp than he was at school, where he was 'mostly lousy' because the teachers 'couldn't hold my interest or couldn't catch it to begin with' and from where he 'barely graduated'.

Having graduated, however, he began working for the New York Telephone Company and joined the 108th Infantry Regiment of the National Guard Headquarters. He became 'a wireman' in the commando platoon, and eventually a squad leader and 'wire chief'. 'It was fun', he says, 'and back then I could go all day and night if I had to'. He 'just missed the draft' for the Korean 'police action', he says, and 'was too old, with too many dependants for Vietnam'.

He has been married three times ('the last one, to Joanne, stuck'), has travelled all over the country indulging his 'proclivity for riding, canoeing, caving, mountain climbing and shooting', has 'squeezed in thirty odd credit hours of college time', and 'after clearing the ground' himself has also built his own house in Kingsville, Missouri, where he now lives. 'Life's been a blast, and I'd probably do it over in much the same way if I had to do it again,' he says.

When he heard about militia groups forming, Bill 'inquired and joined', hoping it wasn't 'too late to start setting the situation right without leading to real bloodshed'. His disillusionment with American politics, however, had begun much earlier after 'money grubbers ruined Joe McCarthy' and after the Vietnam War, when 'some said we were fighting the advance of Communism, but we were just making a bunch of rich fat cats fatter and richer'. 'The Communists', he says, 'took over the reins of our government' and now 'the most financially powerful Communists are in Washington DC and Wall Street'.

Rick Hawkins

Rick Hawkins was born and grew up in Kansas City. He dropped out of high school in the tenth grade, aged seventeen, in order to join the United States Army. 'I remember thinking something like I was tired of people telling me what to do, not exactly rocket scientist material,' he says. During his five years of service in the Signal Corps he worked on digital telephone communications. He was posted to Georgia and Texas and to Germany for three years.

Rick is now forty-three and married with a fourteen-year-old daughter. He lives in Smithville, Missouri, and works for United Telephones 'on the long distance end of things'. A keen outdoors man, his hobbies include rock-climbing, water-skiing, windsurfing, cycling, and shooting ('anything I can whenever I get the chance'), as well as weight lifting, martial arts, photography and 'struggling with learning the classical guitar'.

Rick says that he had always been 'very politically opinionated, but never to the point of actually doing anything about it' until he heard about the 51st Militia. He joined at its first public meeting and has been its Executive Officer for the past three years, with responsibility for the planning and organizing of the 51st's training exercises and classes, including its firearms and rappelling training. 'I joined the 51st because there were certain aspects of the military that I still kind of missed,' he says. He saw the militia, at least initially, as a means 'to get hooked up with other like-minded individuals . . . to run around in the woods and play with my gun'. However, not having 'had much luck' with this he found himself 'much more interested in the political side of things'.

Rick characterizes the militia in military terms as a 'deterrent', as a means of preventing the government from 'doing anything it wants'. It's 'much like our army in Europe was a deterrent to the Soviet Union during the cold war', he explains, 'Yeah, they could wipe us out, but it would be a mess.'

Jim Johnston

Jim Johnston was born in Kansas City in May 1953 and grew up on his family's farm in Unionville, Missouri. He graduated from his local high school in 1972 and married Carolyn in 1981, and helped to raise her three children from a previous marriage. They now have an eleven-year-old grandson. Jim works as a truck driver for the Ash Grove Cement Company. He says that he 'loves to hunt and fish' and is a regular worshipper at his local church, the Church of Christ in Raymore, Missouri.

Jim joined the Missouri 51st Militia in 1996 and is now a 'Captain', responsible for ensuring that both supplies and staff make their way to the local gun shows in good time. He joined, he explains, because he felt it 'was the best way to serve my country'; he was unable to serve in the military because of 'physical problems'. 'If you love your country', he says, 'you will do what you can to serve it.' As a lover of 'freedom and liberty' he saw those ideals as increasingly under threat.

Mike and Jim McKinzey

Mike and Jim McKinzey are two of the founders of the Missouri 51st Militia. Mike was born in 1952 in Phoenix, Arizona, and his younger brother, Jim, was born in Wichita, Kansas, in 1954. The sons of an Air Force Sergeant, many of their early years were spent moving around the country with their father's postings. As they were growing up they spent time in Maine, South Dakota, Oklahoma, Missouri, California, and the island of Guam.

In 1971, after graduating from Ruskin High School in Kansas City and completing a semester at junior college, Mike enlisted in the United States Army. He was trained as a helicopter weapons technician and did a tour of duty in Vietnam. When he finished his Army service he worked nights at the county jail and went to the University of Missouri in Kansas City during the day, where he obtained his degrees in physiology and criminology.

Mike is now a self-employed repairer of photocopiers, fax machines and printers. He married in 1984 and divorced in 1987. He has a twelve-year-old daughter, and says it was his fears for her future and his sense of the general loss of people's personal freedom that led him to get involved in forming the 51st. He is now a 'Major' in the 51st Militia and its Public Information Officer.

Commander Jim McKinzey

'It is my opinion', he says, 'that the freedoms the founders of this country said are God given and should be protected by government are now dead, freedoms like property rights, ethical taxation, self-protection and so on. I don't fight to save this country – it's already gone – but to limit how bad it must get before it turns around.'

Jim McKinzey dropped out of high school in the eleventh grade. He enlisted in the Army in February 1972 as a Combat Engineer and during the whole of his year and a half service he 'never left the state of Missouri'.

After the Army, Jim went to work for the Power and Light Department of the city of Independence, Missouri, first as 'a tree trimmer', then 'unloading coal cars' for the power plant, and finally as a boiler operator in the power plant, a job that lasted eleven years.

In 1984 he joined V. P. Porter Roofing Company and after six years was made vice-president. He and his wife, Paula, now own the company. Jim says that he does 'most of the estimating, manages the crews, orders materials and deals with the day-to-day running of the company', although his wife remains 'the boss'. Jim and Paula were married in 1974 and have two sons, aged twenty-five and twenty-two.

'Forming the 51st', he says, 'was something that after talking about it, just kind of happened, like it was the right time and place.' 'History', he says, 'is full of such examples', when the right men and women came together 'for a purpose when it was needed.'

Kay Sheil

Kay Sheil was born in Evening Shade, Arkansas in June 1943. She lived there with her maternal grandparents for four years while her parents, as part of the war effort, were working in the Kansas City defence factories. A housing shortage in the city meant that her parents were unable to find a home for the whole family until 1947 when Kay and her two brothers moved to live with them. She has lived in Kansas City ever since.

Kay was educated in the local public school system and graduated from high school in the spring of 1961. Shortly after her graduation she married and had two daughters. She now has four grandchildren. After her divorce from her first husband in 1975 she says she found it necessary 'to go back to school' and continue her education in order 'to get the skills I needed to get a good paying job'. She attended Penn Valley Community College and the University of Missouri in Kansas City. Her major was in journalism but she gained enough 'legal credit hours' during her studies for her to be taken on as a 'special investigator' with the Prosecuting Attorney's Office in Jackson County, Missouri, in September 1977.

'My job with the PA's office', she explains, 'was to investigate delinquent child support cases.' This involved locating the parent who 'was out of the home and not contributing to the support of his or her minor children' and then assisting the attorneys in either enforcing existing court orders or working to establish new ones. She worked with the PA's Office until 1987.

In 1980 she married Harold Sheil, a Battalion Chief with the Kansas City Fire Department. Harold retired from the department after thirty-three years of service in 1992. He served in the US Army from 1951 to 1956 and was a veteran of the Korean War.

Both Kay and Harold joined the Missouri 51st Militia in February 1995. Kay says that they 'felt the need to stand up and make a statement about the abuses of the federal government, especially the abuse of the Second Amendment. After the government massacre of the people at Waco both Harold and I felt we would be as guilty as those who carried it out and covered it up if we didn't speak up. The militia seemed to be the perfect organization for us to join and get our point across.'

Harold Sheil was the 51st's first Public Information Officer, and Kay its first Executive Officer. She is now a 'Major in charge of Special Operations', a role she sees as being 'basically public relations'. Harold was planning to run for a position of State Representative when he died in March 1996.

Kay says that she has never regretted her decision to join the militia, she sees it as 'one of the best things' she has ever done. 'Even if we don't make things change', she says, 'at least it won't be said that we stood back wringing our hands and doing nothing while the ideal of individual liberty and freedom died in my country.'

Jackie Wittig

Jackie Wittig is fifty-six years old and married to Chuck, one of the founders of the Missouri 51st Militia. She has four children and six grandchildren. She was raised in a small town in central Iowa called Belle Plaine where she was educated at the local high school. She moved to Kansas City when she was nineteen. Her parents were 'strong supporters of the Constitution and the Rule of Law'. 'All her life' they 'ingrained' in her the importance of the 'right to free and open speech, the freedom of religion, the right to bear arms and all the other freedoms and rights' that she sees as being guaranteed 'first by God and secondly by the Constitution'. These values, she says, simply became part of her 'belief system'.

Jackie says her concerns grew over the years as she saw how these 'precious freedoms were withered due to bad legislation and the compromises of some Congressional members'. When the opportunity came to align herself with 'others of similar beliefs' she joined the 51st 'without reservation'. 'By joining together, people are stronger and more likely to be heard,' she explains.

She says she has a 'hard time' understanding why some people are fearful of the militias when the 'American militia is so basic to constitutional thought'. 'The militia was what was responsible for freeing Americans from oppression in the very beginning of our young country', she says, and now, 'when oppression is rearing its head again, the militia is also here.' Her emphasis though is on 'education and knowledge' – these, she says, are the 'swords we must use today'.

The Good-Ol'-Boys Protest October 1996

INTERVIEW

Mulloy

Let's begin by talking about history. It seems that the contemporary militia movement is a political movement which is very interested in, and very affected by, American history. And I know that because of its role during the Revolution the militia is a very important institution in American history. Can you tell me something about this, about how you feel about the history of the militia, and about how it affects what you're doing at present?

M. McKinzey

Well, I don't think there are many examples in history where the people, the founding people of a country, like the founders of this country, were all armed. I guess the very idea of an armed population was a little bit unique anyway, so I don't know outside of the United States if there are other examples of this . . .

Bingham

There *are*: England and Switzerland primarily. Some of the earlier English kings – after the Magna Carta I think it was – decided that it would be a whole lot cheaper to have the populace armed than it would be to keep a standing army, and so this was what they did. That book, *Safeguarding Liberty*, has some real good information in it about this.[1] And, of course, the Swiss went to it, I guess that was after the Napoleonic Wars – which was the last time that they were invaded – and I think what they have now is what the founders envisioned for this country, but it has gone by the board here.[2]

Sheil

I like the militia – and this is an attitude I've developed over a while – because of the Second Amendment. Most of us started out as Second Amendment advocates, and I think what happened at Waco proved to us that if you have guns and feel it is your right to bear arms that someday the ATF might come and try and take those guns from us, so we ought to have all of this history behind us.

Our Supreme Court has only heard one Second Amendment case and that was *United States v. Miller*, and it came about because two Treasury Agents – or Revenue Agents as they were called then – were following a couple of moonshiners.[3] They thought they were going to catch these moonshiners making illegal liquor. They didn't, but when they arrested these guys they noticed that one of them had a shotgun – and there had been regulations expanding the powers of the Bureau of Alcohol and Tobacco during Prohibition, and having a shotgun barrel shorter than a certain length wasn't a crime exactly, but it was a breach of these new regulations – so they were arrested for that.

This case went all the way to the Supreme Court, but by the time it got there Mr Miller was dead and nobody knows what happened to his lawyer. He never answered the call, so basically it's a default judgement.[4] Now in that judgement the Supreme Court affirmed the right of militias to be armed so I say today, with what's going on with gun control, that we're actually protecting our right to be armed. They say an 'individual' isn't supposed to have a weapon, they say it's a 'group right'. Well, *we're a group*, so we're protected by the Constitution.

Bingham

There's an awful lot of argument about that, too. Because there are people, who are experts in semantics and what have you, that claim that there *is* an individual right; that you can tell from the other numbered rights in the Bill of Rights that where the founders meant 'state' they said 'state', and where they meant 'people' they said 'people', and that the two are not interchangeable in the way they're used. So there is an individual right to bear arms in the Constitution.[5]

M. McKinzey

Yeah, you're right.

Sheil

It *is* an individual right, yes, but for the sake of legalities in the climate today, if they say that I don't have an individual right to have a gun, but I do have a group right to have a gun, then it's 'either/or', you know.

Mulloy

So that even if an individual right to bear arms isn't recognized by the courts in today's climate, you're saying you have a group right . . .

Sheil

Yes. And the Supreme Court in *Miller* ruled that that's correct. So here we have an official position, and if they want to keep pushing it, then it's going to be a face-off.

Mulloy

Do you anticipate a militia taking a case to the Supreme Court in order to get this clarified, in order to make it absolutely clear what rights you do have?

Sheil

Not at this time. Right now I don't want to go anywhere near the Supreme Court with a Second Amendment case.

Mulloy

The political climate isn't right for it?

Sheil

I don't believe it is. And you know, they don't want to hear one either. So it's sort of like another face-off. What we have is this creeping disarming of individual citizens going on. It's got to the point, from some of the things they propose, that it's not just disarmament, it's: 'You can have guns, but you can't have the ammunition,' or 'You can only have so many guns,' 'You can only have twenty guns,' – maybe it's going to be twenty – or you have certain regulations placed on you and so on and so forth. It's like Jim here, he's probably got 100 guns. Now, why would he be any more dangerous tomorrow than he is today?

Bingham

You can't use but one at a time.

[Laughter.]

Sheil

That's right, you know.

Johnston

And they're going to regulate the ammunition as well as the guns. In other words, if you've got over, say, 100 rounds of ammunition they're wanting to regulate that, and if you've got more than 100 rounds then they want you to have a permit so that you'd be in the same classification as a gun dealer – and I'm against that.

M. McKinzey

From a practical point of view, I think that, before that would happen, the problem we're going to run into is that groups like ours and even other groups, other purely Second Amendment groups, like Jews for the

Preservation of Firearms Ownership and Gun Owners of America, aren't going to stand for it.[6] We – our group – has said specifically – openly and publicly – that we aren't going to abide by any additional gun control laws. 'Pass them if you want but we're just going to ignore them.' So we're going to have a practical, hands-on problem before there's a Supreme Court ruling.

Sheil

Ever since we said that, though, they haven't passed any. I don't know if we've had any effect, it just seems strange. In 1995 or 1996 there was a proposal for Brady Bill Two and we started a massive campaign through the Internet and with brochures and things like that, and it just sort of slid away, and what we heard was they weren't going to do it like that any more, they were going to try it piecemeal, a little bit at a time.

There was a Supreme Court case which involved guns which a lot of people thought was a Second Amendment case, but this was about having a gun within a thousand meters of a school building. And this was struck down by the Supreme Court because it didn't fall under the federal government's powers under the interstate commerce and trade clause of the Constitution.[7] But then they placed it back, knowing full well that they can use this against people and harass people until it goes to the Supreme Court again, which is a long and expensive process. So you have it going back and forth while the general population out there doesn't even realize what's going on.

Mulloy

It seems clear then that this is the key issue. The key issue is gun control.

Sheil

The key issue for the militias is gun control, but we're also very interested in our other rights, our First Amendment rights, Fourth Amendment rights, property rights, all these things.

We feel right now that it's the First Amendment we're using and the First Amendment is very important. I would say that maybe it's the most important, but the reason we can do this is because we have some power. The power comes through the weapons.[8]

J. McKinzey

If, through legislation, they take the Second Amendment away from us, we have nothing to back up our other Bill of Rights.

M. McKinzey

I agree. I wouldn't say that I think the Second Amendment is the most important right. I wouldn't say that. I would probably fall on the First. But, if you lose the Second, you lose the rest. I think the right to protest, the right to address grievances is far more important, but unfortunately without a gun you're just screaming against the wind. You're banging trashcan lids together and then they put you in jail.

Sheil

It's a strange concept for anybody from Europe or England because you live without being armed, and it is a strange thing, you know. You really have to try to adjust to it, but think of it this way: Germany disarmed itself when Hitler came to power, and I know Mike asks a lot of people this – anti-gun people, gun control people: 'If you had had a weapon when they were marching Jews off to the concentration camps, would you have used it to help free them?' The irony is that they gave up their weapons so they had no way to protect themselves.

And people believe, here in this country and all over the world – what we call the civilized world – that it'll never happen again. I doubt that, I think it will happen again somewhere. It happens all the time.

M. McKinzey

It's happened *since* then.

Johnston

History repeats itself.

Sheil

One of the greatest groups for getting information about the history of gun-control and genocide is the group called Jews for the Preservation of Firearms Ownership and they have a webpage . . .

M. McKinzey

I think they list eight or ten genocides since the Holocaust.

Sheil

Right, the latest being in Rwanda, and that shows that if people have nothing to defend themselves with, then you can guarantee something bad will happen.

Mulloy

Let me ask you this. Militias obviously existed and were fairly active during the eighteenth and nineteenth centuries, but they haven't been particularly active throughout much of twentieth century – although there is an argument, which I'm sure you're familiar with, about whether the National Guard effectively became the militia during this period – so why is it, at the end of the twentieth century, that you found the militia to be an appropriate vehicle to bring your concerns forward?[9]

M. McKinzey

When the militias were active they were active against tyranny. In this case, the only difference is that the tyrant is our own government.

Sheil

That was the case the first time around as well.

Bingham

Well, that's what the founders said. They said that the greatest enemy was not from outside the country, it was from your own government – always. The National Guard when it was formed, it was the militia – what they call the select militia – and the founders were very much against select militias because select militias were more or less obligated to the government. After the start of World War One they had to change that because they couldn't send the militias overseas. So a militia law was passed which meant they couldn't be sent overseas. They put through some Act – I don't know what Act it was – but they put through some Act and changed it to make the militia a portion of the army. So actually we're a portion of the army.[10]

Mulloy

I think what I'm getting at is: Why did you choose to form a militia instead of another kind of anti-gun control organization?

Sheil

Well, the militia were the ones who stood up in 1776 –

J. McKinzey

Against great odds.

Sheil

– and the militia is an honorable institution, a well-respected institution in the United States, even though the media and politicians try to say otherwise. We hear things all the time and it's pretty amazing. We hear that 'Chinese militia were accused of killing people in Tiannamen Square.' But there's *no* militia in China. There couldn't be because a militia is an armed citizen. We hear about 'militias in Africa'. *What* are they talking about? But they use this word loosely, you know.

Mulloy
So how would you define the militia, in this country, now?

Sheil
It's an armed citizen who's willing to stand up for his community, his state and his country.

[Jackie Wittig arrives.]

Johnston
See, in the state constitution we're legal as a militia group. We're legal in that sense. And we wanted – I don't think I'm speaking out of turn here – we wanted to stay legal and to be law abiding. Now if we named our organization anything other than a militia then we probably wouldn't be legal. And that goes back to what our forefathers did in the early making of this country – they did it with a militia group.

Mulloy
So there's the historical example – and that's very important – but there's also the practical point that if you are going to protest against gun control legislation then you need to have an organization that's legal in order to do it. It's the two things together.

Sheil
I may be being a little arrogant here, but I think that if you search the whole United States you won't find another militia organization like this.

Mulloy
In what sense?

Sheil
In the sense that we aren't trying to put together an army to attack something. Of course, we believe the militias have the right of self-defense, but . . .

J. McKinzey

And we're extremely open. Everything we do is extremely open.

Wittig

You won't find us building bombs to attack a federal building or anything like that.

Sheil

A militia would never take action against the citizens of its own country unless –

Wittig

No, absolutely not.

Sheil

– unless it was called up by the governor or an official sheriff. In fact, in our country, the sheriff is the highest ranking officer who can call up the militia – the sheriff or the governor – and if they did call up the militia then we would do what we would have to do at the time.

But most of our group are just ordinary people, and I think it's important to find out just who we are and what we do for a living because we're pretty ordinary, middle-class people.

To study us is not to study the whole militia movement in the United States – I think that's what I'm trying to say.

Mulloy

Well, that brings me to another of my questions because the militia, nationally, is a very varied movement, with different groups operating in different parts of the country with their own particular concerns and strategies. What I would like to know is: What's your relationship with the wider militia movement? Is it just a case of, 'OK we're this group here and we do what we think is right, and we're open and we're political.' And if that is the case, then do you get any kind of backlash from other parts of the movement?

Sheil

We do get some backlash.

J. McKinzey

When we first got started – some four years ago – there was a lot of effort put into communicating and meeting with these other groups around the country, and Mike and I made several road trips all over the country to attend these meetings. But we decided that that wasn't the route we wanted to go. We are a Kansas City based militia and we're taking care of our area. We still have contact with these other groups just kinda 'FYI' [for your information] but they don't tell us what to do, and we don't tell them what to do.

Sheil

We found that a lot of the militia movement was built on a cult of personality. They came here, to Independence, Missouri, for some meetings of the militias, and they had two meetings here – what they called the Second Continental Congress – but we didn't attend those meetings because we found them to be just so –

M. McKinzey

Silly!

[Laughter.]

Sheil

– Yeah, silly, and just not worth our time with people raving about black helicopters and UN soldiers. We aren't raving about UN soldiers or black helicopters.

J. McKinzey

We outnumber them.

[Laughter.]

Sheil

I mean the UN has no soldiers itself. The biggest bulk of their soldiers come from the United States and then Europe – England and France, places like that. And I don't think the British or the French are going to want to send their military over here. I just don't buy that.

Wittig

And some of the other parts of the militias – not a lot, but some of them – are really white supremacists in disguise. That's not us. We have black members, we have a Jewish member. Our thing is to include everybody.

J. McKinzey

It makes no difference to us.

Sheil

Our militia has lived through a transition from where we were going at the beginning. Now, to be a member of the Missouri 51st Militia – you can just be a supporter, but to be a member – you have to sign a pledge, be open to the public and carry an ID card. The reasons for that are varied, but one of the reasons is that we're not ashamed of what we do.

There is a movement now that goes around and thinks up these single cell groups where they have two or three people and they're spying and things like that – well that doesn't do any good, that only causes more trouble. Then we have the government itself creating *agent provocateurs* who try to incite people into doing illegal things.[11]

So we took this route, and we probably lost a lot of members by doing that.

Mulloy

By staying public?

Sheil

By staying public and being open.

M. McKinzey

The modern militia movement has evolved tremendously in the last three or four years. Like Kay says – not to sound egotistical – somebody's got to lead the curve and the 51st is one of those groups. There are several others: the First Volunteers in St. Louis is one, and New Jersey has got some good groups, and California's got some good groups, groups that are probably very similar in philosophy to ours. But Kay's right, the vast majority of the smaller militia groups unfortunately just haven't kept up.

Wittig

It takes a great deal of commitment: there's time involved, there's money involved and effort involved, and courage because you've got family and you've got friends who are thinking, 'What is *wrong* with you!? Are you *nuts*, or what!? Just go along with the flow.'

Sheil

The first meeting I attended was at a library and Jim spoke, and a gentlemen stood up and said, 'If we join this, will our names go on a list for the government to find?' And Jim said, 'Well, if you aren't willing to stand up for your convictions then you're nothing.' Then Jackie's husband stood up and mentioned John Hancock. You've probably heard the story of John Hancock: 'I'm gonna sign my name large enough that the King won't have to use his specs.'[12] So, yeah, if you don't stand up and put your money where your mouth is, then . . .

M. McKinzey

I think after Waco, in particular, many of the groups started out with a sense of urgency –

Bingham

And so did we.

M. McKinzey

– Yeah, so did we. We were there saying 'Geemanee! This thing is coming apart.' But then, like I mentioned in the kitchen, you've got your gun, you've got your backpack and you're sitting in the woods and nothing happens, and eventually you have to say, 'I gotta go to work,' and then you move on –

[Laughter.]

– Now all that stuff is still important. Preparedness is still important. I mean for political problems as well as for natural disasters, and any other eventuality because self-sufficiency is *key*, I think, to the militia mentality. Self-sufficiency not only from government, but in *all* aspects of life. We like the idea of being able to say to ourselves and to each other that no matter what comes along, we can take care of ourselves.

Wittig

Don't you find it interesting that the Mormons have been doing this for years and years and nobody says anything. But when the militia start putting away some food stores or putting away things in case of an emergency, it's like [gasp] 'What's *wrong* with these people?'

Sheil

We've been expecting legislation from the federal level that would limit the amount of food you could have. You know things like that, it's not only shocking it's pretty disgusting.

Wittig

Well, it shows that they're scared. It shows that they're frightened. I mean why would they be doing that if they weren't scared?

Mulloy

This is something which is particularly aimed at militia groups?

Wittig

I believe it's aimed at anybody who's trying to be independent.

Sheil

I think the ideology comes through when you ask, 'Are you going to move on towards the left, or are we going to pull back, to come back to the republic that we once were?'

M. McKinzey

The left, I think, gains its power from the whole welfare class. People who are self-sufficient don't need government. The whole welfare idea is predicated on the idea of 'the victim'.

Sheil

We have a lot of government, and you know those foolish people of that Second Continental Congress, their cry was, 'The federal government's going down the tubes. Things are gonna fall apart, what are you gonna do?' Well, I've got another government right here in Missouri and actually we're supposed to be governed from our state level.

The federal government's overstepped its bounds. They use corruption and blackmail, whatever it takes, to get what they want. And the citizen's being bled dry by taxes. It's amazing how much we're taxed. I know that they talk about your government in England, that they tax more than we do, well, you have to see what we pay. We're taxed at our local city level, at our county level, at the state level and by the federal government. My phone bill is taxed by the federal government, my electricity bill – all these things are taxed.

Income tax is not the major source of income for the federal government. They just need more money to do the things they do, and as a student of American history I would say – and anybody would have to agree – that our government has got meaner this century, far meaner. We're empire building!

Bingham

If you're not 'politically correct' from the government's standpoint then you are the enemy of the government. Anybody that goes along with them is fine.

Mulloy

And the militias have become 'the enemy'?

M. McKinzey

Self-sufficiency is the enemy.

Wittig

I don't think they're afraid of us as individuals; they're afraid of us because we're taking the stance that our forefathers took some 200 odd years ago. And what's wrong with that? That's what made our country the great country it was from the beginning and has been through the years. The fundamental beliefs of this country are not wrong, and they weren't wrong at the beginning. We need to stay with them.

J. McKinzey

Also, I think they realize that if you have a group of people out there that are standing up and being vocal today, these are the same people that are going to be resisting you tomorrow with force. And they're smart enough to realize that, so that's why they're attacking us now.

Wittig

Plus we're educating, we're trying our darndest to educate people, to get people to think for themselves instead of just going along with the flow and 'Oh well.' My sons and grandkids are coming along. They all need to be educated, they all need to be aware of their heritage.

Mulloy

You were talking earlier about America being a republic. I'd like to come back to that. How would the operation of government differ if it was functioning as an active republic as opposed to how you see it now?

Sheil

We would have an essentially pretty weak federal government and people would be governing themselves in the states. And you might have some states who are very socialistic as opposed to some states who are totally the opposite, but that would be the choice of the people within the state.

Mulloy
So what would the federal government do?

Sheil
They were given the right to coin money, to regulate interstate trade, defend the borders, maintain the navy, deal with foreign nations, borrow money, and enact legislation, and that's basically their job.

M. McKinzey
Well, there's sixteen things.[13]

Mulloy
So you'd go back to the Constitution and say, 'This is what is set out. This is what the government can do. This is what it's limited to doing'?

M. McKinzey
Right.

Sheil
They're not here to care for people's health, their retirement, their education – all these things that they do –

M. McKinzey
The federal government was never meant to be a nanny.

Mulloy
Are you saying that the state government should do these things?

M. McKinzey
Not necessarily. The population of the state would decide if they want to do it or not.

Mulloy
So, if the state government wanted to, they could –

M. McKinzey
That's right. I suspect we've got at least 90 per cent too much federal government now, and that, I think, would be the basic difference in America not being a republic right now.

Wittig

The unfortunate thing is that when we send our representatives to the federal government there in Washington DC, they start out – the majority of them – with very good intentions. And they're supposed to be our representatives. They're supposed to decide on issues based on what their constituency wants from them. Unfortunately, their constituents being apathetic don't care. They don't write to them. It's just, Send Joe Blow to Congress and then forget all about them.

J. McKinzey

A few years ago when NAFTA [The North American Free Trade Agreement] was passed here in the United States, 80 per cent of the country was against it, but the politicians were for it.

Wittig

So they didn't represent their constituencies at all – not at all.

M. McKinzey

One other problem with our federal government – and this is something I've been thinking about recently, and I did a little story for the newsletter about it – is that, as it says in the Declaration of Independence, our founders believed that when you were born, you were born with liberty and freedom, that these were given to you by your Creator. You were born with certain inalienable rights –

Bingham

The right to self-preservation.

M. McKinzey

– That is *one* of them, but there are *others*. And these rights are a zero sum game. They can't be sold. They can't go away. But they can be transferred. And what has happened is that the federal government has enacted laws and regulations (and bureaucrats have done this), and the rights and the freedoms that were the individual's have now been transferred to the federal government. And there's a lot of power that's gone in that transfer. There's a lot of power that's represented by the freedom that *used to be ours*, but now belongs to the federal government.

One of the things we've seen after the federal government has accumulated these powers that have come from the people, is that then they need to protect them. They need to guard them. And in order to do that, the BATF and the FBI have become more and more military-like and less like peace officers – just to protect these liberties that used to be ours and now belong to them. And conflict and tension has increased as a consequence.

Sheil

How many federal agencies did you find which are armed?

Bingham

There's forty-five of them!

Sheil

And they're arming more. And they say individual citizens shouldn't have weapons!

Wittig

Forty-five of them and some of them are not even police officers.

M. McKinzey

They're *bureaucrats*. That's all they are.

Bingham

The Constitution doesn't authorize the federal government to have any police whatsoever.

Mulloy

This growth in the size of the federal government and the trend towards increasing government involvement in American life that you're talking about, you see this as part of the changes which have taken place in America since the beginning of the twentieth century, particularly during the 1930s with the New Deal, and through to the programmes of President Johnson's Great Society, and so on?

Wittig

Well, it's not only been here. Look at pre-Second World War Germany. This is a prime example of a government taking away firearms from some of the ordinary citizens. If those people had had firearms then the Holocaust might not have happened to the extent that it did. But Hitler centralized. He got control, and he was doing what – unfortunately – we see in some cases here in America.

Sheil

And of course, pre-World War Two Germany and pre-Hitler Germany had a Constitution and Bill of Rights that exceeded even ours in respect of individual rights, but it didn't last very long did it?

Johnston

When Pearl Harbor was being bombed I'm sure the reason why the Japs didn't go any further than Pearl Harbor was because American citizens were too heavily armed for them to come in here and take over. I'm confident that that's the reason why they didn't go any further than Pearl Harbor.

Sheil

That's the reason we aren't afraid of UN forces.

M. McKinzey

On Thursday, the local talk shows were talking about an apology that had come down from the Catholic Church, apologizing to Jewish people for not taking more of a stand against the Nazis. Now, my slant on things like this is that I think those type of apologies for things that happened in history are pretty silly anyway. It's like me apologizing for slavery – *well, I wasn't there*. So anyway, what I thought of was if anybody should be apologizing to anybody, it seems to me that the Jewish people owe us an apology for giving up their guns in 1933, requiring my relatives to pick up their guns and go to Europe to save those that they could save.

My father and seven uncles fought in World War Two. I lost an uncle in World War Two, but I haven't got an apology. And that sort of goes back to what we were talking about earlier: if you give up your guns then bad things happen to you. So if anybody needs to apologize to anybody, I think maybe some Jewish people need to apologize to us for giving up their guns.

That's not to say that the Holocaust wasn't terrible. The Holocaust is unimaginably terrible. Six and a half million Jews died in the Holocaust. And then there were the gypsies and many other people who were marked as 'trouble makers'. And that's exactly what cuts.

Sheil

If you want to count them, just count everybody that died in World War Two.

Bingham

If you put them all together, then Stalin killed about 20 million of his own people.

Sheil

But, of course, there were some people and legislation in this country that changed things during the twentieth century. Our federal government probably wouldn't have been involved in World War One if it wasn't for the income tax allowing it to fill its coffers to fight the war. And many historians say that if we had not been involved in World War One and unbalanced the powers in Europe then World War Two might never have happened. You look back and you see these things.

Mulloy

This seems to be taking us back to what George Washington said about not involving the country in 'entangling foreign alliances'. So you would limit the involvement of your government in overseas affairs?

M. McKinzey

Oh, absolutely.

Sheil

People say that we should be isolationists, but if you want to trade with the world you can't be an isolationist. But you can be neutral in the world –

Wittig

You don't need to meddle in other countries' internal affairs.

Sheil

– Unless you want to build an empire. I think one of the worst things that ever happened to the United States was coming out so victorious in World War Two. It went to our heads.

M. McKinzey

We were at a meeting last week with a military officer from Fort Leavenworth – a Lieutenant Colonel – and he bragged, I would say, that last year the United States military was involved in operations in 126 different countries as 'peacekeepers'. I mean, what are we doing!

Wittig

It's outrageous. All these areas – the Balkans? For what reasons are we doing that?

J. McKinzey

We all have our own views about sending our troops out of the country. In my opinion we shouldn't send them over there as '*peacekeepers*'. If our troops leave the United States then they're going over there to be '*ass-kickers*'. You go over there, you take care of the problem and you bring them home instead of going over there and babysitting for five to six years.

Sheil

Now I feel like we've become mercenaries. In the Gulf War, the whole world was mercenary –

Wittig

And they got paid off for it too.

Sheil

– And the British made money on the deal, you know. They made money, they got paid for what they did, and to me that's kind of scary. To me it's empire building. It has nothing to do with our Constitution, our republic or with national security. It's just empire building.

It was disgusting during the Gulf War to see the resources – individuals and money and military resources – being used to support international oil cartels. And that's exactly what it was. No matter what they said about Kuwait and about freedom in Kuwait. There's no more freedom in Kuwait now than there was before Saddam Hussein took the oil fields.

It's always the same, you have this talk of acting 'for the people', or 'for freedom', but for the most part it's about trade and money. It just goes on and on. Why do we continue to do these things when it has very little to do with humanitarian reasons? There's always some money behind it as an ulterior motive.

Mulloy

This is related to what you were saying about a republic being very different from an empire –

Sheil

An empire is *very* different than a republic.

Mulloy

– and also when you were talking about the Declaration of Independence. Now, in some of the material I've read, there's a distinction made which says that the militias aren't anti-government, they're anti-tyranny –

J. McKinzey

Anti-*bureaucracy*.

Mulloy

– So what you're saying, therefore, is that a citizen has the right to resist the state if it becomes tyrannical. Right?

Bingham

Right.

Sheil

It's not just a right, it's a *duty*.

Mulloy

Yes, and that would be part of the idea of a virtuous citizen living in a republic. Now, my question is this: What are the conditions which trigger this resistance? When do you know that a government is tyrannical enough to resist it?

M. McKinzey

It's a moral decision that every each person would make.

Bingham

When they start putting forward enough force to make people kneel that's when we resist.

Sheil

Well, I think we resist *now*.

Mulloy

OK, let me play devil's advocate here. How many people are there in the 51st Militia in total?

J. McKinzey

As members? Less than 100.

Mulloy

Right, now how many people are there in Kansas City?

J. McKinzey

A million, a million and a half.

Sheil

There's about 12 million in the metroplex, but the city itself has less than half a million people.

Mulloy

OK, let's say half a million. So you 100 in the 51st Militia decide that the government's been tyrannical and you decide to resist the government – exercising your rights – but there's half a million Kansas City citizens who are either uninterested, uninvolved, don't know anything about it, or think the government's doing a good job, so –

J. McKinzey

If you can believe what we're being told, even though there's only 100 members of the 51st there are three other militia groups in Kansas City that we know of, plus there are literally thousands of citizens who, when the time comes, will be there. Now if you can count on them and you put all those numbers together we're 20,000 –

M. McKinzey

But there's no doubt, I mean there's no way that . . . we don't have any grandiose vision of collecting together as an army and marching against Washington –

[Laughter.]

– But I think some of it is tit-for-tat. I think that you resist, you push back with equal force when you're pushed on.

J. McKinzey

Look back at Waco. That was just one event, but that one event mobilized 100,000 people in the United States to form militias. Now if the government pulls off another stunt like that, you can times those numbers by five or six.

Johnston

And don't forget Ruby Ridge.

Bingham

Those two things, Waco and Ruby Ridge, also caused a member of the Special Forces to start writing *The Resister* magazine – not the end of what happened at Waco but the beginning of it.[14]

M. McKinzey

The fundamental question though of when and how moral men resist immoral government – we're not gonna decide that this afternoon, but that's the problem.

Mulloy

That does seem to be a problem to me, looking at it from the outside, because you *do* have to make that choice. And you may have a lot of people, both in the Kansas area and nationally, who simply don't agree with you, who say that your impression of what's happening in America is incorrect. At the very least doesn't that cause you problems in terms of your relationship with the wider community, with law enforcement agencies and so on?

Bingham

It does, but if you want to go back to your history, there was less than 3 per cent of the population at the time of the Revolution that fought the war. The vast majority of the people wanted things to go along just the way they were, just the same as they do today.

M. McKinzey

The militia movement is fluid, it's changing. One of the things we did last year was initiate a membership routine with a waiting period and an ID card. We initiated those things because we decided to look out for each other. Now it would be nice if we had the means and the assets and the time and everything so that when we hear about an injustice in Chicago we can run over to Chicago and help out. But we can't. What we can do is band together in this group and say: 'You mess with *one* of us, you mess with *all* of us.' It would be very unlikely for us now to get involved in any significant way for somebody outside the group, and that may sound selfish, or whatever, but it's just very practical.

Mulloy

That's the local emphasis you were talking about?

M. McKinzey

It's that local emphasis. It's, 'We're going to take care of Kansas City and we're gonna help out in Kansas City.' It would take extraordinary circumstances for us to leave this area. It's too bad that injustices occur – that certain elements of the federal government step on ants all over the place – but often all we can do is just say, 'Well it's too bad that person wasn't a member of a good militia group because then they would have some recourse.'

Sheil

There have been changes, though. After Waco we saw a stand-off in Montana and because of the federal government's fear of militias they talked that out. The federal government was getting messages from militias all over the country. Now, the Freemen may have been criminals, they may have committed crimes, and they should have come out and been tried, but they had other people in there and we said, 'Don't pull another Waco, you can afford to wait.'[15]

Wittig

The interesting thing about that was that the local FBI had such respect for our leadership that they called us, they called Jim.

J. McKinzey

At least once every two weeks during this whole thing they would call just to see what the opinion of the militia at large was about their operation. And we had some pretty frank conversations, and I always made it clear to them that if the FBI was fired upon by the Freemen then the FBI had a right to defend themselves, but that we expected *more* out of our federal agents than for them to fire *first*.[16]

Sheil

The Waco thing is a problem that hasn't been resolved in this country. But another problem is just the amount of bureaucracy we have here, with all their rules and regulations. And the thing is, Americans like choice.

M. McKinzey

It's about power. I'm standing behind a counter with a stamp in my hand and I've got the power. If they don't want to stamp your little piece of paper, they're not going to and you're not going to be able to do anything about it.

I built a house about six to eight years ago, and you get these inspectors that come around as you build, and you just learn the game fast. You have to pacify them and kiss their ass, do whatever it takes. You make them think, 'Oh, like, I would never have thought of that!'

[Rick Hawkins arrives.]

Sheil

In Kansas City we have all these inspectors, and we had a hotel that had a skywalk, and about a year ago they were having a dance in there and all the lights came crashing down. One hundred and ninety-four people were killed and there were many injuries – but they *had inspectors.*

I sometimes ask people: 'What does the government do for you? What does the federal government do for you?

'Well, they inspect our food and keep it safe.'

'Oh yeah. Well how come people die with salmonella from fast food chains?'[17]

They don't really protect you. They give a lot of people jobs, but they don't really protect you. Actually, business protects you, because whenever a fast food restaurant or someone has that kind of trouble, businesses all over the United States have a real good look at the way they do business. If you understand business you can't make people sick. 'Business protects you more than the government,' I say, but people just go away shaking their heads.

I sometimes think that people feel they would be stripped naked if they didn't have all these government agencies that they think are protecting them. And then if you ask them, 'Well, if you went to a restaurant and you ate something and you got sick, what would the government do for you?' – They'd do nothing, it's on you.

Hawkins

I have a lot of fun asking people who get into these discussions that question: 'What does the federal government do for you?' And it's just silence because, you know, for the average person in most of our daily lives we don't have anything to do with the federal government.

Wittig

I can answer that question, but most people can't.

Hawkins

Your state government should have more influence on your life than the federal government. Your county government should have far more influence on your daily life than your state. Your state should have more than the federal. It was set up this way. I mean, it's tiered like that. And that way you can decide if you want to live under these laws. There's these laws – I don't think we have any in Missouri but there's a lot of counties in Arkansas where there's no alcohol, 'period'. Now if you want to live in an environment like that, you can go and seek one out and live there. And that's the way it's supposed to be.

Sheil

We have *so much* government in this country.

Wittig

It's like those poor guys in down in Florida who set up an independent broadcasting system. He was broadcasting religious music or something for five or six blocks in one direction. And it's five o'clock in the morning, and he and his wife are sound asleep, and the SWAT team came in. They had the helicopters, they had guys in black with guns. And they busted into their home, threw them on the floor, trashed their house, all because they were broadcasting but they didn't have the license. So what? They were broadcasting for five or six blocks. Why in the world would they do that? That was our tax money.

Sheil

Why did they have to raid them in the middle of the night like that?

Wittig

It's just stupid.

Sheil

The same thing could have been taken care of at Waco if they'd just went to the door and knocked.[18]

Mulloy

We've been talking a lot about self-sufficiency. Can I ask you whether this idea of self-sufficiency is much stronger in the West, or the mid-West where we are now, than it is in the East, and whether a lot of the feelings which you have are a product of your geography?

M. McKinzey

In large cities there are more limitations – possibly, although that might not always be true – on what you could do for yourself and what you can't do.

Hawkins

The more urban the environment, it seems, the more likely people are to depend on things being provided for them.

Bingham

Besides, this part of the country is younger than the country back East.

Sheil

I think one of the things is that where you have a smaller population, you depend on your neighbor more. And from here until you get to California the population is smaller within larger areas, and this means more self-sufficiency. People have to depend on themselves and their neighbors. It's a whole different world out here in the West. And when your lifestyle is based on self-sufficiency, you're going to have more antagonism towards a nanny-type government.

Some people call it a 'parent' and I think our Vice-President said it should be more like a 'grandparent' which makes you think –

[Laughter.]

– you know, *what* are these people on about? Are these people for *real*? Somewhere along the way they have lost their intelligence.

Wittig

What was the term he used for us? Something about 'natives in the hustings'.

Sheil

Well, you know, he's just amazingly dense!

Wittig

He's having wonderful dreams though. He wakes up in the middle of the night with these wonderful dreams like midnight basketball.

Sheil

He came up with this program to keep kids from cities joining gangs. They would have midnight basketball. Midnight basketball for kids? That makes a lot of sense doesn't it? OK, so the Vice-President is at this press conference and the reporter says, 'Vice-President Gore, would you allow your kids to play basketball at midnight in the inner cities?'

And he says, 'Well, not on school nights.'

[Laughter.]

– 'But you're asking other people to let their children go play basketball at midnight. So what do your kids do?'

'Well, they have to be in bed, so they can go to school.'

And that's like another little stab. They are always for the public schools and what they're doing today, but they all send their kids to private schools to get a better education.

M. McKinzey

Another concept which is important – that defines a militia group – is that of responsibility. While we do pound 'freedom and freedom and freedom,' we also recognize that with that comes responsibility. And what we've seen with the liberalization of our society is the removal of that responsibility for our actions and for raising our kids, and so on. And that doesn't come up often enough. Having guns, etc., that's core to what we are, but we also recognize that that comes with a price of responsibility, and that's significant to us. That's where our Code of Conduct comes in.[19] That's the other side of the coin.

Wittig

It's a sad statement that so few people vote in the elections in our country. Particularly among the conservatives and the Christian conservative group of people. Their voting grade is about 25 per cent, which is outrageous.

Bingham

And that's *better* than most.

J. McKinzey

If I had to sum it all up in one statement, it would be about involvement. The problems our country face are due to the lack of involvement by the community at large.

M. McKinzey

And we're looked at strangely just because we are involved! Just the fact that we're involved on any level makes you weird.

Sheil

If you go out and you protest for what you believe in you've got to face being ridiculed because it's not cool. It's not a *cool* way to be. A cool thing is to be on MTV answering questions about what kind of underwear you wear.

[Laughter.]

Hawkins

The cool thing is, and what people worry more about than anything is, who's playing what game this weekend. That's the central focus to most people.

Johnston

If you were to take out football, basketball, baseball and hockey, this country would be *bored*.

Hawkins

That's one of the questions I ask a lot of people: 'If football, baseball and basketball went away tomorrow – if they just turned off the lights and it didn't exist any more – how would your life change?' They stop and think about it, then they say: 'I'd go to the park on Sunday afternoons with my children.' They don't look at that, you know; football is the focus, and yet it does absolutely nothing for them. It's just entertainment but they lose track of that. All of our priorities are turned around backwards.

Mulloy

Are you having any success in getting other people who are not currently in a militia involved?

J. McKinzey

We're not talking big numbers but then we're not out there trying to recruit everybody. Basically, our recruiting philosophy is, If you're interested you come to us and we will take the ball from there and get you involved. We went through that stage at the beginning where we thought numbers were important. It wasn't. We had so many members *nobody* in this room knew who all of us were.

Johnston

When I signed on a year ago – February – I told Jim McKinzey, 'If you think I'm going to sit on my coccyx, you're gonna lose me because I'm not going to sit on my coccyx and do nothing.' And since then – I don't know how active you could call it – but I've tried to do my part.

J. McKinzey

And that's the people we want. We want the *doers*. We don't want the people who are just going to sit back and watch us do it.

M. McKinzey

Although we do recognize that there are a lot of people who support us philosophically, but just don't want to join us. We call them supporters. If you look at our by-laws those people are called 'supporters', and they buy a T-shirt or a hat, and that's OK too because we've got a little mark-up there that pays the phone bill. There are literally thousands of people in that category.

Mulloy
Does your newsletter go out to the supporters as well?

J. McKinzey
They get it if they pay a subscription of $15 a year. It goes to anybody who pays us $15.

M. McKinzey
Once we put it on the website the number of paid subscriptions has gone down, but that's OK. Our website's getting about twenty or thirty hits a day. And we still send out over fifty copies. They go out all around the country. There's very few just in Kansas City. Most of them go out all over the place.

J. McKinzey
And just out of our pocket we send a copy to the FBI. We send a copy to the BATF.

Sheil
You wanted to talk about our relationship with the law enforcement agencies. Local law enforcement we have no problem with, never have, we're able to talk to them. Even the FBI – we've always had a good relationship with their people, from top to bottom.

J. McKinzey
One local FBI agent even made this statement to the media that the 51st is a very upstanding, reliable militia, and I took that as a pretty big pat on the back.

Sheil
He even once told us that he would go with us to any meeting and talk to anybody about us.

J. McKinzey
But, unfortunately, that guy, Agent Welsh [name changed], I think, was from the older school and the newer school is coming up.

Sheil

Mike and I ran into a new type of FBI agent a couple of weeks ago in St. Joseph. We had been invited a year ago to Western Missouri University in St. Jo to make a breakfast morning speech. And when Mike made his speech I found it was respected because they had read James Bovard's book *Loss of Liberty* and they had really been shocked by the confiscation of property reported in the book, because 'property commits crime' right?[20] And that's what this FBI agent who was more of an accountant –

M. McKinzey

He was a lawyer.

Wittig

A lawyer, that's it.

Bingham

Most of them are lawyers.

Sheil

– Lawyers or accountants. He said this – because we asked him a question about it – and he said that 'property commits crime'. Which got a big laugh. But I think more and more people are becoming aware of their loss of liberties. The way it works here in the United States, if somebody says they saw somebody smoking a marijuana joint in your car, they can take your car away from you, even if you weren't in it. And then you have to prove your innocence. You're *guilty* until *proven innocent*. Now this makes no sense in any country's system of law where you're supposed to have right to property. But that's what's going on. It's this whole war on drugs.

M. McKinzey

One of the fundamental principles that our founders recognized was the ability to own private property, and the war on drugs has just gutted that concept.

Sheil

The Fourth Amendment says that you have the right to be secure in your property, and that if a warrant is issued it must be with probable cause and so forth. But the police no longer come to your door and serve a warrant; now they come in the middle of the night and kick the door down, fully armed and ready to shoot you down. It's come down from the federal level to permeate every level of law enforcement we have. Here in Kansas City,

Missouri, we have a little suburb called Stockton [name changed] and about three years ago neighbors called the Stockton police about an older man who was depressed and who they thought had a gun. So the police went and kicked the door in and he did have a gun, and they shot and killed him.

Bingham

That'll save him from killing himself!

Hawkins

Well, he's not depressed anymore!

[Laughter.]

Sheil

So, if you want to be dead, just call the police. If you want to commit suicide call the police and tell them you've got a gun. They'll come right over and shoot you.

J. McKinzey

You know, I've got a bumper sticker on my door that will prevent all that. It says, 'BATF, FBI – Please knock, and come right in.' They don't break my door down.

[Laughter.]

M. McKinzey

This young FBI guy, though, was really interesting. It was interesting to compare him to the older FBI agent who was about to retire. This guy was probably younger than I am. In a nutshell, he said, 'We *do* have a big government. There's no doubt about it, but the reason we have a big government is because that's what the people want. They've elected representatives who have gone to Washington DC and created this monster, and big governments, like elephants, occasionally will step on an ant.' He didn't even try to defend it! He said it's inevitable that an elephant will step on an ant every once in a while and that was scary.

Now another interesting thing is later on he started talking about his Second Amendment attitude, and in his opinion only the military and the police need guns, and that's the end of it.

Sheil

In the hallway outside the meeting I got him engaged in Second

Amendment and gun control issues, and I said, 'Well, Agent Welsh doesn't agree with you on this gun control issue.' And he said, 'I don't think he does. He's one of the older members.'

M. McKinzey

In a sense he believes that we want to be slaves and as long as you *want* to be slaves you don't get a gun.

Sheil

Boys cannot have guns.

M. McKinzey

He made no attempt to defend the handout about the 'lost rights' given out at the meeting. He just said it's inevitable.

Hawkins

The end justifies the means.

Sheil

And your property rights don't mean anything. That was what the Magna Carta was about wasn't it – property rights?

Hawkins

This goes back to the Revolution and before. We were having this problem during the Revolutionary days and the framers wrote the Constitution based on the problem as it was then. And all they really wanted was the rights of English citizens. The colonists didn't have the rights of the people back in England.

Wittig

English citizens got it because they fought for it and got it.

Sheil

It was a progression from the Magna Carta onwards, all the way down. That's why property rights were considered so important to liberty.

Mulloy

What would you say to those who argue that it's not realistic to expect the Constitution, an eighteenth-century document, to provide guidance for people living at the end of the twentieth century?

Sheil

But people never change.

Hawkins

Human beings have not changed in 10,000 years.

J. McKinzey

Look at the Holy Bible, it's a lot older than the Constitution. Are we going to throw it out too?

Sheil

I try to tell people that these ideas didn't just spring from the minds of our forefathers. They were laid down as far back as the Persians, the Greeks and the Romans. Freedom and liberty are a product of western civilization. These things are not new. And although many of our forefathers were just ordinary people, many of them were not, some of them were very educated people, educated in the classics. They *understood* human nature.

And the Constitution is so *simple*. The bare bones of it are so simple. I don't know why it couldn't live for ever. Some country in Africa could suddenly reorganize and say that they want a governing document that would work. They could pull the US Constitution over, and it would work.

Wittig

What our forefathers did say, though, was that this Constitution was written for a moral people and it would not work for an immoral people. And we're coming across problems from that today.

M. McKinzey

We were talking about that today, or yesterday – about the problem with government and society as it becomes more immoral, and I haven't started thinking about it yet myself, but Kay made the comment that Caesar was fascinated by moral men and that even moral men can commit corrupt acts.

Sheil

I think people should read Shakespeare's *Julius Caesar*. What Shakespeare's laying out is how you corrupt moral men. And I see a lot of parallels between my country today and Rome.

They had a great and glorious civilization, a republic, and you hear a lot of stuff about the emperors being so corrupt and greedy and whatever, but whatever they were, they were good governors. We don't even have *that*. They couldn't have been that bad; they governed Rome for 1,000 years.

And the Roman citizens, they pretty much kept their rights intact during that time . . . but I see a lot of parallels. From the time that you stop being a government just simply for your own people and you want to be an empire, to rule the world, to govern the world.

I think the world has a lot less to fear from the UN than they do the United States. I think every person in every country in the world ought to stand up and tell us to 'get out, get away.' I love the French because they always tell us to do that.

M. McKinzey

You ain't gonna mess around with them!

[Laughter.]

Mulloy

I'm interested in what you're saying about moral men, about the need for moral men, because if you had smaller government – the kind of state and county government that you were talking about earlier – would you necessarily get moral men in positions of power as part of that?

Wittig

We would have more access to that.

Hawkins

You have more direct control when your state representative lives three blocks away. If he does something that you really think is wrong, you can just walk up the street and tell him.

Wittig

You can have a relationship with that person, and this is one of the things that Jim and Kay and Mike have done with Agent Welsh. They have – to give credit where credit's due – worked at creating a relationship with him, and that's why he has a lot of respect for the 51st, because of the work they've done. And we can do the same thing with our state representatives. When we go down to Jefferson City, which is the capital of our state of Missouri, when we go down there to lobby for Second Amendment rights we go into every representative's office and talk with them personally. They know us. They see us coming. They say to my husband, 'Hi Chuck, how you doing?' They know him. 'Hi Jim, hi Kay,' they say.

Sheil

But our US Senators, they're very unapproachable unless you've got the money to give to their campaigns. Now that was a change in our Constitution, that was an Amendment to our Constitution that changed the whole shape of our government.[21]

Originally, US Senators were not powerful individuals. They were appointed or elected by the state legislators and they were just sort of errand boys. 'You go to Washington and you vote like this.' 'If this comes up, you vote on it.' 'If you aren't voting on it, you come home.' But after the Civil War they decided to federalize Senators, and they created these powerful individuals that the Constitution never intended there to be. These are people that are more powerful than state governors.

Mulloy

But even if that was the case – even if more powers were given to the states' governments – you would still need to get people who are not currently active in politics involved. How would you achieve that? If they're not currently interested in politics, how would you get those people involved?

Sheil

Well, either they would get involved or it would go on like it is, and it would be a few of us making the decisions.

Johnston

You've got to change a lot of people's attitudes because there's a lot of people out there that's no different than an ostrich that goes and buries its head in the sand. Unless it affects them they're not going to worry about it.

Sheil

It does affect them – they just don't understand that it does.

Johnston

Not on a direct approach.

Sheil

They don't see it that way. You know a lot of people don't vote, and the reason they give – and I hear this more times than not – is that it doesn't make any difference if they vote or not. 'The government will do what they want to do.' And you can't argue with them because we vote and we see the government constantly doing what they want to do.

Mulloy

I think what I'm saying is: Do you have to change the people first or do you change the system of government? If you create the kind of republic you want, for example, but you still have all the same people with all the same attitudes they currently have, would it make any difference? Or would you still have the same problems?

Hawkins

We don't want to *change* the government. All we're really trying to do is keep it the same and maybe roll it back a little bit.

Sheil

It's like a lion tamer with a whip and a chair. We want to whip the federal government back into its cage. That's the problem: to weaken the federal government and send it back to where it's constitutionally supposed to be. It doesn't really make any difference how many voters you have if you can govern yourself. I'm no proponent of democracy. I think democracy is simply rule by the majority and quite often the mob. What famous philosopher called it rule by the mob?

J. McKinzey

Where you really need to start is back where the people pick their representatives. That's where the first domino starts falling over. Today in America the person with the most money gets elected.[22]

M. McKinzey

Once you take the money out of it, you would start drawing a different sort of person.

Hawkins

You need to set and hold – I hate to say moral standards – but you have to set standards that people –

Johnston

Look at Forbes, though, he had a lot of money and he didn't get it. He didn't even get out of the primaries.[23] A lot of it goes to being, quote unquote, 'politically correct'. Look at Pat Buchanan. He would have made an ideal president but due to the fact that they labelled him as an isolationist, he wasn't 'politically correct', and so he never even got past go.

J. McKinzey

What we're talking about here are problems that are in existence now, but were created because people back, say, sixty years ago, quit getting involved. People got into office that shouldn't have been there.

M. McKinzey

You could argue that people get the government they deserve.

Sheil

Income tax came into effect because they sold it to the people as something only the wealthy would pay. And during the twentieth century we've had this idea – the idealism of Marxism and socialism – that 'wealth is evil', that wealthy people are evil and that only the poor are truly morally good and so on and so forth. Where I come in, is for capitalism. I think capitalism is the answer to the world's problems. And not the media's bloated idea of the capitalist as J. P. Morgan and stuff like that.

Capitalism means that you can take it and you run with it. You create wealth. Socialists and Communists try to give you the idea that wealth is finite; that there's just so much of it. If that were true, how come Bill Gates has created so much wealth? Wealth is *constantly* being created, created by capitalists.

Capitalism gave me the good life. My Constitution gave me a form of government and capitalism gave me the good life. I think that even without most people being involved, if you could shove the federal government back into the constitutional box where it belongs, capitalism would reign and we would be prosperous. We would do more for the world by showing what we can do than by running around taking part in all these police actions and taking sides.

Wittig

Also, what we need to do is get more involved in our local school board to change the curriculum for the kids. I think education is key to so many things. They have taken away from our children so much in history and so much in government studies, and perhaps if we were working through the school boards we could get those back in so that our kids were raised up to be involved. I know *I* was. When I was raised we had elections in school, we had government studies and we had mock campaigns, and all that stuff, so we understood what was going on.

Sheil

It's totally unbelievable. Take my granddaughter's class in American government. They started school the last week of August, and I was over her house one day when she came home from school and I noticed the date. It was September 15. She said: 'We had a test on American government today.' So I said, 'What did you have your test about?' And talking to her, they were tested on everything from the discovery of the New World to the establishment of the Constitution. In that length of time? I said, 'What! How could they possibly do this?'

Wittig

These days they're not even talking about D-Day at school. When I was in school to graduate from the eighth grade you had to pass a test on the American and State Constitution. You studied for a whole year.

Johnston

And if you flunked the test, you didn't get through, you didn't get past eighth grade. You stayed another year until you passed it.

Sheil

Is it any wonder with this educational system that at the time of the Civil War we had a higher rate of literacy – and there were no public schools.

M. McKinzey

Back to the question, though, which is kind of interesting. I'm not sure from my point of view that you can go back. It's like the cycle thing – that's the concept I like. That this country and many others were formed on principles of freedom and liberty and from that point on started corrupting. And maybe it's inevitable that it's going to collapse and then you start over again. I don't know – maybe you can slow it down, but I'm not sure you can stop it.[24]

Sheil

You may be right, but there's no reason to stop trying!

Johnston

On the other side of the coin, when you leave God out of the picture, that's when you get people in Congress that are corrupt like Bill Clinton. When you get immoral men in there it's because they've lost sight of God. And as long as God's in the picture this nation will do good. If you go back to the Old Testament you'll see the Jews, and they've always done good when God was right there and they were obedient, and as soon as they disobeyed God, they fell.

M. McKinzey

Those cycles have come and gone. They just go round and round.

Sheil

I think ethics and morals are more important than anything – they have to be there . . .

M. McKinzey

That has something to do with responsibility too. Or even the reason for responsibility.

Sheil

Jim's talking from his viewpoint as a Christian. I can talk from my viewpoint as a Buddhist. It's a different religion but we still agree that we have to have those morals and those ethics.

Johnston

Morals and ethics, I will agree, play an important part.

Wittig

Well, the country was founded on them, unlike some other countries, which were founded on despotic Genghis Khan types of creatures who took all control right from the beginning, which had nothing to with morals. It had to do with power.

J. McKinzey

Regarding the schools, a couple of years ago Blue Valley school district had a test, and I believe it was being handed to seventh- or eighth-graders. One of the questions was, 'Your whole family was on a ship and the ship sank. You and your family ended up in a life boat and you have run out of food and water. Who do you kill first?'

Wittig

It's outrageous!

J. McKinzey

After a period of time this person I know, he wrote down, 'I'd kill none of them. We would all die together.' He got that question wrong. You'd kill your grandparents first because they have lived their life and their usefulness is over with. And they are teaching that type of stuff to our kids in school!

Wittig

Situational ethics is what it's called.

Hawkins

For different reasons I agree with everybody on education. That's how we end up with FBI agents who think that the militia is the National Guard. Because that's what they were taught. They were taught that from the first time they took American history. There was a teacher standing up there saying, 'Two hundred years ago we had militia, today we have the National Guard.' Well, that's not true. That's not in law, that's not *anywhere*. But it's like what they did in Nazi Germany – the 'Big Lie'. If you tell the 'Big Lie' enough it becomes the truth.[25] If you teach these people – year after year after year – this is the way it is, by the time they get to voting age, that *is* the way it is.

Wittig

Then they have children and it goes on and on and on.

Hawkins

And when you have a person educated in that environment who then goes out and becomes a teacher, the cycle just continues to build. Education is such an easy thing to manipulate. It takes generations to make a major difference.

J. McKinzey

We need to step further back from the school to the parents. I'm forty-four years old and until I was thirty-nine I didn't really give a care, but after things like Waco, if I were to just fall back on the morals of the community and stuff it wouldn't have affected me. But it went back to what my parents taught me and how I was raised. That this was wrong; and it all came to life again. It's parents, school and in your own manner.

Sheil

Another area of our government that I find probably the most dangerous is in these areas of what they call 'national security'. And this means keeping secrets from the American people. Now I don't believe that you can have a democracy if you keep secrets from the people. So, in fact, we have a secret government.

Most Americans cannot understand our foreign relations and that's because we don't have an open policy of telling people what's going on in foreign relations. It's run by spies, the CIA and National Security Agency, all these people who are supposed to be subject to congressional oversight.

Well, where was the congressional oversight in the Bay of Pigs? Where's the congressional oversight in anything? The CIA recently had to move out of Northern Iraq, because they were there starting up trouble with the Kurds. And Vietnam. The CIA were involved in Vietnam when the average American had never even heard of it.

The reasons for most of these things we just don't know. You can go to the library and get a lot of books and read a lot of things but you just don't know.

About two years ago I became very interested in these types of things, and I would go to the library every two weeks and load up on books. I got so I would just go back to the index and look for people's names and cross-reference them through books looking for the things that they did. But trying to find heroes in the American government is like trying to find a needle in a haystack because everybody gets dirty over and over and over again. It just piles up. I don't think you'd find enough moral ethics in the whole of Washington to fill a gnat's belly button.

I have no faith in either the Republican or the Democratic party. It's all been corrupted with power and money – money makes power – and now we have President Clinton who's catching all the heat from the women . . . but I think what's going to come down along the road is all these other things, whether it be Chinese involvement or Indonesian involvement in the election process. Maybe the American people will come to understand what treason is, I don't know –

Bingham

I *doubt* it.

Sheil

– And you have these activists, these people in the women's movement saying, 'Oh well, this was wrong for him to do, but we like his programmes so . . .' The morals and ethics go out the window. You know, they've gone.

Johnston

I've been trading with this barber for twenty-five years and it's kind of like it was back in the 1800s or 1900s. It's a place you go to get your hair cut and you talk politics, you talk hunting, you talk about fishing. Over the years this guy and I have cultivated a good relationship. We talk about everything.

Well, one day I walked in there and it was just him and me in there – and he's a Republican and he's got good morals and everything, and he knows who's Republican and who's Democrat and who's got morals and who ain't – and he was telling me about some of the people that come in there. They have said, 'I don't care what Bill Clinton has done. I don't care if the people there in China come over and have a roll. As long as that economy's good, as long as the money keeps coming in, we don't care what he did or did not do.'

Now Orvill makes his living out of this, so he can't really say a whole lot because, if he does, there's enough barber shops within the area that they would go somewhere else – and they're just that type. So there are very few people like us – this group here and some of the people that come into the shop – that have any morals about them at all. And that number is just dwindling.

Sheil

I think they have morals about themselves but they don't expect it from their government and maybe they shouldn't because it's not there. I don't expect the government to do anything moral – not when the situation is like it is. I see too many immoral actions from that part of world. Some people say once you get inside the Beltway it becomes corrupting.[26] It's a strange place. It's the center of the world as far as they're concerned –

Hawkins

It's the center of *their* world.

Sheil

– It's the center of *their* world and they would like to make it the center of *your* world. This country is a danger to the whole world. We're dangerous to ourselves and the rest of the world – same as China is – because of what we're doing. And if liberty fails here, it will fail in the whole world. And we're getting real close to it. Not only do people in the United States not recognize that but people in the rest of the world do not recognize it.

It's still a great country, it's a great place to come. I was reading an article yesterday about how many highly educated French computer people were coming here for the opportunity. I know they come from England because I have two real good friends who came. He was making $5,000 a year in England before he came here in 1970 and soon he was making $20,000.

They come for the opportunity – we have people coming in here legally and illegally all the time for the opportunities – but still it's just gradually ebbing away and it's a shame –

Hawkins

Too many of them come in here.

Sheil

– Well, that's what they say, but I come from the standpoint that I want to live in a country that *has* people coming in. If you can bring yourself here and be a good citizen, I don't care where you came from. My problem is bringing political refugees here that we pay to support, and singling out groups to come.

We bring in some of the poorest disease-ridden people in the world to filter into American society, but we keep strict quotas on Western Europeans – very, very strict. The people that could contribute are kept out. And why? Because immigration is what built this country; it's what made it great.

I'm not a believer that the world is overpopulated, I'm not a believer that immigration is hurting this country. People talk about people coming in from Mexico and Central America and getting our welfare, well, the problem isn't immigration, it's the welfare state –

Hawkins

If it *wasn't* here they wouldn't come.

Sheil

– Well, they would come to *work*. When I was a kid I was really fortunate in that I got to spend at least a month in the summer in California – I had an aunt and uncle that lived there. And every year when I came, what they call the 'wetbacks' would start coming in and everybody was real glad to see them. They didn't want them living next door to them, but they were glad to see them. Why? Because they served a purpose. They did jobs that Americans wouldn't do. And they're still coming and doing it. We shouldn't be afraid of immigrants; they would just come here for the opportunity.

Mulloy

Tell me your views on Bill Clinton.

M. McKinzey

Well, in my opinion, and probably in the opinion of everybody here, Bill Clinton is a criminal scum bucket! And I would be considered wacko by most people for even thinking it, but, I'm talking about drug running, probably murder, prostitution and on and on. And I think in ten years that these things are going to gradually become accepted as true, but what I was wondering was that we hear that in Europe everyone knows this. That it's no big deal . . .

Wittig
In England you get a better picture of our government than we get here.

Mulloy
Because of the media?

M. McKinzey
The media in Europe has nothing to gain by lying about our government.

Mulloy
Well, I wouldn't say that this was something which was well known in the UK.

Hawkins
Is he generally perceived as a great man, a leader of the free world type?

Mulloy
Actually, I think he's perceived as being a fairly popular president over here.

[Disbelieving laughter.]

Sheil
The President was elected with less than 50 per cent of the voters voting.

Bingham
A little over 25 per cent of the people.

Hawkins
Of the registered voters in the first election it was 43% and in the last I think it was 48 per cent or 49 per cent.[27]

I'm a firm believer that you ought to get a license to vote because what we have here is this massive amount of people who don't really give a damn, who watch all the crap on TV and see it as their patriotic duty to go out there and vote, so they go vote for the guy with the nicest hair! Then they have no idea in hell what he actually believes in or what he stands for.

Wittig

It's media controlled.

Sheil

If the media had spent enough time in Arkansas when he first started to run, Bill Clinton would be in a federal prison today. Instead he became President.

Hawkins

The Democrats have done this twice in a row now. They did it with Carter. They went and got a governor that nobody had ever heard of from a small state in the South who had a big smile and nice hair –

Sheil

Well Carter *was* a pretty nice guy.

Hawkins

– Yeah, he *was* a nice guy, but they ran him up the flag pole and everybody liked it. And they did the exact same thing again with Clinton and nobody caught on to the fact that that's what these guys are doing.

Sheil

And nobody caught onto how Bill Clinton campaigned all over the US. Where did he get the money? Where did he get the money to go around Europe? The Democrat Party wasn't even financing for that year. Where did he get the money? I mean, Arkansas is a lowly populated, poor state.

M. McKinzey

I think Jefferson had the idea that if you didn't own land, you couldn't vote. What about that?

Sheil

Well, democracy wasn't a thing in the United States at the beginning. It was good government and self-rule – that was the way it was supposed to be.

Bingham

Democracy started during the twenties. That's when you started hearing about democracy.[28]

M. McKinzey

That's where democracy and morals and government all get tied together, because in my opinion a very serious problem is the fact that almost half of the people born today in the United States are born to single mothers – nearly half. They don't have a husband so who are they going to look for? They're going to look towards the government, to the people running the government, normally in the Democratic Party, the socialists. Those women – and there are millions of them – are looking to the government to supply what a husband and a father and a family used to supply when self-sufficiency came from the family. And now it's coming from the government. So we've got this whole class of women voting for Bill Clinton. I think it's gonna be a problem.

Hawkins

He deliberately pursues that vote. He cultivated that for years.

Sheil

It's disgusting. And he talks about *morals*. You know, they did a poll after he was elected the first time and about 75 per cent of women said they would like to sleep with Bill Clinton.

M. McKinzey

And 70 per cent of those have!

[Laughter.]

Sheil

I thought this was just *disgusting* – even taking a poll.

Wittig

Well, it's foolish, it's just sheer foolishness.

Hawkins

It all goes back to the forty years of liberalism we've had in this country. They got into the schools, they got into everything they could, education and welfare and everything else, to slowly, subliminally, inject this, 'You need us! Where would you be without us? The bigger we are, the better you are. Give us more money, give us more power so that we can get bigger and take better care of you.'

Sheil

And solve more of your problems and you are a victim.

Hawkins

Oh yeah, if you don't have a job it's not *your fault*. If your children are in jail, it's not *their fault*.

Sheil

If you have illegitimate children and don't have a husband, it's not *your fault*.

Johnston

Nobody takes responsibility for nothing.

Sheil

The government doesn't *want* you to. We're taught to be victims. Women are victims. Minorities are victims. We're all victims of someone. The only unvictimized category is middle-class, healthy, white males. They are the *enemy*. White males are the only ones who can't claim to be a victim. But now if they get disabled – and it's not their fault – they're a victim. If you're a drug addict you can get a federal pension. If you're an alcoholic or a drug addict and you become disabled you get social security.

Wittig

Well, you can't work because you're drunk all the time!

Mulloy

I can hear from what you're saying that you feel there are a lot of things which are wrong right now with America. As a politically active group, what can you do to change that? Obviously, you're unlikely here to be able to get rid of Bill Clinton, or to be able to reform the federal bureaucracy by yourself. So what can you do on a more practical level?

Sheil

One of the projects we have here in the state of Missouri is getting a concealed carry law passed.

M. McKinzey

We're involved in that.

Sheil

That's for protection. I don't particularly need to carry a concealed weapon in my everyday movements, but if I want to go by myself to visit my daughter in Arkansas it's nice to get into my truck and have a pistol there with me and not be breaking the law. I have to criminalize myself to do it now.

My late husband owned an apartment building. It was in sort of a bad part of town and he was having to do a lot of work on it. One day he came in and had a little sack with him – and this little sack was what he used to carry his pistol from the car into the apartment building – well, our granddaughter, who was living with us at the time, she said, 'Oh I see you got your sack with your work gun in it Grandpa.' You know, 'your *work* gun' –

[Laughter.]

– And Mike who goes all over the city and everywhere in his job – he could be mugged at any time so he has more of a reason to be able to protect himself.

J. McKinzey

I'm in the same boat as Mike is there. Being a commercial roofer, I have to go downtown and measure buildings, and I can get into some pretty bad parts of town and when I'm going down there I am carrying concealed, illegally. But if somebody approaches me in the hallway and it comes to it, I would much rather – what's the saying? – 'be judged by twelve than carried by six.'

M. McKinzey

I think that your observation is correct, though. We would agree that our effort is very local. We recognize that there's not much we can do about Washington DC – or there's limited things we can do. So we do concentrate on our own backyard – and hopefully if enough people do that then the big picture will take care of itself. Many of the issues we get involved in are very local, even to the point of operating a food pantry so that when we hear of somebody – maybe just two houses down – who needs something, we can help. So yeah, it's a very local –

Wittig

We sent food up to South Dakota.

M. McKinzey

We did that at one time.

Wittig

Kay's husband, Harold, was going to run for State Representative and we had another member, Pat Wyatt, who ran for a State Rep's job. So there is some political thrust that way. It doesn't happen very often and we haven't got anybody in yet, but we do work at it.

M. McKinzey

There were a number of open militia leaders who ran for state and federal offices, and I think that if we were going to run, we would look at local and county and state offices, because that's definitely where we could make a change.

Sheil

Another point about voting that nobody's mentioned – and I know this for a fact – is that there are a lot of people who vote on a state and local level who do not vote in federal elections. And there are many people, like me and Jackie, we punch those libertarian tickets every time.

Wittig

People talk and talk, and people say, 'Think about this and think about that. Pay attention to what they're doing.' My husband Chuck and I worked for Carson Ross last year in his election. He's a black Republican from our district, but we feel like he supports the Second Amendment, he supports a lot of the things that we believe in, so we feel like we can support him.

Sheil

Politics are different on state level than they are on national level – totally. At the state level they're far more open to the citizens. And coming back to how people vote, there are a lot of people who don't vote the top of the ticket any more. And I've come to the point where I would actually consider not voting myself. If there's not a libertarian running, or some independent that I care about, then the top of the ticket's not important any more because they don't listen.

Wittig

The other thing we've done is, we've put out a lot of literature at the gun shows we go to – at the tables we have at the gun shows – we've had patriot days, rallies and we've had speakers, and we have a group of people who we have dealt with called the Mid-West Constitutional Conference, and they've had speakers and we've worked with them.

Mulloy
The Mid-West Constitutional Conference?

M. McKinzey
It's a sister action group, a patriotic organization. It's predominantly retired folks. Their mission is education.

Hawkins
The thing that we do more than anything, and this is maybe all you *can* really do, is to try to educate people and sometimes, or, in fact, most of the time, it's just one on one.

Sheil
To get on our soapbox is very difficult.

Hawkins
Especially without the media. They're against us and they can reach 10 million with one oversimplified catch-phrase and we have to go out and take two hours explaining it to people.

M. McKinzey
At this point in our history, the pen is still mightier than the sword. And that's reflected in our budget. We spend more – well, much of it's donated – but if we had to buy it, then I would say that 90 per cent of our expenditure is on paper and copy machine supplies.

Hawkins
It's like the gun issue – the Second Amendment – that's obviously what we focus on, but we have other concerns beyond that.

Sheil
I was going to say, the next step of what we're planning to do is open carry. Just get that gun and strap it on. So if you don't want to see that gun, then give us a conceal-carry law.

M. McKinzey
What we're fighting against in that situation is just the social stigma of actually having a gun on your leg. But that's where we're going to go with it because we're not going to get the concealed carry law until our governors see this.

Mulloy
So this is a form of protest – walking around with a gun on your leg?

Wittig
That's right.

M. McKinzey
And in Missouri it's legal.

Hawkins
It's another one of those long-term education things. You talk to gun owners, lifelong gun owners, and you ask them, 'Well, how do you take your gun to the range or how do you go deer hunting or whatever?' And they say, 'You've got to take your bolt out of the rifle and the bolt's got to be in the glove box and the rifle's got to be in the trunk, the bullets have got to be in the glove box,' and *all* this crap, and that's what these people really *believe*. But the truth is you can lay it, cocked and locked, you can lay it in the seat next to you and it's perfectly legal.

Missouri not only has no law against that, they have a constitutional protection of that. Except for a few specific places, you can go armed in the state of Missouri – openly.

M. McKinzey
Openly.

Hawkins
But nobody knows that.

Wittig
But you can't carry it concealed!

Mulloy
So it's hunting, it's target shooting, it's self-defence, it's all these things that you use your guns for?

J. McKinzey
All of them.

Mulloy
And do you all hunt?

J. McKinzey

Some of us do.

M. McKinzey

It *is* all those things, but you didn't hit number one yet. The purpose of the Second Amendment is to throw bad bureaucrats out of the government, should that ever become necessary.

Wittig

For me, it's self-defense.

Sheil

It is self-defense. I practise religion. I'm a pacifist, but being a pacifist doesn't mean letting everyone step right over you. Being a pacifist means you don't initiate force. I'm a Buddhist – and you know there's lots of different religions in the world – and we believe that it's your right and duty to protect your own life and others around you. Your soul is precious. It comes from God. And the Second Amendment means it's my right. That's what it is, it's my *right*. Even if I never have a gun, it's *still* my right. I say to people who say they don't want a gun in the house, 'Well, if you don't want a gun in the house, nobody makes you have a gun, but please do not give up your *right* to be armed.'

Wittig

Those same people, they wouldn't put a sticker on their front door saying, 'No guns in this house' though, would they?

Hawkins

Yeah, 'I'm unarmed, come on in!'

M. McKinzey

I used to be kind of embarrassed about it, but I've talked to several other people and it's not apparently that unusual, but there is a very real and powerful feeling that comes with guns. I mean, you put a gun in your hand and that empowers you. You are personally empowered. And I don't know if you're a shooter or not, but every time I put a .45 in my hand, I am empowered.

Shiel

Have you ever shot a gun?

Mulloy

No.

Wittig

You're not allowed to in England?

Mulloy

Well, it's a totally different society, we have very little individual gun ownership –

Sheil

But still in England you have a lot of violence. So not having guns doesn't do away with violence.

M. McKinzey

And you know that stereotype of a 'violent West'? That's just what that is – a stereotype. And even the stereotype of a 'violent America' – if you take the ghettos out of the equation, we have an incredibly peaceful society.

Sheil

They say we're safer than we were twenty years ago.

Hawkins

We *are* if you look at the crime statistics.

Sheil

It's all localized in the inner cities. Guns and drugs. How come the BATF didn't make a raid on one of those buildings in LA where they have all those guns? I'm sure they would have found some illegal weapons. But no, they're gonna shoot up a church in Waco. They could have made a lot of arrests if they had moved in on one of those gangs. And those gangs are what are causing people problems. The people in Waco weren't causing anybody any problems. Their crime was maybe they had something there that they hadn't paid the tax on. That was the bottom of it.[29]

Hawkins

That was what they were anxious about.

Bingham

They haven't even proved that!

Hawkins

I *have* never seen any proof of that.

J. McKinzey

How did English people look at Waco? Did they know about it?

Mulloy

Yes, it got a lot of coverage at the time, and I think that anybody who's aware of the detail of what happened at Waco – as opposed to those who just saw it when it was on the TV – is of the view that it was very severely mishandled by the law enforcement agencies.

Bingham

When you see that tape, *The Rules of Engagement*, you'll understand why too.[30]

M. McKinzey

The plan was – and this is admitted to – the plan was to put enough gas into that church that the parents would have to bring those kids out.

J. McKinzey

Make the kids suffer until the parents gave in.

M. McKinzey

That was the plan. The mentality of those people! And you think we're not dealing with tyrants. And this was in the wake of the Ruby Ridge incident, which is probably not as well known. Are you familiar with it?

Mulloy

I'm familiar with it, yes.

M. McKinzey

The FBI flew out from Washington DC with 'shoot to kill' rules of engagement. With orders to kill any armed adult in the compound.[31]

Bingham

And they shot Vicki Weaver.

Sheil

[Lon T.] Horiuchi [the FBI sharpshooter who shot Vicki Weaver] said that he thought he was shooting at Kevin, but here he is, an expertly trained sniper using one of the best rifles in the world and he shot her right in the head. Now, it seems to me, he had to know where he was shooting. But it wasn't the federal government's fault! There's never any closure or punishment from the federal level.[32]

Mulloy
But there was a congressional investigation into the events at Ruby Ridge.

Sheil
Oh yeah, and into Waco, but they said there was no wrongdoing from law enforcement and, like you said, it was just a story of something being badly handled by law enforcement. But they initiated force and they got force back. You can argue about who set the compound on fire if you want to, but they set up the whole incident. And those people – carried out from what they called 'the compound', but we call 'a church' – you know, they may have been strange but it was their home, too.

M. McKinzey
They called them 'a cult'. They were Seventh Day Adventists. This religion's been in the United States for over 200 *years*.

Wittig
So *what*? It doesn't matter whether they were a cult or not. They had a perfect right to establish their religion.[33]

Hawkins
I think there is a tendency in society at large – one way or another – to attempt to suppress, drive out and ridicule people who are different. We're seeing that more and more. And that's exactly what these people were, these people were different. Yeah, I would definitely consider them Jesus freaks but I wouldn't burn them to death for that.

Sheil
In America you *can* be different, you have a right to be different, you have the right to aspire to whatever you want to be.

Wittig
You ever seen these little guys walking around with their purple hair and earrings all the way up? We don't shoot them! We walk by.

Hawkins

We *want* to shoot them but we don't!

[Laughter.]

Johnston

We can believe in any kind of religion that we want to believe in. That's constitutional. That's what we tore away from when we got away from Great Britain. And to go down there, like Janet Reno and those élite people, thinking we'll just label them 'a cult', heck, you could probably have put that label on just about *any* religion there is to a degree.

We've got religious freedom, probably here more so than in any other country in the world, and when I heard about Waco I was enraged. I was enraged! Because those people weren't out there *bothering* anybody. They weren't *hurting* anybody. And just to go out there and kill the kids and the families. I have a problem with that.

J. McKinzey

Let me ask you this Jim, When you heard about Waco, when you were enraged about it – and you go to church, regularly right? – how much was it talked about at the pulpit?

Johnston

I never heard it.

J. McKinzey

That's another point right there, because the churches are run by the government with their tax exempt status. If you get up in the pulpit and you talk politics, well then, 'We're gonna take your tax exempt status away from you.'

Johnston

There's been threats to do that, you're right about that.

J. McKinzey

So that's another reason why I have a problem with the church.

Wittig

Pat Robertson is losing his tax exempt status for a couple of years for some reason or other. It was in the paper.

M. McKinzey

One of things I'm often asked is, 'What's the driving motivation behind the militia movement?' And I think I've got it narrowed down to that we want to be left alone. Waco and Ruby Ridge were both situations where people wanted to be left alone. Those people moved to Ruby Ridge simply to be left alone.

Sheil

Whether he was a racist or not is not even important. They took the game to Mr Weaver.

M. McKinzey

That's right. They took it to him.

Hawkins

Well, it's not against the law to be racist.

M. McKinzey

And that goes back to what I was talking about earlier – or at least I think it does – about the idea of moving liberties from the people to the government and of moving power and then the federal government's got to protect that power. And when you go out there to stand up for whatever and then those things happen, well . . .

Mulloy

So Waco was the pivotal point for many of you?

Sheil

I was not a believer in the way the system of government was being run at the time of Waco. Like I said, I already spent a lot of time reading and just trying to figure out what was going on. I was active at that time in the Libertarian Party. And I remember my husband and I got up that morning, turned on the TV and saw this massive arrayment around the Davidians' church down there, and we both just looked at it, and we looked at each other, and we knew that the federal government had no point being there.

Those people were condemned. They were going to go down. I knew it as well as I knew my own name. They would have to destroy those people to keep their credibility. And eventually that's what they did.

One of the most poignant things was when they threw out a sheet saying, 'We need the press.' And the press, they were so jovial about it, said, 'God help us, we are the press!'[34]

Now another little thing that I was thinking about Waco, is that they had a trial for some of those members of the Branch Davidians and they were exonerated. The jury, when all is said and done, said that they felt they might be guilty of some weapons violations but they were exonerated of murder because the state law in Texas says no matter who comes, if they start shooting at you, you can shoot back –

J. McKinzey

With reasonable force.[35]

Sheil

– with reasonable force. But the whole thing is, the jury exonerated them and the press weren't there. We didn't get a day-by-day, blow-by-blow account of that, but we get it from OJ, a murder trial on the other side of the nation that did not affect *my life*. This was amazing to me, that the media can even say that they are journalists, that they can do this kind of thing – the TV media, for sure.

There was a lady who worked for our local paper, the *Kansas City Star*, her name's Emma Woolf [name changed]. She was a liberal before Waco. I used to exchange letters with her, even talk to her over the phone about gun rights. And after Waco she wrote a column about gun rights and admitted she'd never been a proponent of the Second Amendment but she pointed out that those people in the compound at Waco had less firepower than the average Texan, their neighbors around them. So what does this mean?

She left the *Star* because of ideological differences, I don't know what happened to Emma after that, but she, finally, was one of those who woke up and started travelling a new road. So it did turn some people's heads, but other people just want to ignore it. Some people, you know, they see that film *The Rules of Engagement* and they walk away crying. Other liberals refuse to look at it.

M. McKinzey

This film was put together, this documentary, by a guy who started out to make a one hour PBS [Public Broadcast Service] pro-government slam, and he was going to cover the last five or six hours of Waco. His thought was, 'Here's a bunch of religious wackos that committed suicide rather than surrender.' But as he got into it, things didn't start adding up. He changed sides during the making of this tape. He doesn't say that there but . . .

Sheil

Actually, somebody brought him that forward looking, infra-red tape – it's in the film – and you can see through the clear enhancement that the BATF are actually firing into the building.

M. McKinzey

As the building burns – but even if that were left out, it would be a very powerful film.

Sheil

It premiered at the Sundance Film Festival, you know, Robert Redford's festival, and he's a liberal. It played in San Francisco, and it made quite an impact in San Francisco with the liberals there. It's been nominated for Academy Awards. But I wonder if we'll ever see it on public TV because there was another film nominated for an Academy Award about Panama and our local PBS station refused to run it.

Mulloy
It played in London and got very good reviews.

M. McKinzey

It's gotten good reviews everywhere it's played.

Wittig

When it came to Kansas City it was scheduled for one week but it got extended for a second week because there were so many people wanting to see it.

M. McKinzey

Our group, the 51st Militia, was named with respect to the fifty-one days of the siege, but early on we also got involved with that Good Ol' Boys Picnic – you may have talked about this before – and we had a heck of a time getting anybody to have a look at that.[36]

Sheil

I faxed that story to every paper or magazine that I could get the fax number for. I spent three or four days sending that out. Finally we made contact with G. Gordan Liddy and through him we got to the *Washington Times* and the *Washington Times* broke the story. But all the story was written for them, it was laid out with pictures, videos, the whole bit.

The other thing about Waco, is that mini Waco's have been happening all over the country. We got involved with a family from southern Missouri, their name is Laura and Michael Burroughs [name changed]. They're very

103

devout and fervent Catholics, and they moved from the east coast, West Virginia, to Arkansas with a group of Catholics to set up a religious society. Then the group received a grant for a large amount of money and decided to move to Kentucky but Laura and Michael didn't like the area they were in, so they went several miles north into Missouri and found five acres and a house there.

They put down their life savings – they paid $30,000 for it – this was going to be their lifetime home. They bought this house from a woman whose son owned the property next door, and he wanted that property and he offered $15,000 for it, something like that, but his mother wouldn't sell it to him. She sold it to Michael and Laura, and that set up a problem right there.

Now Michael's a truck driver so he couldn't always be at home and whenever Michael was gone, Laura and her children were harassed by this man and his daughter.

It came to a head one day when Laura's daughter was riding a bicycle and this neighbor came by and ran her off the road and she fell into a ditch. That would make any mother angry, so Laura called up and said some choice words to him. She said, 'If you want to fight with me, come and fight with me, but leave my daughter alone.'

And in the meantime, the neighbor had been making sexual remarks to Laura. He even made racial remarks. She's a white woman but her father was adopted. They don't even know what her father's background is, but he had a dark complexion and so she was asked by this man, 'Why you're awful dark aren't you, sure there ain't nigger in the woodpile.'

So one day after that incident with the telephone call the neighbors drove down to Laura's house. They sat in front of her house and she was afraid. She picked up the gun her husband had – the neighbors never saw it – and she looked out the window with the gun. The gun had a trigger lock on it so it couldn't be fired.

Anyways, maybe a week after this, her and the kids settled down at about eight o'clock in the evening to watch a video on TV. Four cars pulled up in the yard, men came rushing up – rushing into her house – dressed like a SWAT team, holding guns, automatic rifles on her kids. They told them to sit down, and they pointed guns at their kids, her little girl was crying. And then, finally, a guy came in and identified himself. He was from the local sheriff's office, and they had had a complaint that she had pointed a gun and threatened her neighbor, and that they also had illegal firearms and had been exploding bombs.

Now when it all shook out, we found out that the BATF was involved, our state police, the highway patrol, they had people there, as well as other law enforcement. They even brought – and this is scary – an ambulance. Did they expect to kill those people that night?

Well, while she was waiting for trial, she called every state and federal office she possibly could, asking for protection, because there's nothing worse – think about it – then when law enforcement are the ones who've violated your home. From the Attorney General's Office, right on down, they claimed to have no jurisdiction.

We got acquainted with her because she asked for help from the militia because nobody else would help her. They were just like everybody else, they thought militia people were crazy, but I talked to her.

They thought that we could send armed people down there to protect her. I said, no, we really can't do that, because people have jobs, but I told her the best advice was to take it to the press, to go public with it. Once you've done that then the law enforcement agencies have got to stand back.

Well, as things proceeded she was totally exonerated but they lost their home – they had to sell their home just for money to live on – Michael had to quit his job, the kids were traumatized, you know. All that's happened to them. And when I made a speech at the university at St. Joseph we had this guy who was from the Attorney General's Office in Missouri down there, and he said, 'Well, at least she had her day in court.'

Does this *exonerate* this whole thing that happened to these people? That she had her day in court to clear her name? She hasn't been compensated for any of the other things that happened to her. Is this American justice?

I like to talk about what happened to Laura to people right here in Missouri, because they think that it only happens somewhere else. But it doesn't, it happens right here.

There was another case with a man over in Independence. They went in, the federal agents, absolutely trashed his house, did everything in the world to him and never could find any of the illegal weapons he was supposed to have. And then they claimed that they found a small amount of marijuana to justify it. That small amount of marijuana came out about two weeks after they had done everything else they could to find anything illegal in his home.

It goes on and on and there's been no end to it. And that's one of the things I'd like to stop. I'd like to see people ask for a moratorium on this stuff, on this war on drugs, and look at the bigger picture, but nobody elected will talk about doing anything about changing the drug policy in the United States.

Bingham

I don't know of anybody in office who has got any backbone about them at *all*.

Sheil

Well, it's obviously not about drugs because they haven't even slowed down drug addiction in the United States.

Johnston

But they sure like to confiscate your property!

Sheil

They can take mostly anybody's property.

Mulloy

Can I ask you this: Have you ever thought of changing the name of your organization from a militia to something else, because –

J. McKinzey

We thought about it.

Mulloy

But you decided not to.

J. McKinzey

We want that word 'militia' in there because it makes people look at you. It makes people listen to what we want to say.

Sheil

I've even told members of press, 'If we didn't call ourselves a militia, you wouldn't be here.' *You* wouldn't be here if we didn't call ourselves militia. So, that's the only way we can climb on to our soapbox.

M. McKinzey

We *are* a militia.

Mulloy

But from what you've been saying a lot of your political positions might be characterized as being either libertarian or conservative, and part of what you're saying is that you can't get people to listen to you because they're prejudiced against the word militia.

Hawkins

The Republicans and the Libertarians can't get people to listen either because they just don't stir up anybody. Nobody wants to pay attention to that.

Sheil

The Libertarians get less press than we do!

J. McKinzey

We're talking about the demographics of the militia. There's very few Democrats in the militia. A lot of Republicans, a lot of Libertarians and a lot of that's just third party. The last major election – I vote in all of them – but the last major one we had with the president and everything, I voted all three parties. I take each candidate as an individual and look at what they stand for, but there's so many people out there that'll walk into the booth and just hit that Democrat button and then turn around and walk out.

Mulloy

What about the religious make-up of the group?

J. McKinzey

It's pretty wide.

Hawkins

I'd say it's generally Christian conservative.

J. McKinzey

I don't think we have any atheists, but it wouldn't make any difference if we did.

Sheil

We have some people who are more agnostic, I think.

J. McKinzey

We have Jewish members.

Sheil

But religion, occupation, political affiliations, that's not what the militia's about because the militia is for the *whole* people.

Wittig

The militia's about love of our country. It's got nothing to do with anything else.

Sheil

What was it James Madison said? 'You are the militia, they are us, they are the whole people.'[37]

J. McKinzey

A few years ago, a small group of us was on the *McNeil/Lehrer Newshour*, and the first question they asked me was, 'Which one of your liberties have been infringed upon?' I didn't have an answer for it. Since then, I'm ready. You don't wait for someone to infringe upon your liberties to stand up for it. If you wait until that point, you'd be like the residents down at Waco. It was too late for them to stand up.

Hawkins

It's too late when they're kicking your door in.

Sheil

That was real interesting, that whole *McNeil/Lehrer Newshour*, on which we got about five minutes. Jim was there, my husband Harold was there, and they all talked about problems with the federal government in various different ways, and how it had affected their lives. And after it was over they had these militia experts –

[Laughter.]

– and what I remember most is they had Morris Dees from the Southern Poverty Law Center – I'd never seen him before – and his comment was, 'That's not a militia, those people don't know anything about a militia.' Because he would not accept that we were like we were.[38]

J. McKinzey

But now I'm on his top 120 list, so apparently we learned how to be one.[39]

[Laughter.]

Sheil

I don't even know how they put that list together, because it's just a list of Patriots, of 'prominent Patriots'. Jim's on there and the information is bogus.

J. McKinzey

They got my name right but everything else is wrong.

Sheil

Terry Nichols is on there, McVeigh is on there, those people are on there. Now what do *they* have to do with patriotism?

Wittig

They didn't even *make* a militia. Militias kicked them out.

M. McKinzey

You talked about the image the militia gives, even just the word. Well, to some degree – to a large degree – even the word 'Patriot' is being added to that list of dirty words.

Sheil

It's not *cool* to be a Patriot, it's not *hip*.

Johnston

Back up now and I'll give you an example.

I work part-time for a tool-cutter, and this gal says, 'Are you available to work at such and such a time.'

I said, 'Well, yeah, I can be available here, but I can't be available here, here or here.'

She said, 'Why not?'

I said, 'I gotta go to a gun show with the Missouri 51st.'

'Are you a member?'

And I said, 'Yeah,' and I showed her my ID card.

She says, 'OK.'

Well this went on for a while, and I'd been to about three or four gun shows.

'Jim', she says, 'have you ever thought about getting out of the militia?'

I said, 'No, it'll be a cold day in hell before I get out.'

She says, 'Why?'

I said, 'In the first place, before I answer that question, why don't you back up three steps?'

She said, 'What for?'

I said, 'What do you know about a militia? Tell me what you know. What investigative work have you done to know that being in a militia would make me look bad down the road?'

She said, 'Well, there's been a little bit about it in the news, they're talking about those Arizona Vipers.'

I said, 'Well, what do you know about the 51st Militia?'

And she said, ' I don't know anything about it.'

So then I said, 'How do you know that between now and somewhere down the road that it's gonna make me look bad? If you don't know anything about it, aren't you prejudging the organization without any in-depth knowledge of it.'

I said, 'Now, if this is going to create a problem with me working with you, I'll be more than glad to give you back the truck keys and the gate keys and there won't be no hard feelings. I'll give you back my keys and I'll say sionara, and this will all be over but for the crying, if this is going to create a problem.'

She said, 'No, I never did say it was gonna create a problem.'

I said, 'These guys have been in business for four years and for three years of it I haven't checked them out.'

And I says, 'I talked to my barber and I was going to that opening meeting down there in Kansas City, to the library, and Orvill said something there, he said, "Well, the FBI and the ATF will be there and they'll take a picture of your car license plate and six months down the road they'll come and kick in your door."'

But everything bad that I'd heard about the 51st never panned out, and now like I told him, I wished I'd joined three years ago. But hindsight is '20:20' and I did something a lot of people didn't do. I sat there and observed and looked and I went to the meetings. I thought they were *great*, I found all of them to be law abiding citizens. And religion didn't play a factor in it at all. *Not at all.* They all seemed to be God-fearing people, and whether they go to church or not is not left up to me to decide. I'm not their judge or nothing. I have no quarrels with them.

And since that time, she calls me up and says, 'Hey, can you be available?'

'Yes'

'You ain't got a gun show?'

'No.'

So *she* listened. But most people don't know nothing about the militia groups. They think that whatever the government says is gospel. 'They don't lie, they don't do no wrong.'

Sheil

Actually, when you get right down to the story, it's fear of the government. We had one of those polls recently and the results said that 75 per cent of the people do not trust the government. And they're talking about the federal government. It's fear of government that keeps a lot of people down.

Hawkins

I've had that conversation with people 100 times in the last four years. They'll tell me, 'You gotta quit this or you're gonna disappear. They're gonna come and get you, they're gonna round you up and kick in your door, blah blah blah.' And fortunately, now we can tell them, 'Well, it's been four years and I don't know anybody who's disappeared.'

Sheil

And we're willing to take that risk. 'OK, come and get us, here we are.'

Mulloy

Do you think you've had ATF or FBI agents trying to infiltrate you?

J. McKinzey

Oh yeah, two or three times. Since we're the type of organization that we are, we use our heads a little bit and you can pick these people out, so we'll call up the FBI and say, 'We've got this mysterious guy hanging around us, you might want to check it out.'

Sheil

'Does he belong to you?!'

[Laughter.]

Sheil

– That was the policy at the beginning. If anybody comes in and they talk about doing illegal things we just drop a dime on them. We figure that most of the time they're FBI anyway.

Hawkins

We've had very little of that really, but yeah, anytime anybody's ever come to a meeting and wanted to know when we're gonna blow something up, it's been somebody from law enforcement. They kind of stick out.

Sheil

They might pick on anybody with a federal firearms license. And they talk about minorities that are picked up. That little story I told you about Laura and Michael, well, Michael at one time had a federal firearm license. They had a profile on him. 'Religious convert, moved out with a group, had a firearm license' – obviously he thought the Second Amendment was important.

111

M. McKinzey

I don't want to get into that particular story, but Sam's story fits the profile. That's a whole other story. He was a guy who was from Iran. He had a Ph.D. in Chemistry. He worked for the federal government. Well, two days after the Trade Center bombing in New York, several years ago, his life fell in on itself. I mean he's *not right* yet. They descended on him and I know they just keyed it in on a little keyboard and here's Sam's name flashing, and they ruined his life. They ruined his life.

Sheil

We know of one of our supporters who recently acquired a federal firearms license and he's been approached by a person several times to put a bayonet on an Enfield rifle.

M. McKinzey

This happened two months ago right here in Kansas City and he's just taken an ad in the paper. An Enfield is the old, bolt-action-standard World War One rifle. It's English. And we had a law called the Assault Weapon Ban passed in 1994, and to put a bayonet – this is a little oversimplified – but to put a bayonet on most of these guns is illegal – ten years.

So this guy kept showing up at this guy's house with this bayonet trying to get him to put the bayonet on the rifle. Now, he's gone out of his way to say, 'I'm not gonna put that bayonet on. Buy the rifle, take it home, do what you want to do, but I'm not gonna do it.' But the guy's persistent – an obvious *provocateur* – and these guys go round getting paid by the person they trick.

And the fundamental question is: Does a moral government create laws that put people in jail for ten years for putting bayonets on rifles? And do they send people around to trick you into doing that?

This guy is a member of a militia group – not our group, but a good group – and so he's a threat. Now, if he had put that bayonet on that rifle, several days later here would have come the BATF and he – it's my opinion – he probably would have decided to resist arrest and then he would have asked for help.

And then we would have to make that moral decision that you were talking about earlier. When do people make moral decisions? We would have been put into the position of deciding, Is this where I fight? It's a problem.

Sheil

He might not have resisted if they came to his door, but the chances of that happening, of them knocking on his door, are about as likely as me winning the lottery. They would have come in the middle of the night, kicked in his door, and he would have responded like most people who are ready and armed to defend themselves.

M. McKinzey

And if they hadn't killed him outright, he would have asked for help.

J. McKinzey

If he'd had the opportunity to get the word out, we would have had to make decisions, and since Mike and I are personal friends of his, our decision would have been to grab our guns and say, 'We're gonna go help this guy.'

M. McKinzey

And that's a scary, scary thing.

J. McKinzey

That option could not only end his life, but it could end my life and Mike's life, and other people in the militia, who would have come along, I think, from the 51st to help defend this case.

M. McKinzey

I just don't know that people grasp the seriousness of the situation.

Sheil

One of the most despicable things about these *provocateurs* is that they're only paid informants. They get breaks on charges or they get money for doing this. They don't care. They're scum. They're not honorable people, they're not even from the government.

Mulloy

How do your families feel about the possibility of your getting involved in that kind of situation?

J. McKinzey

In my case, my wife is also involved in the militia. We have talked about it, and because we never know when this moral decision is going to come down the line, I do not own a car, I do not own my house – everything is in my wife's name. And that's just one small thing so that if something happens to me, she can still carry on. But she would trust me to make a right decision. And it's going to have to be an awful good example for me to grab my gun and go. I mean, I'm really going to have to be pushed hard to do that. Because if we have to grab our guns we've lost our cause.

Sheil

There'd be no turning back. You know people talk about the militia as wanting a second revolution. No sane person in this country would want a civil war. That would destroy our government; our government as we've known it would be gone.

J. McKinzey

Mike, Rick and myself, we were all in the Army and we know what it's like to be out in the dead of winter in a tent. Jackie's husband was even a prisoner of war for a short time. It's no picnic out there, and I'm in no hurry to get out there again. And I'm going to do everything I can to keep it from going there.

Wittig

Chuck says says he will never be in that situation again where he's a prisoner of war.

M. McKinzey

The interesting thing is, had that friend put a bayonet on that rifle and the worst case scenario had come down, most people would have just shook their heads. They would have no idea what happened and why.

J. McKinzey

And the reason we would have went, was not because he put the bayonet on to the rifle, but because of the principle that had been violated.

M. McKinzey

Or they would say, 'Well, why doesn't he just surrender and go through the system?' And I would say, 'Well, that's like telling the Jews as they got in to the box car, "Just go for the ride. I'm gonna file a brief, and we'll get you outta there. Trust me."' But you're right, it's a moral dilemma.

Hawkins

You got any Schindlers out there?

Sheil

You know, Hollywood's a strange thing. I picked up two little interesting pieces of obscure history last week about the movies they make. *Schindler's List* – They never mentioned that when these people were let go into Czechoslovakia, Schindler armed them, knowing that people who weren't armed who enter war zones can't protect themselves. But that was never mentioned; it was just like he was a benevolent saviour. The other thing is in that movie *Amistad* – that's a great movie, but do you know what Cinque [the central character in the film] did when he got back to Africa? He became a slave trader, and that's real contradictory, to make a hero out of this man.[40]

Bingham

Another thing that's pretty scary is Congress passing laws which create criminals by legislation like the Lautenberg law.

Mulloy

What was that?

M. McKinzey

This is a law they even snuck through on us, and we're watching them! They tucked it on the end of last year's budget.[41] Basically, it says that if you've ever had a conviction – even a misdemeanour – for anything that could be defined as domestic violence, then you can't own a weapon, and that's even if you were convicted fifteen years ago. It's retroactive, for ever!

Sheil

Even the government can't handle this one because they didn't do what they usually do with laws they pass, which is they usually exempt Congress, the Senate, law enforcement and the military. But they didn't, so they're going to have to reappraise this one because the military were up in arms, because people in the military had their guns taken away from them; there were people in law enforcement that had their guns taken away from them.

Wittig

Just because they got into a bar fight sometime when they were eighteen years old with their brother, or their sister or somebody that they were living with. That's all defined as domestic violence.

J. McKinzey

When this all came down, the 51st had its yearly meeting, and there's like 200 people in the audience, and we had the ATF and the FBI there, and we stood up and told them to their faces that we were not going to comply.

Sheil

We even had a police officer from Independence who stood up and said, 'I can't enforce these laws. I will not enforce these laws.'

Wittig

That was brave of him to do that.

Sheil

Yes, but that's the kind of people we have to have. You've got to be willing to put yourself on the line even if it's only with your mouth. The FBI, they just smiled benevolently; they have no problem with it. The guy from BATF, he just shook his head.

'First', he said, 'I don't pass these laws.'

'Yes, but you're going to have to enforce them. Look at our faces, we're the people that you're going to have to come to.'

And then he says, 'Well, how would I know what you have in your house anyway?'

Bingham

'If you're not out there making bombs', he said, 'we're not gonna bother you.'

J. McKinzey

But that's what distinguishes the 51st from a lot of these other militias. There is no question about where we stand. We tell everybody and anybody and we're not ashamed of it.

Sheil

I said, 'All our lives we've been hard working, law abiding citizens and now you're gonna come and pass more laws and make us criminals.' We just can't go along with it, we'll have to become criminals. And you know that Amnesty International in 1994 said that the US had more political prisoners than South Africa. I thought about getting on to their website and looking that over and seeing what the situation is still like. Most people in this country wouldn't even believe we have political prisoners.

M. McKinzey

Have you read *Unintended Consequences*? It's a book by a guy named John Ross about the history of guns in America.[42]

Sheil

It's a novel. It's got a good story in it, but there's valuable history on the Second Amendment too.

J. McKinzey

All throughout the twentieth century, push, push, push.

M. McKinzey

It's worth looking into to get a feel for the gun culture in the US.

Mulloy

Yes, well I think the gun culture *is* difficult for a lot of people outside the US to understand.

Sheil

Well, there's people who like to shoot those big guns, those fully automatic machine guns for recreation. They collect them and they like to use them. But they haven't committed any crimes with them, so why does our government continue to put pressure on them?

There's a man down in Alabama who spent three years in prison for having some night-sight binoculars he wasn't supposed to have that were sold to him by a government agent, and he went to prison because he had them. *Why*? If you believe the government is benevolent and isn't trying to take all the power from the people, to disarm the people of the United States, then why do they do these things?

M. McKinzey

You have to understand that the BATF is part of the Treasury Department. All the gun laws are parts of the Internal Revenue Code. It's about collecting money. It's not about public safety. Any American citizen without a felony conviction can own a truckload of machine guns. You've just got to pay the taxes. You got to feed the bureaucracy – the monster. It's not about machine guns or the danger. In fact, when I got my Federal Firearms License they practically begged me to get a Class Three License for $600. She must have been getting commission or something. She asked me three or four times. 'Are you sure you don't want a Class Three?' That's $600 as opposed to $90.

Sheil

The policy of the anti-gun movement is to put all the stuff on gun owners. Unfortunately, if you pick up a newspaper they always say, 'the grass-roots organization for gun control', and it's always 'the powerful gun lobby, the powerful NRA'. Yeah, right! There's a joke: Why is Sarah Brady doing what she does for gun control? $600,000 a year.

Hawkins

If you look at the crime statistics – and this is something that people just don't grasp – but if you get a copy of the Justice Department's crime statistics reports – which you can get from any public library – you'll see that all of our crime problems, like somebody was saying earlier, are in the inner cities. But the gun laws they've passed in the past few years are on assault weapons, and even Janet Reno admitted, when they passed that law, that assault weapons were used in less than 1 per cent of all crime. I pulled something off of the Justice Department's webpages just the other night, that said the involvement of assault weapons in crime today is almost incalculable because they're involved in so few.

But the government is not worried about a fourteen-year-old black kid down in the 'hood with a .25 automatic in his pocket – they're not writing laws to stop that, even though that's what they're stating the problem is – the government is worried about 80 million middle-class, tax-paying, property owners with AK47s because we're a risk. Because as taxes go up and our liberties are slowly but surely squeezed, we're the people who are going to cause them a lot of problems. The drug dealers and the punks and all the criminal element, they don't threaten the government, they never have threatened the government. Those people in the government aren't in the least bit worried about that; they're worried about us.

I had a huge argument a couple of weeks ago at the rock-climbing club I belong to, and that's absolutely the other side of the looking-glass from this group. The entire group is made up of doctors, lawyers and teachers. There's very few of us that aren't some type of professional. And I just heard out of the corner of my ear, somebody was talking about, 'There isn't much crime in Canada is there?' and 'Yeah, well, there's no guns.'

And we got into a big one. And about half way through the conversation I find out that this girl's an immigrant, she's from Canada, and they left Canada because taxes were so high. And I'm trying to tell her that the way the government imposes high taxes on you is by taking away your ability to resist.

You go to Europe. In England, Capital Gains Tax is *something*. Most of the rock stars back in the sixties and seventies they came here so they didn't have to pay Capital Gains Tax. Well, with no way to resist that, with no way to turn that back, the government will basically force upon you anything they want.

She was going on and on about the government taking care of people and socialized medicine and how much better it works in Canada. Well, like, 'Why aren't *you* in Canada?'

She left Canada because the economic opportunity isn't nearly as good and the taxes are way too high there, but she stood there supporting large scale government influence in our lives – welfare, socialised medicine, the whole bit – and bitching about our taxes. I thought, 'Are you listening to yourself?'

Sheil

You know, one of the impressions I came away from England with, when I was first there, was how poor the people are and how big the gap was between the rich and the poor. I was shocked at the actual poverty of the whole society.

Mulloy

The whole society?

Sheil

Well, there's just no middle class like we have here.

J. McKinzey

If you look at what influence guns have on society, you take the Jews and the Warsaw ghetto. How many German troops had to be brought in to get that ghetto under control?[43]

Hawkins

That's a perfect example in history you can look at. When Hitler banned guns, if they'd have resisted then, they wouldn't have had a problem, but once the guns were taken away then it was, 'Well, OK, wear this patch on your shirt, stand over here, and go and live in this part of town.'[44]

And that's what's starting to happen here. It's just like I was talking about taxation, it's a slow gradual 'Restrict this,' 'Ban this,' 'Register that' attitude and once you got them all registered you can round them all up. And then 40 per cent to 50 per cent income tax becomes a very realistic possibility because there isn't anything you can do about it. You can elect people to go to Washington to stop it and when they get to Washington and everybody goes, 'Well, you know, if we get them to pay 50 per cent income tax, look how much more money you got to spend.' They're gonna go, 'Oh, OK, well let's do that.'

We have so many modern examples that are in the news right now –

Bosnia is such a textbook example – of what happens when only the government has guns and then the government decides to turn out the lights and go home, or the main powerful central government just leaves the local government with all the guns.

Sheil

Or they leave you with the UN to protect you. A lot of people in the States at the moment are against the UN because they feel it's part of a New World Order or world government. I'm against it because it's been an *ineffectual* organization from the beginning. It has not worked, look at Lebanon.

Johnston

Every place that they have gone to protect they have installed communism.

Sheil

Well, it's not just that – the people that they've been 'protecting' have been nearly wiped out. Lebanon is a perfect example because the Israelis bombed Lebanon for weeks and what did the UN ever do? It doesn't work. It's ineffectual, it's really a silly organization. There's no real power, it takes up money and causes a lot of problems for people who don't need that kind of problem. But about the Warsaw ghetto, I think you expect Americans to choose their heroes from American society but those people in Warsaw that made a stand – I don't even know their names but they're my heroes. They held up a whole German Panzer Division with that little outbreak, that's what that power can do for you, the empowerment of, 'OK, I've got a gun in my hand and I can use it' – and they did.

M. McKinzey

I think you have to make the jump of – we live in a country with a benevolent government or maybe we don't. I mean, I'm not willing to say we do, so I better keep my gun. I don't trust these guys.

Sheil

As a student of history, I've never found any benevolent government. Government in its nature is not benevolent.

M. McKinzey

That's right, government is *force*.

J. McKinzey

To regress a little bit and kind of blow the horn of the 51st, a lot of the militias that are in the United States today are wearing out their equipment going on alert. Def-Con Three, Def-Con Two – some of the militias are on Def-Con Two as we speak here today. Now, the first time we ever went on alert was the day the Murrah building in Oklahoma blew up. I put the 51st on alert to start gathering up medical stuff, blankets, food supplies and we were going to hit Oklahoma City. All these other ones went on Def-Con Three and started heading for the woods, but we were going to go down there and help people. Our philosophy seems to be different from everybody else's.

M. McKinzey

You'll never hear it but during the very first day of the Oklahoma City bombing, a lot of those guys walking round there in camouflage fatigues were militia. They moved right in, but once the smoke cleared and FEMA [the Federal Emergency and Management Agency] was there and the government had taken it over, it was, 'All you rednecks take a walk.' But either the mayor or the governor, or someone did at one point acknowledge the militias' help.

J. McKinzey

It was the mayor of Oklahoma City, I think. He only did it once and he was told, 'Don't do that again.'

Sheil

At the last meeting Mike or somebody said something about that we were on a list as an example of neo-militias. What do they mean by neo-militia?

M. McKinzey

It's on the Militia Watchdog.[45] 'Neo' means new, upcoming, revised. 'Neo' is just Latin for new. They put it on there because it sounds like neo-Nazis.

Mulloy

I think it's just to distinguish you from the eighteenth-century militia.

Hawkins

Yeah, but we're not that old. There's no distinction.

Mulloy

Yes, but *you* didn't exist in the eighteenth century, so you are new now.

M. McKinzey

When I first read it, 'neo-militia', I got out my dictionary and looked it up because I thought, they are tying us in with the Nazis.

Mulloy

I really don't think that's what's intended.

Hawkins

I think the media use it as a buzz word. In reality, it doesn't mean anything bad, but you know what the Militia Watchdog is, I mean they hate us. Just like 'paramilitary' has become an evil word. 'Para' just means 'like'. We are a military-like organization; so are the boy scouts, but 'a paramilitary neo-militia' is a horrible thing now. Nobody gives it a second thought.

Shoot for Larry Gates, June 1997

Notes

1.　Larry Pratt (ed.), *Safeguarding Liberty: The Constitution and Citizen Militias* (Franklin, Tennessee, Legacy Communications, 1995). A collection of essays from various academic and non-academic advocates of the right to keep and bear arms, the book covers issues ranging from the historical, biblical and philosophical roots of the Second Amendment to the practical role gun ownership plays in preventing crime in the United States. Larry Pratt, the book's editor, is the founder of the gun rights organization Gun Owners of America.

2.　The idea of Switzerland as providing a model for how a nation should arm its citizens is discussed in 'The Swiss Report' by George S. Patton and Lewis W. Walt, ibid, 197–212.

3.　307 U.S. 174 (1939). There are several nineteenth-century cases dealing with the Second Amendment, but *Miller* is the only twentieth-century decision in which the Supreme Court has extensively considered the scope of the right to bear arms. Jack Miller and an accomplice were charged with transporting an unregistered sawn-off shotgun in interstate commerce in violation of the National Firearms Act of 1934. They challenged their indictment on Second Amendment grounds before the District Court and won. The case then went to the Supreme Court on the question of whether it was proper to take judicial notice of whether a sawn-off shotgun was a 'militia weapon' and thus protected by the Second Amendment, or whether such a finding required evidentiary proceedings. The Supreme Court reversed the first decision and referred the case back to the District Court for further fact-finding proceedings. It held:

> In the absence of any evidence tending to show that possession or use of a 'shotgun having a barrel of less than eighteen inches in length' at this time has some reasonable relationship to the preservation or efficiency of a well regulated militia, we cannot say that the Second Amendment guarantees the right to keep and bear such an instrument. Certainly it is not within judicial notice that this weapon is any part of the ordinary military equipment or that its use could contribute to the common defense.

Unfortunately, as Glenn Reynolds points out in his 'Critical Guide to the Second Amendment,' the opinion of the Supreme Court in this case is 'somewhat confusing' and partisans on all sides of the gun rights debate have been able to invoke it to support their own particular interpretations of the right to bear arms. *Tennessee Law Review* (Vol. 62, Spring 1995, No. 3), 461–512. On this point, see also David C. Williams, 'Civic Republicanism and the Citizen Militia: The Terrifying Second Amendment,' *The Yale Law Journal* (Vol. 101, 1991–92), 551–615, especially 556–559.

For a restrictive view of *Miller* based on 'a collective rights' interpretation of the Second Amendment, see Keith A. Ehrman and Dennis Henigan, 'The Second Amendment in the Twentieth Century: Have You Seen Your Militia Lately?', *University of Dayton Law Review* (Vol. 15, Fall 1989, No.1), 5–58, and Thomas Halpern et al., *The Limits of Dissent: The Constitutional Status of Armed Civilian Militias* (Amherst, Massachusetts, Aletheia Press, 1996), especially 72–91. For a less restrictive view based on an 'individual rights' interpretation of the Second Amendment, see Robert Dowlut, 'Federal and State Constitutional Guarantees To Arms,' *University of Dayton Law Review* (Vol. 15, Fall 1989, No.1), 59–89, and Sanford Levinson, 'The Embarrassing Second Amendment,' *The Yale Law Journal* (Vol. 99, 1989–90), 637–659.

4.　In the view of Robert Dowlet, Deputy General Counsel for the National Rifle Association, the opinion of the Supreme Court in *Miller* does suffer 'from a fundamental defect' because neither the defendants nor their representatives appeared before the Court, and therefore the Court 'considered only the government's view', ibid,73.

5.   Bingham is referring here to another aspect of the gun rights debate. Advocates of the 'collective' or 'states' rights' theory of the Second Amendment interpret the 'right of the people' in this context as meaning only that the rights of state militias to bear arms were intended to be protected from interference from the federal government. Lawrence Cress, for example, argues that during the Confederation period State Constitutions such as that of New Hampshire used the word 'man' or 'person' to 'describe individual rights such as freedom of conscience', and the use of the term 'the people' in relation to the right to bear arms is intended to refer to the 'sovereign citizenry' collectively organized for the 'common defense'. Lawrence Delbert Cress, 'An Armed Community: The Origins and Meaning of the Right to Bear Arms,' *The Journal of American History* (Vol. 71, June 1984, No.1), 22–42. See also Ehrman and Henigan, 'The Second Amendment,' and Halpern, *Dissent*.

Advocates of the 'individual rights' approach to the Second Amendment reject this argument, because it ignores the fact, they say, that in the First, Fourth and Ninth Amendments of the Constitution, the phrase 'right of the people' clearly refers to individual rights, and that where Congress intended to protect the rights of the states, as in the case of the Tenth Amendment, it explicitly wrote 'the States'. On this see Stephen Halbrook, *That Every Man Be Armed: The Evolution of a Constitutional Right* (University of New Mexico Press, Albuquerque, 1984), 84–87; David B. Kopel, 'Trust the People: The Case Against Gun Control,' in Pratt (ed.), *Safeguarding*, 261–305; Levinson, 'Embarrassing,' 645–647; and Reynolds, 'A Critical Guide,' 466–471.

6.   Jews for the Preservation of Firearms Ownership have a website at 'www.jpfo.org' and Gun Owners of America can be found at 'www.gunowners.org'.

7.   *United States v. Lopez* 115. S. Ct. 1624 (1995). Alfonso Lopez, Jr. was a twelfth-grade student who was charged with violating the Gun-Free School Zones Act of 1990 after he carried a concealed .38 calibre handgun and five bullets into his high school in San Antonio, Texas. Under the Act, Congress had made it a federal offence 'for any individual knowingly to possess a firearm at a place that the individual knows, or has reasonable cause to believe is a school zone'. The Supreme Court held that the Act exceeded Congress's authority under the Commerce Clause of the Constitution (Article I, Section 8, Clause 3) '[t]o regulate Commerce. . . among the several States' because it 'neither regulated a commercial activity, nor contained a requirement in which the possession of such firearms was connected in any way to interstate commerce'.

8.   The First Amendment reads: 'Congress shall make no law respecting an establishment of religion, or prohibiting the free exercise thereof; or abridging the freedom of speech, or of the press; or of the right of the people peaceably to assemble, and to petition the Government for a redress of grievances.'

The Fourth Amendment reads: 'The right of the people to be secure in their persons, houses, papers, and effects, against unreasonable searches and seizures, shall not be violated, and no warrants shall issue, but upon probable cause, supported by Oath or affirmation, and particularly describing the place to be searched, and the person or things to be seized.'

9.   One of the most frequently heard arguments in the gun rights debate is that it is the rights of the National Guard as the 'militia' which are protected by the Second Amendment. However, it is difficult to sustain this argument on the basis of the historical evidence. As Joyce Malcolm writes: 'The argument that today's National Guardsmen . . . would constitute the *only* persons entitled to keep and bear arms has no historical foundation.' This is because, Malcolm explains, the National Guard functions as a 'select militia' and America's founders regarded a 'select militia' as 'little better than a standing army'. The United States Code also makes a clear distinction between the militia and the National Guard. See note 13 of the Introduction to this volume. Joyce Lee Malcolm, *To Keep And Bear Arms: The Origins of an Anglo-American Right* (Cambridge, Harvard University Press, 1994), 163. See also

Reynolds, 'A Critical Guide,' 475–478; David Hardy, 'The Militia is Not the National Guard,' in Pratt (ed.), *Safeguarding*, 99–106; and Levinson, 'Embarrassing,' 39.

10. Bingham is referring here to the National Guard Act of 1933 which allowed the 'militias' to serve overseas. It is not the case, however, that the 51st Militia should therefore be regarded as part of the American Armed Forces, although if they meet the age and citizen requirements set down in the *United States Code* (Section 311), individual members can be said, along with any other Americans meeting these requirements, to be part of the 'Unorganized Militia' of the United States. Indeed this is recognized in the names some militias have given to themselves, *viz*. the Ohio Unorganized Militia, and Linda Thompson's Unorganized Militia of the United States.

11. The existence and operations of single cell groups or 'phantom cells' within the militia movement is one of the major concerns of monitoring agencies such as the American Jewish Committee, the Anti-Defamation League and the Southern Poverty Law Center. See, for example, the extract from *False Patriots* at pages 251–254 of this volume. On the militias' use of this strategy, see the Militia of Montana at pages 351–352.

On the militias' fears of 'infiltration' by the government see the 'Policing the Militias' section of this volume at pages 409–421.

12. John Hancock was the first signatory of the Declaration of Independence and his name is now a common shorthand term used to refer to a signature of any kind.

13. McKinzey is referring to the provisions of Section 8 Article 1 of the Constitution which set out the powers of Congress. This list of powers is regarded literally by the militias as providing a clear and strict limitation on Congress's activities. These powers have become more expansive over time, however, as a consequence of the interpretation placed upon them by the Supreme Court, particularly in relation to the 'supremacy of laws' and 'regulation' of commerce clauses.

14. *The Resister* magazine, describing itself as the 'Official Publication of the Special Forces Underground', is a Patriot publication aimed specifically at military personnel. See pages 413–414 in this volume.

15. The term 'Freeman', John George and Laird Wilcox explain, is a 'euphemism for a kind of anarcho-libertarian lifestyle devoid of taxes, gun control, and other encroachments from the state, such as compulsory education and building codes'. Often referring to themselves as 'sovereign citizens', 'Freemen' feel that they are not bound by the 'federal jurisdiction of the United States'. Unsurprisingly, the Freemen's beliefs often lead to confrontations with the judicial and law enforcement system. One such confrontation, known as 'The Freemen Siege', began on March 25 1996 in Jordan, Montana, when the FBI arrested two Freemen leaders, Leroy Schweitzer and Dan Paterson, on charges that included theft, fraud, and intimidation of government officials. Schweitzer's and Paterson's arrest resulted in an eighty-one day armed stand-off ('the longest' in American history, according to the Montana Human Rights Network) between the remaining Freemen who were holed up in a fortified complex of ranches known as Justus Township, and the FBI. The 'siege' ended peacefully on June 13 1996, a fact which seemed to signal a shift in policy by the FBI, evidencing their desire to avoid 'another Waco or Ruby Ridge'.

See, for example, George and Wilcox, *Extremists*, 261; the Montana Human Rights Network, *Human Rights Network News*, 'Freemen - News & Comment' (1996), 1–3; Tim Cornwell, 'A Softly, Softly Siege,' *The Independent* (June 8, 1996), 18; Joel Dyer, *Harvest of Rage: Why Oklahoma City is Only the Beginning* (Boulder, Colorado, Westview Press, 1997), 193–198; and the views of Montana County Attorney John Bohlman in this volume at pages 228–231.

16. For a discussion of the 'secret contact' between the FBI and the militias during the Freemen stand-off and other 'crises' see 'The Secret FBI–Militia Alliance,' *U.S.News and World Report* (May 12, 1997), 40–41. The 'informal hot line' between the FBI and the

militias apparently grew out of the work of an academic group based at Michigan State University called the Critical Incident Analysis Group. In 1995 senior FBI officials began attending meetings of the group and using its contacts with the militia movement as a means to 'control rumours and head off violent confrontations'. See also, Tim Rhodes, 'Militia Joins Up with FBI to Fight Anarchy,' *The Sunday Times* (August 15, 1999), 20, on the contacts between the Michigan Militia and the FBI.

17. Sheil was referring to a popular chain of fast food restaurants in the United States.

18. One of the criticisms groups like the militias make of the law enforcement agencies handling of events at Waco is that the serving of the original search warrant by the BATF on February 28 1993 was configured as a 'dynamic entry' military-style operation and that no attempt had been made to 'peacefully' serve the search and arrest warrant on David Koresh. On this see Edward Gaffney Jr., 'The Waco Tragedy: Constitutional Concerns and Policy Perspectives,' in Stuart A. Wright, *Armageddon in Waco: Critical Perspectives on the Branch Davidian Conflict* (Chicago, University of Chicago Press, 1995), 338–341.

19. The Missouri 51st Militia's Code of Conduct can be found at pages 348–349 of this volume.

20. James Bovard, *Lost Rights: The Destruction of American Liberty* (New York, St Martin's Press, 1994).

21. The 17th Amendment provided for the direct election of Senators. It was ratified in 1913.

22. On this, see, for example, William Greider, *Who Will Tell The People: The Betrayal of American Democracy* (New York, Simon & Schuster, 1992). This is also the theme of Warren Beatty's recent critically acclaimed film *Bulworth* (Warren Beatty, 1998).

23. The multimillionaire publisher Steve Forbes sought the Republican nomination for the presidency in the 1996 election, and appears likely to run again in 2000.

24. The idea of a republican cycle is a popular one in militia and Patriot circles. It is presented, for example, in Gary Hunt's *Outpost of Freedom – Sentinel* (Vol. II, No. 1, January 31, 1995, 6) as the 'stages through which every Republic goes' in the following terms:

> They begin in BONDAGE.
> They then go from Bondage to SPIRITUAL FAITH.
> With that Spiritual Faith they develop GREAT COURAGE.
> The Great Courage leads to LIBERTY.
> Liberty then leads to ABUNDANCE.
> Abundance then leads to SELFISHNESS.
> This Selfishness then leads to COMPLACENCY.
> The Complacency grows into APATHY.
> Apathy then degenerates into DEPENDENCE.
> This Dependence brings them full circle back to <u>BONDAGE</u>.

25. The concept of the 'Big Lie' is frequently used by the militias and is usually attributed to Hitler or Goebbels. Its use by the militias in this way again illustrates that it is wrong to associate all Far-Right groups with neo-Nazism. However, as John George and Laird Wilcox point out, rather than being the advocate of the 'Big Lie' himself, which is how the militias understand and use the phrase, Hitler, in *Mein Kampf,* accused 'the Jews' of using the technique. George and Wilcox, *Extremists,* 394.

26. The Beltway (Interstate 495) is the road system that surrounds Capitol Hill in Washington DC. To be 'inside the Beltway', therefore, is a metaphor for the perceived isolation of the nation's political institutions in Washington from the rest of the country and their apparent detachment and corruption. Gavin Esler discusses the crisis of confidence in America's political system represented by such attitudes in the 'Why Americans Hate

Washington' section of his book, *The United States of Anger: The People and the American Dream* (London, Penguin, 1997), 277–289. People in 'real America', he says, now joke that 'Washington DC stands for Dysfunctional City.'

27. President Clinton was elected with 43 per cent of the popular vote in 1992 and with 50.1 per cent in 1996. Quoted in Gerald M. Popper et al, *The Election of 1992: Reports and Interpretations* (Chatham, Chatham House Publishers Inc., 1993), 136–137, and Popper et al, *The Election of 1996: Reports and Interpretations* (Chatham, Chatham House Publishers Inc., 1997), 178–179.

28. The beginnings of America's shift from its origins as a 'Republic' to its current status as a 'Democracy' are more usually attributed within the militia movement to the advent of the New Deal in the 1930s. See 'The American Founding' section of this volume at pages 366–367.

29. 'What the public never understood', write James Tabor and Eugene Gallagher, on this point, 'was that the entire legal issue between the BATF and [David] Koresh had to do with paperwork, fees, and registration, not possession of the alleged weapons and materials themselves. . . . Apparently Koresh had converted a certain number of weapons to a fully automatic capacity, which came out in the 1994 San Antonio trail of eleven Branch Davidians. However, even those weapons were not illegal; rather the violation was possession without proper registration.' James D. Tabor and Eugene V. Gallagher, *Why Waco: Cults and the Battle for Religious Freedom in America* (Berkeley, University of California Press, 1995), 100–101.

30. *Waco: The Rules of Engagement* is a documentary made about the events at Waco by Dan Gifford, William Gazecki, and Michael McNulty, and was the winner of the 1997 IDA Feature Award. A copy of the film was given to me by Kay Sheil after the interview. It was given a limited cinema release in the UK and has been screened by BBC 2 as part of its 'Storyville' series, although in a shorter form than the American version. It should not be confused with Linda Thompson's videos, *Waco: The Big Lie* and *Waco II: The Big Lie Continues*, although all three are frequently sold on the militia and Patriot circuit.

31. 'To this day, the reasoning for the loosening of the rules of engagement is hotly contested. Perhaps dispassionate judgement was overcome by the death of Marshal William Degan, or maybe there was another reason,' Kenneth Stern writes. 'Conspiratoralists and Weaver supporters are not alone in questioning the government's actions.' Kenneth Stern, *A Force Upon the Plain: The American Militia Movement and the Politics of Hate* (Norman, University of Oklahoma Press, 1996), 38–39.

32. Horiuchi was subsequently tried and acquitted of the murder of Vicki Weaver.

33. See, on this, James R. Lewis, 'Self-Fulfiling Stereotypes, the Anticult Movement, and the Waco Confrontation,' in Wright (ed.), *Armageddon*, 95–110; and 'The Role of the Anti-cult Movement' section of James R. Lewis (ed.), *From the Ashes: Making Sense of Waco* (Lanham, Maryland, Rowman & Littlefield Publishers Inc., 1994), 121–142.

34. The Davidians' access to the public and the media was severely curtailed by the FBI and BATF during the siege. As a result the Davidians took to writing messages on bedsheets and hanging them from the windows of Mount Carmel. Sheil is referring to one such message in which the Davidians called for the help of the press. In response some members of the press made their own banner which said, 'God help us. We are the press.' The incident is recounted in the *Waco: Rules of Engagement*. Another banner made by the Davidians read, 'Rodney King. Now We Understand.' See Tabor and Gallagher, *Why Waco?*, 63–64 and James T. Richardson, 'Manufacturing Consent About Koresh: A Structural Analysis of the Role of the Media in the Waco Tragedy,' in Wright (ed.), *Armageddon*, 153–176.

35. Judge Smith's instructions to the jurors in respect of the murder charges against the Davidians made this clear. He told them: 'If a defendant was not an aggressor, and had reasonable grounds to believe that he was in imminent danger of death or serious bodily harm

from which he could save himself only by using deadly force against his assailants, he had the right to employ deadly force in order to defend himself.' The relevant section of the Texas Penal Code (Subchapter C, Article 9, 31) reads: 'The use of force to resist an arrest or search is justified; if before the actor offers any resistance, the peace officer uses, or attempts to use, greater force than necessary to make the arrest or search, and; when and to the degree the actor reasonably believes the force is immediately necessary to protect himself against the peace officer's use of or attempted use of greater force than necessary.' On this see, for example, Tarbor and Gallagher, *Why Waco?*, 64–65, and Dick J. Reavis, *The Ashes of Waco: An Investigation* (New York, Simon & Schuster, 1995), 295.

36. The 'Good Ol' Boys Roundup' was a BATF organized gathering of law enforcement agents held at campsite near Ocoee Tennessee between May 19–21 1995. The Missouri 51st and the Tennessee Gadsden Militia obtained video and photographic evidence of the 'picnic' which showed racist literature being openly distributed and attendees participating in anti-black 'skits'. See, on this, 'Officers Allegedly Were At Racist Picnic,' *The Kansas City Star* (July 15, 1995), A8; Lawrence W. Myers, 'Operation Achilles Heel: Exposing Allegations of Racism, Rape, and Drug Abuse Among "Redneck Rouges" in Federal Law Enforcement,' *Media Bypass* (Vol.3, #9, Sept. 1995), 18–27; and George and Wilcox, *Extremists*, 264.

37. Sheil is probably thinking of George Mason's words, spoken during the debate on the ratification of the Constitution in the Virginia Assembly, which are frequently quoted in the gun rights debate: 'I ask, sir, what is the militia? It is the whole people, except for a few public officials.' Quoted in Halbrook, *Armed*, 74.

38. What Morris Dees, Director of the Southern Poverty Law Center said was: 'I looked at the group sitting around a table in Missouri, and the things that they were talking about [were] political issues, minor things, paying taxes or farmland issues. They're not [the] major issues that paramilitary militias are dealing with in this country. This is a new group, and I doubt if they even understand what the [M]ilitia of Montana is doing . . .' *The MacNeil/Lehrer Newshour*, April 26 1995 (transcript obtained by author).

39. In *False Patriots: The Threat of Antigovernment Extremists*, the Southern Poverty Law Center published a list of 'Prominent Patriots,' these being the 'Patriots whose activities contributed significantly to the movement between 1994 and early 1996'. Jim McKinzey's entry reads as follows: 'Commander of the 51st Missouri Militia, McKinzey served on the national common board of the Tri-States Militia until December 1995 when he withdrew his group from that organization.' *False Patriots* (1996), 53.

40. *Schindler's List* (Stephen Spielberg, 1993). *Amistad* (Stephen Spielberg, 1998).

41. The Lautenberg Domestic Confiscation provision was enacted as Section 658 of the Treasury-Postal portion of the Omnibus Appropriations Bill in September 1996.

42. John Ross, *Unintended Consequences* (St. Louis, Accurate Press, 1996). The 863 page novel which chronicles the federal government's 'war on the gun culture' has become a staple of the militia and Patriot circuit.

43. The Warsaw ghetto uprising of 1943 is frequently invoked by gun rights advocates both as an example of the dangers of gun control and as an heroic instance of armed resistance. See, for example, David Caplan, 'Weapons Control Laws: Gateways to Victim Oppression and Genocide,' in Pratt, *Safeguarding*, 319–322, and Wayne La Pierre, *Guns, Crime, and Freedom* (Regnery Publishing, Inc., Washington DC, 1994), 166–170.

44. The main Nazi gun control law was passed in 1938. For criticisms of the militias' assessment of this law see 'Hitler Didn't Do It,' in the Coalition of Human Dignity's report, 'The American Militia Movement' (1995).

45. The Militia Watchdog is a militia and Patriot monitoring and discussion group. Its website can be found at 'www.militia-watchdog.org'. See the extract from its 'Calendar of Conspiracy' in this volume at pages 258–261.

MAINSTREAM TEXTS

FIRST REPORTS :
THE MILITIA MOVEMENT EMERGES

T his section contains some of the earliest reports into the activities of the militia movement. It begins with an extract from the Montana Human Rights Network's *A Season of Discontent: Militias, Constitutionalists and the Far Right in Montana*, first published in May 1994, three months after the formation of the Militia of Montana. The report provides an account of the emergence of the Militia of Montana – one of the most influential of the militias to appear at this time – and its links with other elements of the Far Right. It also offers an introduction to such questions as, 'Which groups make up the Far Right in America?', and 'How exactly do we define political extremism?' It is followed by an extract from the Anti-Defamation League's October 1994 report, *Armed and Dangerous: Militias Take Aim at the Federal Government*, the first national survey of the militia movement to be issued by the 'watchdog' community. The report expresses concern about the conspiratorialism which appears to underpin the ideology of the militia movement and the presence within some militias of 'persons with histories of racial and religious bigotry'. The ADL's concerns are echoed by Morris Dees, Chief Trial Counsel for the Southern Poverty Law

Center, in his letter of October 25 1994 to the Attorney General, Janet Reno, also reproduced here. Dees' letter is accompanied by an extract from Klanwatch's *Intelligence Report* of December 1994 announcing the formation of a Militia Task Force to monitor the militias, with particular attention to be given to the 'racist activists who function at various levels of leadership within . . . the movement at large'. There follows one of the first extensive journalistic accounts of the militia movement: Beth Hawkins' report for the *Detroit Metro Times* of October 12 1994, in which she investigates the formation of the Michigan Militia and considers its impact on the inhabitants of the small towns of Michigan. We conclude with an article by Tennessee University Law Professor, Glenn Reynolds, first published in the *Chicago Tribune* in January 1995, in which he considers both the militias' interpretation of the Second Amendment and the questions which their emergence raises for America's political establishment.

From the Montana Human Rights Network, *A Season of Discontent: Militias, Constitutionalists and the Far Right in Montana* **(May 1994).**

A SEASON OF DISCONTENT

Background

The Far Right is a collection of organizations and individuals that is very difficult to characterize. Although they are commonly placed at the same end of the political spectrum, their views are not the same. Some of the themes that characterize the Far Right are discernible by a review of the positions taken and the literature distributed by Far Right groups. Aryan Nation literature, for example, clearly identifies the Aryan Nation as a Far Right, racist organization, that exists well outside the mainstream.

Racist groups represent the political margins. They embody the most extreme manifestation of anger, frustration and fear. However, those same emotions are feeding a host of more mainstream political efforts to 'take back America.'

The rise of the Religious Right, the success of the Ross Perot organizing effort, the popularity of Rob Natelson [of Montanans for Better Government] and his anti-government rhetoric all find their strength in the same undercurrent of anger and fear. These more mainstream right-wing, groups are a legitimate, accepted part of the political fabric of Montana. However, they rely on anger at public institutions and fear that Americans are on the brink of losing some vaguely defined vision of what our lives should be.

There is currently a marked increase in extremist activities in Montana. Montanans need to recognize that the glue holding these groups together, and enabling them to grow, is a negative attitude about our social institutions.

Several terms used in this report need definition to ensure an understanding of the kinds of groups being discussed and the philosophies they hold.

Christian Identity – A racist theology which holds that white Northern Europeans are God's chosen people, Jewish people are descendants of

Satan, and people of color are non-human or 'mud people.' Christian Identity is a recurrent theme in a number of racist organizations including various Ku Klux Klan groups, the Aryan Nation, and even some skinhead organizations.

Constitutionalists – Groups that view the constitution as a static document which has been misapplied and misinterpreted by the current judicial system. Often these groups also believe that the original constitution applies only to white Christian men and that people of other races have different citizenship rights.

Racist Right – Organizations which believe there are inherent biological differences between groups of people based on their race, ethnicity or religious beliefs and assign a value to groups based on these differences. Racist groups in Montana believe that people who are white, and of Northern European descent, are superior to other groups.

Religious Right – Organizations such as Pat Robertson's Christian Coalition which are part of an ultra-conservative political movement that claims to represent the 'Christian' perspective. Their ultimate goal is to create a theocratic government. These organizations are intensely homophobic but do not generally espouse an overtly racist or anti-Semitic philosophy.

Tax Protesters – People who believe that our current tax structure is inherently illegal. Specifically, these groups tend to focus on federal taxation issues and the income tax. There is heavy cross representation between tax protesters and Constitutionalists.

County Movement – Groups and individuals who believe that county government is the ultimate authority within the boundaries of that county.

Second Amendment Groups – Groups which have formed in response to legislation which they believe infringes upon rights granted under the Second Amendment. Specifically, these groups have focused on the Brady Bill and recent legislation banning certain assault weapons.

Defining Extremism and the Far Right in Montana

What defines the Far Right? The answer is not derived through a formula. It is not that simple. How individuals and groups view democratic processes and how they participate in those processes are key factors. Although numerous groups fall into the broad range of extremist organizations on the right, these groups are often quite different in the positions they hold and the issue areas in which they work. A careful study, however, reveals recurrent themes within Far Right extremist groups.

Far Right extremist groups:

1. Seek to limit or proscribe the rights of specific groups to participate in society.

White supremacy is a clear example of this theme, but there are certainly others which are more subtle. When Religious Right activist Bob Simonds says that the only people qualified to sit on school boards are 'Bible-believing Christians,' the message is that non-Christians are not qualified to serve in these offices.

2. Seek to separate groups along racial, ethnic or religious lines and assign relative values to different groups.

The white supremacist movement is pathological in its fixation on race and ethnicity, and, again, this is an example which most people understand immediately. But there are numerous other manifestations. Pat Buchanan's comments at the 1992 National Christian Coalition Convention reflected the same theme when he said, 'Our culture is superior to other cultures because our culture is Christian . . .'

3. Seek to impose their values on the public at the expense of basic freedoms.

To some degree anyone who is active in the political process seeks to impose his or her positions on public institutions. However, groups on the Far Right seek to do this in an expansive manner, and generally, in a manner that attacks basic freedoms. The white supremacist movement's vision of America is [of] a racially pure white state. Pat Robertson's vision of America is [of] a Christian theocratic state. Both visions are a radical departure from the vision most people have of America – a vision of a nation which values equality, independent of the individual citizen's race or religion.

4. Believe their way is the absolute and only truth.

Far Right groups tend to assert that truth is absolute, knowable, and that they alone know the truth. For example, Christian Identity, a racist theology which states that Jews are descendants of Satan, underlies much of the white supremacist movement. Constitutionalists see the original constitution as a static document which was divinely inspired, and reject many of the amendments for several reasons. The Religious Right sees the Bible (as they interpret it) as the absolute truth and allows for no deviation or questioning of the principles they believe the Bible sets forth.

5. Promote conspiracies.

Conspiracy theories espoused by the Far Right abound. All serve the same purpose – to isolate people and to discount factual information which does not comport with the conspirator's world view. A conspiracy theory allows its believers to deny any fact which challenges their position, usually by claiming that the fact is part of the conspiracy. For example, information which comes from a major news outlet is immediately suspect because the media is dominated by . . . (fill in the blank). Any report from the government or university system is obviously unreliable because the government is filled with . . . (again, fill in the blank). People become isolated because they take all of their information from very limited sources, which, in time, further compounds their isolation.

6. Have disdain for and abuse democratic processes.

Many of these groups reject the democratic processes we all depend on in our society. Ironically, they often use the very processes that they reject to legitimize their beliefs.

This is most clear in the activity of Constitutionalists and their use of the court system. These groups openly state that they do not believe the court system has jurisdiction over them, yet they file document after document in the courts and with local governments. This is costly to the local tax payer and time consuming for government employees. The Constitutionalists participate in these processes for many reasons, but the one thing they do not expect is that the legal system will deliver to them the rights they think they are entitled to.

Another example is the 'stealth candidate.' Activists in the Religious Right encourage people to run for office while concealing their public policy goals. This is in direct conflict with the very basics of representative government. Citizens in a democracy cannot vote for an individual to represent them when they do not even know what the candidate believes.

7. Seek to silence opposition.

White supremacist groups have a long tradition of using fear and violence to intimidate those who oppose their beliefs. The Religious Right in Montana has routinely sought avenues to silence its opponents rather than debate the issues. When the Network announced its 1993 human rights conference, the Christian Coalition of Montana attempted to pressure the College of Great Falls to not allow the conference to occur on its campus. Additionally, they orchestrated a call-in campaign to get US West to withdraw its funding of the conference. Neither effort was successful.

The Fringe Dwellers
and the Linkages Between Them

The most extreme elements in the Far Right are using more benign groups to recruit and radicalize a growing number of individuals. It is one thing when an individual joins a Klan group with a full understanding of the Klan's beliefs. That is clearly a right we all have and a right which is critical to our free society. It is another matter when an individual unwittingly joins a group he believes can help him with tax problems or help save his farm, or because he is concerned about gun control, only to be 'brought along' into increasingly extreme and radicalized philosophies which are destructive to the individual and society.

The following discussion describes the activities of Far Right groups and traces the linkages between them.

Militia Movement

Organizers have been forming militias in Montana since February 1994. The general argument of militia organizers is that the government is out of control and an armed citizenry is needed to keep the government in check. Militia promoters have generally pointed to the passage of the Brady Bill and the restrictions on assault weapons as the first step in a much larger conspiracy to wrest control of America. They attribute the conspiracy to a host of shadowy organizations, though they are generally unclear about the ultimate goal of these conspirators.

It is important to understand that the militia movement in Montana focuses on the government as an enemy and depends on unsubstantiated conspiracy theories. Militias do not seek to supplement the national guard by serving as a home guard to be called upon in times of emergency, as some have claimed. Materials being marketed through militia meetings indicate that the militias are forming to protect the citizens from the government.

The militia movement is not a recent phenomenon, nor is it limited to Montana. During his 1992 presidential bid, Populist Party candidate Bo Gritz actively encouraged his supporters to form militias and praised the organized militia movement in Idaho. Since his failed presidential bid, Gritz has been conducting 'S.P.I.K.E.' (Specially Prepared Individuals for Key Events) trainings which are often termed 'survivalist' but have also been characterized as paramilitary and have included weapons trainings. Gritz has advertised these by stating, 'Both street confrontation and deliberate shooting will be taught along with instinctive "Quick Kill" skills. All guns and ammo will be furnished.' (*Center for Action*, September 1993, p. 4)[1]

The strength of the current militia movement in Montana is troubling. Militia meetings have been held in numerous communities and have consistently drawn substantial numbers. The Network staff are aware of the following meetings:

Place	Date	# of Participants
Hamilton	2-15-94	250
Kalispell	2-24-94	250-300
Eureka	2-25-94	200+
Kalispell	3-10-94	800
Sanders County	3-24-94	70
Big Timber	4-1-94	300+
Billings	4-2/3-94	150
Kalispell	4-7-94	150
Troy	4-20-94	100-150
Eureka	5-6-94	25-30
Great Falls	5-11-94	200

There appears to be a trend emerging. After being exposed to the more extreme positions of the organizers, the number of people who come to a second or third meeting tends to drop off. In Troy, the local paper reported that people started drifting away during the meeting, and by the end as many as half had already left.

The Network has received numerous calls from people who discovered militia materials in other communities. It is clear that militia materials are being distributed through existing networks of like-minded individuals around the state.

[The literature being distributed as a part of the militia movement in this way] represents the most mainstream material produced by the militia movement. If one purchases the materials which are for sale, one sees a far more radical and paranoid picture.

For example, one of the video tapes for sale in the Militia of Montana catalog details foreign troop operations in the U.S. It goes on to say that the U.S. government is currently paying and training the Crips and the Bloods, two notorious youth gangs, to act as a domestic police force and to assist the government in confiscating firearms. Other materials for sale are filled with similar outrageous claims.

Militia links to other groups

Several militia organizers have made conscious efforts to distance themselves from elements in the racist right. There were considerable efforts to manage this issue at several militia meetings. For example, audience members at a meeting in Hamilton said they should issue a statement opposing white supremacist ideas. However, the key organizers' linkages to the racist right are very clear.

The Militia of Montana (MOM) is the most well organized group promoting formation of local militias. MOM literature has been present at many of the organizing meetings in Montana.

The primary organizers of MOM are John, David and Randy Trochmann. They have been active in the Far Right and racist movements for years. The Trochmanns have had a long-standing relationship with the Aryan Nation Church in Hayden Lake. John Trochmann was one of the featured speakers at the Aryan Nations Congress in 1990.

John Trochmann was also the co-chair for United Citizens for Justice (UCJ), a support group for white supremacist Randy Weaver. UCJ was formed in September of 1992 during the standoff between Weaver and law enforcement authorities in the Idaho panhandle. Its primary focus was the alleged misconduct of law enforcement, but the leadership in UCJ was clearly involved in the racist right. One of the mailing lists being used to promote militia material by MOM came from UCJ.

John Trochmann spoke at militia meetings in Troy, Big Timber, Thompson Falls, Great Falls and Bozeman. John's brother, David Trochmann, attended meetings distributing MOM literature. David was featured promoting his Constitutionalist ideas in a Spokane television news series about racist organizations in Montana.

The Trochmanns have held Bible studies with Larry McCurry of Thompson Falls, Chris Temple of Polson and other long-time Christian Identity followers. McCurry has ties with leaders of a variety of factions of the racist movement, including the Aryan Nations, national Christian Identity minister Pete Peters, and Thom Robb, the Grand Wizard of the

Knights of the Ku Klux Klan (the same Klan group which has been active in Billings).

Chris Temple was active in the leadership of UCJ along with the Trochmanns. Temple was a former organizer for the Bo Gritz campaign in Montana and worked with the Populist Party in New York. Gritz and the Populist Party both have well-documented ties to the racist movement. Temple is also a writer for a national Christian Identity publication called *Jubilee* based in Midpines, CA.

MOM materials have surfaced in other areas of the state. Several of the videos they promote are also being circulated among Constitutionalists and tax protesters in central Montana who are convening their own courts, arresting deputies, and threatening to hang the sheriff.[2] Further, tax protester Red Beckman and MOM organizer John Trochmann have appeared together at meetings. . . .

Despite these ties, militia organizers want to portray themselves as mainstream Montanans with legitimate concerns about public policy. It is a portrayal that rings hollow when one considers that they are advocating the formation of a domestic army to fight the government. Unfortunately, these groups are finding far too many sympathetic ears. They are using concerns about gun control and frustration with government to reach people. These individuals are then brought into this movement, are converted to more and more radical ideology and, ultimately, to direct action.

Notes

1. *Center for Action* is the name of the newsletter Bo Gritz produces.
2. See on this the account of Montana County Attorney John Bohlman in this volume at pages 228–231.

From the Anti-Defamation League, *Armed and Dangerous: Militias Take Aim at the Federal Government* (1994).

ARMED AND DANGEROUS

Introduction

Bands of armed right-wing militants, most calling themselves 'militias,' are cropping up across America. They have no centralized structure, but there are linkages among some of them, consisting largely of the sharing of propaganda material and speakers. A survey conducted by the Anti-Defamation League has found evidence of their activity in no fewer than 13 states.[1]

The aims of these militias, often bellicosely stated, involve laying the groundwork for massive resistance to the federal government and its law enforcement agencies as well as opposition to gun control laws. In the view of many such extremists, numbering in the thousands, America's government is the enemy, now widening its authoritarian control and planning warfare against the citizenry.

To the militia ideologues, gun control legislation – the Brady Law, restrictions on assault weapons, etc. – are major stratagems in a secret government conspiracy to disarm and control the American people and abolish their Constitutional 'right to bear arms.' They are also obsessed with the role of government in two recent events – the Branch Davidian confrontation in Waco and the Randy Weaver siege in Idaho – which they interpret as signs of impending tyranny. The answer, say these extremists, is ultimately, necessarily, *paramilitary* resistance. An armed and aroused citizenry must be mobilized and ready for a call to war.[2]

For most, if not all, of the militias, the fear of government confiscation of their weapons is a paramount concern. Samuel Sherwood, head of the 'U.S. Militia Association' in Idaho, states: 'When they come around to collect weapons, we'll have the legal and lawful structure to say "no" to that.'[3] Randy Trochmann of the 'Militia of Montana' gets tougher: 'If and when the federal government decides to confiscate weapons, people will band together to stop them. They are not going to give up their guns.' And the 'enemy' easily becomes nightmarish: Robert Pummer, a leader of the 'Florida State Militia,' says that his group is 'capable of defending ourselves against chemical and biological agents.'

Although thwarting gun control is the chief aim of the militias, they seek to turn the clock back on federal involvement in a host of other issues as well, e.g., education, abortion, the environment.

Case in point: Norman Olson. a regional militia commander in northern Michigan, has envisioned violence erupting if present government policies continue. Olson, a Baptist minister who owns a gun shop, declared: 'We're talking about a situation where armed conflict may be inevitable *if the country doesn't turn around.*' (Emphasis added.) Most often the central issue of the militants has been the legality of guns themselves. Clearly, their deeper suspicions and terrors should be of concern: Is their militant cause merely the alleged gun-toting 'right' of citizens? – or is it the 'turning around' of the U.S. itself from what the militants see as the treasonous' direction of the federal government's present policies? The question which no one can answer just yet is what, exactly, the 'militias' intend to do with their guns.

Might they still, as many observers hope, limit themselves to the time-honored means provided by the Constitution – freedom of expression, the ballot, the courts, the right of petition, or do they intend to resort to lawlessness?

A recent episode in Virginia offers some partial but troubling evidence. Members of a militia group calling itself the Blue Ridge Hunt Club were arrested for possession of illegal weapons. The leader of the group, James Roy Mullins, and three others who were taken into custody, were found to be stockpiling weapons in their homes and storage facilities. Found on a computer disk in Mullins' home was a draft of the group's newsletter stating that it planned a series of terrorist actions in furtherance of its aims. According to an ATF official, the group intended to further arm itself by raiding the National Guard Armory in Pulaski, Virginia.[4]

A further and vexing problem uncovered by investigation of the growing militias is the presence in some of them – even in leadership roles – of persons with histories of racial and religious bigotry and of political extremism. In the Northwest, for example, a militia leader has a background in the Aryan Nations movement;[5] elsewhere we find other erstwhile neo-Nazis and Ku Kluxers.[6]

The militias are of concern and doubtless will remain so in the coming months; they are driven by a combustible issue in American life which remains unresolved – that of gun control, an issue of urgency and passion in a society beset by violent crime. Coming head to head: a cry for weapons restrictions and a perceived Constitutional right. Most of those siding with the latter are law-abiding citizens who feel that guns are desirable for personal defense or for sport.

Many of them feel that the National Rifle Association (NRA) adequately represents their concerns; others who see the NRA as too moderate have sought out more extreme advocates such as the American Pistol and Rifle Association (APRA). Of late, however, still others are resorting to the mustering of a far more desperate and dangerous 'resistance' – the militia movement that is the focus of this report.

[A state-by-state synopsis of militia activity followed.]

*

Conclusion

Given the revolutionary posturing of so many of the militias, and the role in them of hatemongers of long standing, the better part of wisdom dictates that close attention be paid to them. There is a role here for the press and for citizen organizations that monitor extremism. The Anti-Defamation League is pledged to do its part.

The chief responsibility for keeping on top of the militia threat, however, plainly rests with the law enforcement branch of government. That this responsibility must be implemented with all due respect for the legal rights to which everyone is entitled should go without saying. Law enforcement agencies need the requisite resources to monitor these groups and to take appropriate measures, when necessary, to protect the public.

One such tool is paramilitary training legislation already on the books of many states. Those laws (many patterned after a model bill first formulated by ADL, which is appended to this report) should be applied, where appropriate.[7] In states where such laws have yet to be adopted, ADL urges that they be given prompt consideration.

The right to hold and promote one's views on the issues which are agitating the militias – such as gun control, the environment, and abortion – is inviolate under the Constitution. There is no right, however, to use force or violence either to impose one's views on others or to resist laws properly enacted. That is the crux of the problem presented by the rise of the militias.

Notes

1. Arizona, Colorado, Florida, Idaho, Indiana, Michigan, Missouri, Montana, New Hampshire, New Mexico, North Carolina, Ohio and Virginia.

2. The ADL's footnotes which accompanied this section of the report have been omitted in this volume.

3. The United States Militia Association was thought to have disbanded when Sam Sherwood moved to Utah in 1995. However, according to Tim Rhodes of the Ada County Terrorism Taskforce 'six to seven' people in the area still use the name in an attempt to keep the organization alive. 'People are often quick to report that groups break up,' explains Rhodes, and the case of the USMA provides 'a primary reason why the validation of information sources is required' when it comes to tracking the activities of groups like the militias. (Correspondence with editor.)

4. All four were subsequently convicted of federal firearms violations. Mullins was sentenced to a five-year prison term.

5. This is a reference to John Trochmann of the Militia of Montana.

6. In Ohio, for example, there was said to be 'overlapping participation, and a weapons-sale connection' among the Pike County militia, the neo-Nazi SS Action Group and the Ku Klux Klan.

7. Included in this volume at pages 268–270.

Reprinted from the hearings before the Committee on the Judiciary of the United States Senate examining 'Terrorism in the United States: The Nature and Extent of the Threat and Possible Legislative Responses' (April 27 and May 24, 1995).

LETTER FROM MORRIS DEES
TO JANET RENO

THE SOUTHERN POVERTY LAW CENTER,
Montgomery, AL, October 25, 1994.

Hon. JANET RENO,
U.S. Attorney General,
U.S. Department of Justice, Washington, DC.

DEAR ATTORNEY GENERAL RENO: On behalf of the Southern Poverty Law Center and its 350,000 supporters, I urge you to alert all federal law enforcement authorities to the growing danger posed by the unauthorized militias that have recently sprung up in at least eighteen states. Some sources put this number as high as thirty.

We have substantial evidence that white supremacists are infiltrating the leadership of these organizations. In our view, this mixture of armed groups and those who hate is a recipe for disaster.

The Justice Department's own experience demonstrates that the danger is very real. In 1984, for example, federal prosecutors in Seattle obtained convictions of 22 members of the Order, an armed and fanatical white racist group bent on inciting a race war that would lead to the overthrow of the government. Those convicted had robbed armored cars of over $4.1 million, stored caches of military weapons, killed a well-known person from Denver, and planned the murders of many other prominent citizens.[1]

In 1986, the Justice Department helped stop the paramilitary operations of the North Carolina White Patriot Party after our office provided evidence that active-duty military personnel were assisting the group and providing military armament. White Patriot Party members were linked to many crimes, including three murders.

Our office has confirmed the active involvement of a number of well-known white supremacists, Posse Comitatus, Identity Christian, and other extremist leaders and groups in the growing militia movement. Those individuals involved include Louis Beam, once on the FBI's Ten Most Wanted list and now an Aryan Nation leader, James Wickstrom, a Posse

Comitatus leader convicted of conspiracy to pass counterfeit bills to fund a guerrilla army, and James 'Bo' Gritz, a notorious anti-Semite who has been closely associated with David Duke and other white racist leaders.

We have also received reports that active duty military personnel as well as National Guardsmen may be assisting some of the newly-formed militias. Based on our North Carolina experience, these reports are ominous.

Citizens have the right to form peaceful groups to protest gun legislation and to engage in target practice. But they do not have the right to possess illegal weapons, violate state paramilitary laws, or harass minorities. Based on the history of paramilitary operations conducted under the influence of white supremacists, I believe it is highly likely that illegal activity of this sort is already occurring.

I have enclosed a brief biographical sketch of some white supremacist leaders and others who are involved in the militia movement, a list of the militia groups receiving their help and a list of state militia groups that have no known white supremacy involvement at this time. I have also enclosed a press release issued by the Center today to alert the nation to this growing problem.[2]

Please feel free to contact me or my staff if we can be of assistance.

Sincerely,

MORRIS DEES,
Chief Trial Counsel.

Notes

1   For an account of the activities of the Order see, for example James Coates, *Armed and Dangerous: The Rise of the Survivalist Right* (New York, Hill and Wang, 1987, 1995), 41–76, and Kevin Flynn and Gary Gerhardt, *The Silent Brotherhood* (New York, The Free Press, 1988). The murder of the Jewish radio talk-show host Alan Berg in Denver in June 1984 was the subject of the 1988 film *Talk Radio* (Oliver Stone).

The connections and similarities between the paramilitary groups of the 1980s and the militia movement are discussed further in this volume at pages 239–241 in an article from Klanwatch's *Intelligence Report* of June 1995.

2   Omitted from this volume.

From the Klanwatch *Intelligence Report*, 'Racist Extremists Exploit Nationwide Militia Movement' (December, 1994/# 76).

RACIST EXTREMISTS EXPLOIT NATIONWIDE MILITIA MOVEMENT
White Supremacists Linked to Brigades in Nine States

Militant racists have made alarming inroads among the ranks of the rising militia movement now sweeping the United States, according to intelligence developed by Klanwatch.

After months of monitoring the American Patriot Fax Network (APFN), plus numerous militia communiqués and various racist publications, along with reports from law enforcement and human rights sources, Klanwatch discovered numerous links to the white supremacist 'theology' of Identity, the anti-Semitic Posse Comitatus, the Aryan Nations and the Ku Klux Klan.

Militia strategists John Trochmann, Tom Stetson, Pete Peters, Jim Wickstrom and Louis Beam are Identity adherents who have long-standing ties to the Aryan Nations and its leader, Richard Butler. Some are veterans of the Posse Comitatus and the Ku Klux Klan. These, and other racist extremists, are actively involved or associated with militia organizations in at least nine states – Montana, Idaho, Florida, Colorado, Texas, Pennsylvania, Tennessee, Missouri and Michigan.

'The passage of gun-control legislation has fanned the flames of anti-government sentiment and led to the explosion of private militia groups around the country,' explained Klanwatch Director Danny Welch. 'The foot soldiers in these groups are just the type of people that Klan and neo-Nazi leaders have recruited in recent years. Citizen militias are fertile ground for white supremacist recruitment and they have a legitimacy that hate groups can use to present a "patriotic" face to the public and media.'

This situation prompted Klanwatch to form a Militia Task Force, which will use its expertise and experience to monitor citizen militias. The Klanwatch database will be updated to include any racist militia activity and reports from law enforcement agencies.

Based on information developed by the new Klanwatch Militia Task Force, Morris Dees, Executive Chairman of The Southern Poverty

Law Center, wrote a letter to United States Attorney General Janet Reno that called for the Justice Department to be alert to the danger posed by the growing white supremacist involvement in these rapidly growing militias. In his letter, Dees stated that the 'mixture of armed groups with those who hate is a recipe for disaster.'

The anti-gun control activists, tax resisters and anti-federal government groups who comprise most militias are without a racist agenda and are not the concern of Klanwatch. The Task Force will focus on racist activists who function at various levels of leadership within militias and the movement at large.

The white supremacists and anti-Semites taking advantage of this new radical right constituency are following a pattern of organized terrorism that dates back to the days of Reconstruction and the birth of the Ku Klux Klan. In recent years, efforts by Klanwatch were crucial in breaking up two such racist paramilitary organizations.

Until Klanwatch obtained an injunction against him in 1982, longtime racist Louis Beam operated the Texas Emergency Reserve, an off-shoot of the Texas Klan that was training 2,500 paramilitary soldiers in five secret camps. In a 1986 North Carolina case, Klanwatch, working with the U.S. Attorney for the Eastern District of North Carolina, obtained criminal convictions of two leaders of the White Patriot Party for operating an illegal paramilitary army using stolen military armaments. White Patriot Party members were responsible for numerous crimes, including three murders.

Klanwatch has received reports that active duty military personnel as well as National Guardsmen may be assisting some of the newly-formed militias. Based on the North Carolina experience, these reports are ominous.

The influence of white supremacists and their sympathizers spreads beyond their immediate locales to militias nationwide, via a network of fax machines, computer bulletin boards, shortwave radio broadcasts and mail-order videos. New technology has significantly accelerated the ability of racist groups to organize effectively and immediately.

'This is one of the most significant and, potentially, most dangerous developments in the white supremacy movement in a decade,' said Klanwatch Director Welch. 'The popularity of the militias, along with their conspiracy theories, rabid anti-government rhetoric and a willingness to take up arms, makes the movement highly attractive to longtime racist leaders like Beam and Wickstrom. It gives them and their cohorts a public platform for their racist agenda and fertile ground for new recruits. It is a very volatile situation.'

Beth Hawkins, 'Patriot Games'. First published in the *Detroit Metro Times* (October 12, 1994).

PATRIOT GAMES

A sign alongside Highway 31 just outside Pellston, Michigan, describes the village as the ice-box of the nation.

A blink-and-you-miss-it town with a population of 580, the weather used to be pretty much the only news here. Then one Saturday in May, the Michigan Militia Corps came to town. Three dozen men in full battle regalia, their faces smeared with camouflage paint, set up in the village park a few yards from a kids' baseball game. Led by Baptist preacher Norman Olson and his deacon, Ray Southwell, they brought semi-automatics and posted armed sentries.

The group deliberately chose to meet in the park as a way to 'go public' and draw attention, according to Southwell. They hoped to use the resulting publicity to spread their message: that the U.S. government is plotting to strip Americans of their weapons in preparation for martial law and the installation of a socialist one-world government.

'People say, "Why the camouflage and the guns?"' explains Southwell. 'And I say, "Without the camouflage and guns, no one would pay any attention."'

If holding paramilitary exercises in a playground was intended as a publicity ploy, it worked. The militia's first public meeting left Pellston residents frightened and angry – but not about the possibility that the feds will subvert democracy.

'When Rev. Olson called me, I thought he wanted to use the park for a church picnic,' says village President Mary Hessel. 'They asked to use the pavilion, but they didn't say they were going to come with guns, with their faces blacked out and in camouflage.'

Hessel told Olson the group was welcome to meet in the park, but asked that they leave the guns at home next time.

To the leaders of the militia, her request was the first shot in a battle they're likening to Lexington and Concord. Militia leader Olson says village officials are 'fearful peasants' who would rather trash the Constitution's Second and 10th amendments than stand up for liberty.

Hessel says the unofficial militia should know better than to hold paramilitary exercises in a park frequented by families with small children. Sooner or later someone is likely to get hurt, she says. Pellston, both sides warn, could become the next Waco.

Barely six months after its inception, the Michigan Militia Corps has caught on like a brush fire. Organizers say they have no idea how many people have taken the paramilitary oath, but they say brigades have formed in 63 of the state's 83 counties.

Meetings across the state typically draw 50-100 people, more in the Detroit area.

The groups are part of a nationwide militia movement sparked in part by government attempts to regulate firearms. Members' fears have been fanned by two standoffs between federal agents and citizens: The 1993 Branch Davidian conflagration in Waco, Texas, and the siege a year earlier involving Randy Weaver, whose wife and son were killed along with an agent during a shootout at his home in Ruby Ridge, Idaho. Weaver had refused to respond to a subpoena for a gun charge but was later acquitted.

No estimates exist as to how many people nationwide have joined, but brigades have cropped up in at least a dozen states and a recent national rally drew 10,000 people.

Observers aren't surprised that people who previously belonged to other militant right-wing organizations have rushed to embrace the militia movement. What is new, they say, is the number of people who appear to have been motivated to join the paramilitary squads by federal passage of the Brady and crime bills.

Approved last winter, the Brady Law requires background checks and waiting periods on gun purchases. In September, the crime bill outlawed 19 kinds of semi-automatic weapons and accessories.

Often, militia leaders are former members of the Posse Comitatus, best known for bloody skirmishes with federal agents during the mid-1980s. Posse members reject many kinds of federal authority, including the authority to impose an income tax, and believe the United States is a Christian nation and the county sheriff the only legal law enforcement official.

Although militia members say they are sure they will attract supremacists – whom they call 'loose cannons' – to date there is no evidence linking the militia's Michigan leaders to racist, anti-Semitic or supremacist groups. However, the leader of the Montana Militia has ties to the neo-Nazi Aryan Nation.

Militiamen in Detroit have circulated some Posse literature, but most of Michigan's new weekend warriors come from outside of more-established ultra-right movements. They include followers

150

of the religious right, survivalist and anti-tax groups, the Libertarian Party and the presidential campaign of H. Ross Perot.

In the Detroit area, militia recruiting and organizing takes place at popular gun-owners clubs, according to a person who regularly attends meetings of what he describes as the paramilitary right. At a recent town meeting of the Gun Owners of Wayne County, Michigan, 150-200 people discussed organizing militias, he reports. Present at the meeting was state Rep. Deborah Whyman (R), who talked about legislative efforts to make weapons more accessible.

Some 8,000 people, most of them reportedly members of the gun-owners clubs and militias, attended recent gun-rights rally in Lansing. A recent rally hosted by the Gun Owners of Macomb County drew more than 8,000 people.

Most of the people being drawn into the murky world of right-wing anti-government activity were attracted by the group's Second Amendment platform. They say Big Brother wants to strip them of their guns so they'll be powerless during an imminent collapse into tyranny.

Even some staunch critics of the movement concede that its rapid growth shows that U.S. liberals have underestimated the fervor with which gun-rights advocates will protect their right to bear arms.

'The mobilization of gun owners over the last year makes me think that the number of gun owners who are willing to live with that (level of) organization is much larger than we thought,' says Dick Lobenthal, head of the Detroit chapter of the B'nai B'rith Anti-Defamation League. 'The left and the center had no idea how many people out there are staunch supporters of the right to own guns.'

Adding the deadly clashes between federal agents and groups in Waco and Ruby Ridge to the new restrictions on gun ownership increases the number of people who are convinced that it's time to take up arms, says Danny Welch, an analyst at the Alabama-based organization Klanwatch.

'The government going in and overpowering this religious cult,' says Welch. 'It's definitely used as an example of what they've been saying for a long time, that we're in a police state.'

Other policy analysts tracking the militia agree.

'It all comes back to the underlying resentment a lot of Americans have to the outlandish and excessive use of force with the Randy Weaver and Waco situations,' says Chip Berlet, a militia expert and analyst at the Cambridge, Mass.-based Political Research Associates. 'The average American reaction to that is "God help us if that's what we've come to."'

'There are a whole bunch of spinoffs: The sovereignty

movement, the county movement, the wise-use and unfunded mandates movements,' adds Berlet. 'And when the group splinters, you don't end up with no problem – you end up with two problems. This is not going away.'

Real estate agent Ray Southwell took up arms after losing a battle with his local school board over curriculum. He says he was angry that his kids were being taught 'socialistic values.'

A deacon in the Baptist Church, last November Southwell took his frustration and his fascination with citizens' militias in other states to his pastor, Norman Olson. Southwell had heard about the militias through the Patriot Movement – a loose conglomeration of ultraconservative causes. He and Olson, who owns a gun store, set about recruiting for 'God's army.' They say they vowed to keep their militia free of racism and anti-Semitism as well as non-partisan and nondenominational. Nonetheless, they appointed a chaplain, to keep the militia focused on its 'biblical and constitutional intent.'

During a July organizational meeting for prospective recruits, the brigade's chaplain gave a speech that began with a graphic but dubious description of the *in utero* decapitation of a fetus for research purposes. The leaders videotaped the talk for inclusion in a training video for other militia start-ups.

Decrying legalized abortion, the chaplain said he was moved to take up arms after viewing the televised specter of the ATF – the federal Bureau of Alcohol, Tobacco and Firearms – laying siege to the Branch Davidian headquarters in Waco. 'Watching my government burn a church and bury the evidence' propelled him into the militia, he said.

Indeed, among the materials circulated by the Michigan Militia Corps leaders are tracts linking alleged conspiracies to keep abortion legal to the institution of world government, as well as a list of reasons for forming militias that includes protecting the right to life.

Outside the group's Michigan headquarters, cars sport pro-life bumper stickers. Inside, fundamentalist videos and other information fight for space next to information on how to arm a militia.

The Wisconsin militia is headed by anti-abortion crusaders and has enjoyed visits by Operation Rescue leader Randall Terry. The alliance of armed right and religious right has prompted the Planned Parenthood Federation of America to produce a package of material on the ties between militias and religious zealots.

'Different elements in the right-wing community are arriving at similar conclusions for different reasons,' explains Fred Clarkson, a Planned Parenthood researcher in New York. 'They all agree government has become oppressive and that they need to take up arms.'

'In other words, whatever you think is the great evil, you agree that you need to take action.'

Those tracking the militia movement disagree on whether it will remain cohesive after the more radical agendas of some of its members surface. Some speculate that inevitable clashes with officialdom will scare off people whose sole motivation for joining was the Second Amendment. Others say the attention such clashes would draw to the movement would help make its members feel effective.

In either case, they agree, it's unlikely that militias will disappear. With so many taking a paramilitary oath – even if they take it only temporarily – extremist theories will trickle down to thousands of people.

'The bad news is that as more pure Second Amendment people drop out, what you're left with is a core of heavily armed fascists,' warns Berlet. 'And I personally do not sleep well with groups of armed paranoids who believe the government is behind a totalitarian conspiracy. Eventually, they will have a confrontation. It's inevitable and they're going to remain keyed up.'

As Mary Hessel sees it, Pellston's wrangling with the militia demonstrated that the group is primed for a confrontation. After the group's first meeting at the park, village officials asked the troopers

to leave the guns home next time.

Afterward, Hessel was pelted with phone calls at home from gun-rights supporters and militiamen across the country. Tired of explaining that her family owns guns for hunting, she demanded that the militia remove her phone number from its computer bulletin board.

The following month, militia members arrived at the park toting guns its members said were unloaded and thus exempt from the village firearms ban. Pellston officials revoked the militia's permit to use the pavilion. Unbeknownst to the village, the superpatriots scheduled their next meeting at a village-run campground three quarters of a mile from the park, vowing that their 'objective will be the same: Visibility, Organization, and Legitimacy.'

Militia leaders say the unloaded guns they brought to the campground were kept on a rack that was watched constantly. But Hessel says armed militiamen in battle regalia guarded the campground entrance during the confab.

On July 11, Pellston extended its gun ban to the campground, located outside village limits on the banks of the Maple River. Although for decades the village had maintained and administered the 15-site campground, the property is owned by the state Department of Natural Resources.

Olson and Southwell took their case to the DNR, which in August concluded that the group wasn't violating state law. The agency also noted that the agreement allowing the village to run the campground expired in the early 1970s and suggested that any new agreement would have to conform to state policies, including firearms provisions.

In August, the Village Council voted to suspend operation of the campground, and asked the DNR to render it unusable while the future of the property is being considered. State officials removed signs and water spigots at the property, bulldozed dirt berms in front of the campsites and boarded up the outhouses.

Attorney Wayne Richard Smith, who represents Pellston's village government, says the community understands the militia's Second Amendment stance but finds its presence intimidating.

'We won't maintain that campground for the militia and no one else is going to use it if they're there,' says Smith. 'You have this little park where people fish in the Maple River and hunt. But having guys there in blackface is scaring people away from going.'

Smith also advised Hessel not to pick up a stack of letters that arrived via certified mail at the local post office. Although a federal lawsuit Olson threatened to file protesting the village firearms ordinance appears not to have materialized, without referring specifically to the Pellston controversy he has threatened to impanel extra-legal citizens' grand juries to consider offenses against the Constitution.

Ray Southwell and the other patriots now practice on private land. But they've taken the incident as proof that officialdom, whether in its small-town guise or as the massive one-world-government promoting New World Order, will be back to get them.

The militia's belief that a confrontation with officialdom is inevitable may become a self-fulfiling prophecy if government and political circles ignore the movement, say analysts following the development of the militias. For proof, one need only consider the Branch Davidian and Randy Weaver standoffs, they and the militiamen agree.

'This is the kind of situation in which you look at something where governmental conduct really is horrific. Then you have people who say, "Well, if this is how the government is going to treat its people, then we better get guns,"' says Chip Berlet. 'And when government does go after these people, it does so in a dangerous, authoritarian manner that violates their rights.'

Michigan militia members sense confrontation at every turn. Echoing claims made by armed groups across the country, they say they are watched by mysterious helicopters. The militia's headquarters in Harbor Springs, Michigan, is located adjacent to a small airstrip, but the government helicopters that land there are searching for marijuana fields in the northern part of the state.

More plausibly, Southwell also asserts that at last summer's organizing meetings, men with guns and badges took down license plate numbers in parking lots in the area. Shouting numbers at one another across the lots, the men knelt behind each car, holding a video camera at plate-level, he says.

Southwell suspects the authorities are trying to make him and his comrades feel like they're being watched.

State police deny they spied on militia, but Berlet, Lobenthal and others say there may be truth to the group's claim about the license plates.

'It's called "The Game" . . . doing a parody of surveillance,' says Berlet. 'The object is to let the victim know, and I find that ostentatious. The sole purpose is chilling free speech.'

Both the militia and its critics insist that such episodes only serve to heighten paranoia all around, sometimes forcing such conflagrations as the one in Waco. But neither is the solution to ignore the militia.

'There has to be a middle ground that pursues the issue using available legal means, but that also addresses it in the social arena,' says Berlet. 'Let's have a discussion on appropriate police response to armed groups. Government doesn't want to have that discussion because it doesn't want to admit its mistakes. These people have a legitimate grievance. It's their response that's perverted.

'We're talking about a group of heavily armed people who see themselves as patriots saving America from fascism. That's why the government needs to confront this.'[1]

Dan Levitas, who studies racist and anti-Semitic groups for the Atlanta-based Center for Democratic Renewal and Education, says the hardliners in the militias see the atmosphere of paranoia as an opportunity to prove their case against the government.

'The ATF may well come and there may well be some bloody shootout. They (the militia) may stage some kind of confrontation.'

In Ray Southwell's case, the government's silence only makes him all the more convinced that the group needs visibility. Otherwise, he says, when the Michigan militia runs afoul of the government, he'll need his guns.

When Southwell describes the confrontation he believes is inevitable for the militia, the scenario is far uglier than a war of words with Mary Hessel. Rather, he says, it'll be the Bureau of Alcohol,

Tobacco and Firearms that appears in the woods outside the Michigan militia's headquarters one day.

Inside the headquarters, established in the home of a militiaman who owns several rooms of high-tech multimedia equipment, four computers hum and warble as they intercept communications from both far-flung members and the curious.

Callers reach a computer-operated voice-mail service offering a menu of options. The system functions as a kind of electronic hot line, spitting out computer-generated faxes detailing the rumor of the day. Naturally, most of the rumors concern the ATF. Not only is it the federal agency that regulates guns, its commands were involved in the Waco and Randy Weaver cases. And although there have been plenty of other skirmishes between government agents and armed groups in recent years, it's those two incidents that provide the militia movement with its martyrs.

Toying with a Pillsbury doughboy salt shaker in the command center kitchen, Southwell says he has a feeling he's going to be the latest martyr.

'We have to let the tyrants, the politicians and the bureaucrats know that we're taking a stand,' he says. 'When martial law is declared, I'm gonna have my neighbor there helping me.'

When he began organizing the militia, he lost his job as a real estate broker. He says he understands why the brokerage he used to work for didn't want to become the focus of national controversy. He's taken steps to insure that his family will survive what he sees as an inevitable confrontation.

Southwell even has a vision of how the end will be. He says that at the battle of Lexington and Concord when British soldiers came to get the colonists' guns, they found a preacher and a deacon. The famous 'shot heard round the world' was fired and the deacon lost his life.

Deacon Southwell imagines the ATF will come for him one day soon, sending the local sheriff to his door to disguise its arrival.

'I have to accept the idea that my life will never be the same. I sold everything I own and turned my house over to my son. I'm ready to take whatever abuse comes,' he intones. 'We are taking a stand and are prepared to lose everything.'

Note

1. The militias' fears of government surveillance are discussed in the 'Policing the Militias' section of this volume at pages 409–421. For examples of the government and law enforcement agency response to the militias see the evidence presented to the congressional hearings into the militias, reproduced in this volume at pages 205–231.

Glenn Harlan Reynolds, 'Up in Arms about a Revolting Movement'. First published in the *Chicago Tribune* (January 30, 1995).

UP IN ARMS ABOUT A REVOLTING MOVEMENT

Recently, a steady drumbeat of print reports and network news stories has given national attention to what many in the South and West already knew: that some Americans are arming themselves and organizing into militia companies. Part of a so-called 'Patriot Movement' that some number at 5 million members, the militia movement is estimated by press accounts as having somewhere between 100,000 and 300,000 members under arms. Their fear, based on all sorts of rumors about 'black helicopters' and foreign forces maneuvring in remote areas, is that the feds, perhaps in conjunction with the United Nations, will seize their guns and establish a 'new world order' dictatorship that will take control over their lives. Some are even talking about armed revolt.

Militia members believe their action are authorized by the U.S. Constitution. They're silly to worry about the UN, which can't even handle the Serbs. They're half right about the Constitution – but the part they have wrong could mean trouble. Militia advocates point to the Constitution's 2nd Amendment, which addresses the right to keep and bear arms, and to the framers' general views in favor of an armed citizenry as a check on tyrants. Here they're on solid ground. There is no question that the framers supported an armed citizenry as a way of preventing tyrannical government.

But the militia groups haven't thought about how the framers defined tyrannical government. The fact is that though there is plenty to complain about with regard to the expansion of government in the last half-century, just about all of it was with the acquiescence – and often the outright endorsement – of the electorate. That makes a big difference. Although many militia supporters can quote the framers at great length on the right to bear arms, few seem aware that the framers also put a lot of effort into distinguishing between legitimate revolutions – such as the American Revolution – and mere 'rebellions' or 'insurrections.' The former represented a right, even a duty, of the people. The latter were illegitimate, mere outlawry. The framers developed a rather sophisticated political theory for distinguishing between the two.

The most important aspect of this theory was representation. Those who were not represented lacked the citizen's duty of loyalty. A government that taxed its citizens without representation was thus no better than an outlaw, and citizens enjoyed the same right of resistance against its officers as they possessed against robbers.

But revolting against taxation without representation is not the same thing as revolting against taxation, period. Like it or not, the government we have now is the government that most citizens at least thought they wanted.

If you want to know what the framers considered grounds for revolt, read the list of complaints about George III in the Declaration of Independence.[1]

The framers understood what a dangerous thing a revolution was. They embarked on their effort with trepidation, and they would not have been surprised to learn that most revolutions that came after theirs either failed or produced a new tyranny worse than the old. They knew that once let out, the genie of revolution often proves both destructive and hard to rebottle. As the militia movement says, the framers did believe in the right to revolution. But they believed that such strong medicine was a last resort against tyranny. Today's militia members would be better advised to organize a new political party, or to work at increasing voter turnout.

Such counsel may seem bland beside the very real romance of revolution. But those on the political right (from which most, though not all, of the militia movement comes) should know better than to yield to that romance. Ever since the idolization of Che Guevara, a large chunk of the American left has succumbed to revolutionary romance while those on the right have focused on workaday politics. The relative fortunes of those two movements over the last 25 years, especially after November's elections, suggest which approach works.

Having said this, I also have a cautionary note for those who are not part of the militia movement. When large numbers of citizens begin arming against their own government and are ready to believe even the silliest rumors about that government's willingness to evade the Constitution, there is a problem that goes beyond gullibility. This country's political establishment should think about what it has done to inspire such distrust – and what it can do to regain the trust and loyalty of many Americans who no longer grant it either.

Note

1. See the Militia of Montana's adaptation and application of the Declaration of Independence at pages 327–331 of this volume.

THE OKLAHOMA CITY BOMBING

The horrific bombing of the Alfred P. Murrah Federal Building in Oklahoma City on April 19 1995 and the intense attention that was suddenly directed towards the militia movement are addressed in this selection of documents. It opens with President Clinton's remarks from the White House on the day of the bombing, in which he promises 'swift, certain and severe' justice for the bombers. Clinton's remarks are followed by an account of the bombing and its aftermath from the weekly news journal, *U.S.News & World Report*. The report captures the sense of shock which engulfed much of America because such an act of terrorism had taken place in the nation's 'heartland'. On April 23 1995 President Clinton was interviewed from the grounds of the Oklahoma State Fair for the American television programme *60 Minutes*. During the interview, the text of which is reproduced here, the President discussed some of the many issues which had arisen as a consequence of the militia movement's suspected involvement in the bombing, including the need for more extensive anti-terrorism powers to be given to the nation's law enforcement agencies, his own experience with political extremism while Governor of Arkansas, the legacy of America's frontier past, and its apparent current fascination with violent films. Two days later the President addressed the militias directly in a speech at Michigan State University when he warned them not to try to 'appropriate our sacred symbols for paranoid purposes'. The speech also provides an illustration of the powerful rhetorical style that Clinton brings to the presidency. The section closes with Paul Glastris' account for *The Washington Monthly* of his journey to Michigan to search for the militia movement's 'amateur soldiers'. What he discovers is a diverse mix of people and a wide range of views reflecting the disparate nature of the Far Right in America.

President Clinton, 'Remarks on the Oklahoma City Bombing'. Reprinted from the *Weekly Compilation of Presidential Documents* (Vol. 31, No. 16, 1995).

REMARKS ON THE OKLAHOMA CITY BOMBING

APRIL 19, 1995

The bombing in Oklahoma City was an attack on innocent children and defenseless citizens. It was an act of cowardice, and it was evil. The United States will not tolerate it. And I will not allow the people of this country to be intimidated by evil cowards.

I have met with our team, which we assembled to deal with this bombing. And I have determined to take the following steps to assure the strongest response to this situation:

First, I have deployed a crisis management team under the leadership of the FBI, working with the Department of Justice, the Bureau of Alcohol, Tobacco and Firearms, military and local authorities. We are sending the world's finest investigators to solve these murders.

Second, I have declared an emergency in Oklahoma City. And at my direction, James Lee Witt, the Director of the Federal Emergency Management Agency, is now on his way there to make sure we do everything we can to help the people of Oklahoma deal with the tragedy.

Third, we are taking every precaution to reassure and to protect people who work in or live near other Federal facilities.

Let there be no room for doubt: We will find the people who did this. When we do, justice will be swift, certain, and severe. These people are killers, and they must be treated like killers.

Finally, let me say that I ask all Americans tonight to pray for the people who have lost their lives, to pray for the families and the friends of the dead and the wounded, to pray for the people of Oklahoma City.

May God's grace be with them. Meanwhile, we will be about our work. Thank you.

NOTE: The President spoke at 5.30 p.m. in the Briefing Room at the White House.

From *U.S.News & World Report*, 'The End of Innocence' (May 1, 1995).

THE END OF INNOCENCE

A Grim Tally

It fell to President Clinton and Reno to sound the larger themes from the tragedy. Despite the stunning success of the police investigation, rescue workers in Oklahoma City soldiered on through the weekend, continuing the dangerous work of removing the dead from the shattered Murrah building. Dozens had been confirmed killed, but in the horrible crumble of steel and concrete many bodies were dismembered, others disfigured beyond recognition. Days after the bombing, many families still had no confirmation that loved ones had died. The police had to list them as 'missing.' In their hearts, the families knew the awful truth.

It was President Clinton who best tempered the heady note of success with a reminder of the grim tally in Oklahoma, calling for a national day of mourning and then planning a trip to Oklahoma City with first lady Hillary Rodham Clinton to lead the nation in a memorial ceremony.

It was not just those who lost friends and loved ones in Oklahoma City last week who needed consoling and reassurance. Across the nation, parents clutched children to their breasts fiercely, weeping as the latest small body was pulled from the crumble of rubble illuminated by the TV lights. To the world, the outrage of Oklahoma City was summed up in a single image, at once terrible and tender. Firefighter Chris Fields had rushed to the Murrah building minutes after the explosion. A police officer who had arrived just before him was already clawing through the wreckage, trying to reach a baby. The child was covered in building insulation, and the police officer extricated it quickly, handing the tiny body to Fields. The firefighter cradled the child, rushing her toward waiting emergency vehicles. 'I couldn't tell if the skull was cracked,' Fields said, 'But the head was cut open. It almost made you just want to throw up.' The baby girl in Fields' arms had just turned a year old. She died soon after Fields turned her over to rescue workers. Long after the fates of those responsible for the bombing are decided, America will find it hard to forget the image of Chris Fields and his tender care for a dying child.

Getting Through

That Oklahoma City has now taken its place at the top of the list of terrorist attacks on Americans on American soil scarcely begins to describe the enormity of the tragedy or its effect on the nation's psyche. In an emotional address at week's end, President Clinton made a point of speaking directly to children about the tragedy, attempting to reassure them that the world was not the cruel place the attack in Oklahoma City suggested. 'We're going to get through this,' the president said. 'We're going to get through this.'

It may not be easy. The memorial service this week in Oklahoma City marks an official beginning to the healing process. But overcoming such a grievous shock will take time. . . .

What's Next?

Clearly, the brightest star to emerge from the Oklahoma City tragedy was Louis Freeh. He shunned all public appearances, except for a brief press conference at which Reno announced that McVeigh was in custody. With Potts and Bryant, Freeh quickly put together a team of more than 180 agents.[1] Though it was based partly on luck, the stunningly quick success of the investigation last week reflected well on a newly invigorated FBI and on its director, whom many in

Washington are calling the Clinton administration's most shining political appointee.

The FBI's work is not done, however. With McVeigh in jail, the FBI team has its work cut out for this week and beyond. It has not been ruled out that the Oklahoma City bombing somehow could have ties to a foreign terrorist group, although investigators say that possibility is remote.[2] In Oklahoma City, agents still have a long way to go on the all-important forensic investigation. Working with technicians at the FBI laboratory on the second floor of the J. Edgar Hoover building, the forensic teams quickly determined the kind of chemicals used in the bomb. They have yet to learn what kind of detonator was used and whether a timing mechanism was involved. Detonators and timers would provide hard evidence about whether the alleged bombers had more professional help in assembling the massive 1,500-to-2,000-pound bomb. Can those questions be answered? That depends on whether the huge explosion reduced parts of the detonator and any timing device to pieces too small to be recovered and evaluated.

There are other questions. Within hours of the explosion in Oklahoma City, senior law enforcement officials were privately downplaying the idea that it was related in any way to the FBI raid in

Waco. The raid was exactly two years earlier, to the day, on April 19,1993. To a handful of federal investigators who track the doings of violent militia groups the April 19 date was a portentous clue. Survivalists and members of the most extreme militias regard April 19 as something of a hallowed date. On April 19, 1992, FBI agents raided the homestead of a militia leader named Randall Weaver at a place called Ruby Ridge, Idaho. An FBI sniper killed Weaver's wife; his son died in a separate shooting by a federal agent. Weaver was subsequently acquitted of criminal charges. His case is a *cause célebre* among many militia and survivalist groups. Exactly one year after Weaver, of course, was Waco. And on April 19 of this year was still another event energizing many militia groups and their members. A white supremacist named Richard Wayne Snell was convicted in Arkansas in 1987 of the murder of a pawnshop owner he thought was Jewish, and he was sentenced to death by lethal injection. Bill Clinton, then the governor of Arkansas signed the death warrant.

Snell's appeals had all run out. While he waited on death row, a group related to the Michigan Militia, the Militia of Montana, denounced the impending execution as a 'grand climax' orchestrated by the U.S. government. The Murrah building blew up at 9:04 a.m. Nearly 12 hours later, at 9:16 p.m.,

Richard Snell was pronounced dead by a prison doctor at the state prison at Varner, 60 miles from Little Rock.

The biggest question, of course, concerns the nature of the militia group to which McVeigh and the Nichols brothers appear to belong. In the small rural towns that dot Sanilac and Tuscola counties in the center of Michigan's thumb, on the eastern side of the state above Detroit, the secretive men of the Michigan Militia Corps prepare for doomsday. They train each other to shoot guns and rifles, sometimes wearing military fatigues and with their faces blackened, preparing for what they believe is the inevitable day when they will be forced to defend themselves against a hostile U.S. government.

'We are preparing to defend ourselves from the government and some other groups that are being brought in from overseas,' says William Fischer, who until four months ago was the commander of the Tuscola County chapter of the paramilitary group. Tuscola is approximately a mile from the site of the FBI raid late last week at the Nicholses farmhouse in the rural village of Decker. 'There are all kinds of Russian troops in the U.S., training,' Fischer says. 'And we hear a lot of reports that concentration camps are being set up in this country.' Camps for whom? 'For American citizens who do not believe in what the government believes,' Fischer replies. 'They are camps for anyone the government says is radical.'

The talk may sound crazy, but the FBI is taking it very seriously. A senior law enforcement official says the FBI opened an investigation into the Michigan Militia only last month. 'We were certainly aware of them,' the official says. The Bureau inquiry focused on the militia members suspected of plotting to blow up Soviet-bloc tanks at the National Guard base in Grayling. The militia's commander, Norman Olson, who lives in Pellston, a hamlet in the northern part of the state, was questioned by the FBI but denied his organization was involved. Olson, a gun-shop owner and Baptist minister, could not be reached for comment. But John Ulrich, a member of the militia from Pellston, says Olson recently wrote Michigan's attorney general and the FBI asserting that a few militia members, acting secretly and independently, were suspected of conspiring to blow up the tanks.

Separately, Ulrich says, during two brigade meetings 'an agitator' whom he refused to identify denounced the Bureau of Alcohol, Tobacco and Firearms. He says the man was affiliated with an organization known as the Patriots. FBI officials now are trying to determine whether McVeigh, the Nichols brothers and perhaps other violent men claiming membership in the Michigan Militia are actually members of a more extremist splinter group such as the Patriots.

Several members of the Michigan Militia say such a group may be linked to a man named Mark Koernke. Reportedly a former Army intelligence officer, Koernke is known by an alias, 'Mark from Michigan,' Michigan Militia members say. They disavow any association with Koernke. 'We are not an organization that is trying to hide everything,' Ulrich says. 'We are trying to be upfront with everyone.' Koernke could not be reached for comment. Other militia activists described as 'security aides' to Koernke were arrested in Fowlerville, Mich., on weapons charges in September 1994 after loaded rifles, handguns, gas masks and night-vision binoculars were found in their car. Asked about Koernke and any ties he may have to the Oklahoma City bombing, or to McVeigh and the Nichols brothers, senior law enforcement officials declined to comment.

The Michigan Militia was formed last April 29 by Olson and others. The organization claims to have more than 10,000 members spread across 66 of Michigan's 83 counties. Members say they stockpile weapons and ammunition, in addition to conducting regular military exercises. According to a report by the Anti-Defamation League of B'nai B'rith, Michigan Militia members believe the U.S. government will ban firearm ownership in this country. 'An essential additional ingredient, though,' the report states, 'is (members') conviction that the government intends to wage war on citizens who refuse to give up their weapons.'

In separate interviews last week, militia leaders said the FBI raid on the Branch Davidian complex in Waco is strong evidence that the government intends to wage war on citizens who refuse to give up their guns. One of the militia members arrested in Fowlerville, Mich., last year with assault weapons, gas masks and night-vision goggles was a 27-year old man named James Alford. 'If it takes force when the United Nations takes over America,' Alford told Gary Krause, the Fowlerville police chief who detained him, 'we will use force.'

Guns, gas masks and assault weapons are bad enough, but tolerable perhaps if they are used only by grown men playing war games somewhere back in the woods. If a 2,000-pound bomb is targeted at innocent civilians, however, that raises the threat to an entirely different level. That is the threat that the FBI, and the nation, must now assess.

Unlike previous terrorist attacks, the fireball that engulfed the Murrah building on a quiet spring morning as Americans went about their normal routines consumed more than its victims. The World Trade Center bombing largely failed to shake the presumption of most Americans that in their own homes, in their own cities, they were safe, far from the violence plaguing the rest of the world. New York was a seething, violent place, a place of too many immigrants, too many misfits. It was, in other words, foreign. Not so Oklahoma City. It is the nation's heartland, a locus of normalcy far removed from the nastiness and nuttiness of New York and Los Angeles. Call Oklahoma City's upbeat Chamber of Commerce, and a reassuring male baritone sings a happy little ditty: 'It's a wonderful life in Oklahoma City. A place to raise your family right. Rest assured you can sleep at night. Everybody's so polite.' Not everybody, it turns out.

Notes

1. Some of the evidence presented to Congress by Louis Freeh and Robert Bryant along with other prominent government and law enforcement officials is included in this volume at pages 205–218.

2. An interview with McVeigh's lawyer, Stephen Jones, can be found in this volume at pages 302–306.

From an interview between President Clinton and *60 Minutes*, **C.B.S. Television (April 24, 1995). Reprinted from the** *Weekly Compilation of Presidential Documents* **(Vol. 31, No. 16, 1995).**

PRESIDENT CLINTON AND *60 MINUTES*

Mr. Kroft

You said immediately after the attack that we will find the people who did this, and justice will be swift, certain, and severe. If it had turned out that this had been an act of foreign-sponsored terrorism, you would have had some limited but very clear options. You could have ordered bombing attacks. You could have ordered trade embargoes. You could have done a lot of things. But it seems almost certain now that this is home-grown terrorism, that the enemy is in fact within. How do we respond to that?

The President

Well, we have to arrest the people who did it. We have to put them on trial. We have to convict them. Then we have to punish them. I certainly believe that they should be executed. And in the crime bill, which the Congress passed last year, we had an expansion of capital punishment for purposes such as this. If this is not a crime for which capital punishment is called, I don't know what is.

Ed Bradley

Mr. President, this is Ed Bradley in New York. There are many people who would question our system of criminal justice today in the United States – in fact, many people who have lost faith in our criminal justice system. With so many people languishing on death row today for so many years, how can you say with such assurance that justice will be certain, swift, and severe?

The President

Well, let me say first of all, it's been a long time since there has been a capital case carried through at the national level. But our new crime bill permits that. Now, when I was Governor, I carried out our capital punishment laws at the State level. We just pursued the appeals vigorously.

I do believe the habeas corpus provisions of the Federal law, which permit these appeals sometimes to be delayed seven, eight, nine years, should be changed. I have advocated that. I tried to pass it last year. I hope the Congress will pass a review and a reform of the habeas corpus provisions, because it should not take eight or nine years and three trips to the Supreme Court to finalize whether a person, in fact, was properly convicted or not.

Mr. Bradley

But without a change in the law, you think that is what will happen?

The President

It may not happen. We can still have fairly rapid appeals processes. But the Congress has the opportunity this year to reform the habeas corpus proceedings, and I hope that they will do so.[1]

Mike Wallace

Mr. President, Mike Wallace. Are we Americans going to have to give up some of our liberties in order better to combat terrorism, both from overseas and here?

The President

Mike, I don't think we have to give up our liberties, but I do think we have to have more discipline and we have to be willing to see serious threats to our liberties properly investigated. I have sent a counter-terrorism piece of legislation to Capitol Hill, which I hope Congress will pass. And after consultation with the Attorney General, the FBI Director, and others, I'm going to send some more legislation to Congress to ask them to give the FBI and others more power to crack these terrorist networks, both domestic and foreign.[2]

We still will have freedom of speech. We'll have freedom of association. We'll have freedom of movement. But we may have to have some discipline in doing it so we can go after people who want to destroy our very way of life.

You know, we accepted a minor infringement on our freedom, I guess, when the airport metal detectors were put up, but they went a long way to stop airplane hijackings and the explosion of planes and the murdering of innocent people. We're going to have to be very, very tough and firm in dealing with this. We cannot allow our country to be subject to the kinds of things these poor people in Oklahoma City have been through in the last few days.

Mr. Wallace

People are wondering, Mr. President, if you're going to close down Pennsylvania Avenue in front of the White House to regular traffic. There are barriers there, of course, all the time. But there are those who suggest, particularly because of the man who tried to shoot up the White House, that maybe Pennsylvania Avenue itself should be shut down.[3]

The President

Well, I hope that they won't have to do that. I hope that ways can be found to make the front of the White House secure without doing that, because millions of Americans go by Pennsylvania Avenue every year and see the White House and the overwhelming number of them are law-abiding, good American citizens, and I hope they won't have to do that.

Mr. Wallace

Lesley Stahl has been out in Michigan with the Michigan militia for the past 24 hours. Lesley.

Lesley Stahl

Mike. Mr. President, what I kept hearing from the militia men there – and I gather this is true among all these so-called patriots – is the Waco incident. It seems to be their battle cry. It's their cause. They say that the Feds went into a religious compound to take people's guns away. They say no Federal official was ever punished, no one was ever brought to trial. I'm just wondering if you have any second thoughts about the way that raid was carried out?

The President

Let me remind you what happened at Waco and before that raid was carried out. Before that raid was carried out, those people murdered a bunch of innocent law enforcement officials who worked for the Federal Government. Before there was any raid, there were dead Federal law enforcement officials on the ground. And when that raid occurred, it was the people who ran their cult compound at Waco who murdered their own children, not the Federal officials. They made the decision to destroy all those children that were there.

And I think that to make those people heroes after what they did, killing our innocent Federal officials and then killing their own children, is evidence of what is wrong. People should not be able to violate the law and then say if Federal law enforcement officials come on my land to arrest me for violating the law or because I'm suspected of a crime, I have the right to kill them and then turn around and kill the people who live there. I cannot believe that any serious patriotic American believes that the conduct of those people at Waco justifies the kind of outrageous behavior we've seen here at Oklahoma City or the kind of inflammatory rhetoric that we're hearing all across this country today. It's wrong.

Ms. Stahl

But, Mr. President, there are tens, maybe more – tens of thousands of men and women dressing up on weekends in military garb going off for training because they're upset about Waco. Despite what you say, we're talking about thousands and thousands of people in this country who are furious at the Federal Government for what you say is irrational, but they believe it.

The President

Well, they have a right to believe whatever they want. They have a right to say whatever they want. They have a right to keep and bear arms. They have a right to put on uniforms and go out on the weekends. They do not have the right to kill innocent Americans. They do not have the right to violate the law. And they do not have the right to take the position that if somebody comes to arrest them for violating the law, they're perfectly justified in killing them. They are wrong in that.

This is a freedom-loving democracy because the rule of law has reigned for over 200 years now, not because vigilantes took the law into their own hands. And they're just not right about that.

Mr. Kroft

Mr. President, you have some personal history yourself with right-wing paramilitary groups when you were Governor of Arkansas. You considered proposing a law that would have outlawed paramilitary operations. Do you still feel that way? And what's your – what, if anything should be done? Do we have the tools? What should be done to counteract this threat?

The President

Well, let me say, first of all, what I have done today. I've renewed my call in the Congress to pass the antiterrorism legislation that's up there, that I've sent. I have determined to send some more legislation to the Hill that will strengthen the hand of the FBI and other law enforcement officers in cracking terrorist networks, both domestic and foreign. I have instructed the Federal Government to do a preventive effort on all Federal buildings that we have today. And we're going to rebuild Oklahoma City.

Now, over and above that, I have asked the Attorney General, the FBI

Director, and the National Security Adviser to give me a set of things, which would go into a directive, about what else we should do. I don't want to prejudge this issue.

When I was Governor of Arkansas, this is over ten years ago now, we became sort of a campground for some people who had pretty extreme views. One of them was a tax resister who had killed people in another State, who subsequently killed a sheriff who was a friend of mine and was himself killed. One was the man, Mr. Snell, who was just executed a couple of days ago, who killed a State trooper in cold blood who was a friend of mine and servant of our State, and got the death penalty when I was Governor. One was a group of people who had among them women and children but also two men wanted on murder warrants. And thank God we were able to quarantine their compound. And that was all resolved peacefully.[4]

But I have dealt with this extensively. And I know the potential problems that are there. I don't want to interfere with anybody's constitutional rights. But people do not have a right to violate the law and do not have a right to encourage people to kill law enforcement officials and do not have a right to take the position that if a law enforcement officer simply tries to see them about whether they've violated the law or not, they can blow him to kingdom come. That is wrong.

Mr. Bradley

Mr. President, do you think that what happened in Oklahoma City is an isolated incident carried out by a handful of people or is part of a larger, more coordinated effort involving a larger network of these groups?

The President

I don't think the evidence that we have at the present time supports the latter conclusion. And I think we should stick to the evidence. Just as I cautioned the American people earlier not to stereotype any people from other countries or of different ethnic groups as being potentially responsible for this, I don't want to castigate or categorize any groups here in America and accuse them of doing something that we don't have any evidence that they have done.

I do want to say to the American people, though, we should all be careful about the kind of language we use and the kind of incendiary talk we have. We never know who's listening or what impact it might have. So we need to show some restraint and discipline here because of all the people in this country that might be on edge and might be capable of doing something like this horrible thing in Oklahoma City.

Mr. Kroft

Mr. President, do you think that we are a violent nation, that violence is part of the American way of life?

The President

Well, we've always had a fair amount of violence. But organized, systematic, political violence that leads to large numbers of deaths has not been very much in evidence in American history except from time to time. That is, we're a nation – we're still a kind of a frontier nation. We're a nation that believes, indeed, enshrines in our Constitution the right to keep and bear arms. A lot of us, including the President, like to hunt and fish and do things like that. And then, of course, the number of guns in our country is far greater than any other, and a lot of them are misused in crimes and a lot of them lead to deaths. And there are a lot of knives and other weapons that don't have anything to do with guns that lead to death.

So we've had a lot of crime and violence in our country, but not this sort of organized, political mass killing. And we have got to take steps aggressively to shut it down. And I'm going to do everything in my power to do just that.

Mr. Wallace

Final question – do we see too much violence in movies and television in the United States?

The President

Well, I have said before, I said in my State of the Union Address, that I think we see it sometimes when it's disembodied and romanticized, when you don't deal with the consequences of it. I think when a movie shows violence, if it's honest and it's horrible and it's ugly and there are human consequences, then maybe that's a realistic and a decent thing to do. That movie *Boyz N the Hood*, I thought, did a good job of that.[5]

But when a movie – when movie after movie after movie after movie sort of romanticizes violence and killing and you don't see the human consequences, you don't see the faces of the mothers and the children that I saw today, the husbands and the wives, then I think too much of it can deaden the senses of a lot of Americans. And we need to be aware of that.[6]

But it's not just the movies showing violence. It's the words spouting violence, giving sanction to violence, telling people how to practice violence that are sweeping all across the country. People should examine the consequences of what they say and the kind of emotions they are trying to inflame.

NOTE: The interview began at 6:03 p.m. from the Oklahoma State Fair Arena in Oklahoma City. The President was interviewed by CBS correspondents Steve Kroft, Ed Bradley, Mike Wallace, and Lesley Stahl.

Notes

1. Sections 102 to 107 of the Antiterrorism and Effective Death Penalty Act of 1996, the legislation which eventually resulted from President Clinton's proposed Omnibus Counterterrorism Act of 1995, amended the Federal judicial code to establish a one-year statute of limitations for habeas corpus actions brought by State prisoners.

2. See the views of FBI Director Louis Freeh and Deputy Attorney General Jamie Gorelick in this volume at pages 205–209 and 210–212.

3. President Clinton did subsequently close Pennsylvania Avenue to traffic. He was the first president in American history to do so. See Gavin Esler, *The United States of Anger: The People and the American Dream* (London, Penguin, 1998), 296.

4. The Covenant, the Sword and the Arm of the Lord's 'commune' called Zarepath-Horeb in the Ozark area of Arkansas was raided by the FBI and Arkansas State police in 1985. For an account of this and of the arrest of Richard Wayne Snell, a CSA adherent, see James Coates, *Armed and Dangerous: The Rise of the Survivalist Right* (New York, Hill and Wang, 1987, 1995), 136–140.

5. *Boyz N the Hood* (John Singleton, 1991). The film tells the story of three young black men growing up in a violence ridden area of south central Los Angeles.

6. The issue of the impact of film violence on 'real' life has been re-opened in the wake of the school shootings in Littleton, Colorado, with President Clinton ordering the Federal Trade Commission and the Justice Department to examine the entertainment industry's marketing of violence.

President Clinton, 'Remarks at the Michigan State University Commencement Ceremony', East Lansing, Michigan (May 5, 1995). Reprinted from the *Weekly Compilation of Presidential Documents* (Vol. 31, No. 16, 1995).

MICHIGAN STATE UNIVERSITY ADDRESS

You who graduate today will have the chance to live in the most exciting, the most prosperous, the most diverse and interesting world in the entire history of humanity. Still, you must face the fact that no time is free of problems, and we have new and grave security challenges.

In this, the 20th century, millions of lives were lost in wars between nations and in efforts by totalitarian dictatorships to stamp out the light of liberty among their subjects. In the 21st century, bloody wars of ethnic and tribal hatred will be fought still in some parts of the world. But with freedom and democracy advancing, the real threat to our security will be rooted in the fact that all the forces that are lifting us up and opening unparalleled opportunity for us contain a dark underside. For open societies are characterized by free and rapid movements of people and technology and information. And that very wonder makes them very, very vulnerable to the forces of organized destruction and evil. So the great security challenge for your future in the 21st century will be to determine how to beat back the dangers while keeping the benefits of this new time.

The dark possibilities of our age are visible now in the smoke, the horror, and the heartbreak of Oklahoma City. As the long and painful search and rescue effort comes to an end with 165 dead, 467, injured, and two still unaccounted for, our prayers are with those who lost their loved ones and with the brave and good people of Oklahoma City, who have moved with such strength and character to deal with this tragedy.

But that threat is not isolated. And you must not believe it is. We see that threat again in the bombing of the World Trade Center in New York, in the nerve gas attack in the Tokyo subway, in the terrorist assault on innocent civilians in the Middle East, in the organized crime plaguing the former Soviet Union now that the heavy hand of communism has been lifted. We see it even on the Internet, where people exchange information about bombs and terrorism, even as children learn from sources all around the world.

My fellow Americans, we must respond to this threat in ways that preserve both our security and our freedoms. Appeasement of organized evil is not an option for the next century any more than it was in this century. Like the vigilant generations that brought us victory in World War II and the cold war, we must stand our ground. In this high-tech world, we must make sure that we have the high-tech tools to confront the high-tech forces of destruction and evil.

That is why I have insisted that Congress pass strong antiterrorism legislation immediately, to provide for more than 1,000 new law enforcement personnel solely to fight terrorism, to create a domestic antiterrorism center, to make available the most up-to-date technology, to trace the source of any bomb that goes off, and to provide tough new punishment for carrying stolen explosives, selling those explosives for use in a violent crime, and for attacking members of the uniformed services or Federal workers.

To their credit, the leaders of Congress have promised to put a bill on my desk by Memorial Day. I applaud them for that. This is not and must never be a partisan issue. This is about America's future. It is about your future.

We can do this without undermining our constitutional rights. In fact, the failure to act will undermine those rights. For no one is free in America where parents have to worry when they drop off their children for day care or when you are the target of assassination simply because you work for our Government. No one is free in America when large numbers of our fellow citizens must always be looking over their shoulders.

It is with this in mind that I would like to say something to the paramilitary groups and to others who believe the greatest threat to America comes not from terrorists from within our country or beyond our borders but from our own Government.

I want to say this to the militias and to others who believe this, to those nearby and those far away: I am well aware that most of you have never violated the law of the land. I welcome the comments that some of you have made recently condemning the bombing in Oklahoma City. I believe you have every right, indeed you have the responsibility, to question our Government when you disagree with its policies. And I will do everything in my power to protect your right to do so.

But I also know there have been lawbreakers among those who espouse your philosophy. I know from painful personal experience as a Governor of a State who lived through the coldblooded killing of a young sheriff and a young African-American State trooper who were friends of mine by people who espoused the view that the Government was the biggest problem in America and that people had a right to take violence into their own hands.

So I ask you to hear me now. It is one thing to believe that the Federal Government has too much power and to work within the law to reduce it. It is quite another to break the law of the land and threaten to shoot officers of the law if all they do is their duty to uphold it. It is one thing to believe we are taxed too much and work to reduce the tax burden. It is quite another to refuse to pay your taxes, though your neighbor pays his. It is one thing to believe we are over-regulated and to work to lessen the burden of regulation. It is quite another to slander our dedicated public servants, our brave police officers, even our rescue workers who have been called a hostile army of occupation.

This is a very free country. Those of you in the militia movements have broader rights here than you would in any other country in the entire world.

Do people who work for the Government sometimes make mistakes? Of course, they do. They are human. Almost every American has some experience with this, a rude tax collector, an arbitrary regulator, an insensitive social worker, an abusive law officer. As long as human beings make up our Government there will be mistakes. But our Constitution was established by Americans determined to limit those abuses. And think of the limits: the Bill of Rights, the separation of powers, access to the courts, the right to take your case to the country through the media, and the right to vote people in or out of office on a regular basis.

But there is no right to resort to violence when you don't get your way. There is no right to kill people. There is no right to kill people who are doing their duty or minding their own business or children who are innocent in every way. Those are the people who perished in Oklahoma City. And those who claim such rights are wrong and un-American.

Whenever in our history people have believed that violence is a legitimate extension of politics, they have been wrong. In the 1960s . . . many good things happened, and there was much turmoil. But the Weathermen of the radical left who resorted to violence in the 1960s were wrong.[1] Today, the gang members who use life on the mean streets of America, as terrible as it is, to justify taking the law into their own hands and taking innocent life are wrong. The people who came to the United States to bomb the World Trade Center were wrong.

Freedom of political speech will never justify violence – never. Our Founding Fathers created a system of laws in which reason could prevail over fear. Without respect for this law, there is no freedom.

So I say this to the militias and all others who believe that the greatest threat to freedom comes from the Government instead of from those who would take away our freedom: If you say violence is an acceptable way to make change, you are wrong. If you say that Government is in a conspiracy to take your freedom away, you are just plain wrong. If you treat law enforcement officers who put their lives on the line for your safety every day like some kind of enemy army to be suspected, derided, and if they should enforce the law against you, to be shot, you are wrong. If you appropriate our sacred symbols for paranoid purposes and compare yourselves to colonial militias who fought for the democracy you now rail against, you are wrong. How dare you suggest that we in the freest nation on Earth live in tyranny! How dare you call yourselves patriots and heroes!

I say to you, all of you, the members of the Class of 1995, there is nothing patriotic about hating your country or pretending that you can love your country, but despise your Government. There is nothing heroic about turning your back on America or ignoring your own responsibilities. If you want to preserve your own freedom, you must stand up for the freedom of others with whom you disagree. But you also must stand up for the rule of law. You cannot have one without the other.

The real American heroes today are the citizens who get up every morning and have the courage to work hard and play by the rules: the mother who stays up the extra half hour after a long day's work to read her child a story; the rescue worker who digs with his hands in the rubble as the building crumbles about him; the neighbor who lives side-by-side with people different from himself; the Government worker who quietly and efficiently labors to see to it that the programs we depend on are honestly and properly carried out; most of all the parent who works long years for modest pay and sacrifices so that his or her children can have the education that you have had and the chances you are going to have. I ask you never to forget that. . . .

So, my fellow Americans and members of the Class of 1995, let me close by reminding you once again that you live in a very great country. When we are united by our humanity and our civic virtue, nothing can stop us. Let me remind you once again that our best days as a nation still lie before us. But we must not give in to fear or use the frustrations of the moment as an excuse to walk away from the obligations of citizenship.

Remember what our Founding Fathers built. Remember the victories won for us in the cold war and in World War II, fifty years ago next week. Remember the blood and sweat and triumph that enabled us to come to this, the greatest moment of possibility in our history.

Go out and make the most of the potential God has given you. Make the most of the opportunities and freedoms America has given you. Be optimistic; be strong. Make the choices that Theodore Roosevelt and Ernest Green made.[2] Seize your moment. Build a better future. And redeem once again the promise of America.

Notes

1. The Weathermen – named after a line in the Bob Dylan song *Subterranean Homesick Blues* ('You don't need a weatherman to know which way the wind blows') – were a paramilitary-style underground terrorist group which endorsed the use of random violence against establishment institutions as a means of bringing about 'the Revolution' during the late 1960s. See, for example, James Miller's *Democracy is in the Streets* (New York, Simon & Schuster, 1987), 311–13.

2. Theodore Roosevelt had been the last president to address the University in 1907.

Paul Glastris, 'Patriot Games'. First published in *The Washington Monthly* (June 1995).

Patriot Games

Our Roving Reporter goes in search of the militia movement's amateur soldiers and finds something even scarier – amateur lawyers.

BY PAUL GLASTRIS

One June day two years ago, James Douglas Nichols was pushing 70 miles per hour down a country road not far from his Decker, Michigan farm when he was caught in the crosshairs of a sheriff deputy's radar gun. The deputy pulled Nichols over and issued him tickets for speeding and for driving without a valid license.

Soon after, before a courthouse hearing in Sanilac County in eastern Michigan's 'thumb,' Nichols offered a bizarre defense of his actions. The government, Nichols insisted, does not have the constitutional power to regulate private citizens in their cars. 'I have put everyone concerned here on notice of what is going on here,' declared Nichols with paranoid melodrama, 'to violate my rights to free travel as cited in the Constitution of the United States and the Constitution of Michigan.'

Presiding District Court Judge James A. Marcus patiently explained to Nichols the long-accepted legal distinction between a private citizen's constitutional right to travel freely and the government's legitimate right to regulate the operation of a motor vehicle. But Nichols was not about to buy the judge's fine distinction;

he had done plenty of his own research. Nichols continued his losing protests, citing Supreme Court case after Supreme Court case. 'He'd lift a sentence or phrase that he thought was applicable, but he'd do so out of context so that the meaning was completely incorrect or nonsensical,' recalls Judge Marcus.

The Sanilac County courthouse, a gracious brick edifice with a hideous concrete-block addition stuck on the back, is no stranger to twisted logic. Earlier that year, James's brother Terry Nichols had tried his own hand at finding his salvation in do-it-yourself legal reasoning. He didn't really owe that $31,000 in bank credit card debt, he announced to the court, because the banks had lent him 'credit,' not 'legal tender.' He offered to pay with what he called a 'certified fractional reserve check' – a worthless piece of paper. 'You can't follow their arguments,' explains Judge Marcus, 'because they're listening to a different music no one else hears.'

But now, after the Oklahoma City bombing, plenty of people are straining to hear the melody. James and Terry Nichols were both picked up after the bombing, though only Terry, and their friend Timothy McVeigh, have been charged with being directly involved. The search for possible motives behind the worst terrorist attack in the nation's history has turned the nation's attention to the so-called 'patriot movement,' the subculture of shadowy paramilitary groups and screwball ideas to which all three men were drawn.

The media has portrayed the movement as full of gun-loving right-wing extremists, and Timothy McVeigh, given his obsession with weapons and Waco, certainly fits that description. But that portrayal obscures a key fact: Most members of the patriot movement are less obsessed with guns than with laws. (James Nichols, for one, never joined a militia.) For every camouflage-wearing amateur soldier drilling on weekends there are several amateur lawyers sitting at home reading federal statutes.

The patriot movement is a loose, motley affair. It includes plenty of racists and anti-Semites, but also a good number of people who are not. Much of their ideology can be safely classified as extreme versions of contemporary conservative, anti-government dogma. Yet their absolutist notions about personal liberties put them closer to the ACLU and the New Left than to William Bennett and the Heritage Foundation.[1]

What all 'patriots' do seem to share, beyond the well-publicized fear that the federal government is stealing their rights, is a passionate devotion to the precise language of the nation's founding documents. Imagine Robert Bork and Nat Hentoff dropping acid in the woods and you begin to get the picture.[2]

Better yet, imagine a fundamentalist revival meeting where the Bible is replaced by *The Federalist Papers*. As I chased the Nichols story around the prairie-flat eastern Michigan farm country on the wind-swept shores of Lake Huron, time and again friends and neighbors of James Nichols would bring up the Constitution, the Declaration of Independence, or *The Federalist Papers*, chide me for not having studied them, and quote from them as if from scripture. The religious parallels were unmistakable, even down to the millenarian belief, almost universally shared, that Washington's attack on individual liberty is a prelude to the imposition of a 'New World Order': a totalitarian, one-world government controlled by the United Nations.

Suspicious, even dismissive, of the interpretations of scholarly priests (i.e. judges), patriots prefer an extreme version of Martin Luther's 'priesthood of all believers' in which each individual can clearly grasp the framers' intent by reading the sacred texts for themselves. But like Christian fundamentalists, these patriots are guided by an idiosyncratic political agenda. They tend to quote selectively and read literally, 'isolating the part from the whole and pretending that there can be only one reading,' notes University of Chicago theologian Martin Marty. They are Constitutional fundamentalists.

One of the movement's gentler, more thoughtful members is James Nichols' neighbor and friend Phil Morawski, a bearded, pudgy, vaguely hippyish-looking farmer who sports a cowboy hat with a large silver crucifix and the words 'To Live in Christ' scrawled on it. Morawski became a familiar figure on network television in the days after the raid on the Nichols home, speaking to reporters in a Foster Brooks-like hiccupy slur ('He doesn't drink,' swears another neighbor, 'he just talks that way.') Morawski lives with his mother and brother only a mile south of the Nichols place, on a farm complete with braying goats and a red, American Gothic-style barn. On the barn, in large, faded-white letters, are the words 'Happy Birthday America.' Though not a militia member, Morawski says he has attended some of their meetings where he 'swore an oath to the Constitution.'

Like most 'patriots,' Morawski's frustration with the federal government arose from a personal trauma. Along with millions of other farmers, he took out large expansion loans at the urging of U.S. Department of Agriculture in the seventies, then found himself buried in debt in the eighties, when land and commodity prices plummeted. He spent years in and out of court fighting the farm credit system, and managed to hold onto his land only by learning the intricacies of agricultural law with the help of various grassroots farm groups, many of which eventually evolved into patriot organizations.[3]

In the process he picked up some odd ideas. Nailed to the front of his farmhouse is a copy of the farm's title, or 'patent,' which the land's first settlers received from the federal government in the nineteenth century. Morawski and many other patriot farmers firmly believe that the language of these patents exempts them from local zoning ordinances. (Only the courts disagree.)

James Nichols, too, was drawn into the orbit of the patriot movement after a bitter personal legal battle. During a nasty divorce settlement in the late eighties, his ex-wife Kelly accused him of child abuse. Nichols passed a lie detector test and the charges were dropped. But the episode, which included a police search of his house, left him feeling both furious and humiliated.

After that, Nichols plunged into the literature of the newly emerging patriot movement. He read the Constitution and *The Federalist Papers*, along with 'Spotlight,' a *National Enquirer* – like patriot paper, which runs pieces such as an exposé about concentration camps being constructed to hold domestic political prisoners. During the winters, with little farm work to do,

Nichols curled up with *Black's Law Dictionary* and the Uniform Commercial Code – an encyclopedia-length volume of rules that regulate commercial transactions. He was looking, he told friends, for legal means to take himself 'completely out of the system.' He attended meetings of We the People, a tax-protest group whose members believe the Federal Reserve system is unconstitutional. Soon, he, too, was marking all his money with a red stamp that said he is not responsible for its value. He even tried to get the county clerk to expunge his marriage license from the public record, and claimed to be 'no longer one of your citizens of your *de facto* government.'

Nichols' notions were not exactly original. Virtually all of them had roots in the Posse Comitatus, a radical anti-federal-government movement founded in Oregon in 1969 and popular in the rural Midwest during the eighties farm crisis. Posse members believed, among other things, that the Federal Reserve is in the pockets of a cabal of Jewish international bankers and that all constitutional amendments other than the first ten – the ones written by and for white Christians – are suspect. The Posse died out in the mid-eighties after some of its leaders were jailed or killed in shoot-outs with federal authorities. But the movement's legalist protests, such as refusing to carry drivers licenses and paying debts with 'fractional reserve checks,' made their way into the patriot movement and into the minds of the Nichols brothers.[4]

Although he never joined the militia, James Nichols attended several of their meetings, usually to give informational speeches on how to 'drop out of the system.' He won few converts. 'He's a little bit farther than we are,' admits Art Bean, commander of the Michigan Militia of Tuscola County (just west of Sanilac County). Not that the militia members are middle-of-the-roaders. Bean, among others, is 'very disturbed' by the Federal Emergency Management Agency's statutory language, which he says gives the president the power to declare martial law: 'Read the law and make up your own mind.' He fully expects Clinton to use that power before the 1996 elections, in part to stop the militias.

In his search for ways to drop out of the system, Nichols came upon the teachings of a radical constitutionalist named Karl Granse. A self-professed legal expert, Granse runs an outfit called Citizens for a Constitutional Republic, headquartered in Apple Valley, an upscale Minneapolis suburb. In the fall of 1994, Nichols and several friends traveled to Minneapolis for one of Granse's seminars on how to shuffle off the legal coils of taxes and licenses. Nichols returned to Michigan $600

poorer, the price of the weekend lecture plus various books and videotapes.

Eager to watch one of the videotapes, I went to visit a Nichols friend, Jim LeValley, who had borrowed one. A member of the Michigan Militia, LeValley raises flowers and herbs in a commercial greenhouse next to his home on the banks of the Cass River. He greeted me in a camouflage cap, his boots caked with dirt. We settled into the Ethan Allen furniture in his living room and flipped on the videotape.

On the tape, Granse points to the wall behind him, where an overhead projector displays fragments of statutory language defining those people subject to the federal income tax as 'residents of the United States.' He then posits that no one in the room meets the criteria because they live in the individual states. 'The "United States" implies more than one,' he proclaims with great flourish, teasing an audience member from Illinois to illustrate his point: 'You can either live in the United States or in Illinois. Which is it going to be? . . . You see, we have to stop and analyze the words,' Granse instructs. 'Law is a precise language.'

As the tape played on, LeValley told me why he finds Granse's ideas so appealing. 'If you are not part of the corporate entity of the United States you don't have to worry about the laws set forth by the United States to govern its people,' LeValley explained. 'It makes life a whole lot easier.' I thought of W.C. Fields, who once insisted that he had studied the Bible scrupulously for 18 years, looking for loopholes.

When the tape was over, LeValley pulled a dollar bill from his pocket, flipped it over, and pointed to the Latin words beneath the Masonic eyed-pyramid: NOVUS ORDO SECLORUM. 'You know what that means?' he asked me. 'That means "New World Order." It means eventually they want us to be in a one-world government. That's why they want to take away our guns.'

As I drove off, I wondered whether LeValley and his self-taught colleagues would someday see through the patriot movement's paranoid misreadings of history and the world. It might help if they knew that the words on the dollar bill, a quotation from the Latin poet Virgil meaning 'New Order of the Ages,' were chosen not by international conspirators, but by a committee of this country's first patriots, the revolutionaries who wrote the Constitution.

Notes

1. William Bennett is a senior conservative Republican politician. The Heritage Foundation is a right-wing 'think-tank' founded by Joseph Coors in 1973.

2. Robert Bork is a conservative judge and Nat Hentoff is a columnist for the *Village Voice*.

3. The roots of the anti-government movement 'farm crisis' of the 1980s is explored in Joel Dyer's *Harvest of Rage: Why Oklahoma City is Only the Beginning* (Boulder, Colorado, Westview Press, 1997).

4. For an account of the activities of the Posse Comitatus see, for example, James Corcoran, *Bitter Harvest: The Birth of Paramilitary Terrorism in the Heartland* (New York, Penguin, 1990, 1995).

CONGRESSIONAL INVESTIGATIONS:
THE MILITIA HEARINGS

Following the Oklahoma City bombing there were three hearings in Congress either directly concerned with, or substantially related to, the activities of the militia movement. In April 1995 the Senate Judiciary Committee held hearings concerning the 'Nature and Extent of the Threat of Terrorism in the United States and Proposed Legislation to Enhance and Extend the Penalties for Terrorist Acts'. In June 1995 the Senate Judiciary Subcommittee on Terrorism, Technology and Government Information held hearings into the 'Scope of Militia Organizations in the United States' and the 'Extent to which they Pose a Threat to American Citizens'. And in November 1995 the Subcommittee on Crime, of the Judiciary Committee of the House of Representatives, held hearings into the 'Nature and Threat of Violent Anti-Government Groups in America'. Some of the evidence presented at these hearings is reproduced below. It is divided into three parts. The first part consists of an extract from the 'question and answer' session between Senators Specter, Kohl, Thompson and Feinstein and five prominent militia figures (Norman Olson, Bob Fletcher, James Johnson, John Trochmann and Ken Adams) taken from the

June hearings. The militia members are questioned, among other things, on their attitudes towards the Oklahoma City bombing, the law, their apparent advocacy of violence and their conspiratorial beliefs. This is followed by the evidence presented to the April hearings by two senior government officials, Louis Freeh, Director of the FBI and Jamie Gorelick, Deputy Attorney General of the United States. They place the emergence of the militia movement in the context of the wider terrorist threats faced by the US as they lobby for greater powers and resources to combat such threats. Also included here is the evidence of the FBI's Assistant Director, Robert Bryant, and the BATF's Deputy Associate Director for Criminal Enforcement, James Brown, given at the June hearings, in which they recount their respective organizations' experience of policing Far Right groups. We conclude with the experiences and concerns of county attorneys, sheriffs and police officers from around the US. Drawn from all three hearings these provide a compelling series of first-hand accounts of the dangers faced by those who, in the words of Richard Romley, County Attorney for Arizona, are 'on the front line in the battle against crime and extremism'.

PART ONE
QUESTIONING THE MILITIAS

From the hearing before the Subcommittee on Terrorism, Technology and Government Information of the Committee on the Judiciary of the United States Senate examining 'The Militia Movement in the United States' (June 15, 1995).

The participants:

Senator Specter, Pennsylvania, Chairman
Senator Kohl, Wisconsin
Senator Thompson, Tennessee
Senator Feinstein, California
Norman Olson, Michigan Militia
Bob Fletcher, Militia of Montana
James Johnson, Ohio Unorganized Militia
John Trochmann, Militia of Montana
Ken Adams, Michigan Militia

Senator Specter

Mr. Olson, I heard you say on national television that you could understand why someone would bomb the Oklahoma City Federal building. How can you say that? How can you understand why someone would bomb a building and kill so many innocent men, women, and children?[1]

Mr. Olson

I don't believe that is the correct context, Senator Specter. I believe the context was when they were asking me about the dynamics that occurred following the bombing of the Oklahoma City Federal Building, I was asked by Lesley Stahl and I responded that I understand what took place.

The Senator from Montana [Senator Baucus] here earlier said that he understood why people hate their Government.[2] I don't think it is uncommon for us to seek understanding because unless we understand a problem, we

187

have no way of solving it . . . What I said was that I understand the dynamic of retribution. Revenge and retribution are a natural dynamic which occurs when justice is taken out of the equation.

Back in the Old Testament, there were cities of refuge. You who are students of the Old Testament know that those cities of refuge were placed in the promised land to allow a place for a person to run if someone's life were taken; that a relative would not avenge the life of that one awaiting justice. When justice is removed from the equation, then the dynamic of revenge, retribution, and retaliation will take place. I understand the dynamic, sir. That is what I meant.

Senator Specter

You talk about vengeance and you talk about retribution and you talk about many factors, but what I want to understand from you is whether you . . . think there is any justification whatsoever . . . for the bombing of the Oklahoma City Federal Building.

Mr. Olson

Well, you are a clever attorney, sir, and I give you credit for trying to wrap my thoughts around your axle, but I am not going to allow you to do that. Sir, it has not been proven that that person did that, nor has it been proven that that was, in fact, an act of retaliation, retribution, or revenge. We still have to await the ongoing investigation.

It very well may be that there was a conspiracy at higher levels, people behind those people whom we have been fed by the press to accept or to believe that perhaps it was one angry individual. I say wait. Let's do the investigation. Let's wait.

Three days after John F. Kennedy was killed, everybody believed that Lee Harvey Oswald did it. Today, many of us doubt that he alone did it, and you are the single-bullet theorist and you believe that he alone did it.[3] We don't necessarily hold to that opinion, sir.

Senator Specter

Well, if we can leave the single-bullet theory for another day –

[Laughter.]

Mr. Olson

That is your choice.

188

Senator Specter

No. I will stay and discuss the single-bullet theory with you when the hearings are concluded, and I will be glad to do that on the record and in public. I am not trying to put any words in your mouth. I am just asking a direct question and I am trying to understand what you understand.

I cannot understand how anybody could understand why someone would bomb the Oklahoma City Federal Building as a matter of retribution.

Mr. Olson

Well, then, you don't understand the problem that we have had in Northern Ireland, you don't understand the problem that we have had in South Africa, you do not understand the hatred and the retaliation and the retribution and the revenge that has been going on around this globe since time immortal. Then you don't understand the dynamic, sir.

Senator Specter

Well, Mr. Olson, I may not understand, and that is why we have had these hearings so that you could have a full opportunity to express yourself.

Mr. Olson

May I make a correction for the record, too? Senator Kohl raised a poster a moment ago showing Hitler with his hand raised in the air.[4] Sir, that is a copyrighted poster produced by Jews for the Preservation of Firearm Ownership. It is not the work of some militia organization, just to make that comment for the record.

Senator Specter

Well, we will pick up your comment about copyrights and about Jews in a few minutes.

Mr. Olson

No, sir. I believe you are trying to lay at the feet of the militia some culpability, responsibility. You are trying to make us out to be something that we are not, much as the press has tried to do over this last year. We are not what you think we are. We are not what the press wants to feed to the American people.

We are people who are opposed to racism and hatred. We are people who love our Government and love the Constitution. It has been the design and the blueprint for governments around this world and we are proud of the United States of America, but the thing that we stand against is corruption. We stand against oppression and tyranny in government and we, many of us, are coming to the conclusion that you best represent that corruption and tyranny.

There are millions, 40 to 70 million Americans out there on the other side of the Alleghenys, and there is intelligent life west of the Alleghenys, sir, and I believe that you have to talk to those people out there. . . .[5]

Following the Oklahoma City bombing, Louis Freeh, on April 27, came out and said that the Michigan Militia Corps had nothing to do with the bombing in Oklahoma City. However, the press did not pick up on that. When you talk about, or when the Senators talk about, or Carl Levin talks about how terrible it would be to even consider that the Federal Government had anything to do with killing Americans, I submit to you, sir, that the Central Intelligence Agency has been in the business of killing Americans and killing people in the United States and around the world since 1946.

I submit to you, sir, that the Central Intelligence Agency is probably the grandest conspirator behind all of this Government, and I submit to you, sir, that perhaps the puppeteer strings of the CIA reach even into the Senators perhaps before us and perhaps also in the Senate of the United States of America.

Senator Specter

Well, as long as you say 'perhaps,' Mr. Olson. Senator Kohl.

Senator Kohl

Thank you very much, Mr. Chairman.

I would just like to read to you, Mr. Olson, a fax that you sent out on April 28 to the American people, and it said this: 'The wrath of the country has been directed toward the brave men and women of the Michigan militia. Now, here is the truth. On April 19, 1995, a day that will live in infamy, the government of Japan, in retaliation for the United States gas attack on the subway in Japan, blew up the Federal Building in Oklahoma City.' That is a fax from you to the American people on April 28, 1995. Would you care to comment on it?

Mr. Olson

I have a 40-page document that I have prepared, a transcript of an audio tape, that is available to the press. We encourage the press to see me at the press conference this afternoon, at 3 o'clock at the White Room on the 13th floor of the National Press Club Building, and I will be happy to provide you with 40 pages of transcript. . . [I]f we wait and the investigation is done, I believe that we will find collusion between governments in the involvement in the Oklahoma City bombing if we will wait and allow the investigations to be conducted.

Senator Kohl

All right. Mr. Fletcher, as I mentioned in my statement, the Militia of Montana claims that there are 'lesbians, sex perverts, child molester advocates, Christian haters, and the most doctrinaire of Communists heading the FBI and the IRS.'[6] Now, Mr. Fletcher, with respect to the IRS, I have no quarrel with you. [Laughter.]

Mr. Fletcher

So be it, sir.

Senator Kohl

But my friend, Louis Freeh, is a different matter. So I would like to ask you, are you suggesting that he is a lesbian, a sex pervert, a child molester advocate, a Christian hater, or a Communist?

Mr. Fletcher

Well, first off, that is not my quote. For the record, we clear that, and I think that comes out of a singular book [sic] that we carry the same as the library carries, and that is the extent of that.

Now, those people that live inside the Beltway have to select their own friends and figure out what their sexual status is, and there is a huge variety at the highest levels of this Government in that direction. What I would like to point out, though, is that you bring up Mr. Freeh and an interesting thing has taken place, actually, almost one year ago, July 2.

Mr. Freeh was in Poland and he made a Nazi-related speech and it was a memorial to the Jewish camps and the holocaustic action that took place there, and he said an interesting statement. He said that what happened 50 years ago is not just history as much as it is a warning, and Mr. Freeh said that, in fact, at any time that any nation of the world starts to utilize local police with their Federal enforcement and starts to federally arm the police at a local level, as Adolf Hitler did as he slowly came in and did his outrageous acts back in 1940 and 1938 – he said that any time we see this, it is an immediate red flag that that nation is probably moving into a dictatorship.

Well, within one single year, we start supplying local police agencies with armored personnel carriers. This, by the way, is just the sheriff's department. Those are not military. This is the sheriff's department in Everett, WA. These armored personnel vehicles are being supplied by Federal enforcing agents to a whole variety of local police agencies. This is exactly part of what Mr. Freeh was telling the folks in Poland and the rest of the world to be aware of as a sign of moving to a dictatorship. This is only one small part of that, sir.

191

This is what I would refer to as a terrorist. These are FBI enforcing agents dressed in their black outfits. This, sir, is an ATF agent in his black outfit. This used to be a terrorist. If an American saw this character going down the street, any American, 10 or 15 years ago, they would have shot this sucker because this is a picture of a terrorist. This is now the ATF agents [sic].

We have questions, going beyond Mr. Freeh's point, of hundreds of flat cars of United Nations Russian equipment all over the United States. We have questions as to why the U.S. Army, with this document I have here, has put together the regulations to create civilian inmate labor prison camps inside military bases. Those are the questions. We have questions why, under executive orders, the President of the United States sends $200 million to build Russian homes for Russian soldiers overseas.[7]

Senator Kohl

Thank you. I would like to just get on, Mr. Fletcher. In an interview with the *Los Angeles Times* on April 21, you told the Associated Press that the American Government has created weather-tampering techniques so that the New World Order will be able to starve millions of Americans and control the rest.

Would you explain what you were trying to say?

Mr. Fletcher

Well, what I was trying to say is exactly what I said. There are weather-control techniques. We have a complete package on that which I did not bring, but I, certainly, will see to it that it is brought in for the record. . . .

Senator Kohl

You are saying that the Government has created weather-tampering techniques so that the 'New World Order' will be able to starve millions of Americans –

Mr. Fletcher

Worldwide.

Senator Kohl

– And to control the rest?

Mr. Fletcher

Yes, sir, and that is my belief, as bizarre as that sounds. If somebody had told me that that equipment even existed ten years ago, I would have thought they were nuts, sir; and at this point in time we have all the documents to prove it. And if you think that eighty-five tornadoes take place in the middle of our growing area by simultaneous accident, I am sorry. The equipment that is already set up internationally – and as bizarre as that is, it is proven and documented. We will supply you with those documents. . . . So, yes, I do stand on that.

Senator Kohl

Thank you, Mr. Fletcher. Thank you, Mr. Chairman.

Senator Specter

Thank you very much, Senator Kohl. Senator Thompson.

Senator Thompson

Mr. Johnson, whether or not one agrees with your [opening] statement, I think you gave a very thoughtful statement, thought-provoking, as to what you perceive to be going on in the country and the concerns. You mentioned the problems, as you see them, with our Government. You talk about the tax rates being too high. You talk about the Government being too big, too intrusive, and all those things, many of which many of us are also concerned about and are trying to do something about.

You talked about the British, our Revolution, and other places around the world. But, you know, we couldn't vote King George out of office. The difference between us and other countries is that we do have a democratic society and one in which huge numbers of people don't even bother to vote, but we have an opportunity to change just about all of the things that you listed that are a problem.

I take it that you think that our system is broken down, our electoral process in some way has broken down; either is it not really free and open, or maybe we shouldn't go by democratic processes. What is your problem with working through the process to solve these problems?

Mr. Johnson

You know, there was an organization that I believe came out back in September and said that the militias' aim was clearly the democratic process itself, and my response to that was that our aim – our target was right on target right around November 8 when a whole new Congress came in here.[8] Fine, granted.

Now, we advocate that more than everything, voting, but we seem to have a problem here during these campaigns when all of these wonderful politicians, God love them, say whatever they are going to say and they get inside the Beltway and everything is, how do we say, politics as usual. Now, what is going on?

As this trend continues – and you guys have to listen to this – you are pushing people's backs against the wall out there. We have got people out there hungry, like I was talking about, people out there starving, and people tired of getting terrorized by law enforcement. I will support law enforcement whenever they support the law. I will just call them enforcement.

They are getting outright economically terrorized, socially terrorized. I mean, the political correctness is getting out of hand. What this militia is now is it is a mindset. It is the civil rights movement of the 1990s. It is people sitting there with 'don't tread on me' stamped across their foreheads. There are people drawing a line in the sand. That is what it is.

Nobody is going to go out there and shoot things. Nobody is going to go out there and blow up things. We are not baby killers; we are baby boomers. We are not terrorists; we are taxpayers. We are not extremists; we are just extremely ticked off at the way the Government is deviating away from what is going on around here.[9]

When I say 'we' as this militia, as this little covert group out there – no. It is everybody. Just because you say we are going to form ourselves a militia doesn't make you the militia. What we stand for here is the Constitution. That is it. . . .

Senator Thompson

I take it, then, basically, you think the system doesn't work, that the problems are not being addressed, that politicians promise one thing and deliver another. You are not the first one to come up with that idea, I assure you.

Mr. Johnson

It is becoming a real general consensus around the country, sir.

Senator Feinstein

This is my first occasion to be able to talk with militia members, so I am a newcomer and I listened very carefully to what has been said here today. What I gather from it is that, as you put it, Mr. Johnson, people are ticked off, irritated, annoyed, upset, whatever you may say, about a variety of things having to do with 'government,' whether it is law enforcement or decision makers or anything else.

What I would like to have each one of you answer is, assuming this is correct, do you believe there are circumstances in which you can take the law into your own hands?

Mr. Trochmann

No, ma'am, I don't. Nobody should be an island unto himself, nor a law unto himself.

Senator Feinstein

So you believe there are no circumstances where individuals should take the law into their own hands?

Mr. Trochmann

There is one.

Senator Feinstein

What is that?

Mr. Trochmann

When someone comes to destroy my family, I won't have a choice. If that were ever to happen, I would defend to the last drop of blood, and I would expect any other American to do the same thing. . . .

Senator Feinstein

Mr. Fletcher, do you believe there are any circumstances under which you or your followers can take the law into their own hands?

Mr. Fletcher

Commonly, absolutely not, and we do not at any time espouse that in any way, shape, or form. However, we are and, again, it is totally as in the Militia of Montana. We are predominately educational in nature, and by that I mean that is what we do, mostly. You will not find us out in our camouflage and that type of thing very regularly at all. No, and at no time have we ever espoused any such action.

We are, however, a defensive kind of a concept, if you will, and I suppose there could be some bizarre situation like the unconstitutional suspension of the Constitution that might therefore appear that people are going to take things into their own hands, yes.

Senator Feinstein

Mr. Adams.

Mr. Adams

There is no time for any people to go against the laws of their government and to take those laws into their own hands. That is totally unacceptable in any society, and we certainly fully agree with that.

One of the questions that was brought up about this particular meeting here today was, you know, how many people are involved with the militia, and I think in some earlier testimony that was kind of hard to put a finger on.[10] I can personally tell you that from my office alone, we have helped establish over 1,000 lawful militia units throughout the country in all fifty States.

I know that all of these people that I have talked to and that I talked to throughout the Nation agree with the statements I am making right now that we must be law-abiding. The only exception to that, which I believe has already been stated, is for self-preservation and self-defense of our persons and family if an unlawful act were being perpetrated against us.

Senator Feinstein

Mr. Johnson.

Mr. Johnson

I would say there would only be two occasions. The first one is, once again, if you come into somebody's house shooting.

Senator Feinstein

Without a warrant and without reasonable cause?

Mr. Johnson

Yes, without a warrant and without reasonable cause, and it would be awfully nice if they came in the house with the warrant, it would be nice if they would knock politely. But other than that, I don't see a reason for using any kind of force to justify your actions. Of course, once again, you suspend the Constitution. For that reason, I don't have to recognize anybody in Federal law enforcement. If we are invaded for some reason and our Government is overthrown by a foreign power, we are going to have to take the law into our own hands to save it.

Senator Feinstein

Mr. Olson.

Mr. Olson

I would agree completely with what James Johnson has said, that there is no other reason to take the law into one's own hands unless it is for the preservation of himself or the property, his family. . . .

Senator Feinstein

Mr. Olson, you are wearing a uniform and that uniform says you are a commander. What is it that you command?

Mr. Olson

Ours is an organization of command communication. Serving in the military, we understand what is called command control communication because there is a control that must be exercised in the organized military. We in the militia have command communication in that we convey information down to the lowest level so that reasonable, intelligent human beings can make an informed decision.

Senator Feinstein

Do you command people?

Mr. Olson

No. I am a commander only in what is called a unity of command, so that a person reports to another person all the way up and down the chain. That is called a simple line of communication or echelon communication. There is no command control, ma'am.

Senator Feinstein

What do these people communicate about?

Mr. Olson

They communicate information. The information now available to the American public is extraordinary in that we are available now through alternative sources of news to convey truth to the American people. I believe that what you are seeing in America in the last three or four years is a phenomenon of informed Americans now waking up. A new conscience is building in America.

Senator Feinstein

I don't mean to stop you, but I have got so many questions I want to ask you about what it is –

Mr. Olson

Forgive me. I am a preacher.

Senator Feinstein

– Practically, what is it you do? Do the people in your organization stockpile weapons?

Mr. Olson
I wouldn't say stockpiling. No one should have more than they should need.

Senator Feinstein
How many weapons does an individual need?

Mr. Olson
It depends upon the threat that they perceive.

Senator Feinstein
So is it fair to say that there could be unlimited numbers of weapons?

Mr. Olson
Possibly. The old adage in the military is that accuracy is everything.

Senator Feinstein
What do you do with these weapons?

Mr. Olson
Prepare ourselves to defend ourselves, ma'am. We are not offensive. We are defensive, purely defensive.

Senator Feinstein
So everybody is trained in how to use these weapons?

Mr. Olson
No, ma'am. In the community that we call the militia, there are two parts of the militia: that which we call the patriot body – those people that are more concerned about information, seminars, videotapes, information – and then there is the militia who may be involved in the weekend maneuvers. That is what you see in the press, often.

What you don't see in this vast grouping of Americans concerned about the Constitution is the religious right, for example. They are very much concerned. The patriot community, the information community – they are very much concerned. What you do see is that small portion of people called the militia who exercise on the weekends.

Senator Feinstein
Under what circumstances would this command operation that you have

sanction the use of these weapons?

Mr. Olson

Excellent question, ma'am. We will defer to the lawful historic authority, which is the county sheriff. He indeed is the commander of the local militia, and when a situation erupts in which we would be deputized –

Senator Feinstein

Does he participate with you?

Mr. Olson

No, he cannot, because, of course, of his political nature. He cannot always, but he is normally in support of – knowing the historic role of our sheriffs, in the event that the county were to be endangered, he could deputize a ready posse and he could form the militia to defend the people. That is what the historic militia is all about.

Senator Feinstein

What would this county be afraid of?

Mr. Olson

The county could be afraid of – for example, there are fifty three Federal agencies right now that employ deadly force, that carry weapons and they can make arrests using deadly force.

Senator Feinstein

But supposing they had warrants?

Mr. Olson

That may not necessarily be what the county – the best interests of the people in the county. For example, our county sheriff does not know when Federal officials come into the county to search, seize or arrest until he sees it on the nightly news. We have a bill before our house, and we are trying to seek support for it. Perhaps you have heard of it, the 'no-more-waco's' bill, or the sheriff empowerment legislation, which would require Federal agencies to get permission from the local county sheriffs before they could come into the county; in other words, coordinate their activities with the county sheriff. There are, of course, some exceptions to that rule which would involve necessarily the investigation of the sheriff himself, for example.

Senator Feinstein

Do you believe there are any circumstances in which an individual has a right to blow up a building? Let's start with you, Mr. Trochmann.

Mr. Trochmann

Absolutely not, Mrs. Feinstein; absolutely not. We are, plain and simple, a neighborhood watch, watching out for problems. When we encounter what we perceive as threats to a peaceful society, we do something about it. We alert the proper officials.

Senator Feinstein

Well, let me ask you this: If you are plain and simple, why do I read constantly these violent quotes, this hatred for other people, this anti-Semitic, anti-black – I mean, driving people to have this intense fear and antagonism?

Mr. Trochmann

Would you like my black friend to answer that for you?

Senator Feinstein

No, no, no. I asked you.

Mr. Trochmann

I am sick and tired of these questions constantly.

Senator Feinstein

I asked you why? –

Mr. Trochmann

We have gone over it and over it and over it, and if you want to blame somebody about it, take a look at the press. We are telling them one thing, they are telling you something else. I already addressed that.

Senator Feinstein

So you are saying you don't say these things?

Mr. Trochmann

No, ma'am, I do not say that.

Senator Feinstein

OK. That is all I wanted to know.

Mr. Trochmann

We are all in this together.

Senator Feinstein

So all those comments are wrong?

Mr. Trochmann

I am sorry, Mrs. Feinstein. What we are saying is we are all in this together. America had better put away its differences or we will cease to have a country. We shouldn't be your side and my side. We should all be for the same – the betterment of our country and our fellow countrymen. That is all I am saying.

Senator Feinstein

Mr. Fletcher, the circumstances under which –

Mr. Fletcher

The same answer. No, absolutely not. And I don't mean that your question is ludicrous, but it is a little bit, and I don't mean that as an insult. I don't think anybody could perceive that point in time where that would make sense, particularly if we are talking the housing of infants and that type of thing.

The press which Mr. Trochmann refers to shows Mr. Trochmann's face and one of the other patriot leader's face and the blown-up babies, and then just leaves it hang there, and that is unfortunately, we can't sue for that, and if we could, it would look like the national debt in terms of the legal action.

As far as the racial thing is concerned, that is garbage. Those folks in the extreme radical fringes of the patriot movement, which is a cross-section of Americana, the same as the police forces. Ten per cent of every police force is either racially motivated, racist persons; they are doing drugs, doing prostitution, or stealing on the side. It is probably the same in the militia movement because it is a cross-section of Americana.

We stand down from any hate kind of rhetoric whatsoever, period. And my wife of twenty-five years who is Jewish and Italian – my business partners for four or five different years were blacks, and my granddaughter is half American Indian. So if I am racist, I am doing a lousy job of it.

Senator Feinstein

OK; thank you. Mr. Adams.

Mr. Adams

We certainly in no way would ever condone, as I said earlier, any type of violence and, of course, that would include a bombing. I would ask each of you that as you watch the media report upon us – and you have probably seen many of our faces many times – listen for those words of racism from our mouth. You have not heard it. You will not hear it.

If we hear of anyone in our organization speaking of hate or speaking of racism, they will be asked to leave and never return because we do not condone it. The press will go out and find some fringe element out there that may say something, but trust me and believe me: It is not part of our mainstream organization. And, as I said earlier, there are going to be some people that will try to ride our coat tails because we are before the press.

My gosh, we are before you today and that is a lot of public knowledge. And they are going to try to grab some of that, and we will try to eliminate it wherever we can. But you pay very close attention to what the media has to say. Certainly, as politicians, you have been sound-bited and you know exactly what we are talking about. But you watch what we say out of our own mouth and that is what is true.

Senator Feinstein

Mr. Johnson.

Mr. Johnson

Yes. First, it is a question about blowing up a building?

Senator Feinstein

Are there any circumstances under which an individual is justified to blow up any building?

Mr. Johnson

After you have evacuated it and you wanted to cover up the evidence. Other than that, let me talk about the racist aspect now. It is getting old; I am getting real tired of being called a Klan member. I am getting tired of being called a member of the Aryan Nation group.

I spoke two weeks ago down at the Lincoln Memorial along with two other black people and the Jews for the Preservation of Firearms, and I believe there was somebody else Jewish who had helped organize it. The reports came out that a racist, anti-Semitic militia group held a rally at the Lincoln Memorial. Are these people blind or is there an agenda afoot here?

There are more black people showing up every day. A lot of the things that the people sit around in these meetings – these so-called right-wing wackos – and talk about happen daily in black communities, and black communities know this. The first people concerned seriously about neighborhood house-to-house searches and seizures were over in Chicago. They were black. Good grief, almost half the people in Waco who got killed were black.

This movement isn't about guns and skin color. It is about liberty, it is about freedom. The same kind of legislation we are seeing down on everybody now came down on blacks just after the Civil War. That is why they are getting involved in this thing, and it is going to come eventually to somebody as you keep ignoring us and saying, well, these guys are just a bunch of angry white men.

Senator Feinstein

Mr. Olson, would you respond to that?

Mr. Olson

The answer is absolutely not; absolutely not. Our record stands for itself. The FBI will give you all the evidence concerning the Michigan Militia Corps on that question.

Mr. Adams

I can assure . . . all Members of Congress and all the people of this Nation that the militia does not constitute any threat to this Nation.

Senator Specter

Well, we have that assurance, Mr. Adams, but you will forgive us if we don't want to accept it at face value. We want to look further.

Mr. Fletcher

Mr. Specter, if it please – I wonder if we would be able to have an assurance that we would have an open door to get to you folks. Relative to the same fear that we have relative to a government that maybe the people are no longer trusting.

Senator Specter

You have an open door to this subcommittee. Any additional information you wish to provide to us we would be glad to have. . . .

There is in the Constitution beyond the more frequently quoted freedom of speech, religion, and press, the right of the citizenry to petition the Congress, and we are interested in what you have to say. Much of it, you have already heard – there is disagreement with the panel, and I would express that same disagreement. My own view is that whatever ideas you have, let's get them out in the open.

I believe, if I may say just one or two words in a conclusory fashion, that much of what has been said here today will fall of its own weight, but let's hear about it. I think if we hear you out, we may decrease your membership, but it is a free society. We all have a right to speak, and let the American people draw their conclusions. My own sense is that it is healthy and that America will applaud letting you speak your piece, no matter how much we disagree with you.

Notes

1. These hearings were severely criticized by some monitoring agencies. Daniel Levitas of the Kansas City-based Institute for Research and Education on Human Rights Inc., writing in *The Nation*, for example, saw them as 'a soapbox for the "patriots" rather than the critical forum that was so badly needed', and criticized the chairmen, Arlen Specter, for 'greatly underestimating the rhetorical skills of the militia leaders' and for failing to expose the 'racist and anti-Semitic agenda of many militia activists.' Daniel Levitas, 'Militia Forum,' *The Nation*, (July 10, 1995), 42. See also the Montana Human Rights Network report, 'Militia Drama Plays Out in Washington DC', in *Network News*, (Vol.5, No. 1, July 1995), 2.

2. In his opening statement Senator Baucus commented: 'I understand anger with government. The government is not perfect, and often people are right to be angry, but those who express their anger through hate rhetoric and violence are few. The vast majority of Montanans reject hate, obey the law, treat each other with courtesy, and cherish our peaceful democratic values. This is true for conservatives, liberals, Democrats, Republicans, property owners, environmentalists, gun controllers, NRA members, everybody. Militia groups are the exception, and they are a small exception.'

3. Specter was an Assistant Counsel to the Warren Commission enquiry into the assassination of President Kennedy.

4. The poster features a drawing of Adolf Hitler with his arm raised in a Nazi salute and the words 'All In Favor Of Gun Control Raise Your Right Hand' below. Senator Kohl expressed the view that such 'language is unacceptable, as well as sophomoric'.

5. The Allegheny Mountains form the western part of the Appalachian Mountains, running from northern Pennsylvania to south-western Virginia. They are traditionally seen as one of the dividing lines between the 'East' and the 'West' in the United States.

6. Senator Kohl was reading from an advertisement for a video in an issue of the Militia of Montana's newsletter *Taking Aim* during his opening statement.

7. See the 'Conspiracies and the New World Order' section of this volume at pages 423–446.

8. Presumably this is a reference to one of the monitoring agencies' reports.

9. See Johnson's 'Heartfelt Invitation to Black Americans' at pages 361–363 of this volume.

10. See, for example, the evidence presented by James Brown of the ATF reproduced in this volume at pages 215–218.

PART TWO
NATIONAL LAW ENFORCEMENT CONCERNS

From the hearings before the Committee on the Judiciary of the United States Senate examining 'Terrorism in the United States: The Nature and Extent of the Threat and Possible Legislative Responses' (April 27 and May 24, 1995).

LOUIS J. FREEH

Director, Federal Bureau of Investigation

I testified about terrorism earlier this month before Chairman Hyde and the House Judiciary Committee. At that time, I stated that the threat of terrorism is very real, is a deadly menace that seems able to strike nearly anywhere in the world, and that it knows no boundaries.

As America is covered in blood in Oklahoma City, it is appropriate to pause a moment and recall some of the immense suffering which Americans have endured at the hands of terrorists:

> In April, 1983, the United States Embassy in Beirut, Lebanon was bombed, resulting in 16 deaths and over 100 injured.
>
> A suicide truck-driver bombed the United States Marines Barracks in Beirut in October, 1983, resulting in 241 deaths.
>
> In June, 1985, TWA Flight 847 was hijacked. U.S. Navy diver Robert Stethem was brutally murdered by the hijackers and his body was dumped on the airport tarmac in Beirut.
>
> Marine Lieutenant Colonel William Higgins, part of the United Nations peacekeeping force in Lebanon, was kidnapped in February, 1988. He was subsequently murdered.
>
> Pan Am Flight 103 was blown up over Lockerbie, Scotland in December, 1988. As a result, 270 people were killed.

In February, 1993, terrorists exploded a bomb beneath New York City's World Trade Center, resulting in six deaths.

Just last month we witnessed the killing of American diplomatic personnel in Karachi, Pakistan.

Terrorism has now exploded into Middle America.

Other Terrorist incidents should also be recalled. The horror at the 1972 Summer Olympics in Munich. The terror plotted in the Philippines in January of this year against U.S. Air Carriers servicing the far east region. We must be mindful that one of those charged in that plot – Ramzi Ahmed Yousef – was also charged with the bombing of the World Trade Center. Last month, the world witnessed a terrorist in Tokyo's subway system.

In my testimony earlier this month, I stated that 'The face and the hand of terrorism are changing dramatically. . .' The most prominent international terrorist threat has been the emergence of international extremist groups that use crime and violence to further their political, social, and economic objectives.

As the bombing in Oklahoma City makes clear, however, Americans with such aims must also be considered in our profile of a terrorist. We cannot protect our country, our way of life, our Government and the democratic processes that ensure our freedoms and liberties if we fail to take seriously the threat of terrorism from all sources – foreign and domestic. There is no real difference between attacks planned or perpetrated against U.S. citizens here or abroad. Our law enforcement response must be the same, regardless of whether the plan or attack is organized and deployed by an American or a citizen of another country, whether the funds supporting the attack are raised locally or provided by foreign governments.

However, as I testified previously, the current scope of Federal criminal laws does not reach some very possible and truly frightening terrorist activity. Such activity could easily be the basis of a campaign to affect the operation of the United States Government and destroy the safety and confidence of the American public.

For example, if, acting within a single State, a terrorist organization entered into a campaign of assassination, killing non-Federal officials, leaders of private interest groups and members of the general public, this activity could fall entirely outside of Federal criminal jurisdiction.

Similarly, if a terrorist organization puts up posters threatening to kill or injure non-Federal officials, leaders of private interest groups and members of the general public, the FBI would be hard pressed to articulate a legal basis for investigating this activity.

Perhaps most frighteningly, if a terrorist or terrorist organization acting within a single State constructed bombs or incendiary devices with ingredients that did not cross State lines and proceed to bomb or burn non-government owned abandoned buildings, or many private residences, the FBI probably could not investigate.

Federal jurisdiction for the terrorist attack in Oklahoma City is plainly based on Title 18, *United States Code*, Section 844(F). That law prohibits the destruction, by means of fire or an explosion, of any building in whole or in part owned, possessed, or used by the United States or any department or agency thereof. Because death resulted, the death penalty applies.

The examples I mentioned before, however, illustrate the serious gap in the Federal criminal laws presently used to combat terrorism. There is a need, therefore, for a comprehensive Federal law against acts of terrorism committed in the United States.

With last week's tragedy in Oklahoma City, we must intensify our focus on the threat to America from within – by individuals and domestic groups which may have no foreign connections.

Terrorism is best prevented by acquiring, through legal and constitutional means, intelligence information relating to groups and individuals whose violent intentions threaten the public or our nation's interests.

Since the 1970s, the FBI has operated in accordance with the guidelines issued by attorneys general. Those guidelines were issued in response to prior performance by the FBI. Since then, intelligence gathering and investigative authorities have depended, in large part, on whether those who engage in terrorism are identified as a domestic group or an international group.

A domestic terrorism investigation may be initiated only when the 'facts or circumstances reasonably indicate that two or more persons are engaged in an enterprise for the purpose of further political or social goals, wholly or in part, through activities that involve force or violence and a violation of the criminal laws of the United States.' As you know, the specific requirements for international investigations are classified.

There is a broad range of threats confronting the United States. Many are external. Some, as we have always known, are internal. We must be as concerned about an individual or a group of Americans planning to bomb an office building as we are of an individual or group of foreigners planning to do the same thing.

Unfortunately, there are individuals and several groups in the United States that are arming themselves for potential conflicts with law enforcement or gathering weapons to further a social or political cause. I am greatly concerned about terrorist attacks here on American soil. The attacks are not only against one or two individuals – the effort, as in Oklahoma City, will be to murder as many as possible through a single blow.

207

For two decades, the FBI has been at an extreme disadvantage with regard to domestic groups which advocate violence. We have no intelligence or background information on them until their violent talk becomes deadly action. I do not support broad and undefined intelligence collection efforts – but law enforcement has to know something about those individuals and groups advocating deadly violence in the furtherance of their causes. The first rule of self-defense is to know the enemy who intends to destroy you.

Intelligence serves a very useful purpose and helps to protect the American people. It should not be considered a 'dirty word.'

I do not want my remarks to be interpreted as advocating investigative activity against groups exercising their legitimate constitutional rights or targeting people who disagree with our government. The FBI is entirely comfortable with the Constitution, due process rights, congressional oversight, legal process, and the American jury system. They each protect the American people and the FBI.

Law enforcement is not interested in investigating lawful activity. Law enforcement is not concerned with a group simply because of its ideology or political philosophy. The fact is – we do not need the business. The FBI has lots of important work to do in protecting people and the United States.

The FBI cannot and should not, however, tolerate and ignore any individuals or groups which advocate violence – which would kill innocent Americans, which would kill 'America's kids.' They are not just enemies of the United States, they are enemies of mankind. . . .

The FBI needs to meet the challenges of terrorism. For example:

> As I testified before, there is no comprehensive Federal anti-terrorism law.
>
> There is a need for a single counterterrorism center to be run by the FBI and supported by other agencies. To date, the United States Government has never had such a concentrated ability and focus.
>
> There is no prohibition on terrorist fund-raising – the lifeblood of any terrorist organization.
>
> Law enforcement must be able to trace money, explosives, nuclear materials, and terrorists.
>
> The use of pen registers and trap and trace devices in counterterrorism and counterintelligence investigations must be eased.
>
> It is absolutely critical for investigators to have increased access – short of a full-blown grand jury investigation – to hotel, motel, and common carrier records for counterterrorism and counterintelligence investigations.
>
> The FBI strictly obeys the law. As we heard the Congress and successive Presidents and attorneys general tell us, it is clear that we

were told to investigate domestic terrorists differently from foreign terrorists. If that is not what the American people speaking through its Congress and President now want, then tell us and the FBI will obey.

In order to conduct effective counterterrorism investigations, there is a continuing need to recruit sources, informants, agents, and support employees from a broad cross-section of society – here and abroad. That type of recruitment effort, however, costs money.

As we enter the 21st century, the FBI must have forensic capabilities on the street and in the laboratory that are on the 'cutting edge' of technology.

Law enforcement must have the ability to communicate rapidly by radio and other forms of wireless communications. Local, State, and Federal law enforcement officers and agencies must be able to talk among themselves, so that a State trooper on America's highways – like Oklahoma – has the full benefit of law enforcement's knowledge as he approaches a car with a suspect in it.

There must be funding for logistical support in counterterrorism operations and activities. The FBI currently relies on the Department of Defense for this support. Although the Department of Defense has been extremely cooperative, the FBI has been required to reimburse it for support.

Although Congress last year enacted the digital telephony legislation to ensure law enforcement's continued ability to conduct court-authorized wiretaps, the funding for carrier compliance has not been approved. In addition, the FBI needs funding for essential digital telephony research which it must undertake.

Encryption capabilities available to criminals and terrorists endanger the future usefulness of court-authorized wiretaps. This problem must be resolved.

There are no legally available means to exclude and remove alien terrorists without compromising vital national security information.

Rewards should be increased for those who provide information leading to the arrest and conviction of persons who commit acts of terrorism.

In connection with the bombing of the Federal building in Oklahoma City, we have thus far had some excellent investigative results. I will not be able to provide much information to the committee about this investigation, because it is ongoing and I do not wish to jeopardize the investigation or the prosecutive efforts that will ensue.

I urge anyone with information about this tragedy to come forward. Our success depends, in large part, on your help.

To everyone, I promise to pursue this matter with all available resources.

From the hearings before the Committee on the Judiciary of the United States Senate examining 'Terrorism in the United States: The Nature and Extent of the Threat and Possible Legislative Responses' (April 27 and May 24 1995).

JAMIE S. GORELICK
Deputy Attorney General, Department of Justice

The terrible event of eight days ago challenges all of us to prove that we have the will and the power to fulfil a fundamental responsibility set out for us in the first sentence of our Constitution: to 'insure domestic tranquility.'

Few experiences in our two centuries of government under that Constitution have tested our resolve in such a dramatic way. The Oklahoma City bomb sent shock waves across the nation, affecting people far removed geographically from those who lost their lives, who suffered grievous injury, who saw their families torn apart in an instant. But just as it showed the darkest impulses of human nature, it has also shown the fundamental goodness and strength of the American people, exemplified by the thousands of rescue workers who still are risking their lives in the shadow of that bombed-out building.

For us, today's hearing and the process it commences represent an opportunity to show that we as a government and as a people can stand up to terrorism while preserving our precious constitutional rights. Working together, we can honor the memory of the victims and ease some of the pain of their families by taking steps to stop terrorists, in a way that preserves both our domestic tranquility and our liberty. . . .

The President has urged the Congress to pass the Omnibus Counter-terrorism Act of 1995 – S. 390 – which he transmitted to the House and Senate of February 9. This bill will, for the first time, provide clear Federal criminal jurisdiction for any international terrorist attack that might occur in the United States.

Specifically, the bill will provide Federal criminal jurisdiction over terrorists who use the United States as the place from which to plan terrorist attacks overseas; provide a workable mechanism, utilizing United States District Judges, appointed by the Chief Justice, to deport alien terrorists expeditiously, without risking the disclosure of national security information or techniques; provide a new mechanism for preventing fund-raising in the United States that supports international terrorist activities overseas; and implement an international treaty requiring the insertion of a chemical agent into plastic explosives when manufactured to make them detectable.

The President has also called for more tools for federal law enforcement agencies investigating terrorism cases:

> We need approximately 1000 new agents, prosecutors, and other federal law enforcement and support personnel to investigate, deter, and prosecute terrorist activity. This and other proposals enunciated by the President which I will discuss will require an additional $150 million in fiscal year '95 ($100 million for personnel and $50 million for infrastructure) and an additional $500 million in fiscal year '96 ($400 million for personnel and infrastructure, together, and $100 million for digital telephony costs). The five year cost for these investments is approximately $1.25 billion (including digital telephony outyear costs).
>
> We should create an interagency Domestic Counterterrorism Center headed by the FBI that will establish a single point of contact for intelligence relating to terrorism. It will serve as a collection and dissemination point as well as provide analytical support. It will be available to all law enforcement agencies – federal, state, and local – and to agencies that deal with international terrorism.
>
> We should ease access to financial and credit reports in anti-terrorism cases. While banking records can be obtained under current law through appropriate legal procedures, credit records – which show where suspected terrorists do their banking – are not currently accessible through those very same legal procedures. The House has before it a bill which we support that would allow us to use the same process to obtain records from credit firms as is currently available to obtain bank records.
>
> Similarly, we should have the same legal standard in national security cases that we currently use in standard criminal cases for obtaining permission to track telephone traffic with 'pen registers' and 'trap and trace' devices.
>
> The national security letter process, which is currently used for obtaining certain categories of information in terrorism investigations, should be available to obtain records critical to such investigations from hotels, motels and common carriers.
>
> We should fund the 'digital telephony' bill passed by Congress last session. This technology will assure court-authorized law enforcement access to electronic surveillance of digitized communications.
>
> We need an FBI counterterrorist and counterintelligence fund to pay for extraordinary logistical and other expenses arising from terrorism crises.
>
> We should require, within one year, the inclusion of taggants

– microscopic particles – in standard explosive device raw materials which will permit tracing of the materials post-explosion.

We should require the BATF to study and report on: (1) effective means of tagging explosives for purposes of identification and detection, (2) whether certain common chemicals used to manufacture explosives can be rendered inert, and (3) whether controls can be imposed on certain precursor chemicals used to manufacture explosives.

We should permit military participation in crime-fighting when chemicals, biological or other weapons of mass destruction are concerned, just as the military can assist in such efforts currently when nuclear weapons are concerned.

We should, within constitutional limitations, expand, in a number of ways, the authority of law enforcement to fight terrorism through electronic surveillance. Examples of such increased authority include expansion of the list of felonies which could be used as the basis for a surveillance order, and authority to obtain roving wiretaps where it is not practical to specify the number of the phone to be tapped (such as when a suspect uses multiple cellular phones).

We should criminalize the use of chemical weapons in solid and liquid form, just as they are currently criminalized for use in gaseous form.

We should make it illegal to possess explosives knowing that they are stolen.

The current penalty of up to five (5) years imprisonment for anyone who transfers a firearm or explosive materials knowing that it will be used to commit a crime of violence should be increased to a mandatory penalty of not less than ten (10) years; and

The enhanced penalties for terrorist attacks against some federal employees should be extended to protect all current and former Federal employees, and their families, when the crime is committed because of the official duties of the federal employee.

Mr. Chairman, I want to stress two important points in closing. First, the President, the Attorney General, and the entire Administration want to work with the Congress in a bipartisan manner to meet the challenge of terrorism. This is an American problem, and it calls on all of us to set aside political considerations to achieve a response that is effective and comprehensive.

Second, I am certain you share our conviction that we can take decisive and forceful action against terrorism without sacrificing our nation's fundamental freedoms. The choice between civil liberties and a safe society is a false choice. We need not – and we will not – trade off the guarantees of the Bill of Rights in order to uphold our duty to 'insure domestic tranquility.'

From the hearing before the Subcommittee on Terrorism, Technology and Government Information of the Committee on the Judiciary of the United States Senate examining 'The Militia Movement in the United States' (June 15, 1995).

ROBERT M. BRYANT

Assistant Director, National Security Division, F.B.I.

L et me assure you that the FBI is doing everything within its mandate to prevent acts of terrorism from occurring. If an incident does occur, the FBI will mount whatever lawful effort it takes to solve the crime and apprehend the individual terrorists or terrorist group. The swift and effective investigation of terrorist acts, culminating in arrests, convictions, and incarcerations, sends a powerful message to terrorists and helps deter future acts of terrorism. . . .

FBI domestic counterterrorism investigations under the [Attorney General's] guidelines are limited to occasions when there is a reasonable indication 'that two or more persons are engaged in an enterprise the purpose of furthering political or social goals wholly or in part through activities that involve force or violence and a violation of the criminal laws of the United States.' A consideration the guidelines prescribe in determining whether an investigation is warranted is the danger to privacy and free expression posed by an investigation.

In addition, we may investigate individuals under the general crimes portion of the guidelines. Full investigations under these provisions may be initiated when 'facts or circumstances reasonably indicate that a federal crime has been, is being, or will be committed.' For investigations of groups under the domestic security provisions and of individuals under the general crimes provisions, there must be an objective, factual basis regarding criminal activity. More limited inquiries may be conducted when information is received which, although short of a reasonable indication of criminal activities, responsible handling requires some further scrutiny beyond the prompt and extremely limited checking out of initial leads.

One recent example of the type of investigation we do conduct led to the arrests and convictions of two men from Minnesota: Duane Baker and Leroy Wheeler, who claimed to be members of a tax protest group called the Patriots Council. Baker and Wheeler manufactured a quantity of ricin, a highly toxic derivative of the castor bean. They planned to use the ricin to kill a police officer who had served eviction papers on one of the group's members. Following their arrests on August 4, 1994, they were convicted of violations of the Biological Weapons Anti-Terrorist Act of 1989.

A second example involved individuals linked to a militia group who learned that Russian-made tanks were located at a local military base. Apparently fearing that these tanks were the prelude to a Russian-led invasion of the United States by the United Nations, some individuals took it upon themselves to plan to destroy these tanks. In fact, the tanks were captured by the United States Army from the Iraqis during Desert Storm and are being used for training our own soldiers, as well as for research and development to improve United States tanks and combat tactics. These misguided individuals were foiled before any damage could be done.

Finally, in the mid 1980s, some groups, which could now be viewed as paramilitary in nature, engaged in a wide range of criminal activity, including bank robberies, counterfeiting, seditious conspiracy, homicide, bombings, threats to Federal authorities including judges, and illegal possession and use of weapons and explosives. These are the types of activities that will receive the full investigative attention of the FBI. Organizations that are peaceful and do not plan to violate the laws of the United States are of no investigative interest to the FBI.

From the hearing before the Subcommittee on Terrorism, Technology and Government Information of the Committee on the Judiciary of the United States Senate examining 'The Militia Movement in the United States' (June 15, 1995).

JAMES L. BROWN

Deputy Associate Director, National Security Division, B.A.T.F.

Since the tragic bombing of the Alfred P. Murrah Building in Oklahoma City on April 19, much of the American public has learned for the first time through the media about the militia movement.

ATF has a long history of working to prevent violence associated with firearms. ATF's unique jurisdiction over the Federal firearms laws allows us to focus on armed career criminals and drug traffickers, and international firearms traffickers. Our expertise in explosives led to the discovery of a key piece of evidence in the World Trade Center bombing, ultimately bringing the perpetrators to justice.

Paramilitary terrorist activity within the United States is not a new phenomenon. Its origins in the second half of this century date back to 1960, with the establishment of the Minutemen Organization. The organization, founded and coordinated by Robert Depugh, was reportedly intended to resist the spread of communism in the United States by the use of guerrilla tactics. ATF conducted over 60 investigations nationwide of members of the Minutemen from the late 1960s to the early 1980s.[1]

From 1976 to the mid-1980s, ATF conducted forty-three investigations of members and associates of the Posse Comitatus, a group opposed to government 'intrusion.' On February 13, 1983, Gordon Kahl, a member of the Posse Comitatus in Medina, North Dakota, succeeded in bringing the group to national notoriety. On that date, Kahl and others engaged in an armed confrontation with Federal and local law enforcement officers, resulting in the death of two U.S. marshals and the wounding of three other Federal, county and local enforcement officers. Before he was finally apprehended, Kahl shot and killed the sheriff of Lawrence County, Arkansas. The ideology of the Posse Comitatus is very similar to that of many of today's militias.[2]

At this point, I'd like to give you some examples of the types of allegations that have been found in some of the militia propaganda in this country. These are not necessarily representative of the views of all militia members, however. Certainly there are members of militia groups who are upstanding, law-abiding citizens.

As a result of criminal investigations conducted by ATF, along with information received from other law enforcement agencies, open source documents, and publications distributed by militias, ATF estimates militias exist in approximately forty states.

A May 11, 1995 Gannett News Service article quoting the Center for Democratic Renewal, a private Atlanta group that monitors militias, reports that there are up to 100,000 militia members in at least thirty states.

Accurate estimates reflecting the total number of militias, the number and specific states involved, and the total militia membership nationwide are not available.

As you are aware, the incident in Oklahoma City has generated much speculation in the media about militia groups and antigovernment views. While we do not investigate groups based on their beliefs, we do pursue investigations on individual suspects based on evidence of violations of the law. Through these investigations we have gained some insight into militias.

During the past decade, several national and global events provided the environment for the formation of militias. Militias include members with a spectrum of views. They range from ideas which are extreme, violent and paranoid to active opposition to the firearms laws. Some militias believe that they are the 'people's response' to a wide range of issues that include the supposed takeover of the United States by the United Nations. Most are primarily concerned about firearms laws.

In April 1994, a militia promoter called for an armed march on Washington DC to arrest members of Congress unless they complied with a list of demands including the repeal of gun control legislation. Although the march was later canceled, this proposed march fostered the concept of militias nationwide.[3]

One theory promoted by some of today's militia members is that the democratic United States will be replaced by the 'new world order.' A national Militia speaker furthers the notion that the 'illuminati' (a group of national and international government and military officials) will round up all 'Christian patriots' confiscate their guns, and haul them off in black helicopters to concentration camps. A 1994 news article quotes this spokesperson as saying that urban street gangs would be part of the home invasion of the 'patriots.' Also included in this invasion force would be foreign mercenaries, including Nepalese Gurkhas and Royal Hong Kong Police. The Operation would supposedly be controlled by the Federal Emergency Management Agency; a multijurisdictional task force comprised of the 'Fincen police,' ATF, and the FBI; and other Federal enforcement agencies.[4]

Militias, apparently forming independently across the United States, are able to share many of the same philosophies and agendas, due to an efficient networking system. This system utilizes militia-oriented publications, computer bulletin board services, commercial radio stations, videos, public forums, and short-wave radio to spread their rhetoric.

Federal authorities are likened to Nazis and are called 'baby killers' by some militia advocates. Hateful descriptions of the President and the Attorney General of the United States, found in some militia-related letters and literature, are so vile that they cannot be repeated here. The most recent propaganda circulating among some militia supporters is that the President ordered the Oklahoma City bombing.

Federal and local enforcement personnel have been threatened, harassed, assaulted, and shot. A white supremacist with militia leanings shot and wounded a Missouri State trooper in September 1994.[5] In November 1994, an adherent of a militia philosophy shot Nashville Metro police officers when they stopped him on suspicion of drunken driving.

ATF has successfully investigated and charged several members of the present-day militia movement with violations of Federal firearms and explosives laws. I want to emphasize that we do not investigate these people based on their beliefs; we pursue investigations on individual suspects based on violations or intended violations of the law. I would like to highlight a couple of those investigations:

American Patriots. On March 24, 1994, the Las Vegas Metro police responded to a report of shots being fired on a Las Vegas street. The officers then encountered two armed suspects with a MAK-90 semiautomatic rifle and numerous handgrenades. ATF's assistance was requested, and a Federal search warrant was executed at the suspects' residences, yielding numerous handgrenades, pipe bombs, and other explosives, along with drugs, illegal firearms, and thousands of rounds of ammunition. Upon questioning, the suspects claimed membership with the American Patriots and affiliation with the ARM (presumably Aryan Resistance Movement). The suspects stated that war had been declared against the police. They were hostile toward the ATF agents and made several references to Waco. Both have been convicted of possession of unregistered machine-guns.

American Citizen Alliance and the Liberty Group. While purchasing 50 ammunition magazines from a firearms dealer in Maitland, Florida, a suspect made references to militia activity while in the presence of a police detective. He spoke about a plan in place to kill Federal judges, members of Congress, and special agents. He also advised that he had sixty Ruger rifles. An inquiry into the suspect's background revealed his status as a convicted felon, and he was arrested by ATF on October 15, 1994. At the time of his arrest, he had a Ruger rifle with a silencer. The suspect has five associates, also members of the American Citizen Alliance, who are defendants in Federal cases as the result of their role in placing unlawful liens against the properties of Federal District Court Judges. The original suspect pled guilty to possession of an unregistered machine gun and was sentenced on April 19, 1995.

ATF has joined with the Department of Justice agencies (FBI and DEA) and other Treasury agencies in the fight against violent crime. ATF has been at the forefront of that battle due to our unique position of being vested with the enforcement of the Federal firearms and explosives laws and the regulation of those industries. . . .

In conclusion, the men and women of ATF investigate and apprehend some of the most violent criminals in America on a daily basis. During our extensive planning for the execution of search and arrest warrants, we anticipate – and expect – violators to be armed with firearms or to have in their possession destructive devices. In fact, the possession or use of a firearm or bomb is the primary element of proof for many of the statutes we enforce. Unfortunately, and sadly, the responsibility of apprehending the nation''s most violent criminals has taken its toll on our agency, resulting in the deaths of 183 special agents in the line of duty.

Notes

1. For an account of the activities of the Minutemen, see, for example, John George and Laird Wilcox, *American Extremists: Militias, Supremacists, Klansmen, Communists and Others* (Amherst, New York, Prometheus Books, 1996), 221–246.

2. The story of Gordan Kahl is told by James Corcoran in *Bitter Harvest: The Birth of Paramilitary Terrorism in the Heartland* (New York, Penguin, 1990, 1995).

3. Linda Thompson, Adjunct General of the Unorganized Militia of the United States, called for the march, and for a view on it from within the militia movement see the editorial reproduced from *Common Sense* at pages 393–395 of this volume.

4. See on this the extracts from *The Freedom Networker* in this volume at pages 435, 436 and 437–439.

5. See the account of Missouri Highway Patrolman Fred Mills in the following section.

PART THREE
POLICING THE FRONT LINE

From the hearing before the Subcommittee on Terrorism, Technology and Government Information of the Committee on the Judiciary of the United States Senate examining 'The Militia Movement in the United States' (June 15, 1995).

RICHARD R. ROMLEY
Maricopa County Attorney, Phoenix, Arizona

As Maricopa County attorney I am the chief prosecutor in a county whose population is approximately 2.5 million people. It encompasses twenty-three cities and towns, including the city of Phoenix. I am responsible for more than 250 prosecuting attorneys whose primary role is to investigate and prosecute the more than 40,000 felony offenses reported to my office each year.

The horror of Oklahoma City has unfortunately thrust Arizona onto the front pages of our nation's newspapers. As most of us know, the accused bomber – Timothy McVeigh – lived in Arizona. We also know that numerous associates of Mr. McVeigh also reside in Arizona and it has been reported that they have connections with various militia organizations.

Arizona, like other States, is experiencing a proliferation of militias. Thirteen groups have recently been identified. Some leaders of these groups spew messages of hate and conspiracy. Messages rooted in anti-Semitism and racism. Messages which create images of 'black helicopters' and international military troops hiding in caves waiting for a signal to usurp our democracy. However, these messages are so outrageous that they often fall on deaf ears, even among their own members. Therefore, we must be careful not to label all members of militias as supporters of the rantings of these extremists. Our focus must be on the fanatic fringe of the militia movement who maliciously seek to sow the seeds of violent discontent.

It is this fanatical fringe – claiming to be patriotic Americans – who attack by intimidation and violence the very core of our democracy. In my jurisdiction we have had direct experience with some of these extremists. My office has prosecuted numerous individuals whose fanaticism was based on racial or religious prejudice and a desire to violently destroy confidence in our democratically elected government. Let me tell you about one case. It involved a member of a white-supremacist group called the 'Arizona White Battalion' who was also associated with a group called 'The Freemen', a tax-protesting, anti-government organization. This person conspired to place bombs at more than 37 locations. His targets included synagogues, day care centers and government buildings. His plan was to detonate the bomb during peak occupation of these buildings. Fortunately, he was apprehended before he could carry out his plan, and is now serving a long prison sentence. As horrible as his intentions were, they become even more troublesome when we consider that this potential mad bomber was only sixteen years old when he first laid down his plan of destruction. Sixteen years old when the seeds of hate had already taken root.

So-called 'patriots' refuse to acknowledge that in a representative democracy you do not challenge laws by insurrection, you bring your grievances to the ballot box or to the courts. In their quest for notoriety, power and financial gain these fanatical individuals shroud their insurrection in patriotism. It is difficult to explain their underlying motives. They have declared war on the very system that guarantees them the freedoms they demand. It is as if, in the absence of a real threat or enemy, they have turned inward against their own government.

In the face of such attacks it may be tempting to react quickly and harshly. This is where I urge caution. We must not be stampeded into quick, but ill-conceived action because of the horror of immediate events. We must engage in calm and thoughtful deliberation before we choose our course of action. It must be consistent with our constitutionally guaranteed freedoms. For we, as Americans, have the right to question and criticize our government.

If there is one common denominator among the extremists in these groups, it is that they all strive for the opportunity of martyrdom. We must be careful not to give them that opportunity. If our decisions are made in haste, we help create false martyrs around whom they could rally the disaffected and misguided. We must ensure that government does not self-fulfil the prophecy of those who seek to destroy.

However, we in law enforcement must be vigilant. When these extremists encourage change through violent means rather than just talk, we need to step up and say enough is enough. If an individual steps over the line of lawlessness, we must act swiftly. As a prosecutor I have no patience with those who break the law or who encourage others to do so.

As one who is on the front line in the battle against crime and extremism, I applaud the Senate's passage of the anti-terrorism legislation. You have given law enforcement tools with which to combat this menace . . . This legislation will help ensure that our citizens need not live in fear that horrors such as the World Trade Center bombing or the Federal courthouse bombing in Oklahoma will occur in their communities.

From the hearing before the Subcommittee on Terrorism, Technology and Government Information of the Committee on the Judiciary of the United States Senate examining 'The Militia Movement in the United States' (June 15, 1995).

FRED M. MILLS

Superintendent, Missouri State Highway Patrol

Hate groups and extremism always have been a part of Missouri's history as far back as before the Civil War, in which Missouri's citizens were torn by the slavery issue. Factions of the Ku Klux Klan have existed in Missouri since that time, and continue to attract members even today. Other extremist groups have surfaced in Missouri over the past century only to disappear and then resurface again, or re-emerge under a different name with a slightly different philosophy. This has been the history of extremism in Missouri. Discontent within society over a variety of issues has spawned new groups, only to see those groups subside as the issues were resolved.

Groups, such as the Christian Patriot Defense League, an ultra right-wing movement, have been visible in the Midwest since the 1950s. The CPDL settled into a paramilitary training camp on a farm near Licking, MO, in 1980 and began hosting 'Freedom Festivals,' which drew members of various Christian Identity organizations, the KKK, CSA, and Posse Comitatus to train to defend themselves and their freedoms. In 1984 Missouri passed an antiparamilitary law, which prohibited this kind of activity, resulting in the CPDL being limited only to martial art-type training (574.070 RSMo.).

The impact of extremism in Missouri was first felt by the Missouri State Highway Patrol in 1985, when Tpr. Jimmie Linegar was shot and killed by a member of the Aryan Nations, a white supremacist group. This incident led the Highway Patrol, in conjunction with federal and local law enforcement agencies, to raid a training compound on the Missouri-Arkansas border for the Covenant, Sword, and Arm of the Lord, a paramilitary survivalist group of 'Christian Patriots.' The violence associated with the shooting, and firepower confiscated from the camp, surprised many Missourians and some law enforcement agencies. This seemingly singular event, however, merely highlighted an evolving trend toward extremism, not only in Missouri but across the nation, as well.[1]

The 1987 shooting of Tpr. Russell Harper, again, demonstrated the power of hate espoused by extremist groups. While the man who shot Tpr. Harper was not directly tied to any particular hate group, he did espouse white supremacist and hate group philosophies, as well as collect Aryan Nation literature and paraphernalia. When officers raided his farm in Ozark County, located near the former CSA compound, they seized a variety of weapons, many of which were illegal.

In July 1992 the Missouri State Highway Patrol formed its organized Crime Unit within its Division of Drug and Crime Control. One of the Unit's tasks was to gather information about extremist and hate groups in Missouri, as well as street gangs, outlaw motorcycle gangs, and organized crime. The Unit has focused on three extremist groups: the KKK, Christian Identity religious movements, and militias.

Again, in September 1994, a Missouri State Highway Patrol officer was struck at by an extremist group. Cpl. Bobbie Harper was shot and seriously injured by a 'patriot' for the 'Citizens of the Kingdom of Christ,' a Christian Identity religious movement, in retaliation for the arrest of one of its principals. Harper was forced to retire from the Highway Patrol due to his injuries and continues to have health problems associated with them. Meanwhile, the 'patriot' has disappeared, probably protected by the network of extremist groups that stretch across the country.

The escalating level of violence in 1994, in Missouri as well as across the nation, was felt personally by many members of the Missouri State Highway Patrol. The Patrol recorded six officer-involved shootings in 1994. Luckily, none were fatal for the Patrol officers involved. Missouri, however, did have six law enforcement officers killed in 1994, ranking it sixth in the nation for number of officers killed. While none of these incidents were directly related to extremist movements in Missouri, they do represent a growing tendency toward violence.

Each day Missouri State Highway Patrol road officers come into contact with a variety of people traveling on Missouri's highways. While the officers are trained to provide courteous and friendly service to all citizens, they also are taught to treat each traffic stop, whether for a traffic violation or service rendered, as if it could develop into a critical incident. Assaults on officers, such as those that led to the deaths of Tprs. Jimmie Linegar and Russell Harper [sic], are becoming all too prevalent in today's society.

Extremism has become more evident in Missouri in the past decade, and many of the militias gaining national and local media attention were begun by people with extremist views. To say that all militia members are extremists, however, is overstating today's movement. Many people who attend militia meetings would be considered law-abiding, God-fearing citizens – farmers, entrepreneurs, former military personnel, and some who simply are curious as to what these groups are about.

222

Most of Missouri's 'militias or extremist groups' have not evolved much past the stage where they organize into formal groups to discuss their concern and displeasure with the current state of government and society, and to practice skills believed to be needed to protect themselves. Our concern and fear is focused on those whose motives and objectives are to spread the cancer of hatred and criminal conduct, who will utilize these groups as a vehicle for their efforts or as a cover for their activities. We are seeing these seeds of discontent being planted, and the rhetoric is becoming more and more violent and distrusting of all government.

The Highway Patrol continues to collect information about extremist groups in Missouri. Due to a shortage of manpower and money, however, the Patrol's Organized Crime Unit is staffed by only one officer. Law enforcement officers across the country need the support of their legislators and Congress – through supportive legislation and funds – to help turn the tide of extremism across the country and ensure the safety of its citizens.

Missouri has long been considered a good place to work, raise a family, and retire. Only recently has its peaceful demeanor been disrupted by the acts of violence of extremist groups. While we take these acts very seriously, the Patrol does not want to infringe on the rights of Missouri citizens to gather to discuss their perceptions of problems within our society and government. When violence does erupt, threatening Missouri citizens and the state, however, the Patrol stands ready to quickly and effectively protect those we are sworn to serve.

In closing, let me say while things in this country have obviously changed and some areas of our communities may have lost that sense of pride and caring, all is not lost. We have a majority of citizens, although sometimes quiet, that truly care about and support law enforcement. We saw it when Cpl. Harper was the victim of a cowardly assault. We also saw our nation pull together in mourning for the tragedy that occurred in Oklahoma City.

We in Missouri are blessed with a Governor, Mel Carnahan, who is an outspoken supporter of law enforcement and who has joined in the battle to remove the cancer of crime from our communities. We need Congress to demonstrate on-going courage and the commitment to support the officers who strive to keep American citizens safe and our country the special place it is to live, work, and raise our families.

Note

1. For an account of the activities of the CSA see James Coates, *Armed and Dangerous: The Rise of the Survivalist Right* (New York, Hill and Wang, 1987, 1995), 136–148.

From the hearing before the Subcommittee on Crime of the Committee on the Judiciary of the House of Representatives examining the 'Nature and Threat of Violent Anti-Government Groups in America' (November 2, 1995).

TED ALMAY

Superintendent, Ohio Bureau of Criminal Identification and Investigation

I am here this morning to provide testimony in regards to recent confrontations that Ohio law enforcement have been involved in with domestic threat groups.

The Ohio Unorganized Militia is named in both the Ohio Constitution and the Ohio Revised Code. The original premise that all citizens between the ages of 18 and 65 were in the Ohio Unorganized Militia relates to the minute-man concept that in the event of war, and the armed forces were deployed overseas, there would be no militia to defend our state borders if an invasion was to occur. This brief mention of the Unorganized Militia has given credibility to the present day militia and its belief that they must defend Ohio against government whose elected officials have committed treason by breaking their oath of office to support and defend the Constitution.

It is believed that current militia membership in Ohio is approximately 500 members, which has doubled since the Oklahoma City bombing. In recent weeks, it appears, however, that the militia is becoming even more disorganized as members become disenchanted with the political beliefs and frustration as government fails to meet their demands. The state command level of the Ohio Unorganized Militia is all but disbanded and the county level groups are in a general state of disarray, primarily over internal leadership disputes. Due in part to the lack of organization and leadership, Ohio law enforcement has had several confrontations with militia members.

In July 1994, a rural county sheriff's office received a complaint of automatic weapons fire in the middle of the night. Upon arrival, the sheriff was confronted by several people dressed in camouflage fatigue uniforms who claimed to be a 'gun club'. After further investigation, it was determined that the Ohio Unorganized Militia was conducting night training maneuvers.

In January of 1995, information was received that the militia movement was looking for a means to draw national media attention to their cause. A plan was discussed that involved charging a local sheriff or judge with treason and arresting them in a rural county adjacent to a media market [sic]. Local militia members were directed to determine the location of their electoral officials' private residences and work locations. When it became known that law enforcement was aware of this plan, it dissolved.

In March of 1995, a militia member, Joseph Mann, was conducting a training seminar of the new Ruger 9mm pistol to a group of militia recruits in his home. In an effort to demonstrate the safety mechanism, Mann loaded the weapon, put it to his head and pulled the trigger. The safety was not set properly and Mann died at the scene in front of his training class.

In June of 1995, Agents from ATF along with the Parma Police Department were attempting to serve a search warrant on weapons violations at the local residence of an alleged militia member. The man had left the house prior to the search and notified the militia. Approximately ten members came in vehicles and communicated via CB radio. They advised ATF that they were present to 'monitor the situation.'

On June 25, 1995, militia member Michael Hill was stopped for a traffic violation in rural Frazeysburg, Ohio. Hill had removed his Ohio license plates and replaced them with homemade militia tags. Hill told the officer he had no right to stop him and sped away. After a brief chase, Hill stopped again and exited his vehicle. Hill then drew a .45 caliber semi-automatic pistol and pointed it at the officers, who fired, killing Hill.

It should be noted that Hill was the self-proclaimed Chaplain of the militia, chief justice of the so-called 'one supreme court' for the republic of Ohio, and a former Canton police officer.

As the militia continue to unravel, a relatively new and disturbing group calling themselves the 'one supreme court' has arisen. This small but radical group is composed mostly of former or current militia members. They have based their jurisdiction as a common law court from the 1933 Bank Emergency Act instituted to restore America's financial crises. This emergency act gave the federal government power over the states to regulate commerce and banking, along with the Federal Reserve Board. This state of emergency has never officially ended, and the common law court movement use this language as a foundation for their beliefs. This notion that the federal government has taken away the rights of citizens of each state for its own benefit, is their call to action.

To state their cause publicly, their members will file a motion of 'quiet title' with the one supreme court, and declare themselves 'sovereign human beings.' To do this, the person must appear before the 'court' with their birth certificate and two witnesses to swear that the a subject was born in the United States, but not born in Washington DC. They believe that the federal courts have original jurisdiction in Washington DC, therefore if you are born there, the federal government has jurisdiction over you. Once the witnesses have testified and the birth certificate has been examined, a motion of quiet title is granted. The subject declares himself a sovereign human being exempt of all state, federal, and local law.

The concept is that the federal government, by removing states' rights have influenced all law by forbidding the people to have a voice in government since parts of the Constitution have been suspended by the Bank Act of 1933. The persons must then run a newspaper ad for three consecutive days to declare themselves sovereign and alert local government and law enforcement that they have no jurisdiction over them. This includes the IRS, all courts of record, the banking profession, specifically including foreclosures and liens. Also included is law enforcement, especially in the area of traffic enforcement as this violates their right of free passage, licensing boards, and virtually any government regulated industry. Once a person is charged criminally or becomes involved in a civil matter, their eagerness to file dozens of meritless motions prevail. Gene Schroder of Colorado has published a book of 'fill-in-the-blank' type motions that challenge every aspect of the proceeding from the constitutional issue of jurisdiction to a change of venue to the one supreme court. These documents put a tremendous strain on the legal system, and upon ultimate failure can result in attempts to intimidate and even threaten Judges. According to a recent survey conducted by Chief Justice Tom Moyer of the Ohio Supreme Court, 22 judges reported recent filings from this group. In addition, several judges have received threats and one judge has received police protection for himself and his family as a result of his denying these motions.

In addition, the constitutional study group of the one supreme court has 'indicted' several people for treason, including all members of the Ohio Supreme Court. To date, no known action to serve the indictments, other than by mail has occurred.

The one supreme court has also drawn significant media attention and most major newspapers in Ohio have run stories. In fact, the television program *20/20* filmed the court in Columbus earlier this month. There is concern among law enforcement that as the media displays the actions of a small group of people who have elected to exclude themselves from the law, more individuals may selectively ignore current law and the judicial system. It is important to note that these groups are closely linked via the Internet computer network, and events that occur anywhere in the nation can be twisted and sent out within minutes.

It is my belief that this movement will dissolve as its members become frustrated with the lack of progress and government's refusal to acknowledge their beliefs. The next major concern, however, will be the trial of Timothy McVeigh. If convicted they will claim a government conspiracy to frame a militia sympathizer. If acquitted, we anticipate that they will still claim a conspiracy to indict him and discredit their movement. These dates will be added to the list of Waco, Ruby Ridge, and in Ohio, the Frazysburg shooting of Mike Hill.

In conclusion, the First Amendment rights of all citizens are paramount to our survival. There is a system of change that has been present for over 200 years and every piece of legislation that you debate in these chambers is about change. The process is slow to provide time for thought and discussion. If the militia and common law courts have the support they claim, then they should work within the system. Until such time as the law is changed, no American has the right to selectively exclude themselves from the laws that protect us all. The irony of this situation is that these individuals under the cry of patriotism have chosen to exclude themselves from selected laws while screaming that their rights under the Constitution must be protected.

From the hearing before the Subcommittee on Terrorism, Technology and Government Information of the Committee on the Judiciary of the United States Senate examining 'The Militia Movement in the United States' (June 15, 1995).

JOHN BOHLMAN

Musselshell County Attorney, Roundup, Montana

Even prior to my taking office as county attorney, I was aware that the militia activity in Montana was primarily taking place in the western part of Montana. As Noxon, Montana, is over 500 miles northwest of my hometown of Roundup, Montana, I was not very attentive to Militia of Montana activities. I was much more concerned with the eastern Montana 'Freemen' who were very active in Musselshell and Garfield Counties. I believe that one of the reasons that the 'Freemen' made their most violent threats and took their most aggressive actions in Garfield County is the fact that Garfield County has a total population of less than 1,500 people and that the total law enforcement presence consists of a sheriff and his undersheriff. Fugitives from state and federal warrants are currently making their base of operation a log home in Musselshell County where the total population is about 4,400 people and the Sheriff's Department consists of five officers.

In spite of the absence of a militia organization in Musselshell County, I have had direct dealings with the Militia of Montana and other militia and 'patriot' group members since March 3, 1995. During the week beginning February 27, 1995, the Musselshell County Sheriff's Department was on alert that an organization known as the 'Freemen', and/or members of similar organizations, were planning to kidnap a judge and/or county prosecutor in eastern Montana. As the information was related to me by the Sheriff of Musselshell County, the federal agency supplying the warning stated that it was believed that Garfield County Attorney Nick Murnion, the District Court Judge that served Garfield County, and Musselshell County's District Judge Roy C. Rodeghiero were considered the most likely targets, and that the victim was to be put on trial before the organization members, convicted, executed by hanging, and that the whole event was to be videotaped. Based on that information, the Musselshell County Sheriff placed reserve deputies in the Musselshell County Courthouse to increase security for Judge Rodeghiero. The Judge was also accompanied to work in the mornings and home in the evenings by Sheriff's deputies.

On the afternoon of March 3, 1995, two men were arrested for violation of the state's concealed weapon law, a misdemeanor, after they had been stopped by a deputy for driving a pickup with no license plates. (Earlier, one of the two men had been in the county courthouse and had spent time on each floor, including being just outside the judge's office.) That stop led to the deputy finding that the driver also had no driver's license. When the two men exited the pickup, the deputy learned that both men were carrying concealed weapons without permits, and both men were placed under arrest. Shortly after the arrest, the sheriff's deputies learned that the two men had in their possession a large amount of weapons and ammunition which included bullets that would pierce class II body armor commonly worn by law enforcement officers, approximately 30 plastic 'flex-cuffs' and a role of duct tape, approximately $26,000 in cash and approximately $60,000 in gold and silver coins, a video camera and film and a 35mm. Minolta camera with additional lenses, and sophisticated radio communication equipment . . . At the time of this discovery, the deputies concluded that they had disrupted the attempt to kidnap and kill a judge about which we had been warned by a federal agency. A few days after the arrest, a hand drawn map carried in the pocket of one of the men, Frank Ellena, was identified as a map of the town of Jordan, Montana. The map clearly marked for identification the home of the Sheriff and the home of the county prosecutor, Nick Murnion, who had successfully convicted a member of the Freemen group who was sentenced to ten (10) years in prison.

At approximately 6 o'clock p.m. on March 3, 1995, and only about 90 minutes after the first two men were jailed, two vehicles containing six men entered the parking area of the Musselshell County Sheriff's Department and parked facing the door in what appeared to the deputies to be an effort to control entrance to the Sheriff's Department. The first deputy to see the vehicles believed that when the vehicles entered the parking area, at least one occupant in each vehicle was speaking into a remote, hand-held radio transmitter/receiver. (When the first two men were stopped, they too were talking into a remote, hand-held radio transmitter/receiver.) Two men remained in one car, and three men entered the jail and made what the deputies described as a demand that the evidence recently taken be turned over to them. The jail lacks security due to its age and design so the evidence (guns, etc.) was in clear view of the three men. As the demand or request was being made, one of the deputies saw a gun concealed on one of the men when that man's jacket opened. The two deputies immediately placed the three individuals under arrest. It was believed by the deputies that these three men and the two men in the car outside were co-conspirators of the first two men arrested.

After securing the three individuals arrested inside the jail, the two deputies went outside to the white car which contained two men. According to the deputies, one of the two men was speaking into a hand-held radio transmitter/receiver as the deputies approached and both men locked the doors of the two-door car. The officers had their weapons drawn and demanded that the two men exit the car. The two men refused and one continued to talk into a radio. One deputy saw a gun tucked into the front of the passenger's pants and the driver began unzipping his jacket as if reaching for a gun. The driver's side window was broken by one deputy and the passenger then opened his door. Both men were placed under arrest and a check of both men showed that both men were carrying handguns and that the driver did have a handgun in a shoulder holster under his jacket.

I learned later that night that the passenger in the two-door car was John Trochman [sic], a founder of the Militia of Montana. I did not know anything about him until I read the newspaper the following day and then read an *Esquire* magazine interview with John Trochman. Within an hour after the arrest of John Trochman, telephone calls began coming into the jail from all over Montana, and from other states as well. In the week that followed, the jail received hundreds of telephone calls from all over the United States demanding that the arrested individuals be released and making threats against the Sheriff and his deputies. . . . I received approximately forty threats on our lives and threats that included my secretary's family. One caller identified himself as being with the Militia of Montana and made threatening comments about my secretary's adopted Korean daughter. Because of the racial comments made by some callers, my secretary drove to another state during the night to hide her daughter. One of the deputies sent his family out-of-town after he received a call that neither of the two arresting deputies could find a hole deep enough to hide in. Some callers stated that armed men from militia organizations in various states would come to Roundup to see that justice was done to those of us responsible for the arrest of the 'fine patriot John Trochman.' Many callers stated that they knew my phones were 'bugged' by the F.B.I. and that these seven men had been arrested on false charges as part of an F.B.I. scheme to get John Trochman into custody. Interestingly, Randy Trochman, a co-founder of M.O.M., gave press releases disavowing any link between John Trochman and M.O.M. and the 'Freemen' organization. He stated that the 'Freemen' were extremist and that John Trochman was in Musselshell County to attempt to negotiate a settlement of the tensions between the 'Freemen' and local law enforcement. However, facts sharply contradict those press releases. In the January 24, 1995, issue of *Taking Aim*, M.O.M.'s newsletter, John Trochman wrote an extensive article explaining how to set up replacement governments at the county level and how to create the so-called assets that are the basis of money crimes being actively committed by at least two of the 'Freemen' operating out of Musselshell County. Mr. Trochman even thanked three 'Freemen' leaders for teaching these techniques and he encouraged readers to go and study with the 'Freemen' so that the techniques could be implemented. The article went so far as to state that M.O.M. would help interested individuals make arrangements to spend the necessary time with the 'Freemen'.

In concluding . . . I want to state that on a personal level I am opposed to such organizations [as the militias] because I believe they are attempting to impose their political will by force and the threat of force. It is impossible to lump them into a single classification at this time because the different groups have some common ground, but they also have very distinct variations. My opinion is that they are predominately racist and that they are composed of members who do not fundamentally agree with equality of citizens and the principle of one-person, one-vote. However, as a prosecutor for the State of Montana, my only public concern is that laws not be broken and that when the laws are broken, those criminals responsible are apprehended and dealt with fairly by our criminal legal system. I am concerned that militias will spawn lawbreakers who will be immune from prosecution due to actual violent resistance by the lawbreakers' militia associates or due to the threat of violence readily projected by M.O.M. and the North America Militia. I believe my fear has been realized already in the person of John Trochman. Mr. Trochman and an associate recently committed what I consider to have been misdemeanor assaults on Shaun McLaughlin and his cameraman, both TV news reporters from Oklahoma City, while the two reporters were on a public road. I believe that no charges resulted from that event. When Mr. Trochman was in the Musselshell County Jail he claimed to have a concealed weapon permit. However, the permit had no expiration date when state law requires a four-year expiration on such permits, 'none' fills the space where the person is to identify a social security number, and the permit was not recorded as required with the Montana Department of Justice. However, the State Attorney General's office declined prosecution. At M.O.M. meetings and in public statements, Mr. Trochman has made it clear that he and the Militia of Montana are protecting Gordon Sellner from arrest. Gordon Sellner is charged with shooting a deputy sheriff. The use of force, deception, or intimidation to purposely prevent or obstruct anyone from performing an act that might aid in the apprehension of Mr. Sellner is a crime in Montana. Similarly, Calvin Greenup was able to avoid arrest for crimes he committed in Rivalli County, Montana, for quite some time because of his violent threats and leadership position with the North America Militia.

WATCHING THE MILITIAS

This section is divided into two parts. In the first part the principal concerns of those organizations that monitor the Far Right in America are addressed. We begin with an extract from *Beyond The Bombing: The Militia Menace Grows*, the Anti-Defamation League's second report into the militia movement. Following this, the militias' 'deep roots' in the racist and anti-Semitic paramilitary Right of the 1980s are outlined in an article reproduced from the June 1995 issue of Klanwatch's *Intelligence Report*. Concerns over the conspiracy theories expressed by some militias and the tendency of such thinking to lead to anti-Semitism and racism are then described in two extracts from the ADL's 1996 report, *Vigilante Justice: Militias and 'Common Law Courts' Wage War Against the Federal Government*. The dangers of 'underground terrorist cells' operating on the principle of 'leaderless resistance' are highlighted next in a report from the Southern Poverty Law Center's *False Patriots: The Threat of Antigovernment Extremists*. This is also the source for the critical assessment of the militias' interpretation of the Second Amendment which follows. The first part of the section ends with an excerpt from the Militia Watchdog's 'Calendar of Conspiracy', an on-line documentation of criminal acts committed by members of the Patriot movement. In the second part of the section, monitoring agencies' recommendations for dealing with the problems posed by the militias, not only for Federal and State governments, but also for the local communities in which they appear, are discussed. They include proposals for legislation intended to restrict the militias' paramilitary training and the activities of Common Law Courts.

PART ONE
THE WATCHDOGS' CONCERNS

From the Anti-Defamation League, *Beyond the Bombing: The Militia Menace Grows* **(1995).**

BEYOND THE BOMBING

Continued monitoring by ADL in the months after publication of the October 1994 report [*Armed and Dangerous: Militias Take Aim at the Federal Government*] reveals that the militia movement has grown – with some of the growth taking place after the Oklahoma City bombing. In this new survey, conducted through ADL's regional offices and completed six weeks after the bombing, militias have been found to be operating in at least forty states, with membership reaching some 15,000. A continued flow of information indicates that these numbers could rise still higher. While these findings are not a definitive indication of the militias' future prospects, they do point to the need for ongoing close attention to this movement.

In California, more than thirty militias are presently operating, apparently having benefited from the large amount of publicity the movement has received in recent weeks. Other states in which militia activity has increased are Michigan, Georgia, Alabama, New Hampshire, Missouri and Arizona. In a few states – Ohio, Indiana and Colorado, for example – activity has declined since the bombing. For some groups, such as the Northwest Oregon Regional Militia, a factor in their decline has been the belief that the government, having engineered the blast, is now poised to take extreme measures to destroy the militia movement.

Since the militias are mainly located in rural and small town communities, the burden of monitoring them falls largely on state and local law enforcement agencies. In the course of the current ADL survey, it became evident that many of these agencies – in large measure for lack of adequate investigative resources – have not yet managed to rise to this task. That job will be made even more difficult if, as some militia strategists are counseling, the groups adopt a strategy of organizing into small units designed to be less susceptible to detection, monitoring and infiltration by law enforcement. This approach echoes a strategic concept known as 'leaderless resistance' that has been promoted in recent years by several far-right figures, including Tom Metzger of Fallbrook, California, who leads the White Aryan Resistance, and Louis Beam, a former Texas KKK Grand Dragon who has been 'Ambassador-At-Large' of the Idaho-based Aryan Nations.[1]

Weapons and Conspiracy Fantasies

The most ominous aspect of the militias' program is the conviction, openly expressed by many of them, that an impending armed conflict with the federal government necessitates paramilitary training and the stockpiling of weapons in preparation for that day of reckoning. According to the militias' conspiracy view, the federal authorities are enacting gun control legislation in order to make it impossible for the people to resist the imposition of a tyrannical regime or a 'one-world' dictatorship. Many militia supporters believe that the conspiracy involves not only federal authorities, but also the United Nations, foreign troops and other sinister forces.

Sometimes mentioned among these sinister forces are Jews. ADL's first report on militias noted that a number of militia figures have histories of bigotry. The current survey confirms that some militia propaganda continues to exhibit an anti-Semitic strain that could well become more pervasive among militia groups as a result of the movement's obsessive conspiracy-mongering.

In this connection, the role of America's leading anti-Semitic organization, Liberty Lobby, and its weekly publication, *The Spotlight*, merit attention. In April 1995, ADL revealed that one of the Oklahoma City bombing suspects, Timothy McVeigh, advertised for sale in *The Spotlight* a military-style rocket launcher. On May 28, *The New York Times* reported that Terry Nichols, the other bombing suspect, and his brother James were readers of *The Spotlight*. Many of the conspiracy fantasies fueling the militias were promoted heavily in a September 1994 eight-page supplement of *The Spotlight*. The supplement, widely distributed among militiamen, intoned: 'Is America on the verge of war? Is a "national emergency" about to be declared and America placed under martial law? Is America on the brink of occupation by military troops under United Nations control?' In addition, the Militia of Montana has been promoting for sale in its catalog a comprehensive bomb-making manual entitled *The Road Back*, which was produced by Liberty Lobby's publishing arm, Noontide Press. The catalog describes the book as 'a plan for the restoration of freedom when our country has been taken over by its enemies.'[2]

Spreading their Message

The militia movement's continued growth is due – at least partly – to an effective communications network. Militia organizers have promoted their ideology not only at militia meetings, but also at gun shows, 'patriot' rallies and gatherings of various groups with anti-government 'grievances.' Some militia firebrands reach their audience through mail-order videotapes and through computer bulletin boards and the Internet. Exploiting yet another medium, the pro-militia American Patriot Fax Network disseminates material from well-known hate group figures and conspiracy theorists, including some who proclaim that the government orchestrated the Oklahoma City bombing.

Of course, the fact that the men charged with the Oklahoma City bombing have had some association with one militia group does not make the entire movement responsible for the crime. But even if no further connection is established between the bombing and the militias, it should be clear by now that these extremists, particularly those engaged in paramilitary training, present a serious danger. The formula they have concocted – belief in menacing conspiracies, hatred of the government, and the conviction that an armed showdown is coming – is a prescription for disaster.

For these reasons, the Anti-Defamation League urges the vigorous enforcement by the states of existing statutes outlawing specific types of paramilitary training. Many of these measures, currently on the books of 24 states, were patterned after a model bill formulated by ADL (see ADL's recent Law Report, *The ADL Anti-Paramilitary Training Statute: A Response To Domestic Terrorism*). The League has written to the governors of the remaining 26 states, urging them to work with their legislatures to adopt such a statute. In addition, ADL has called for federal legislation to address the terrorist threat associated with both international and domestic extremism. We are encouraged at the rapid progress that appears to be taking place on a bipartisan basis toward the adoption of a comprehensive anti-terrorism bill.[3]

MILITIA ACTIVITY IN THE UNITED STATES

Number of 🔫 indicates level of activity in 40 states with known Militia groups

© Anti-Defamation League June 1995

Notes

1. See on this 'Underground Terror' from the Southern Poverty Law Center's 1995 report *False Patriots*, reproduced in this volume at pages 251–254. See also the extract from the Militia of Montana's *Information and Networking Manual* at pages 351–354.

2. For further details of the ADL's concerns about the conspiratorialism and anti-Semitism of the militia movement see the extracts from their 1996 report, *Vigilante Justice*, reproduced in this volume at pages 242–245 and 246–250.

3. To date no anti-Paramilitary Training legislation has been passed at the federal level.

From the Klanwatch *Intelligence Report*, 'Contemporary Militia Movement more than 30 Years in the Making' (June, 1995/ #78).

CONTEMPORARY MILITIA MOVEMENT MORE THAN 30 YEARS IN THE MAKING

White Supremacist Paramilitaries Flourishing by the Early 1980s

Today's militias have deep roots in right-wing extremist movements that formed in the United States 30 years ago.

Radical racist and anti-Semitic groups have flirted with paramilitary training for decades in anticipation of a Communist takeover or a race war.

It began in the early 1960s when Californian William Potter Gale founded a racist paramilitary organization called the California Rangers. The state's attorney general called the group 'a threat to the peace and security of our state' and recommended outlawing such organizations.

The organization soon disbanded and Gale went on to stronger stuff. He was an early leader in the American version of the racist, anti-Semitic Christian Identity 'faith' and was chief architect of the militant tax protest movement called Posse Comitatus. At his Identity church in California, Gale mentored the man who is today the country's most prominent Identity patriarch – Aryan Nations founder Richard Butler.

Gale dedicated much of his adult life to teaching paramilitary and survivalist skills to white supremacists.

In 1987 he was convicted of threatening Internal Revenue Service agents, mailing threatening letters and attempting to interfere with the administration of federal tax laws. Gale died in 1988.

The most notorious follower of Gale's Posse Comitatus ideology was North Dakota farmer Gordon Kahl. In 1983, the fiercely racist and anti-Semitic Kahl killed two U.S. marshals and wounded three others when they attempted to arrest him for violating his probation on a tax evasion conviction. Kahl died later that year in a shoot-out with federal agents at his Arkansas hideout. Kahl's death Kahl galvanized militant white supremacists and fueled the contemporary militia movement.

One of the earliest signals of the radical right's new militancy was the growth of paramilitary training in the early 1980s. Neo-Nazis, survivalists, Identity followers, militant tax protesters, and Klansmen trained with assault weapons, grenades, rocket launchers, and explosives throughout the decade. They studied hand-to-hand combat, guerrilla warfare and survival techniques in preparation for what they believed was an impending race war.

• In 1980, Invisible Empire Imperial Wizard Bill Wilkinson operated a paramilitary training camp in Alabama where Klansmen and their children were instructed in weapons use.

• In 1981, more than 1,000 people trained in advanced guerrilla warfare techniques at a paramilitary training camp sponsored by the Christian Patriots Defense League in Illinois. That year, neo-Nazis and Klansmen were convicted of plotting to overthrow the government of Dominica, and the Texas Klan, headed by the flamboyant radical racist Louis Beam – today a major militia strategist – ran a paramilitary camp for white supremacists and led a terrorism campaign against Vietnamese fishermen in Galveston Bay.[1]

• In 1982, a Posse Comitatus 'survival school' offered instruction on the demolition of roadways, dams and bridges.

• In 1983-84, a band of racist terrorists later called The Order committed a string of murders and robberies and attempted to start a race war patterned after the one chronicled in the notorious racist novel, *The Turner Diaries*.[2]

• In 1983, the Covenant, Sword and Arm of the Lord, a paramilitary survivalist group linked to The Order, stockpiled weapons and explosives, and trained in urban warfare, martial arts and wilderness survival in preparation for race war. That year, CSA members firebombed a synagogue, burned a church and attempted to blow up a natural gas pipeline. An FBI raid on the compound in 1985 yielded hundreds of weapons and bombs, and enough cyanide to poison the water supply of an entire city.

• From 1983 to 1986, North Carolina Klan and White Patriot Party leader Glenn Miller and his followers recruited active-duty military personnel and purchased stolen military weapons and explosives to stockpile and use in paramilitary training. Miller, an associate of The Order, had visions of building a white racist army to take over the Southeastern United States.

• In 1986, a violent band of Aryan Nations militants called The Order II attempted to follow in the footsteps of the original Order. The group killed a man, bombed federal buildings and houses in Idaho and circulated counterfeit money. All were captured and pleaded guilty.

• In 1987, longtime neo-Nazi activist Harold Covington outlined revolutionary tactics and gave detailed descriptions of assault techniques in his book, *The March Up Country*. Shortly after the Oklahoma City bombing, Covington, who operates out of Seattle, speculated that someone 'in the movement' was involved.

• In 1988, Identity minister and virulent anti-Semite James Wickstrom – today a prominent militia strategist – was charged with conspiring to pass counterfeit money, buy stolen weapons and set up a paramilitary camp in Pennsylvania. Convicted in 1990 and sentenced to prison, Wickstrom was released in 1993.

• In 1989, Oklahoma Klansman and former weapons dealer Joe Grego gave detailed instructions on weapons and explosives to Klan members and neo-Nazi Skinheads in his newsletter, *The Oklahoma Separatist*.[3]

Aggressive law enforcement and Klanwatch lawsuits effectively halted much of the paramilitary training that began in the early 1980s, but white supremacists continued throughout the decade to advocate arms training and preparation for a race war.

Then came the Weaver incident on Idaho's Ruby Ridge, and militant white supremacists saw their chance.

Capitalizing on the furor over the Weaver affair, they quickly organized a militia strategy meeting at Estes Park, Colo., in 1992. Over 160 men from Aryan Nations, various Klan groups, Posse Comitatus and Identity organizations attended the meeting. Speakers included some of the country's top racist leaders – Louis Beam, Richard Butler and longtime Identity minister Pete Peters.

During the meeting, strategists adopted the revolutionary tactic called 'Leaderless Resistance' as the operating policy for underground militia units. The tactic calls for small, leaderless terrorist cells to carry out violence aimed at provoking a revolt against the federal government.

The invitation-only gathering in Estes Park led to the formation of most of today's hardcore racist militias.

Six months later, Waco became a flashpoint, and the current militia movement was born.

Notes

1. These events are captured in Bruce Springsteen's song 'Galveston Bay' from *The Ghost of Tom Joad* (Columbia, 1995).

2. *The Turner Diaries* is believed to have been the book which Timothy McVeigh used as a blueprint for the Oklahoma City bombing. See on this, for example, Kenneth Stern, *A Force Upon the Plain: The American Militia Movement and the Politics of Hate* (Norman, University of Oklahoma Press, 1997), 53–54.

3. For further details of the paramilitary activities of the Far Right during the 1980s see James Coates, *Armed and Dangerous: The Rise of the Survivalist Right* (New York, Hill and Wang, 1987, 1995).

From the Anti-Defamation League, *Vigilante Justice: Militias and 'Common Law Courts' Wage War Against the Government* (1997).

CONSPIRACY THEORIES: THE BEDROCK OF MILITIA BELIEF

Militia and 'common law court' ideologues insist that gun control legislation – especially the Brady Law and restrictions on assault weapons – are major components of a secret and evil government conspiracy to disarm and control the American people. They are also obsessed with the government's handling of two events – the 1993 Branch Davidian confrontation in Waco, Texas, and the 1992 Randy Weaver siege in Ruby Ridge, Idaho – and interpret both as signs of impending tyranny. The militias' conspiracy-haunted views are regularly voiced in their publications. They see an evil Federal government working in league with the United Nations to strip Americans of their constitutional rights. Their allegations are often absurd, outrageous and even dangerous to the health of American democratic society. These conspiracy-ridden activists are, in the words of the late Columbia University Professor Richard Hofstadter, practitioners of 'The Paranoid Style in American Politics,' the title of his essay on the subject. In it, Hofstadter wrote that the distinguishing characteristic of the 'paranoid style' was:

> A vast and sinister conspiracy, a gigantic and yet subtle machinery of influence set in motion to undermine and destroy a way of life. . . . The distinguishing thing about the paranoid style is not that its exponents see conspiracies or plots here and there in history, but that they regard a 'vast' or 'gigantic' conspiracy as the motive force in historical events . . .

In order to get a clear picture of the 'paranoid style' of activists in the militia and 'common law court' movements, some of their conspiracy fantasies should be examined:

• Conspiracies alleging the illegality of the Federal system of government are particularly attractive to the militias and 'common law court' activists. Russell Dean Landers, one of the

242

Montana Freemen, has insisted that the Freemen were targeted because they told the world about the 'illegal' U.S. Government. Landers has asserted that he has papers proving that the Federal Government was set up illegally by European bankers and other conspirators in 1881. He has said that he will file motions claiming that the FBI had no right to make arrests in the Freemen's compound called Justus Township. Landers and his cohorts have refused to cooperate with any part of the Federal legal system including judges, prosecutors or public defenders.

• According to several reports, Oklahoma City bombing suspect Timothy McVeigh believed that the U.S. Army had inserted a 'bio-chip' into his hip in order to monitor his activities. Many in the militias similarly believe that the government plans to put a large scale 'big brother' spy system in place to control all of its citizens.

• Militia figure Mark Koernke, also known as 'Mark from Michigan,' told an audience at the 'Great Ohio Preparedness and Self-Reliance Expo of 96' that the Federal Government blew up the Alfred P. Murrah Building in Oklahoma City as part of a plan to cast the militia movement in a bad light. He offered no proof for this allegation but it is still generally regarded as gospel by many militia activists. John Trochmann, co-

founder of the Militia of Montana, told the Florida Panhandle Patriots that a general of the U.S. Army, whom he would not name, informed him that the Oklahoma City bombing was 'an inside job.'

• Militias believe that the United Nations is at the core of a 'New World Order' operation, whose goal is the subjugation of U.S. citizens. John Trochmann asserted that Retired Chief of Staff General Colin Powell would be Bob Dole's Vice Presidential candidate. Powell, Trochmann said, would aid the U.N. in its plot to become the ruling body of the world. In a lecture to the Florida Panhandle Patriots, Trochmann displayed photos of tanks, helicopters and armored troop carriers with 'U.N.' insignia, and implied that they were being secretly stored all over the U.S.

• Weather control by the U.S. Government is another favorite theme. Anti-government conspiracy monger Robert Fletcher (formerly of the Militia of Montana) has said that 'it was no coincidence' that 85 tornadoes 'took place simultaneously' in the Midwest on one day during 1994. One source of the conspiracy theories animating militia members has been *The Spotlight*, publication of Liberty Lobby, the leading anti-Semitic propaganda organization in America today. A September 1994 eight-page supplement of the paper widely distributed among militiamen intoned: 'Is America on the verge of war? Is a "national emergency" about to be declared and America placed under martial law? Is America on the brink of occupation by military troops under United Nations control?' *The Spotlight,* in its August 15, 1994, issue, carried the following story about weather manipulation:

> Extreme Weather Patterns May Not be Acts of God. Is Someone – or a group of someones – fooling around with the weather? Why would anyone do this? The answer is simple . . . to create starvation conditions for selected segments of the world's people on demand, and to eliminate many if not most of the world's food producers, mainly U.S. farmers and rancher. . . . Now, through a controlled program of weather modification on an international scale, the 'internationalists' may have the ultimate weapon .
> . .

• Many militias are opposed to Federal regulation of firearms, tax collection and land use, and believe they are evidence of a 'hidden hand.' Among the agencies regarded with the most suspicion is FEMA, the Federal Emergency Management Agency. The Norwela Common Militia of Louisiana puts out a publication solely about the dangers of FEMA which they see as the 'secret government' of the United States and its 'most powerful entity.' The Norwela Militia warns 'it was not even created under Constitutional law by the Congress. It was a product of a Presidential Executive Order. It is not the U.S. Military nor the Central Intelligence Agency. These organizations are subject to the control of Congress.' The Norwela Militia has also written:

> The scenarios established to trigger FEMA into action are generally found in the society of today: economic collapse, civil unrest, drug problems, terrorist attacks, distrust of the government by a majority of the people . . . with all of these premises existing, it could only be a matter of time until one of these triggers the entire emergency necessary to bring FEMA into action. And then it may be too late, because under the FEMA plan, *there is no contingency by which Constitutional power is restored.*

• The government's 'war on drugs' with its use of Federal law enforcement, electronic monitors and increased police search and seizure options, is considered suspect. Many militias contend that the country's drug problem has been exaggerated by the Federal Government as part of its war against American citizens.

• Black helicopters figure prominently in militia literature as the sinister vanguard of military forces for the New World Order. In 1994, Jim Keith wrote a book entitled: *Black Helicopters Over America: Strike Force for the New World Order*, and dedicated it 'to those who resist the New World Order.' It alleges that black U.N. helicopters are part of the conspiracy to take over the United States. And, his theory continues, they are part of a larger scheme which includes concentration camps and combat units to be used against American citizens.

While each of these conspiracies seems ludicrous, a recent national study on mistrust of government conducted by James Davison Hunter at the University of Virginia, found that one-quarter of Americans believe that the U.S. Government is run by a conspiracy, and 'one in ten strongly subscribes to this view.' More disturbingly, 64 percent of those polled believe that the 'governing elite' is insensitive to the concerns of its citizens. These numbers suggest a suspicious electorate open to the wildest and most deceitful conjecture.

From the Anti-Defamation League, *Vigilante Justice: Militias and 'Common Law Courts' Wage War Against the Government* (1997).

ANTI-SEMITISM AND RACISM

Today's right-wing extremists depend on conspiracy theories to fuel enthusiasm among their supporters. Without the belief that an evil 'New World Order' is upon us, militias would lose their *raison d'être*. The 'common law courts,' too, would be in permanent recess if not for their outrageous belief that our government suspended the Constitution long ago. History has shown that such obsessive conspiracy-mongering often ultimately fingers Jews or other minorities as scapegoats for the nation's ills.

It is hardly surprising, then, that anti-Semites and racists have found a comfortable home in segments of the anti-government extremist movement. Indeed, much of the movement's activity is directed by groups that promote anti-Semitism and racism along with their more visible agitation against the government. Propaganda materials that are passed around at meetings, conventions, gun shows and over the Internet often promote the view that Jews or Jewish institutions are co-conspirators in the New World Order. With disturbing frequency, classic tracts of anti-Semitism are hawked at militia-oriented events or are available from the catalogs of anti-government extremist organizations.

Some bigots in the movement are wise to the public relations problems presented by their beliefs. Rather than present these views openly, they camouflage them, dressing them up as history or religion. Occasionally, standard code words such as 'international bankers,' or 'Zionists' are used to refer to the alleged Jewish role in the conspiracy.

Much of the ideology of today's anti-government extremists traces its roots to the anti-Semitic Posse Comitatus which had its heyday in the 1980s. Like many militias and 'common law courts,' the Posse rejects Federal and state government agencies in favor of what it views as 'legitimate' authority, usually the county sheriff.

The Posse adheres to the beliefs of the Christian Identity 'church,' an anti-Semitic pseudo-religion that preaches that whites of Northern European extraction are the true children of Israel and that Jews are the descendants of Satan. Several former Posse members are active in today's 'common law courts,' including Leonard Ginter, an Arkansas Posse member who spent five years in prison for harboring Federal fugitive Gordon Kahl, a Posse activist. Ginter currently serves as a 'justice' in an Arkansas 'common law court.'

Identity-oriented ideas permeate many 'common law court' documents and propaganda. One 'Common Law Affidavit' originating in Kentucky, for example, refers to 'the White race of People of the Posterity a/k/a Israel (sic).' The Christian Identity name for God – Yahweh – is often used in 'common law court' oaths and frequently appears in their pseudo-legal documents.

As ADL detailed in *The Freemen Network: An Assault on the Rule of Law*, a number of the Montana Freemen hold Christian Identity beliefs. One of their manifestos proclaimed 'It is the colored people, and the jews (sic), who are the descendants of Cain . . . when We move into a new land, We are to kill all of the inhabitants of the other races. . . . We are not to allow women nor foreigners (colored people, jews, and/or citizens of the United States) to rule over us (sic).' The Freemen spread this creed of hatred – along with lessons in 'common law court' – type activity – to hundreds of people who attended their seminars in Montana.

John Trochmann, a leader of the Militia of Montana (M.O.M.), has long tried to play down his ties to Christian Identity as well as his experience with the Aryan Nations, a neo-Nazi group. In his frequent speeches around the country, he insists that he has been wrongly accused of anti-Semitism and racism. Yet his organization persists in promoting the work of some of the country's most rabid anti-Semites.

In the July 1996 issue of *Taking Aim*, M.O.M.'s monthly newsletter, six pages were devoted to a rambling conspiracy tract by Christian Identity propagandist George Eaton. Editors of the newsletter described Eaton as 'a very honorable man a close friend ours (sic) here at M.O.M.' *Taking Aim* continues to market works by other noted anti-Semites including James Wickstrom, a convicted counterfeiter and leader of the anti-Semitic Posse Comitatus, and John Weaver, a Christian Identity 'Pastor.' Returning the favor, Wickstrom promotes and sells M.O.M. videos as well as tapes by Eugene Schroder, a leading 'common law court' promoter.

John Trochmann himself has continued to maintain his close ties to the anti-Semitic Liberty Lobby. He was interviewed by *Spotlight*, the group's propaganda organ, and he attended a 1995 convention celebrating Liberty Lobby's 40th

247

anniversary. In a 1995 interview, David Trochmann of M.O.M told the *Nashville Tennessean* that he agrees with aspects of Christian Identity doctrine and that he believes that the number of Jews killed during the Holocaust has been exaggerated considerably.

The 1996 arrest and conviction of Oklahoman Ray Lampley brought to the surface the most disturbing manifestation of anti-Semitism in the militia movement. Lampley, leader of the now defunct Oklahoma Constitutional Militia, conspired to bomb the Houston office of the Anti-Defamation League as well as other targets. Lampley expressed intensely anti-Semitic and anti-government views and said that it is the duty of militia activists to rescue American citizens from Federal rule.

Anti-Semitic and racist material is routinely distributed at 'Preparedness Expos,' in cities across the country. . . . These gatherings purport to be trade-shows for survivalists and gun enthusiasts but, in fact, they serve as opportunities for anti-government extremists – including racists and anti-Semites – to spread their propaganda among sympathizers and potential recruits. Over the last two years, 'Expo' participants have sold or distributed a wide range of anti-Semitic works including Christian Identity literature.

United Sovereign Citizens, a leading propaganda and organizing group for the 'common law court' movement whose leaders include Identity follower Darrell Frech, peddles the notorious *Protocols of the Elders of Zion*. Earl Jones of New Mexico, who has spoken at numerous Identity-oriented events, told a United Sovereigns audience in February 1996 that Americans are living 'under Talmudic Law.'

The Free American, an extremist magazine popular among militia supporters and 'common law court' activists, has also promoted *The Protocols*, which it described as 'the blueprint used for the New World Order.' In addition, the Identity publication, *The Jubilee*, mixes its anti-Semitism with pro-militia and 'common law court' propaganda for an audience of both racists and anti-government extremists.

Some 'common law court' adherents believe that there are two classes of citizens – 'sovereign' white citizens, whose rights are God-given, and 'Fourteenth Amendment' citizens, nonwhites who are subject to the laws of the illegitimate Federal Government. This racist nonsense is repeated in countless pseudo-legal documents distributed throughout the country. Johnny Liberty (real name – John David Von Hove), author of *Sovereign American's Handbook*, a bible for many 'common law court' activists, affirmed his belief in the theory in a 1996 newspaper interview.

Hardcore anti-Semites in the

'common law court' movement often blend their bigoted views into their pseudo-legal ramblings. For example, an Arizona-based 'common law court' agitator has contrived a bogus legal action against 'Tamuldic Jews from A to Z in State and Federal Govts.' He accuses the Jews of, among other things, persecuting the Arizona Governor because he voted against a hate crime bill.

More frequently, however, the anti-Semitism and racism found in the 'common law court' movement is more subtle. For example, *Why a Bankrupt America?*, a document widely quoted in the movement that was distributed at a recent 'court' meeting in Oregon, camouflages its anti-Semitism as economics. Purporting to discuss the country's economic problems, the booklet pins the blame on the Federal Reserve Bank and promotes the myth that several Jewish banking families (along with the Rockefellers) are its beneficiaries:

> Is this what you work your fingers to the bone for – to pay usury to a private group of bankers who make up the Fed? Some of its stockholders are identified as: Rothschilds of London and Berlin; Lazard Brothers of Paris; Israel Moses Reif of Italy; Kuhn, Loeb and Warburg of Germany; and the Lehman Brothers, Goldman, Sachs, and the Rockefeller families of New York. The shareholders are not you nor I, not America, not the U.S. Government. They are a consortium of private international banking families and their stockholders!

The booklet recommends for further reading the blatantly anti-Semitic *Secrets of the Federal Reserve* by Eustace Mullins.

Paradoxically, some of the material promoted by 'common law courts' has been found in the African-American community as well. At a New York rally held by the Nation of Islam's Louis Farrakhan in October 1996, booksellers promoted 'common law court' materials – including a 'handbook' by Johnny Liberty – along with such classic anti-Semitic works as Martin Luther's *The Jews and Their Lies*, and *The Protocols of the Elders of Zion*.

Bo Gritz leads survival and weapons training sessions popular among militia supporters and is forming a 'Constitutional Covenant Community' in Idaho. In the October 1996 issue of his *Center For Action* Monthly Newsletter, Gritz alludes to the accusation – historically exploited by anti-Semites – that Jews 'demanded the crucifixion of Jesus Christ.' He then suggests that 'Jews are still reaping the bitter harvest of bad blood even today.' Gritz continues to promote his book, *Called to Serve*, in which he asserts that Jewish families control the Federal Reserve system.

Eustace Mullins, a longtime anti-Jewish propagandist, is a frequent speaker on the militia and anti-government circuit. His obsession with the Federal Reserve system – and his belief that it is a private institution owned by eight Jewish families – make him popular with the conspiracy crowd. Mullins' support for militias is intertwined with his anti-Semitism: in a recent essay, he said that militias are 'the only organized threat to the Zionists' absolute control of the U.S.'

The National Association for the Advancement of White People (NAAWP) – a racist and anti-Semitic organization founded by David Duke – is itself attempting to organize militias. A leader of one of these groups, Dan Daniels of Florida, views the goals of the militia in racial terms:

> We are becoming the voice of White Resistance. . . . We invite you to join or start an NAAWP Militia. . . . Take a hand in determining the destiny of your race!

Many, perhaps most, anti-government extremists reject the blatant racism of groups like the NAAWP. Yet the movement itself persists in allowing other – usually more subtle – bigots to use Jews, Blacks and other minorities as scapegoats for the nation's problems, both real and imagined.

From the Southern Poverty Law Center, *False Patriots: The Threat of Anti-Government Extremists* (1996).

UNDERGROUND TERROR

Secret Units Prepare for Guerrilla Warfare

The greatest danger posed by militant Patriots comes from the movement's underground terrorists. Although their locations and identities are usually hidden, the fact of their existence is beyond doubt. Popular materials distributed by Patriot organizations detail the workings of guerrilla cells whose purpose is to launch clandestine attacks on government targets. During 1994 and 1995, these forces went into action with numerous efforts at large-scale sabotage, including the Oklahoma City bombing, the Amtrak train derailment in Arizona, and the theft of large quantities of explosives in California and Georgia.

Terrorist Attacks

• The April 19, 1995 bombing of the federal building in Oklahoma City that left 169 people dead was the worst act of terrorism on U.S. soil. Details from indictments issued by the federal grand jury against suspects Timothy McVeigh, Terry Nichols and Michael Fortier,

volumes of media reports and other sources have led authorities to suspect they were connected with a Patriot terrorist unit.

• The October 9, 1995 derailment of Amtrak's Sunset Limited passenger train left one passenger dead and eighty-three injured. The derailment had all the earmarks of an underground terrorist action. The site of the Arizona derailment was remote and strategically located at a bridge to maximize the potential for injury and damage. The effort required planning, surveillance, knowledge of railway procedure and the cooperation of at least two individuals. Sabotage to rail lines is one of the operations recommended in at least three guerrilla manuals circulated in the militia movement.

• On the night that the Sunset Limited plunged from its tracks, a Fayette County, Ga. company was robbed of a quarter-ton of premixed ANFO (ammonium nitrate/fuel oil) explosives and a significant amount of dynamite and blasting caps. It was the second large theft of explosive ingredients in that area in less than ninety days. Not long after the April bombing in Oklahoma City, 1,500 pounds of ammonium nitrate was stolen from another site in Fayette County. None of the material has been recovered.

• In March 1995, four members of the Minnesota Patriots Council, an extremist Posse Comitatus faction with ties to Identity, were convicted of conspiracy to produce and possess ricin – one of the deadliest known toxins – in order to kill IRS officials and law enforcement officers. The four had learned how to manufacture ricin through a manual marketed to Patriots.

• The Tri-States Militia, comprised of militias from at least 30 states, was linked to at least five would-be terrorists whose bomb plots were thwarted by federal and state law enforcement. Oklahoma militia leaders and Identity 'prophets' Ray Lampley and Larry Crow had been involved with Tri-States since April 1995. The two, along with Lampley's wife Cecilia and J.D. Baird, were arrested in November 1995 on federal explosives charges. The four were allegedly part of a terrorist cell that planned to blow up the Southern Poverty Law Center, offices of the Anti-Defamation League, federal buildings, abortion clinics and sites in the gay community.

Instructions for Sabotage

Patriots' plans for terror follow the prescriptions for guerrilla warfare outlined in numerous Patriot publications.

The Road Back, a book written by William Potter Gale and reissued by Patriot Robert Pummer, outlines the reasons for acts of sabotage:

> Direct confrontation with a militarily superior enemy will result in defeat. Sabotage does not require this tactic. . . . The Resistance forces must convince a large portion of the passive population of their potential for the success of their movement. Unless this can be accomplished, the most effective weapon in the hands of the enemy will be apathy.

Sabotage acts are 'like a snowball going downhill. News of success of neighbor units generates more activity.'

The M.O.D. Manual suggests that urban guerrillas sabotage telephone lines, oil and gas lines, fuel plants, ammo depots, military camps, commissaries, army trucks, military and police cars.

'The military and police repression centers and their specific and specialized organs, must also claim the attention of the urban guerrilla saboteur,' M.O.D. says. It suggests that Patriots 'place homemade mines in the way of the police, use gasoline, or throw Molotov cocktails to set their vehicles on fire. . . . Public offices, centers of government services, government warehouses, are easy targets for sabotage.'

Another readily available Patriot manual, *Citizen Soldier*, describes three phases of guerrilla warfare: The 'organization and buildup phase' during which 'the resistance undertakes a campaign of widespread propaganda'; the 'guerrilla warfare phase . . . characterized by continuous, organized combat operations on the part of the resistance'; and the 'open warfare or general uprising phase,' in which guerrillas 'directly engage the enemy in decisive combat.'

The terrorists' message is getting through to a wider group of Patriots, online discussions indicate. A message on the Internet newsgroup 'misc.activism.militia' in 1995 led one Patriot to observe that weekend warriors who dress in camouflage, do newspaper interviews and call themselves militias are useful only as distractions from the real Patriot movement.

The true activists, said the writer who identified himself only as 'anonymous,' are not interested in publicity, and in fact take great pains to disguise their Patriot activities. Instead, he said, they are 'the smart boys who have hidden in the crowd . . . walking around on the busy street looking harmless – while setting fires, planting bombs, creating sabotage, dispersing poisons, murdering stragglers, disrupting data, monkey-wrenching utilities, assassinating politicians and media 'personalities,' robbing banks, spreading rumors, intimidating government sympathizers and creating random perturbation ops among the populace.'

Leaderless Resistance

The underground strategy used by the Patriot movement was described by revolutionary white supremacist Louis Beam in the 1992 edition of his newsletter *The Seditionist*. Beam proposed that Patriots who were 'serious about their opposition to federal despotism' should stop holding public meetings and start organizing underground 'phantom cells' – small independent units that could instigate actions against the government without having to coordinate plans with a central leadership.

The idea was to 'weed out' the 'groupies' – Patriots who are not willing to take action – and at the same time create an 'intelligence nightmare' for law enforcement authorities, whose attempts to infiltrate the movement would be stymied by the lack of a unified network and a clear hierarchy of leadership.

The guerrilla strategy, called 'leaderless resistance,' was not new, but Beam was the first to promote it openly to white supremacists and antigovernment Patriots.

Since then, several militia manuals have outlined the secret cell strategy in detail. One of them, *Citizen Soldier* by Robert Bradley describes how to set up a guerrilla unit with four layers of activists: the 'full-time soldiers who . . . come out to strike against the occupying power, and disappear;' the auxiliary, 'to provide for and organize civilian support' through recruiting, propaganda, counterintelligence, providing safe houses; the auxiliary's 'home guard,' small armed units who guard weapons caches and train recruits; and the 'underground,' secret auxiliary units. 'Once a Home Guard combat 'cell' reaches ten or twelve members,' Bradley writes, 'it is divided to form a new 'cell.' Old members do not discuss the identities of their former cell members with new members. As the resistance grows, this system will result in the resistance becoming 'compartmented' – which enhances security by restricting the number of resistance members a single person can compromise if he is captured or turns informant.'

'The cell structure is extremely, extremely important,' Militia of Montana leader John Trochmann said in 1996. 'If the enemy forces have no idea what's in store for them if they come to our back yard,

they may think twice.'

The cell system allows Patriots to act quickly. 'Since the entire purpose of Leaderless Resistance is to defeat state tyranny,' Beam wrote, 'all members of phantom cells or individuals will tend to react to objective events in the same way through usual tactics of resistance. Organs of information distribution such as newspapers, leaflets, computers, etc., which are widely available to all, keep each person informed of events, allowing for a planned response that will take many variations. No one need issue an order to anyone. Those idealists truly committed to the cause of freedom will act when they feel the time is ripe, or will take their cue from others who precede them.'

Thanks to such 'cues' as the Oklahoma City bombing, the Amtrak train derailment, and the various bombing and poisoning plots of 1995, underground resisters may have paved the way for a new era of Patriot terror.

From the Southern Poverty Law Center, *False Patriots: The Threat of Anti-Government Extremists* (1996).

JUSTIFYING THE GUNS
Patriots Re-Interpret the Second Amendment

Chapter Three of the Militia of Montana's Field Manual opens this way:

> *Memorize:* 'A well regulated Militia, being necessary to the security of a free state, the right of the people to keep and bear Arms, shall not be infringed.'
> – *Second Amendment to the Constitution of the United States*

Patriots commonly believe that these words guarantee their unlimited right to use combat weapons and form private armies.

But court rulings and legal authorities disagree. In fact, the Second Amendment was written in part to ensure that the federal government would not interfere with the individual states' establishment of militias. (State militias were established in 1792 to provide security for the new nation so that it would not require a large standing army. They proved ineffective and by 1900 were replaced with National Guard units.)

The Second Amendment was never intended to permit private armies. Nor does it guarantee unrestricted gun ownership. But, according to Patriots, owning weapons and forming militias is not just an individual's right but his duty.

The Militia of Montana, based in Noxon and headed by John Trochmann, claimed that in 1994 it sent out about 200 militia information packets a week to people nationwide. Its Field Manual offers followers practical weapons advice as well as theological encouragement in chapters like, 'Choose Your Weapon!' 'Enemy Capabilities and Countermeasures,' and 'Jesus Christ Was Not A Pacifist.' The manual also details the weapons and supplies a Patriot should own and describes how to set up militia cells.

The manual's first 50 pages are devoted to 'Principles Justifying the Arming and Organizing of a Militia.' Summing up those principles, it explains on page 47 that the 'Second Amendment is the teeth of the Bill of Rights, and assault rifles are the teeth of the Second Amendment. . . . At a minimum, you should purchase and learn how to effectively use a firearm, preferably a so-called assault rifle. The more citizens that own guns, the less willing the government will be to threaten us. Ideally, you should also join a local militia, committed to Constitutional principles. You need to be organized, equipped, trained, and coordinated. . . . So arm yourself. Organize yourselves. And prepare to fight if you have to.'

As early as 1886 the United States Supreme Court firmly established that the Constitution does not grant individuals the right to form private armies: 'The right voluntarily to associate together as a military company or organization . . . is not an attribute of national citizenship. Military operation and military drill and parade under arms are subjects especially under the control of the government of every country.' *Presser v. Illinois*, 116 U.S. 252, 267 (1886).

Not only do the Patriots ignore the original intent of the Constitution and the U.S. Supreme Court's rulings, they ignore numerous state laws that forbid private armies.

Patriots also justify private armies by pointing to a federal law, 10 U.S. C. § 311, that states that able-bodied male citizens between the ages of 17 and 45 who are not members of the active Armed Services, National Guard or Naval Militia are members of the 'unorganized militia.' But this membership is of little practical

significance. No court or statute has ever held that membership in the unorganized militia confers any rights or duties on its members. (see *United States v. Oakes*, 564 F 2d 384 (10th Cir. 1977).)

The Second Amendment is also misinterpreted by Patriots to mean that individuals have a right to own firearms. In fact, most Patriots believe that the Constitution and Bill of Rights are divine directives based on Biblical truths. Larry Pratt, executive director of Gun Owners of America, explains, 'What I see in scripture is not that we have a right to keep and bear arms, but that we have a responsibility to do so.'

But the federal courts have always held that the Second Amendment does not provide a constitutional guarantee of individual gun ownership. The Second Amendment's 'right to bear arms' protects only state-sponsored 'well regulated militias' from undue federal interference. See *Lewis v. United States*, 445 U.S. 55 (1980); *United States v. Miller*, 307 U.S. 59 (1939); *Quilici v. Village of Morton Grove*, 695 F.2d 261 (7th Cit. 1982), cert. denied, 464 U.S. 863 (1983).

Although a few scholars maintain that these judicial interpretations are wrong, most legal commentators agree with the courts that the Constitution's 'right to bear arms' applies only to members of official state militias acting in an official capacity and not to unregulated individual citizens.

Still, the Patriots object. The Militia of Montana Field Manual insists that the Second Amendment expressly forbids all types of gun licensing and regulation. The manual recommends that Patriots purchase guns with cash and never give their real names. 'Don't buy guns through dealers since they require you to fill out paperwork.'

Assault rifles, the weapon of choice for Patriots, are especially protected by the Second Amendment, according to the Militia of Montana. 'The more militarily effective a firearm is, the more it is protected by the constitution. . . . Select-fire assault rifles like the M-16 are the most constitutionally protected firearms precisely because they are standard infantry weapons.'

Among the assault weapons recommended are the IN9 .45-caliber, 'the ideal machine gun for the urban guerrilla.' The Militia of Montana also likes the Ruger Mini-14 because, among other advantages, 'It uses the .223 caliber cartridge which packs a high muzzle velocity of over 3000 feet per second and is therefore capable of penetrating most Kevlar body armor.'

It wouldn't take long for a novice Patriot to figure out what the guns are for. Militia of Montana members in 1995 could order a 'M.O.D. Manual' giving them step-by-step instructions on how to wage urban guerrilla warfare against the police and public officials.[1]

Note

1. Examples of the militias' interpretation of the Second Amendment and their attitudes towards gun ownership in general are provided in this volume at pages 377–389 and 391–408.

From the Militia Watchdog, 'Calendar of Conspiracy: A Chronology of Anti-Government Extremist Criminal Activity, April to June 1999' (Vol. 3 No. 2, 1999).

A MILITIA WATCHDOG SPECIAL REPORT: CALENDAR OF CONSPIRACY

May – June 1999

The following is a chronology of some of the events surrounding anti-government criminal activity in the United States during the second quarter of the year 1999. It illustrates both the scope of such activity – from large-scale acts of terrorism to local acts of harassment and intimidation – and its geographic extent – from major cities like Los Angeles and Orlando to remote rural areas in North Dakota and Pennsylvania. The chronology is not comprehensive. Although all major events are included, no systemized reporting system exists for smaller scale events. As a result, arrests or convictions for charges such as placing bogus liens, impersonating public officials, committing tax-related crimes or similar offenses are considerably underrepresented in this report. Such activities occur with a very high level of frequency across the nation. Some examples are included in this chronology to give some indication of the type of activities of this sort that take place. This report also generally does not include hate crimes, although occasionally extraordinary hate crimes are reported, because the line sometimes blurs between hate crimes and other extremist criminal activity. This report includes events from thirty-one states (and one foreign country) but activity occurs in every state in the country.

MAY

May 6, 1999, New York, Vermont: Anti-abortion activist James Kopp, recently from St. Albans, Vermont, but currently a fugitive from justice, is charged second-degree murder in the assassination of abortion doctor Barnett Slepian in October 1998.

May 7, 1999, Ohio: Aryan Nations member Kale Kelly pleads guilty to illegal possession of firearms as a convicted felon, but backs out of a written plea agreement to cooperate with federal authorities investigating a possible bomb or assassination plot. He faces up to ten years in prison.

May 11, 1999, Connecticut: Seven people are arrested (and one more will be arrested on May 12) at the headquarters of a small group calling itself 'the Brotherhood of White Supremacists.' Suspects allegedly robbed two people in their apartment and are charged with various offenses related to the robbery. Strangely, one of the suspects is African-American.

May 13, 1999, Colorado: Following a high-speed chase, police arrest anti-government extremist Jack Modig after authorities spotted him near the Denver-area Colorado Islamic Center. Modig had a numerous weapons and bomb-making materials in the car, leading police to suspect he was planning to destroy the Center. Modig is an active member of the common law court movement in Colorado. He is charged with possession of explosive devices, carrying concealed weapons, eluding a police vehicle and three counts of attempted vehicular assault.

May 15, 1999, Alaska: Palmer, Alaska, police officer James Rowland is killed during a shootout following a traffic stop. The suspect in the killing, Kim Cook, is allegedly an anti-government extremist. He is subsequently charged with first-degree murder.

May 17, 1999, Florida: Francis J. Gilroy is arrested in West Palm Beach following a traffic stop confrontation. Gilroy was pulled over for failing to signal a turn, but refused to provide identification or cooperate with deputies. Police then seized assault rifles and a hoard of ammunition in his van. Gilroy was associated with various groups, including the 'Florida Patriots' and the 'North Carolina Patriots,' as well as various militia groups.

May 20, 1999, Michigan: North American Militia member Kenneth Carter is sentenced to five years in prison for his role in a bombing plot. Carter had pled guilty in 1998 to conspiracy charges. His sentence is considered lenient because he cooperated with the government following his arrest.

May 25, 1999, Michigan: North American Militia leader Brad Metcalf receives a forty year prison sentence, without the possibility of parole, for his role in a plot to blow up government buildings and to threaten to assault and murder federal officers.

May 26, 1999, North Dakota: Avone Kukla, of Dickinson, North Dakota, pleads guilty to one count of tax evasion for failing to pay more than $57,000 in taxes during the 1990s. Instead, Kukla sent the Internal Revenue Service a bogus check from the Montana Freemen for $536,000, along with a demand for a refund of the excess. The plea was part of a bargain with prosecutors.

JUNE

June 3, 1999, Oklahoma: White supremacist Michael Lee Wiggins is arrested for selling a handgun to another felon cooperating with police. Wiggins was buying and selling so many weapons that he had a second gun vault in another house to store all of them.

June 8, 1999, California: Eric Lance Dillard, a member of the white supremacist Nazi Low Riders gang, is sentenced to three years in prison for his role in attacks on black men in the Antelope Valley in 1996. A second defendant had earlier received a fifty-seven month sentence.

June 9, 1999, Ohio, Bangkok (Thailand): Police in Bangkok, Thailand, arrest Robert Alan Smith, a white supremacist wanted for a murder of an African-American in Cleveland, Ohio. Also known as Matthew Stedman, Smith reportedly shot his victim, then burnt him in a metal barrel. He will be extradited to the United States.

June 9, 1999, North Dakota: Lynda Kukla, a tax protester and associate of the Montana Freemen, is sentenced to a year of probation on a tax evasion charge. Her husband (see above) had previously pled guilty.

June 10, 1999, Michigan: Randy Graham is sentenced to 55 years in federal prison for his role in plots to kill government officials and commit terrorist acts. Graham, a member of the western Michigan North American Militia, receives the longest sentence of all four militia members arrested.

June 10, 1999, Alabama: A plumber from Foley, Alabama, is arrested following his purchase of grenades from an undercover ATF agent. Chris Scott Gilliam, charged with possessing an unregistered firearm, told the agent he wanted to send mail bombs to Washington, DC Gilliam is a member of the neo-Nazi group The National Alliance.

June 11, 1999, Missouri: Nine common law court activists in Missouri are convicted of tampering with a judicial official. Jury members recommend four-year sentences for eight defendants, and a seven-year sentence for leader

Dennis Logan (sentencing will not be until August 6). The defendants had previously been convicted in 1997, but an appeals court overturned the decision. In the interim, many defendants had pled guilty.

June 14, 1999, Texas: State officials seize a dry cleaning business owned by Republic of Texas member John E. Parsons for nonpayment of almost $127,000 of back taxes. Parsons claims that the government of Texas is illegitimate and he does not have to pay federal or state taxes.

June 14, 1999, California: Nicholas Victor Fleming, Jr., receives a fifteen-month sentence for having tried to intimidate a U.S. district judge by placing a $10 million bogus lien on the judge's property.

June 18, 1999, California: Three Sacramento-area synagogues are nearly simultaneously set on fire, causing moderate damage. A leaflet left behind blames the 'International Jews media' for the conflict in Kosovo. Police do not know the individuals responsible for the crimes.

June 21, 1999, Pennsylvania: Horace E. Groff pleads guilty to fraud in Lancaster, Pennsylvania, for trying to send bogus Montana Freemen checks to the Internal Revenue Service. Groff sent the IRS a Freeman check for $4.4 million, asking for a $1.8 million refund after his $2.6 million tax bill was paid.

June 24, 1999, South Carolina: Two former Ku Klux Klan members, John England and Clayton Spires, Jr., are sentenced to twenty-five years in prison for state charges related to their shooting of three black teenagers outside a nightclub in 1996. However, the two white supremacists, already serving 25-year federal sentences for the incident, will serve the state sentences concurrently.

June 29, 1999, Illinois: William G. Gustafson, of Palatine, Illinois, is charged with resisting a police officer, disorderly conduct, criminal damage to property and assault following an incident in which he damaged a Hispanic neighbor's fence and threatened to kill her (he has already been charged with a hate crime for the June 14 incident). The self-proclaimed white supremacist swung part of the fence at police officers who arrived at the scene. Officers had to use pepper spray to subdue him. Gustafson, already on probation for aggravated assault, has been under medication and so consequently is ordered to be taken to a hospital to determine if he was sane at the time of the offense and mentally fit to stand trial.

PART TWO
THE WATCHDOGS'
RECOMMENDATIONS

From the Southern Poverty Law Center, *False Patriots: The Threat of Anti-Government Extremists* (1996).

RESPONDING TO ANTI-GOVERNMENT EXTREMISTS

Recommendations of the Militia Task Force

In light of what we now know about the antigovernment movement, these are the recommendations of the Militia Task Force:

1. States should prosecute those who violate anti-militia and anti-paramilitary training statutes. States without such laws should enact them.

Most states have laws that either ban militias completely or at least prevent them from training others to commit violence. These statutes have been used in the past to stop white supremacist paramilitary training, and they can be used today to curb militia activity.

Two types of laws are available. Anti-militia laws, on the books in 24 states, are the most sweeping. These laws ban all private military organizations except those authorized by the state. Anti-paramilitary training laws prohibit private paramilitary training with weapons or explosives when carried out with the knowledge or intent that the training will be used in a civil disorder. Twenty-four states, including seven with anti-militia laws, have anti-paramilitary laws.

'These laws have been proven to work,' said Morris Dees, chief trial counsel for the Southern Poverty Law Center. In Texas, Center attorneys used a state anti-militia statute to close down paramilitary camps operated by the Ku Klux Klan. *Vietnamese Fisherman's Ass'n v. Knights of the Ku Klux Klan*, 543 F. Supp. 198 (S.D. Tex. 1982). In ruling that the camps were illegal, the court defined military organizations in a way that would distinguish them from Scouts and hunters. In North Carolina, the Center used state anti-paramilitary training laws to enjoin the White Patriot Party from operating as a paramilitary organization. *Person v. Miller*, 854 F2d 656 (4th Cir. 1988).

'The problem with these state laws is that they have almost never been enforced,' said Dees. Following the Oklahoma City bombing, Dees sent letters to the attorneys general in the fifty states urging them, to use their state laws to put an end to militia activity. 'States with laws against militias or paramilitary training should vigorously enforce them. States without such laws should enact them,' Dees explained.

Courts have ruled that the government has control over military-type organizations like militias. As the U.S. Supreme Court observed as early as 1886, 'Military organization and military drill and parade under arms are subjects especially under the control of the government of every country. They cannot be claimed as a right independent of law.' *Presser v. Illinois*, 116 U.S. 252, 267 (1886). Indeed, the U.S. Supreme Court has specifically upheld a state law

prohibiting unauthorized militia organizations, finding that it did 'not infringe on the right of the people to keep and bear arms.' *Presser*, 116 U.S. at 264.

Anti-militia and anti-paramilitary training laws give police and prosecutors potent tools to prohibit dangerous militia activity. States can also consider using their public nuisance laws to put militia groups out of business. States also have the clear authority under existing criminal statutes to prosecute those who make specific threats. Taken together, these efforts can shut down militias and reduce the risks of future militia-led violence.

2. A federal statute should be enacted that prohibits private militias not specifically authorized by the states.

State anti-militia laws have the potential to be useful tools in the fight against private militia groups. Still, they are in effect in less than half the states. And the fact remains that those states that have anti-militia laws are not enforcing them.

To back up state law enforcement efforts and to provide the public with another layer of protection, Congress should give federal prosecutors a tool of their own – a federal anti-militia statute.

A federal anti-militia statute would not conflict with the Second Amendment. The Amendment protects only state-sponsored militias from undue federal interference, not private armies that have not been authorized by the state. If a state chooses not to sponsor a militia, the Second Amendment would not bar the federal government from prohibiting unauthorized militias from operating.

3. The current federal anti-paramilitary statute should be broadened.

Although there is no federal anti-militia law currently in effect, there is a federal anti-paramilitary statute. See 18 U.S.C. §231-233. Unfortunately, it is quite limited. Its key provision punishes only those who teach or demonstrate paramilitary techniques to others 'knowing or having reason to know or intending that the same will be unlawfully employed for use in, or in furtherance of, (various types of) civil disorder(s).' 18 U.S.C. § 231(a)(1). It does not punish those who receive paramilitary training when they have the same knowledge or intent. The law should be amended to cover such persons.

4. Federal legislation should be passed regulating the dissemination of dangerous substances used to make weapons of mass destruction, like ammonium nitrate.

Today, anyone can buy a book like *Improvised Weapons of the American Underground* and learn how to make an ammonium nitrate and fuel oil bomb like the one that killed 169 men, women, and children in Oklahoma City on April 19, 1995. What's more, anyone can go to a farm supply store and a gas station and buy most of the ingredients necessary to actually manufacture such a deadly device.

It doesn't have to be this easy for domestic terrorists. While everyone may have a right to read and write what they please under the First Amendment, no one has a right to go to the local hardware store and purchase bomb-making chemicals and equipment.

There are three main ways that dangerous materials can be better controlled. First, dangerous materials can be 'tagged' with chemical agents that make it possible to identify their origin. Second, many dangerous materials – including ammonium nitrate – can be rendered harmless through the use of special additives. Third, restrictions can be imposed on the sale of dangerous substances. For example, regulations could be enacted that would allow only licensed individuals to purchase certain kinds of chemicals or equipment. Restrictions could also be imposed that would limit the quantity of the purchase or that would require a statement about the intended use of the material.

5. The Department of Defense should prohibit military personnel from involvement in unauthorized militia activity.

Military personnel have ready

access to modern weapons and equipment. To help prevent such material from falling into the hands of private militiamen, the Department of Defense should issue a regulation prohibiting members of the armed force from having any involvement in militia activity.

There are signs that military involvement in the Patriot movement may already be a serious problem. In 1992, an underground organization of veteran and active duty Special Forces personnel with Patriot sympathies was formed at Ft. Bragg in North Carolina. Called the Special Forces Underground, this clandestine group combines a racist, anti-democratic agenda with sophisticated tactical skills and military weaponry. Though the precise number of active duty soldiers in the Special Forces Underground is unknown, estimates range between 35 and 100.

The military has prohibited soldiers from associating with certain kinds of groups before. In 1986, Southern Poverty Law Center investigators uncovered a dangerous connection between U. S. Marines from Camp Lejeune in North Carolina and the White Patriot Party (WPP), then the most dangerous Klan group in the country. At secret locations around the state, the Marines were training WPP members in the art of warfare. WPP members also had access to stolen military supplies.

At the Law Center's urging, the Department of Defense instructed military commanders that they could discharge personnel who took part in white supremacist group activities. 'Military Personnel, duty bound to uphold the Constitution, must reject participation in such organizations,' the Defense Department emphasized. 'Active participation, including public demonstrations, recruiting and training members, and organizing or leading such organizations is utterly incompatible with military service.'

The same considerations make military service incompatible with participation in antigovernment militia groups. Members of the armed forces sworn to defend the Constitution simply cannot be allowed to roam the woods in their off hours preparing for war with their government.[1]

6. Law enforcement agencies at all levels should prohibit their personnel from involvement in unauthorized militia activity or groups that promote violence against the government.

The Militia Task Force has received numerous reports of law enforcement officials working closely with Patriot organizations. While active duty personnel typically work clandestinely to protect their careers, ex-law enforcement officers operate in the open.

Gerald 'Jack' McLamb, a former Arizona police officer, uses his law enforcement background to recruit both current and former police officers and military personnel to the Patriot movement. Through his *Aid and Abet Police Newsletter*, McLamb promotes the formation of a national network of law enforcement and military officials sympathetic to the Patriot cause. He also focuses on recruiting county sheriffs and police officers willing to defend their jurisdictions from the encroachment of such federal police agencies as the FBI, the BATF, and the U.S. Marshals Service.

If our law enforcement agencies are to respond effectively to the militia threat, we cannot allow their ranks to include officers who have pledged allegiance to the antigovernment cause.[2]

7. Federal authorities should be allowed to collect data from public sources about people who call for violence against the government.

Because of law enforcement excesses during the Vietnam War and civil rights protest eras, the FBI has been very restrictive in allowing its agents to collect information on antigovernment activity. While we should continue to insist that First Amendment freedoms not be sacrificed in the name of preventing domestic terrorism, some of the restrictions could be eased without infringing on constitutional guarantees. In particular, the federal government should be allowed to collect information on those who call for antigovernment violence – even if the calls for violence are wrapped

in the Patriot rhetoric of 'self-defense' as long as the information is gathered only from publicly available sources.

8. Law enforcement officials nationwide should develop systems for monitoring and sharing information on antigovernment terrorists.

There are thousands of police agencies in the United States. Communications among them are typically poor. While the Patriot world is connected on the Internet, law enforcement officials typically are not. If law enforcement is to respond effectively to the danger presented by the Patriot movement, better communications are essential.

9. Each state should establish a special law enforcement task force to respond to militia activity.

Many local law enforcement officials are unwilling or unprepared to respond to the militia threat. Some are sympathetic to the Patriot cause. Others are fearful of meeting the same fate as the lawmen who tried to arrest Gordon Kahl and Randy Weaver.

Failing to enforce the law in one community risks harm far beyond that community's borders. To back up local police agencies, every state should have a specially trained antimilitia unit.

10. Government employees should be trained in identifying extremist

threats and drilled in emergency procedures.

Government employees – high on the list of Patriot targets – should be informed about the nature of the Patriot threat and its likely forms. Because terrorists often give themselves away, government workers should be trained in what to look for. For example, they should know the telltale signs of letter and package bombs. They should also be trained in responding to bomb threats, evacuation procedures, and first-aid.

11. Journalists should be careful not to present Patriot views of the Constitution without balancing them with prevailing legal interpretations.

It is common for news articles to report Patriot Second Amendment rhetoric without noting that courts have consistently adopted a contrary view.

12. Local clergy should build interfaith allegiances to challenge Identity teachings in their communities.

Religious leaders in our communities should join together to expose the perverted ideology that underlies the Identity movement. They should not simply dismiss Identity adherents as a powerless, fringe element.

13. Schools should promote civic ideals.

Schools have a vital role to play in responding to the Patriot threat. They can help students gain respect for the democratic process by encouraging participation in local affairs. They can help students understand constitutional guarantees. They can teach the values of tolerance and cooperation.

14. Charges of governmental misconduct must be investigated promptly and thoroughly.

The Patriot movement was fueled not simply by events at Ruby Ridge and Waco, but by the failure of the federal government to conduct searching, independent investigations into the tragedies in a timely manner. Although Randy Weaver's wife and son as well as a U.S. Marshal were killed on Ruby Ridge in August 1992, Congress waited three years before holding hearings on what happened. If we are to restore faith in the government, the public must be assured that government misconduct will not go unchecked.

Notes

1. See the extract from the Special Forces Underground's magazine *The Resister* in this volume at pages 413–414.

2. See the extracts from Jack McLamb's *Aid and Abet Newsletter* and *Operation Vampire Killer 2000* in this volume at pages 358–360 and 404–408 and 426–434.

From the Anti-Defamation League, *Vigilante Justice: Militias and 'Common Law Courts' Wage War Against the Government* (1997).

ADL MODEL ANTI-PARAMILITARY TRAINING STATUTE

A. (1) Whoever teaches or demonstrates to any other person the use, application, or making of any firearm, explosive, or incendiary device, or technique capable of causing injury or death to persons, knowing, or having reason to know or intending that same will be unlawfully employed for use in, or in furtherance of, a civil disorder; or

(2) Whoever assembles with one or more persons for the purpose of training with, practicing with, or being instructed in the use of any firearm, explosive or incendiary device, or technique capable of causing injury or death to persons, intending to employ unlawfully the same for use in, or in furtherance of, a civil disorder –

Shall be fined not more than $ __ or imprisoned not more than __ years, or both.

B. Nothing in this section shall make unlawful any act of any law enforcement officer which is performed in the lawful performance of his official duties.

C. As used in this section:

(1) The term 'civil disorder' means any public disturbance involving acts of violence by assemblages of three or more persons, which causes an immediate danger of or results in damage or injury to the property or person of any other individual.

(2) The term 'firearm' means any weapon which is designed to or may readily be converted to expel any projectile by the action of an explosive; or the frame or receiver of any such weapon.

(3) The term 'explosive or incendiary device' means (a) dynamite and all other forms of high explosives, (b) any explosive bomb, grenade, missile, or similar device, and (c) any incendiary bomb or grenade, fire bomb, or similar device, including any device which (i) consists of or includes a breakable container including a flammable liquid or compound, and a wick composed of any material which, when ignited, is capable of igniting such flammable liquid or compound, and (ii) can be carried or thrown by one individual acting alone.

(4) The term 'law enforcement officer' means any officer or employee of the United States, any state, any political subdivision of a state, or the District of Columbia, and such term shall specifically include, but shall not be limited to, members of the National Guard, as defined in section 101(9) of title 10, United States Code, members of the organized militia of any state or territory of the United States, the Commonwealth of Puerto Rico, or the District of Columbia, not included within the definition of National Guard as defined by such section 101(9), and members of the Armed Forces of the United States.

*

ADL MODEL 'COMMON LAW COURTS' STATUTE

A. (1) Any person who deliberately impersonates or falsely acts as a public officer or tribunal, public employee or utility employee, including but not limited to marshals, judges, prosecutors, sheriffs, deputies, court personnel, or any law enforcement authority in connection with or relating to any legal process affecting person(s) and property; or

(2) Any person who simulates legal process including, but not limited to, actions affecting title to real estate or personal property, indictments, subpoenas, warrants, injunctions, liens, orders, judgments, or any legal documents or proceedings; knowing or having reason to know the contents of any such documents or proceedings or the basis for any action to be fraudulent; or

(3) Any person who, while acting falsely under color of law, takes any action against person(s) or property; or

(4) Any person who falsely under color of law attempts in any way to influence, intimidate, or hinder a public official or law enforcement officer in the discharge of his or her official duties by means of, but not limited to, threats of or actual physical abuse, harassment, or through the use of simulated legal process –

Shall be guilty of __ and fined not more than $ __ or imprisoned not more than __ years, or both.

B. (1) Nothing in this section shall make unlawful any act of any law enforcement officer or legal tribunal which is performed under lawful authority; and

(2) Nothing in this section shall prohibit individuals from assembling freely to express opinions or designate group affiliation or association; and

(3) Nothing in this section shall prohibit or in any way limit a person's lawful and legitimate access to the courts or prevent a person from instituting or responding to legitimate and lawful legal process.

C. As used in this section:

(1) The term 'legal process' means a document or order issued by a court or filed or recorded for the purpose of exercising jurisdiction or representing a claim against a person or property, or for the purpose of directing a person to appear before a court or tribunal, or to perform or refrain from performing a specified act. 'Legal process' includes, but is not limited to, a summons, lien, complaint, warrant, injunction, writ, notice, pleading, subpoena, or order.

(2) The term 'person' means an individual, public or private group incorporated or otherwise, legitimate or illegitimate legal tribunal or entity, informal organization, official or unofficial agency or body, or any assemblage of individuals.

From Ken Toole, *What to Do When the Militia Comes to Town* (November 1995).

WHAT TO DO WHEN THE MILITIA COMES TO TOWN

Foreword

The main impact of the militia movement has been its thuggish intimidation of grassroots democracy in small communities across America. In some counties the fear created by the militia is akin to that produced in the South by the Ku Klux Klan in the 1960s. Public officials and private citizens actually have to weigh whether speaking their minds will result in an armed response from the local private armies. That is, of course, the state of political discourse the militias desire – a matter of great concern to the American Jewish Committee and other groups working for the preservation of democracy.

Because this threat continues to grow in the aftermath of the Oklahoma City bombing, the American Jewish Committee commissioned Ken Toole to write this hands-on guide to countering militias on the local level. Ken Toole is director of program for the Montana Human Rights Network, a group dedicated to combating hate and to promoting civil rights. Montana had the first active militia group – the Militia of Montana, which formed in February 1994. The Montana Human Rights Network, under Ken's leadership, helped the state organize against this latest hate group. What Ken and his colleagues put into practice in Montana is reformed into general principles here, and win enable people of goodwill in any part of America to combat armed groups and their hateful political agendas.

Kenneth S. Stern
*Program Specialist on
Anti-Semitism and Extremism
The American Jewish Committee*

What to Do When the Militia Comes to Town

Policy makers at the federal, state, and local levels are struggling to identify statutory tools to address the illegal activities of radical groups that promote violence as a means to change public policy. These efforts are important, but they do not resolve the underlying problem.

Ultimately, the solution does not rest in the law or with law-enforcement agencies. The solution rests with people. Until membership in a militia or similar extremist group is looked upon as something that is, at its root, antidemocratic, unpatriotic, and unpopular, communities will be vulnerable to the activities of these groups. The goal should be to inform the public and to call into question the premises that underlie extremist movements – in the process, initiating meaningful community discussion of pluralism, tolerance, and the values necessary to the conduct of public business in a free society.

This publication is intended to be a tool for individuals working at the local level to confront organizations that promote bigotry and intolerance. While the analytical focus at the beginning is on the militia movement, the community-organizing strategies later presented are useful in building a long-term community effort to counter any organizations that use antidemocratic tactics, including fear and intimidation.

*

Organizing a Community Group

Timing

Many local organizations formed in response to the presence of radical groups in their community have come into being around specific events: a militia group had a meeting or a racist group said they were moving to town or a Jewish family was being harassed. In such instances a local group forms quickly and involvement by a broad spectrum of the community is easily obtained. The problem for groups that form in this environment is that there is almost always a calm after the precipitating event when the group is forced to struggle with identity issues.

On the other hand, some groups have formed out of general concern about the issues rather than in response to a specific incident. These groups will often have a more difficult time in initial recruitment because the need for their existence is not readily apparent to many people. These groups have the luxury of discussing their identity at the outset.

Allies

There are many groups that are naturally inclined to be of great assistance in a community organizing effort to counter extremist-group activity. In beginning a community effort, it is often helpful to approach *individuals* within various constituency groups rather than the groups themselves. When an organization is new and not yet well defined, established community groups are rightfully hesitant to commit themselves to it.

Organizers should recognize that putting together a local group to counter the radical right is often controversial. There are often charges and countercharges and high profile public debate about the activities of extremist groups. After all, part of the task is to expose these groups and they don't like that. This controversy can be difficult for people involved in the organizing effort. More important, this controversy can be difficult for other community organizations and institutions to deal with.

There are two subsets of groups that will be helpful in a community effort to counter extremist groups. Tier A groups are likely to be helpful in establishing a sustained long-term organization dedicated to responding to bigotry and intolerance. In a most general sense, these tend to be groups that associate social justice with structural and political issues in society. Tier B groups will cooperate for specific purposes for fairly limited times. These groups often have a more limited view of social justice, focusing instead on individual advocacy or service to the community.

Tier A Groups

Minority organizations (racial, ethnic, gay/lesbian, etc.). These groups are often the first to recognize the presence of far-right groups in the community. Further, members of these organizations understand the threat posed by radical-right groups and the need to be active in countering their rhetoric.

The Jewish community. For the same reasons as minority groups, Jewish organizations fully understand the need for action in the face of intolerance. In addition, members of the Jewish community are very well informed about far right activity because of national groups like the American Jewish Committee. The Jewish press also devotes substantial coverage to these issues.

Churches. Churches can play a critical role in developing community responses. Often, radical-right organizations claim scriptural justification for the positions they take. Churches are the most effective voice to counter this rhetoric. It is important to understand that in many churches the level of involvement will be dictated by the nature of the congregation. In

273

approaching churches, be flexible and understand the constraints of local church leadership. Take some time to figure out which congregations in a community are most involved in social-justice issues and begin there.

Labor unions. Labor unions are critical to community responses. Right-wing activists often target union members for recruitment, particularly when economic times are tough. Because labor organizations understand this phenomenon, they have education programs in place and mechanisms for delivering their message. More important, most union activists understand right-wing activity and are very experienced at organizing. They are an important asset.

Gay and lesbian advocacy groups. These can be very helpful because people in this community are among the first targets of extremists.

The education community. Teachers, the PTA, the school administration, and, in larger towns, the university community are usually concerned about manifestations of bigotry and intolerance. Thanks in large part to organizations like the National Education Association and the National School Administrators Association, there has already been a great deal of discussion about bigotry and intolerance in the world of education.

Also be aware that there are curriculum or subject-specific associations of teachers within the education community. There is likely to be a state association of social-studies teachers with local members who will be informed about and interested in extremist groups.

Peace groups. In many communities there are groups formed around peace and justice issues. Members of these groups understand the connection between violence and politics that is fundamental to the militia mindset.

Environmentalists. Increasingly, environmental groups and activists have become targets for harassment in communities. As that has occurred environmental activists have become more interested in participating in community groups that counter bigotry.

Good-government groups. Groups such as the League of Women Voters that support democratic principles and processes are good candidates for an antiextremist group, particularly to the extent that the group deals with issues affecting participation in government.

Women's organizations. Women's organizations are often very concerned about right-wing groups because they are often hostile to women's rights.

Tier B Groups

Service clubs. Groups like Kiwanis and Rotary that dedicate themselves to community-improvement projects can be very helpful in providing volunteers and organizing events. In addition, these groups often include community leaders who have a great deal of credibility in the 'mainstream.'

Business groups. Local groups concerned with economic development or business improvement can also be particularly helpful in establishing the credibility of a new organization in the community.

The law-enforcement community. Early contact should be made with the law-enforcement community. Such contacts are critical if confrontations develop or if individuals begin to receive threats. More and more often, law enforcement officials are themselves becoming targets of extremist groups, giving them a clear interest in working with a community group.

Local-government officials. These folks are our elected representatives and they often articulate the 'position' of the community. They should be invited early to participate in the effort. They too are often the targets of extremist groups.

The media. The media should be approached as members of the community and asked to participate. Often local media will decline on the grounds of preserving their objectivity. But sometimes events in the community may cause them to reconsider their position and become involved.

As individuals set about forming a community organization and begin approaching these groups and individuals, it is important not to be restrictive. Very valuable group members may come from groups in Tier B while individuals in Tier A groups may be decidedly uninterested. The key is to be flexible and encourage as much involvement as possible.

*

Developing Campaigns

A campaign is a set of planned activities designed to achieve a specified goal over a defined (usually fairly short) period of time. Community groups will often develop campaigns to address specific issues surrounding militia activity.

Developing a campaign goes like this:

Problem: Militia supporters are aggressive in the community and engaged in some petty criminal activity. Government officials are receiving threats from militia groups. Law enforcement is hesitant to react to militia activity. The local sheriff has said that he agrees with the ideas of militia groups but disagrees with their tactics.

Goal: To create an environment in which law enforcement feels empowered to confront illegal militia activity and which proscribes militia activity.

Themes: Violence and threats are unacceptable; We are a society of law; We are all part of the government and support our elected officials.

Activities: Rally for Democracy in the park to be held on the Fourth of July. Invite dignitaries and local officials to make brief statements: governor, attorney general, mayor, sheriff, etc.

Full-page endorsement ad in the paper with a statement about democracy with as many signatures as possible. Minimum of 500 signatures to run on the Fourth of July.

Letter-to-the-editor campaign during the month of June – letters per week on themes.

'We support our elected officials' signs in local businesses last two weeks of June.

Local petition drive expressing support for local government to be presented at the rally. Goal of 1,500 signatures.

Radio and TV public-service announcements to run last throughout June on themes.

Local radio and TV talk-show appearances by board members/spokespersons last week of June.

Once the group has established a plan with goals and activities, it is important to delegate tasks to assure that the plan is executed. This is often most effectively done by setting up committees to do specific activities. The committee members can do the planning and execute the activity. This is the group's opportunity to expand its base of workers and activists. The campaign plan provides tasks that are well defined and have a discrete beginning and end. For example:

Activity: Rally for Democracy in the park to be held on the Fourth of July. Invite dignitaries and local officials to make brief statements.

Tasks: Reserve park and get permit; send out invitation to guests; arrange for security; get public-address system; decorate the area; print up a program; get volunteers for cleanup.

There should be a mechanism for checking to ensure that things are getting done and that people have the help they need to get things done. This is often done by members of a steering committee or ad hoc committee.

(Planning a campaign is best done by working backward. Take a calendar and mark your target date. Work backward day by day specifying what needs to be done when.)

Warning! Warning! Warning! While this all sounds simple, rest assured that there will be bumps along the way. Plan to be flexible and recognize that some elements of a campaign may have to be dropped because they just aren't getting done.

Other activities. There are a host of activities that a group may want to engage in, in a community. Whether lobbying for some specific item with local government or raising public awareness in a community event, the power of citizens coming together is enhanced by the community's recognition that the group is a credible force and accomplishes what it sets out to do. Most people find the more a group does, the more recognized it is by the community leaders, the easier it is to maintain the organization.

Conclusion

The modern-day militia movement is a chilling echo of groups like the Silver Shirts and the Christian Front that were active in the 1930s. And before the 1930s, following the Civil War, hate groups like the Ku Klux Klan flourished. Then, as now, such groups preyed on people using bizarre conspiracy theories and antigovernment sentiment. Then, as now, violent terrorist acts were planned by these groups as they sought to change the political character of America. We now struggle with these groups just as preceding generations have.

There is a tendency to view extremist activity as a law-enforcement issue. But the law addresses the symptoms and ignores the cure. Law-enforcement agencies confront the illegal acts committed by extremist groups and their members. Throughout history law-enforcement action has sometimes unintentionally increased public support for these groups by creating martyrs. The law does not, and should not, deal with the ideology that drives these groups.

The lesson that emerges from history is that these groups are hindered more by the attitudes of the community than they are by laws. Fear and silence allow hate groups to flourish. People coming together, organizing and speaking out – saying 'Not in my town!' – make the extremists' tasks that much more difficult.

CIVIL LIBERTIES

AND

'WHO WATCHES THE WATCHDOGS?'

For two of the three pieces in this section we return to the November 1995 hearings into the 'Nature and Threat of Violent Anti-Government Groups in America'. Gregory Nojeim, legislative counsel for the American Civil Liberties Union, first describes the ACLU's concerns that 'any potential legislative or law enforcement response to violent anti-Government groups' not infringe upon Americans' First Amendment rights, and expresses its fears that anti-paramilitary legislation of the kind favoured by monitoring agencies such as the Anti-Defamation League and the Southern Poverty Law Center will do just that. David Kopel of the Washington-based Cato Institute voices similar concerns during his testimony, reproduced here. He also complains of the difficulties of obtaining 'hard data' on militia groups, and criticizes some of the monitoring agencies for their response to the appearance of the militias. This latter theme is picked up in the extract from political researcher Laird Wilcox's report, *The Watchdogs: A Close Look at the Anti-Racist 'Watchdog' Groups*, in which he asks the question, 'Who watches the watchdogs?'

From the hearing before the Subcommittee on Crime of the Committee on the Judiciary of the House of Representatives examining the 'Nature and Threat of Violent Anti-Government Groups in America' (November 2, 1995).

GREGORY T. NOJEIM

Legislative Counsel, American Civil Liberties Union

I testify before you today on the behalf of the American Civil Liberties Union, a nationwide, nonpartisan organization of more than 275,000 members devoted to preserving the freedom set forth in the Bill of Rights.

Our primary concern here is that the First Amendment rights of every person in every group, including anti-Government groups, not be sacrificed in the effort to investigate potential criminal activity. Potential responses to anti-Government groups should start with an acknowledgement that the First Amendment protects speech, no matter how provocative, racist, or anti-Government. It even protects advocacy of violence, provided that such advocacy does not cross the line to incitement to imminent lawless action.

Under the standards set forth by the Supreme Court in *Brandenburg v. Ohio*, and ever since, a statute may proscribe advocacy of violence only when such advocacy is directed to inciting or producing imminent lawless action, and is likely to do so.[1] As applied here anti-Government speech advocating violence cannot be proscribed or punished unless it incites, and is likely to produce, lawless action imminently, not some time in the distant future.

In addition, the First Amendment protects the freedom to associate with others. As interpreted by the Supreme Court, a person may not be punished merely on account of membership in an organization, members of which advocate violence or illegal activity, unless the person has at least the specific intent to further the group's violent or unlawful aims.

The leading case in this area, *NAACP v. Claiborne Hardware*, involved a boycott of white-owned stores by the NAACP.[2] Though most of the boycott activities were peaceful, some NAACP members committed acts of violence in furtherance of the boycott. The Supreme Court held that the right to associate does not lose all constitutional protection merely because some members of the group may have participated in conduct or advocated doctrine that itself is not protected. The Court also held that an organization

280

cannot be held criminally responsible for a call to violence issued by a limited subset of the organization. These principles should guide any potential legislative or law enforcement response to violent anti-Government groups.

One bill introduced in the House, H.R. 1544, would subject to a ten-year prison term any person who knowingly participates in a paramilitary organization. In our view, this proposed legislation would unconstitutionally chill and outlaw the expression of political speech and association by proscribing mere participation in a paramilitary organization, rather than the incitement or endorsement of imminent, lawless activity, or participation in such activity, as required by the Supreme Court in *Brandenburg* and *Claiborne Hardware*. Under this bill, it would be a crime to participate in a voter registration drive conducted by an anti-Government, paramilitary organization.

Another bill, H.R. 1899, would amend the Federal civil disorder statute to proscribe training in the use or making of firearms or explosives, while having reason to know or intending that they will be unlawfully used in a civil disorder or a civil rights violation. It would move the point of criminal responsibility back from commission of a violent act to mere training coupled with bad intent.

Under the bill, a person who trained – and training is not defined – to use a Molotov cocktail or a gun in an anti-Government demonstration, but ultimately decided not to when he understood the tremendous risk of personal injury he would create, would still be criminally responsible. Alternatively, if after prayerful reflection, an anti-abortion protester who had trained to commit an act of violence against an abortion clinic decided not to do so, he, too, would be criminally responsible for a civil disorder under this bill.

Finally, we hasten to add that training to engage in many of the techniques used by members of the NAACP to enforce the boycott in *Claiborne Hardware* would have been a crime under this bill, even if they did not result in violence. The legislation comes too close to punishing bad thoughts, instead of bad acts. And the bad acts are already Federal crimes under existing law.

Legislation creating crimes triggers new law enforcement investigatory authority to punish or prevent that criminal activity. Any potential legislative response to violent anti-Government groups ought to be considered not just for the conduct it would proscribe, but in view of the Federal investigatory authority it would trigger.

It has been said that the power to tax is the power to destroy. Likewise, the power to conduct intrusive investigation of protected activities is the power to stifle those activities, including the advocacy of anti-Government views.

The Attorney General guidelines governing such investigations need to be tightened. Instead, the FBI has decided to loosen the guidelines by issuing a reinterpretation that could result in investigation of more protected First Amendment activities. Until that reinterpretation is public, and its impact measured, no new legislation, including the legislation discussed above, and the pending terrorism bill making more activity related to First Amendment protected activity a crime, should be considered.

Though Federal law enforcement authority has expanded dramatically in the past few years, the expansion has not been coupled with increased law enforcement accountability. Nearly two years ago, the ACLU, joined by the National Rifle Association and others, asked President Clinton to appoint a national commission to monitor Federal police policies and practices. Nearly two weeks ago, these same groups and others issued a call on Congress for adoption of a 24-point reform program distilled from what we called the lessons of Waco and Ruby Ridge. The program included common-sense reforms about executing search warrants, use of informants and consultants, penalties for law enforcement misconduct, and rejection of the pending terrorism bill and efforts to weaken the exclusionary rule.

For many anti-Government groups, Waco and Ruby Ridge offer evidence of law enforcement overreaching. Rather than enacting constitutionally-suspect legislation, or legislation that has unintended results, we urge the subcommittee to conduct hearings to look into Federal law enforcement accountability generally, with an eye toward adopting the legislative reforms we proposed.[3]

Notes

1. 395 U.S. 444 (1969).
2. 458 U.S. 886 (1982).
3. The ACLU, in conjunction with other concerned groups such as the American Jewish Committee and the National Association for the Advancement of Colored People, successfully campaigned to remove many of the original proposals in Clinton's Counterterrorism Bill of 1995, including those which would have expanded the government's wiretapping powers. However, the resulting Antiterrorism and Effective Death Penalty of 1996 was still seen by the ACLU as an 'attack' on Americans' civil liberties. For further details see the ACLU website at 'www.aclu.org'.

From the hearing before the Subcommittee on Crime of the Committee on the Judiciary of the House of Representatives examining the 'Nature and Threat of Violent Anti-Government Groups in America' (November 2, 1995).

DAVID B. KOPEL
Associate Policy Analyst Cato Institute

From my own family background, people who threaten violence against government employees are particularly frightening. For most of my childhood, my father's twenty-two-year career on the Colorado House of Representatives was in progress. When he chaired the Colorado House Judiciary Committee, he steered to house passage the only major gun control, a ban on so-called Saturday Night Specials, that has passed any house of the Colorado Legislature in the last twenty-five-years.

My mother served, during the 1970s and the 1980s, as the Colorado and Kansas director of the Federal Government's US Bankruptcy Trustee Program.

Before I went to work for a think tank, I served as an Assistant attorney general for the Colorado Attorney General's Office handling enforcement of environmental laws. And, a while before that, I worked for one of the law firms, Holme, Roberts & Owen, which is named in the frivolous indictment and warrant for citizens' arrest shown to you earlier by Sheriff Sullivan [of Littleton, Colorado].

The cowardly criminals who killed so many innocent people in Oklahoma City could just as well have killed my mother, my father, or myself. Just as much as any other citizen of the United States, Government employees are absolutely entitled to live their lives free of criminal violence and criminal intimidation.

Today, there are many tens of millions of people who are frightened of the Government, and many thousands, or perhaps more, who participate in militias. Some of them may have incorrect beliefs about the Brady Bill or the ban on so-called assault weapons, or the United Nations or other political issues.

Within these groups, as within almost any other group, there are a few criminals. . . . Just as citizens should not imagine that because a few Members of Congress are found guilty of felonies, most Members are criminals, Members of Congress should not imagine that because a few persons with anti-Government viewpoints are criminals, many or most militia members, or other Government critics are criminals. Let us not be panicked into hasty action that history will judge harshly.

One of the reasons that so many people have become fearful of the Federal Government, and some have become angry, has been the virtually uninterrupted expansion of Federal laws at the expense of civil liberty. The cycle of misleading media sensationalism, a couple of congressional hearings, and another broad and intrusive Federal remedy has become all too familiar.

It is possible to assemble before any given congressional panel a half dozen very sincere witnesses who will claim that any given topic is, one, an immense problem; two, rapidly spiraling out of control all over the Nation; and, three, desperately in need of an immediate sweeping Federal remedy. Sometimes these witnesses are incorrect.

We have no reliable hard data about how often Government employees are being threatened or attacked. Still less do we have any hard data about how often existing State and Federal laws are inadequate to punish the criminals involved. Instead, we have, quite frankly, a lot of misinformation or misunderstanding.

For example, the written testimony of the Southern Poverty Law Center, a group for which I was a monthly donor from 1984 through 1995, giving to them 12 times a year, as well as the testimony from the Anti-Defamation League, includes the claim that Sam Sherwood of the United States Militia Association told his followers to look Government in the face because 'they may have to blow it off some day.'

In fact, that quote is a direct distortion of what Mr. Sherwood said. According to *Reason* Magazine, in an article written by a journalist who was actually there when Mr. Sherwood said the words, Mr. Sherwood 'made an impassioned plea for using political action, rather than violence in correcting the wrongs that the members of the United States Militia Association see in Government. He suggested that if his listeners wanted to grab the gun and shoot their legislator, they should first go look them in the face and recognize that legislators are also American citizens who are fathers, mothers, husbands, and wives. The audience not only understood that he was arguing against violence, they applauded his remarks.'[1]

We shouldn't assume that States are necessarily helpless or unwilling to act against criminals who harm Government employees. Certainly there's no State in which these criminals have working control of the State legislature and prevent the States from taking any action. Indeed, there are many problems which are absolutely inappropriate for a Federal remedy. Abuse of State courts and filing frivolous writs in State courts is properly a matter for reform by the States.

Sheriff Sullivan and I have already talked about, when we both get back home to Colorado, reforming our State's uniform consumer credit code and uniform commercial code so as to require notice before liens are filed on property.

The spirit of the Tenth Amendment suggests that before the Federal legislature acts, it considers what the State legislators and the people of the States decide to do. Whatever's going on in Montana, wouldn't it be more sensible to look for a remedy to the dozens of legislators who were in the State Senate and State House of Representatives in Montana, rather than devising some national solution with 535 people in Washington, DC, only three of whom are from Montana?

In regard to anti-Government violence, proposals for broad new conspiracy statutes or for broad new judicial authority to destroy or just ban organizations have not been shown to be necessary, particularly at the Federal level. We know from history that injunction and conspiracy laws have often been used unfairly against political dissidents, including labor organizers.

Some of the new proposed mandatory minimums for 'violent, anti-Government extremists' would impose a two-year mandatory minimum on someone who shoved a policeman during an argument over a traffic ticket, a two-year mandatory minimum on a jilted teenage girl who sent her rival an anonymous letter, 'I'm going to tear your eyes out,' and an eight-year mandatory minimum on an homeowner who waved a baseball bat at a zoning inspector. . . .

According to Section 7 of the Republican Form of Government Guarantee Act, when county governments enforce State and local laws against what they believe to be illegal conduct by Federal employees, the Federal Government will become the judge of its own case. Rather than having the dispute settled by a neutral arbiter, the courts, the dispute will be investigated by the Federal employee's own chief lawyer, the Attorney General, who may then unilaterally withhold payments in lieu of taxes from the county.

Equating all militias with white supremacists is nonsense. Like the Los Angeles Police Department, some militias may have members, or even officers, who are racists, but that does not mean that the organizations as a whole or the vast majority of their members are racists. It is a sad testament to the bigotry of certain segments of the media that totally unsubstantiated, vicious conspiracy theories, of the type that were once employed against Catholics and Jews, are now being trotted out against militia members, patriots, and gun rights organizations.

Militias and patriot groups have been understandably ridiculed for a paranoid world view centered on the United Nations and international banking. But, ironically, many of the people doing the ridiculing share an

285

equally paranoid world view. Some members of the media and the gun control movement have no more idea what a real militia member is like than militia members have about what a real international banker is like. In both cases, stereotyping substitutes for understanding and familiar devils – the United Nations for the militia, the National Rifle Association for the media – are claimed to be responsible for all sorts of ridiculous crimes.

The Southern Poverty Law Center has begun promoting a Federal ban on group firearms training which is not authorized by State law. But State governments are perfectly capable of banning or authorizing whatever they want.

The proposal for Federal ban amounts to asking Washington for legislation which the majority of States have already rejected. The right to keep and bear arms necessarily includes the right to practice with them, just as the constitutional right to read a newspaper editorial about political events necessarily includes the right to learn how to read, even if one learns how to read in a group, and that group happens to promote incorrect political beliefs.

Government is the great teacher, Justice Brandeis told us. Without the unjustifiable, illegal, militaristic, deadly Federal violence at Ruby Ridge and at Waco, there would be no militia movement. The Federal Government should set a better example. If Ruby Ridge had led to a real investigation and corrective measures right away instead of leading to years of coverup by both the Bush and Clinton administrations, then we wouldn't be in the current situation. Ruby Ridge and the Waco tragedies were not the fault of a few bad officials, but the inevitable result of a culture of lawlessness, militarization, and violence that has permeated far too much of the Federal law enforcement establishment.

When corrective measures are undertaken, as a coalition ranging from the American Civil Liberties Union to the Citizens Committee for the Right to Keep and Bear Arms has suggested, then we will begin to see a massive reduction in the tension between millions of American people and their Government.[2]

Notes

1. See Mack Tanner, 'Extreme Prejudice: How the Media Misrepresent the Militia Movement,' *Reason* (July 1995), 42–50.

2. Details of the ACLU's campaign in this regard can be found at their website at 'www.aclu.org'. The Cato Institute's website can be found at 'www.cato.org'.

From Laird Wilcox, *The Watchdogs: A Close Look at Anti-Racist 'Watchdog' Groups* (1998).

THE WATCHDOGS: A CLOSE LOOK AT ANTI-RACIST 'WATCHDOG' GROUPS

In the 35 years that I've been studying extremist groups of the far left and far right, including acquiring material for my collection at the University of Kansas Library,[1] it's become obvious to me that the various 'Watchdog' organizations that monitor these groups often develop a strange symbiotic relationship with them. Watchdog organizations tend to define themselves in terms of their opposition to the various individuals and organizations they call 'extremist,' and depend upon this opposition to justify their existence and their fundraising activities. . . .

In addition to obsessive preoccupation with their enemies, watchdog organizations tend to adopt the position that the end justifies the means . . . [T]he most troubling aspect of this opportunism is their infiltration of law enforcement. The watchdog organizations feed law enforcement agencies information in order to set them on their enemies, real and imagined. By alleging 'dangerousness' on the basis of mere assumed values, opinions and beliefs, they put entirely innocent citizens at risk from law enforcement error and misconduct.

For example, following the Oklahoma City bombing in 1995 the Southern Poverty Law Center gave the FBI a list of several thousand alleged members of militias and 'hate groups' culled from its files. None of them had anything to do with the bombing. These names came from letters to newspapers expressing right-wing political views, lists of 'members' supplied by informants, names from license plate numbers collected outside public meetings, pilfered mailing lists, and so on. The possibility of a mere curiosity seeker or an individual with no criminal intent whatsoever being suggested to the FBI as 'dangerous' seems highly likely. . . .

Watchdog groups can have a profound influence on law enforcement tactics in a number of ways. Both the Anti-Defamation League and Southern Poverty Law Center publish newsletters and other material directed at law enforcement, often giving these agencies names from their files accompanied by suggestions of dangerousness. Both groups, particularly the

ADL, hold law enforcement conferences, seminars and training sessions in dealing with their enemies and critics. . . .

The Anti-Defamation League and the Southern Poverty Law Center practices of acquiring undue influence to advance their agendas with law enforcement agencies and the use of civil law to accomplish de facto criminal prosecutions without the benefit of appropriate constitutional guarantees, is simply wrong, and would be wrong no matter who did it. The rules of evidence and procedural practices in criminal cases are far more protective of civil liberties that those civil cases. In civil prosecutions, for example, a defendant is not entitled to legal counsel unless he can pay for it, whereas in criminal prosecutions legal counsel is guaranteed, regardless of ability to pay. It has not gone unnoticed that most of the defendants in civil cases brought by the Southern Poverty Law Center are either indigent or of very modest means.

While they may give lip service to freedom of expression and other constitutional guarantees, Watchdog groups often operate just on the edge of those protections, often advocating formal censorship or government reprisals against their ideological opponents simply because of their values, opinions and beliefs. Their uniform policy is to avoid debate and make every effort to keep their opponents' views out of the marketplace of ideas. This is not the behavior of someone wanting to promote civil liberties and bona fide human rights.

*

Problems for Journalists and Academics

Watchdog organizations represent a special problem for journalists and academics. Often they are the only source for quotable information about the groups they monitor. Where does one go for information on the paramilitary militia groups or so-called 'hate groups'? Sociologists Betty A. Dobratz and Stephanie L. Shanks-Meile observe that watchdog groups engage in claims making in which they draw attention to certain causes in order to promote their agendas:

> We relied on the SPLC and ADL reports for general information, but we have noted differences between the way events were sometimes portrayed in Klanwatch Intelligence Reports as more militant and dangerous with higher turnouts than we observed. Also, 'watchdog' groups promote 'claims' that are compatible with their political agenda and neglect other ones as they attempt to wield political influence among policymakers.[2]

With respect to the huge media feeding frenzy following the Oklahoma City bombing, writer Adam Parfrey comments:

> The ADL and SPLC boast that they are the media's primary sources on information regarding militias and patriot groups. Their information is usually absorbed whole into establishment news sources as unimpeachable and objective news sources. In truth, the coffers of the ADL and SPLC bulge when constituents are led to believe they're fighting an enemy of enormous evil and mounting strength. Despite their altruistic claims, the ADL and SPLC profit directly off the sensationalism that acts as a sparkplug for Hollywood and the weekly tabloids.[3]

*

Watchdogs and Oklahoma City

[O]ne of the most extensive FBI investigations ever undertaken has failed to implicate any militia group (or *any* group of any kind). The FBI agent in charge of the Oklahoma City Bombing Task Force recently said:

> The investigation, as thorough as it was, was not able to identify other individuals involved other than those who admitted their knowledge or were convicted through two trials.[4]

During the early days of the media feeding frenzy following the bombing militia organizations were widely suspected and even charged with complicity in the crime. Watchdog groups were regularly quoted by the media as 'experts' on the militias and made fantastic claims of vast membership and influence.

Militias had nothing to do with the bombing, but the incredible onslaught changed their composition considerably. Some militias folded and many of their less committed members quit. This had the effect of 'radicalizing' the movement, increasing their paranoia, and before long – in a typical self-fulfiling prophecy – the militias began to mimic the journalism that described them. This stereotype of the violence-prone radical probably attracted individuals of that disposition. Many militia members who have gotten into trouble with the law joined after the bombing. Combine that with harassment by police agencies from the FBI to the local sheriff, negative media publicity, pressures on family and friends, and you have a prescription for disaster. You create the very monsters you claim are out there.

There are hard-core extremists in the movement, but by no means in large numbers, including some of the Jewhaters and racists the ADL and SPLC have attempted to portray as commonplace. In any event the evidence is in now and as far as Oklahoma City was concerned, the militias got a bum rap at the hands of these Watchdogs. A week after the bombing the op-ed section of *Newsday* contained my contribution in which I made the following points:

> Not since the Red Scare of the 1920s has a political minority been under as much hostile scrutiny as the right-wing militia movement is today. The Oklahoma City bombing – the worst incident of domestic terrorism in American history – quickly focused on a man with ephemeral links to a militia group in Michigan. This link, however, consists largely of the fact that he was denied membership in the group, not that he was an active member acting under its direction. The bombing, in fact, appears to be the action of a psychopathic ex-soldier and a few confederates acting on their own.
>
> It's difficult to imagine what the average militia member felt as events unfolded last week, but it must have been excruciatingly uncomfortable for them. Sure, militia members spout conspiratorial rhetoric and uniform hostility toward a federal government they feel is getting out of hand. But I think it's safe to say virtually none of them condoned the bombing and all were horrified to find their movement linked to it. . . . Already they are being called 'baby killers' and treated like pariahs in some communities.
>
> Right now, we're at a dangerous crossroads. The media linkage of the Oklahoma bombing with right-wing politics has the makings of a witch hunt on a scale we haven't seen since Joe McCarthy. Even our president has tried to link conservative talk-show hosts to the bombing. This means that anyone with an American flag on the lawn may soon be suspect, and this kind of paranoia is not something to inflict on the already afflicted.
>
> I hope we take some time to think this through before we start making mistakes, but so far I'm not encouraged.[5]

One does not need to be a right-winger or a militia sympathizer to identify the issues involved in the demonization of the militias. Ritual defamation as a technique is much the same no matter who the victim. In *Faces of the Enemy: Reflections of a Hostile Imagination*, Sam Keen notes:

> In all propaganda, the face of the enemy is designed to provide a focus for our hatred. He is the other. The outsider. The alien. He is not human. If we can only kill him, we will be rid of all within and without ourselves that is evil.

> Paranoia creates a self-fulfiling prophecy, a vicious circle in which suspicion breeds suspicion, threat brings counterthreat. Passive aggressive victims bring on themselves the aggression they obsessively fear.
>
> Paranoids begin with imagined enemies and end up with real ones as the cycle of reaction turns into a complex historical conflict. In *paranoia á deux* hostility becomes synergistic, enemies become hypnotized by each other and become locked in a prison of mirrors.
>
> We scapegoat and create absolute enemies, not because we are intrinsically cruel, but because focusing our anger on an outside target . . . brings our tribe or nation together and allows us to be part of a close and loving in-group.[6]

Nothing, it seems, energizes the mind and perfumes one's ego as much as having some bad people to hate. Watchdog groups are congregations of individuals who collectively hate people with opposing values, attitudes, beliefs and interests. Absent actual physical combat, name-calling is the next best thing. . . .

[W]hen two men were charged in the 19 April 1995 bombing of the Federal Building in Oklahoma City – a ghastly crime that killed 168 people – the SPLC was ready with it's disinformation and fundraising apparatus in place.

The SPLC began a massive mailing fourteen days after the Oklahoma City bombing. This was followed up two weeks later by letters stating, 'We need your help now with the most generous special gift you can make to help us expand our Militia Task Force.' Another SPLC mailing dated 27 April and which appeared to have been prepared before the bombing also asks for funds for their Militia Task Force. 'You know, that's interesting. That was timely wasn't it. I mean, we didn't know the bomb was going to go off,' Dees is quoted as saying.[7]

The SPLC's Klanwatch *Intelligence Report* of June 1995 claimed that 'over 200 militia and support groups operate nationwide.'[8] Three months later, in September 1995 the SPLC issued a report that identified seventy-three 'militias or militia support groups nationwide, with a total of 30,000 to 40,000 members.' The SPLC also claimed that about forty-five have 'ties to the Ku Klux Klan.'[9] One hundred and twenty seven 'militia and support groups' suddenly disappeared. Moreover, even Dees' more modest figures were way off base. Many of the 'support groups' were just groups – some with only a few members – who shared some views with the militias (such as opposition to the income tax or gun control), but conducted no paramilitary activities themselves.

As for 'ties to the Ku Klux Klan,' there were a few cases where this was true, but it constitutes only a small percentage of militia membership. Often these 'ties' were nothing more substantial than the claim that Klansmen had attended militia meetings or that Klan literature was found there.

As for the impressive '30,000 to 40,000' figure, an actual count is impossible, but there is good reason to believe that actual, bona fide membership in the militias may have been no more than 20 per cent of that at the time of the Oklahoma City bombing. (The Anti-Defamation League claimed only 10,000 militia members). Moreover, SPLC claims of a massive increase in membership after the bombing are unsupported except by absurd claims of publicity seekers in the militias themselves, who in some cases claimed wholly unsupportable figures of a million members.

In part the controversy surrounding alleged membership figures rests on what constitutes a 'militia,' a 'militia support group,' and on what constitutes a 'member.' The SPLC uses these terms as broadly as possible. It routinely includes every possible listing, including groups that are alleged to exist but not verified. As 'support groups' the SPLC includes every listing that has interests even vaguely similar to militias. For 'members' they use unverified rumored figures estimated from meeting attendance (which include a large number of curiosity seekers, not to mention journalists, police and informants), and reports on mailing lists, which are always larger than bonfire membership lists. Of course, the financial fortunes of the SPLC depend entirely on claims of a large and growing 'threat' of one kind or another.

Militia 'Support Groups'

The concept of a militia 'support group' is particularly troubling. Using this kind of logic, one might suppose that the NAACP was a 'support' group for the Communist Party, USA, merely because they had some interests in common. This argument has been used against the American Civil Liberties Union, which has defended leftists of all varieties as well as a few right-wingers. Moreover, in the highly individualistic and idiosyncratic far right even similar points of view do not necessarily not spell cooperation or 'support.' Far right groups are constantly feuding with one another and real cooperation on any issue is always problematic. To imply that the 'right' is a monolithic and coordinated entity with 'support groups' is simply not true.

As for militia complicity in the bombing itself – after more than three years of intensive investigation neither the FBI nor any other law enforcement agency has produced evidence that the perpetrators were members of or in any substantial way connected with any militia, anywhere, anytime. No militias were implicated by government prosecutors at Timothy

McVeigh's or Terry Nichols' trials. Militias had nothing to do with the Oklahoma City bombing. The perpetrators were acting entirely on their own.

*

These considerations. . . are what motivated me to ask the question of 'who watches the watchdogs?'. . . I do not mean to imply their concerns are without merit, that they do not focus on groups and individuals that probably bear watching, or that they do not do valuable work in fostering improved interracial and intergroup relations. I have no quarrel with much of what they claim to stand for. A good example is the SPLC's position on capital punishment and prison reform, which I support wholeheartedly.

What I object to in the 'watchdog' organizations are their tactics, their often hidden agenda, and their contempt for the rights of those who disagree with them. My hope is that they will reconsider their behaviors and 'humanize' the watchdog milieu. Also, as a writer I believe other writers and journalists need to be aware of the questionable validity of Watchdog groups as primary sources. Watchdog groups are agenda-driven special-interest groups, whose interests are economic as well as ideological, and not 'experts' in the sense of objective and disinterested scholarship.

I would encourage readers to contact the Watchdog groups for their response to my criticism. Their response may confirm some of what I have written about them.

Laird Wilcox's Notes

1. Wilcox Collection of Contemporary Political Movements, Spencer Research Library, University of Kansas, Lawrence, KS, 66045.

2. Betty A. Dobratz and Stephanie L. Shanks-Meile, *White Power, White Pride!: The White Separatist Movement in the United States* (New York, Twayne Publishers, 1997), 2–3.

3. Adam Parfey, *Cult Rapture: Revelations of the Apocalyptic Mind* (Portland, OR, Feral House, 1995), 327.

4. Diana Baldwin, 'Some Still Hunt For John Doe 2,' *Sunday Oklahoman* (December 13, 1998), A8.

5. Laird Wilcox, 'Don't Fear Militias, Fear Their Fringes,' *Newsday* (April 27, 1995).

6. Sam Keen, *Faces of the Enemy: Reflections of a Hostile Imagination* (New York, Harper, 1986), 18, 23–24, 27.

7. Dan Morse, 'Marketing The Militias,' *Montgomery Advertiser* (26 June, 1995).

8. Southern Poverty Law Center, 'Over 200 Militias and Support Groups Nationwide,' Klanwatch *Intelligence Report* (June 1995).

9. Dick Foster, '10 Militias at Home in Colorado,' *Rocky Mountain News* (September 6, 1995).

CURRENT ISSUES AND
CONTINUING TENSIONS

T he final section of this part of the book begins with Michael Winerip's
account of the 1996 trial of Ohio militiaman Larry Martz for *The New
York Times*. Although the trial failed to attract much international or
national attention, Winerip sees it as 'typical of the daily cat-and-mouse
confrontations that go on between members of the Patriot Movement and
government officials'. It is followed by an interview with Timothy
McVeigh's lawyer, Stephen Jones, conducted by Peter Hancock for the
Kansas *Pitch Weekly*. Jones contends that there was an extensive conspiracy
behind the Oklahoma City bombing and that the federal government has had
to 'reinvent history' in order to sustain the 'official position' that no
conspiracy existed beyond McVeigh and Terry Nichols. The Southern
Poverty Law Center's fear that the imminence of the year 2000 is fuelling a
renewed growth in the Far Right is expressed in an article taken from the fall
1998 issue of their *Intelligence Report*. It is accompanied by an interview
with the head of the FBI's Domestic Terrorism and Counter-Terrorism
Planning Unit, Robert Blitzer, in which he assesses the state of the anti-
government movement in America at the century's end.

Michael Winerip, 'Ohio Case Typifies the Tensions Between Militia Groups and Law'. First published in *The New York Times* (June 23, 1996).

OHIO CASE TYPIFIES THE TENSIONS BETWEEN MILITIA GROUPS AND LAW

CANTON, Ohio. – It is a question that comes up all the time nowadays in small-town America: 'Is the local militiaman as dangerous as he sounds?'

Or is so much of the defiant, anti-government rhetoric that comes from these members of the Patriot movement just talk?

The case of 53-year-old Larry Martz, a paramilitary enthusiast from a well-respected family in Stark county, Ohio, who was voted most likely to succeed in the Lake High School class of 1959, is as complex to judge as the Patriot movement itself.

Martz was convicted recently of assaulting a state trooper during a routine traffic stop and transporting concealed weapons. He was returning from a weekend paramilitary gathering on the night of Jan. 29 when he was pulled over on Interstate 77 near Cambridge, Ohio, for a turn-signal violation so minor that the state trooper did not intend to issue a ticket.

The two briefly scuffled, but the jury, rejecting part of the assault charge, concluded that the 5-foot 8-inch, 140-pound Martz had caused no physical injury to the 6-foot 2-inch, 200-pound trooper.

Martz, who had no previous criminal record, was also convicted of possessing four loaded, concealed weapons in the cab of his pickup. Yet if had stored them properly in the rear of his truck – as he had with six other guns that night – transporting the weapons would have been legal. Indeed, the Republicans who control the Ohio Legislature were about to pass a law permitting the carrying of concealed weapons this year when their fellow Republican, Gov. George V. Voinovich, derailed them.

At his trial in late May, Martz often spoke boldly, then acted meekly. He repeatedly told the judge that the court had no jurisdiction over him, that like the militiamen at Bunker Hill, 'I am a man of action.' But as he represented himself at the five-day trial, he looked nervous and his hands shook. And when the judge asked why he was late the first morning, Martz's response was barely audible. 'I lost my breakfast on the way over,' he said.

The trial of Martz did not attract national attention. Still, it is more typical of the daily cat-and-mouse confrontations that go on between members of the Patriot movement and government officials than the dramatic standoff recently resolved between the Freemen and the FBI in Jordan, Mont.

The movement is a collection of grassroots groups operating in every state with people who call themselves Patriots, Militiamen, Freemen, Common-Law Advocates and Strict Constitutionalists. Sometimes the groups are loosely affiliated; in other cases they are not connected at all.

'Most are law-abiding people who are fed up with government,' said Sgt. Michael Dailey of the Columbus, Ohio, Police Department, an expert on the paramilitary groups. 'Of course, there always is a concern with these people. Unfortunately, a number live on the edge.'

While they tend to be labeled 'right-wing,' their backgrounds touch all points on the spectrum. That is the case with Martz, who has run for office as a Republican, campaigned for Ross Perot and been a member of environmental groups usually identified as liberal.

The movement is so fragmented that membership estimates are unreliable. The Southern Poverty Law Center says that there are 441 paramilitary groups and that they can be found in all 50 states. Dailey says there are '35 to 40 militias' in Ohio, with more than 1,000 active members.

Dailey estimates that among Ohio's 11 million residents, the Patriot movement has 'several hundred thousand sympathizers,' a lot of them 'average people discontented with the two major parties.' There are plenty of those here in Stark County, a place that mirrors national politics. Perot collected 24 percent of the presidential vote here in 1992, and won the backing of 20 percent of county residents in a recent poll.

In 1992 Martz campaigned for Perot, and several of Martz's supporters who watched the trial said they, too, had voted for Perot. In Stark County, Perot's United We Stand chapter is heavily populated by members of the Patriot movement.

Court Performance
Shows Several Sides

At the start of the trial in Common Pleas Court, Martz, who chose to defend himself, stood defiantly in the court's spectator section. He said he would not cross into the main part of the courtroom because the judge had no jurisdiction over him. He argued that the courtroom's U.S. flag had fringes and that a fringed flag was a military flag, meaning he would be subjecting himself to a military tribunal and losing his full constitutional rights.

After 45 minutes of such

argument, Judge David Ellwood ordered the bailiffs to seat Martz and warned that if there was resistance he could be bound and gagged. The courtroom tensed. But then Martz allowed himself be led to the defense table. Soon he was thanking Ellwood at every motion and calling him 'sir' so often, that the judge told him it was not necessary to be so reverential.

Martz would not drink the bottled water in the courtroom, saying he could have an allergic reaction. Instead, he carried a gallon jug with him everywhere. He nodded off at times, and his sympathizers worried that he was not eating. At one lunch recess he stood alone in the parking lot by his pickup, spooning cold oatmeal from a saucepan.

Yet he often performed capably. He succeeded in having the judge remove a juror for bias, correctly pointed out that his indictment was improperly worded, raised many objections that were sustained by the judge and produced witnesses to support his self-defense claim.

Those who know Martz describe him as a bright, eccentric, solitary soul. Twenty-five years ago he was near the top of a 500-person Civil Service list for firefighting jobs in Everett, Wash. He was a good firefighter, said the chief, Terry Ollis, though he stayed only a year and acted strangely at times. 'If someone at the firehouse lit a cigarette, Larry would put on an oxygen mask – he wasn't joking,' Ollis recalls. 'He wouldn't sleep with the rest of the men. He slept in the basement.'

Dangerous Incident, Same Stories

There was not much disagreement about what happened in the confrontation between Martz and the trooper, William Fulton, only about the motivations of each man. Fulton testified that he had first noticed Martz's pickup parked in a rest area with a turn signal blinking, which struck him as a bit unusual, and he later noticed Martz had re-entered the highway without signaling.

Martz contended that the real reason the trooper stopped him was because of a sticker that read, 'Abolish the Unlawful Federal Reserve Bank.'

Fulton said that after talking to Martz he walked back to his patrol car to write a warning, then realized that Martz's driver's license had expired. When the trooper approached a second time, he said, he saw part of a gun in the pickup's cab and asked Martz to step outside. As they headed toward the squad car, Fulton moved to hook his flashlight back on his hip beside his holstered gun.

Martz said he feared that Fulton was going for his gun and that he was about to be murdered.

'It's not as strange as it sounds,' Martz told the jury. Seven months earlier, in June of 1995, Martz had been a witness in a nearby southeastern Ohio town when a Patriot leader, Michael Hill, was shot and killed by a police officer after having been stopped for driving without a license plate.

In that case, Martz told a grand jury that the paramilitary leader had been unarmed. The police officer said he fired because the man had pointed a gun at him. The grand jury did not indict the officer.

Martz said that when Fulton stopped him it was like reliving the earlier shooting. In self defense, he said, he grabbed Fulton from behind in a bear hug, putting his hand over the trooper's gun to prevent him from using it.

Fulton testified that he believed Martz was trying to get the gun to shoot him. 'The thought going through my head was, 'I have to retain this weapon at all costs,' said the trooper.

Fulton said he got Martz to relax by assuring him that this was only about a turn signal and that he did not plan an arrest. It was a lie of convenience, the trooper testified, 'so I could get him to let go.'

The trooper said that when Martz let go, he drew his gun and called for backup. While they waited, the trooper testified, Martz said: 'I don't have anything personally against you; this world's a messed up place. I'm part of the militia. I could have killed you at any point.'

Throughout the struggle Martz had his own loaded handgun in his waistband. He told the jury that if he had been trying to kill Fulton, he could have used his own gun.

Long Search for his Place

Members of the Martz family, who did not want to be interviewed, are well respected in Hartville, a rural Stark County village of 2,031 people. One of Larry Martz's brothers runs the G.L. Martz Mold and Dye factory in Hartville, his mother owns a well-maintained 48-unit apartment complex there, and his father was on the Hartville Planning Council.

Larry Martz played football, ran track and graduated from Lake High when he was 16. He attended Humboldt State University of California, studying forestry, then quit to join the Army, hoping to qualify for Special Forces. Instead he served three years as a medical laboratory technician.

He never did get a degree, attending a few colleges, including Kent State, where he was a Young Republican in the late 1960s.

After working for two fire departments near Seattle, he said during a break in the trial, 'I tried selling different things like real estate, but I was never successful.'

'I was here and there,' he said, traveling widely and living in Costa Rica. He said he returned to California in the late 1970s, working as a tree surgeon and becoming a paying member of the Natural Resources Defense Council and

299

Greenpeace, two environmental groups.

In the mid-1980s, he said, he joined a study group of California 'Patriots' who explored the many ways they believed government officials regularly violated the Constitution.

He said he was a volunteer Congressional district coordinator for Perot in Southern California in 1992. Asked how Perot had done in his district, Martz said, 'We don't know, with the rigging of the computers.' Initially, he said, 'I felt Perot was extraordinary until I learned more about him.'

In 1994 Martz joined an effort to recall a California State Senator, David Roberti, who had supported a ban on assault weapons. The recall failed. Of the five candidates hoping to take Roberti's place, Martz, running as a Republican, received the fewest votes, 1,289 out of 33,078 cast for the losers. 'They rigged the computer count,' he said, 'I had a friend who worked at the polls. She said I seemed to have the most votes where she was.'

In early 1995 he returned to Ohio, living in his mother's apartment complex. He sought out fellow members of the Patriot movement, attended their constitutional study group in Canton and, he said, 'advanced to the rank of major in the militia.'

'These people are precious,' he said. 'They put in their own time and money. A lot of us are going broke. I had savings; about the time I was arrested, it was exhausted.'

Acquaintances say that in the months before the arrest Martz played and replayed a video produced by a paramilitary group that highlighted the mistakes of federal agents at the Branch Davidian compound in Waco, Tex., when more than 80 members of the sect died in a fire.[1]

Seeking Links to Glory of Past

In his closing argument, Martz talked of the sacrifices of the militiamen at Valley Forge in the Revolutionary War. 'The militia' today, he said, 'should be in a position of respect, not the derision we've received.'

He called the 'militia very similar in character and motivation to volunteer firefighters.'

'We have a PR problem, and maybe God put me in this situation for that,' he said.

'How many of you have not made mistakes?' he asked. 'I've never harmed anyone intentionally. I apologize to Trooper Fulton if I misjudged that incident.'

He said that in his 53 years his worst offense came in the Army: 'I wore my medical whites on guard duty and was not allowed to go on pass for a week.'

C. Keith Plummer, the prosecutor, reminded the jurors of what was found in the pickup. There were two assault rifles, a shotgun and a .45-caliber handgun, all loaded, and

1,337 rounds of ammunition in the cab, plus six more guns and 3,800 rounds in the truck bed.

Fulton 'found a time bomb ready to go off,' said the prosecutor. 'Fortunately, he got to it before it did.'

'Did Mr. Martz think Trooper Fulton was after him that day? Right. Mr. Martz thinks everyone's after him. He's out here to protect us. From what? From whom? I submit that we need to be protected from him.'

Plummer's final thought: 'Are we to enforce these laws, or are we to give Larry Keith Martz back his guns and send him up the Interstate?'

In his charge to the jurors, Ellwood reminded them that Martz could claim self-defense if he believed his life was in danger – even if that was not the case.

Quick Verdict, Faster Sentence

Awaiting the verdict, Martz said, 'I hope the jury will think, 'What is this guy doing in a situation like this?' I want them to think, 'How would you vote if George Washington was standing up there instead of me?' Now I don't mean to sound arrogant.'

He felt confident, but worried that there were 10 women on the jury and that they might be too willing to follow a male prosecutor. 'Women aren't as good about standing up to authority,' he said, adding that he did not understand women very well. 'I

never really had a relationship long term with a woman. There are a few women in the militia, but not many. It's hard work, it's a lot of hours, you have to make sacrifices.'

After deliberating three and a half hours, the jury returned at 9.45 pm, finding Martz guilty of both felonies. The judge had said several times that would not let the militia intimidate the judiciary,' and he exercised his option to sentence Martz immediately, giving him two years in prison.

Martz looked stunned. When he tried to speak, his voice cracked. He handed his pickup keys to one of his supporters, then was led away in handcuffs.

The half-dozen paramilitary men who gathered by the pickup in the parking lot afterward spoke angrily about what had happened and what needed to be done. Taking the pickup home for Martz, they drove north along I–77, and though the speed limit was 65 miles an hour and cars kept whizzing by, they did 55 mph, to be safe.

Note

1. Probably Linda Thompson's *Waco: The Big Lie* or *Waco II: The Big Lie Continues*.

Peter Hancock, 'McVeigh's Lawyer Insists Others Unknown Were Involved In OKC Bombing.' First published in the Kansas *Pitch Weekly* (December 24-30, 1998).

MCVEIGH'S LAWYER INSISTS OTHERS UNKNOWN WERE INVOLVED IN OKC BOMBING

Only two people were charged with carrying out the deadliest act of domestic terrorism in U.S. history, the April 19, 1995, bombing of the Alfred P. Murrah Federal Building in Oklahoma City: Timothy McVeigh, who was convicted and sentenced to death for the murder of four federal agents who died in the blast, and Terry Lynn Nichols, a former Army buddy of McVeigh's who was convicted of second-degree murder and sentenced to life in prison for his role in the conspiracy to build the bomb and carry out the attack.

But as McVeigh's lawyer, Stephen Jones, asserts in his recently published book, *Others Unknown* (Public Affairs, $25), it is a virtual certainty that many more people were involved in the plot, people who have never been identified by the government or brought to justice.

'The government coopted the mainstream media almost immediately and held a sort of solid line on what the official story was,' Jones said in an interview during a recent visit to Kansas City. Then they were able to prevent some depositions in some civil cases, then they got the judge (Richard Matsch) to order that discovery material – witnesses' statements, etc. – would have to be filed under seal. They couldn't be filed under public record. There were hours upon hours of secret proceedings in the judge's conference room where these matters were thrashed out, and then they were able to prevent the introduction of significant evidence that undermined the government's case.'

All that, combined with actions the government continued to take after the trial was over – including, according to Jones, pressuring lawmakers into not allowing him to testify before a subcommittee of the Senate Judiciary Committee that was investigating domestic terrorism – prompted Jones to write a book detailing what he claims was a larger conspiracy to blow up the federal building and the government's own effort to cover it up.

But if readers pick up the book thinking they will hear from McVeigh himself about who those other people involved were, they will be disappointed. Jones does not divulge any confidential information that was spoken to him by McVeigh, whose conviction and death sentence are still under appeal. Nor does he make any attempt to proclaim McVeigh's innocence.

What the book does describe, however, are indicators of a larger conspiracy uncovered by the defense team's own investigation, and the lengths to which the government went in keeping evidence of that conspiracy from being admitted into court or reported to the American public.

The existence of 'others unknown' who were involved in the plot would be important, from a legal standpoint, because under federal rules of criminal procedure, a court may consider that as a mitigating factor in deciding whether to impose the death penalty.

The idea of a larger conspiracy comes as no surprise to local law enforcement officials in northeast Kansas where Terry Nichols lived and where the truck bomb was allegedly built. For two years prior to the bombing, police and sheriff's departments in Topeka and surrounding counties had been keeping a close eye on a local outfit of the anti-government 'Freemen' organization.

In the weeks and months after the bombing, there were rampant reports around Pottawatomie and Shawnee counties that at least one, possibly two, yellow Ryder rental trucks had been seen driving to and from the small farm of Ronald A.A. Griesacker, the leader of the local Freemen group who would later become involved in other high-profile incidents involving anti-government groups.

Griesacker, who is currently awaiting sentencing in Wichita on unrelated federal charges for bank fraud and weapons violations, was also known to be associated with another local resident who, according to area investigators, bore an uncanny resemblance to the description and sketch of John Doe No. 2, the mysterious figure who was reportedly with McVeigh when he rented the Ryder truck, but whom the government now claims either never existed or was a case of mistaken identity.

Officials in Shawnee County have told reporters that they showed FBI agents a photo of the man they suspected of being John Doe No. 2, but were told that the man had already been investigated and had been cleared. Later, when local investigators discovered that the man's work records indicated that he was not at work at any of the times John Doe No. 2 was spotted elsewhere, they were told that no one from the FBI had ever made a similar inquiry.

But according to Jones, who maintains a computer index of more than 30,000 names that surfaced during the investigation, neither Griesacker's name nor that of the possible John Doe No. 2 ever appeared in any of the documents the FBI provided to the defense team.

As the trial of Timothy McVeigh approached in 1997, the government changed its story about John Doe No. 2 and stated, at least to the public, that there probably was no such person. The man described as being with McVeigh when he rented the truck was in fact Pvt. Todd Bunting, a U.S. Amy soldier who, the government said, just happened to be at Elliot's Body Shop in Junction City around the same time as McVeigh. The person behind the counter who identified the men, the government said, simply got confused.

But Jones insists that Todd Bunting doesn't look anything like John Doe No. 2. Furthermore, he says, Bunting and McVeigh were there on different days.

'And perhaps most deadly to that ridiculous argument,' Jones said, 'is the fact that Vicki Beemer, who actually handled that transaction, is a good friend of the

man Todd Bunting was with, Robert Hurtig. Clearly, Vicki Beemer would be expected to remember that Bunting was there on Tuesday with her friend and not on Monday but, they (prosecutors) had to take care of the John Doe 2 argument some way.'

According to Jones, government prosecutors had to do away with the idea of a conspiracy the moment they cut a deal with their two key witnesses, Michael and Lori Fortier, the couple from Kingman, AZ, who testified that McVeigh had talked to them about his plans to build the bomb.

'How much more central to the conspiracy can you be, than to be Lori Fortier and manufacture a fake ID for Robert Kling (the alias McVeigh used to rent the truck on April 15, 1995)?' Jones asked rhetorically.

The problem was that the government had no case against Lori Fortier, except her own statement. There wasn't even enough evidence to indict her. Michael Fortier, however, had made some 'careless statements' to investigators, Jones said, but while there may have been enough evidence to indict him, they could never have gotten a conviction.

Still, Jones said, the president and the attorney general had promised the American people to seek the death penalty against all the conspirators.

So, Jones contends, the

government had to 'reinvent history.' There was no conspiracy beyond McVeigh and Nichols. There was no John Doe No. 2. There was no involvement by any Michigan-based militia unit with which McVeigh was known to be associated. There was only Nichols and McVeigh.

It was a prosecution theory that Jones says is impossible to believe. For one thing, he said, it would be physically impossible for McVeigh to build the truck bomb single-handedly, as the government claimed, without passing out and dying from the noxious fumes emanating from the tons of ammonia nitrate fertilizer and fuel oil that was used to make the bomb.

For another thing, Jones insisted there were too many other people closely associated with Nichols and McVeigh who were known to be involved in planning the bombing.

Besides the Fortiers, Jones said, one of the other conspirators was Terry Nichols' brother James, who still lived on the Nichols family farm outside Decker, MI. James Nichols had actually been indicted by a separate grand jury in Michigan in 1995 as a co-conspirator with Terry Nichols and McVeigh in the building and detonation of homemade bombs. That indictment dated the conspiracy from 1988 through April 21, 1995.

Furthermore, when McVeigh was arrested by Oklahoma Highway Patrol troopers about an hour after the bombing, he gave his address as the Nichols family farm in Michigan.

Then there was John Doe No. 2, bringing the total number of conspirators to at least six, Jones said. And there was a possible seventh person who was seen accompanying Nichols in October 1994 to buy ammonium nitrate fertilizer from a co-op in McPherson, KS.

Finally, Jones said, there was the person who may or may not have been with McVeigh when the bomb was actually set off. One survivor of the blast reported seeing McVeigh pull up to the front of the federal building in the Ryder rental truck, accompanied by a second man, who may or may not have fit the description of John Doe No. 2.

According to medical records, a human leg was pulled from the rubble of the blast that could not be matched to any of the known victims.

In his book, Jones also makes the assertion – although the evidence is far from compelling – that Terry Nichols played a much more central role in the conspiracy, with help from people with connections to Middle East terrorist groups.

But throughout his book, Jones alludes to something that makes the idea of an international conspiracy even more compelling. Over the last thirty-years, Americans have grown accustomed to international terrorism. It is natural to believe that murderous acts of such ghastly proportions would be carried out by terrorist groups tied to geopolitical movements. America, after all, is the biggest economic and military power in the world, so surely any attack that succeeds in wounding this country must come from a force that at least purports to rival this country in greatness. It may have been difficult for the FBI or the American public to fathom that the single deadliest act of domestic terrorism in U.S. history could be the work of Midwestern militia nuts – a group generally perceived as lower-class, uneducated right-wing zealots who like to go out on weekend-warrior junkets to drink beer, shoot their guns and complain about the 'gumment'.

For its part, because of its years of experience in such matters, the FBI may have found it easier to buy into the lone-gunman scenario that made McVeigh the perpetrator and Nichols the relatively minor sidekick.

Jones' book, on the other hand, feeds well into the notion held by many people that says surely there must have been more.

From the Southern Poverty Law Center *Intelligence Report,* 'Millennium "Y2Kaos"' (Fall, 1998 /# 92).

MILLENNIUM 'Y2KAOS'

Fears of Computer Bug Fueling the Far Right

'Prepare for war. It's coming!'

With those words, hardline racist preacher James Wickstrom warned an August gathering of extremists in Pennsylvania of the end-times battle he expects in the year 2000 – a battle he believes will be set off by the so-called 'Y2K' computer bug.

Across the extreme-right spectrum, such fears of a societal breakdown sparked by computer date-change problems have set activists afire. While Wickstrom's prophecies may be the most explosive, similar millennial fears are dominating the headlines of the radical press. The airwaves are reverberating with warnings to head for the hills and hunker down for possible riots and race war. The Internet is replete with similarly dire scenarios.

When the crash comes, Wickstrom enjoined some 30 followers, 'get out of the way for a while and then go hunting, O Israel!' Like the biblical figure of David, godly whites must 'fill our shoes with the blood of our enemies and walk in them.' Wickstrom, lives, he said, 'for the day I can walk down the road and see heads on the fence posts.'

If the race war scenario such men envision is a fantasy, the computer problem they believe will set it off is not. Authorities ranging from President Clinton to leaders of industry around the world believe that Y2K – which is short for 'Year 2000' – could lead to major social and economic snarls, even a worldwide depression.

The problem originated with early computer programmers who abbreviated date references to two digits – as in '98' for 1998 – in order to save then precious bytes of computer memory. At the turn of the century, experts say, many computers could crash or spew nonsensical data as they confuse '00' for 1900. While predictions vary hugely, many officials and experts believe there could be serious problems in banking, food supplies, air traffic control, nuclear and electrical power, defense and any number of other sectors.

Many fear a recession. And there are those who forecast even worse.

'Something will Happen'

Regardless of the actual result – and many experts see the headline-making Y2K story as a tempest in a teacup – there is no question that a large number of extremists have pegged the year 2000 as a critical date. For many, it will be the time when Christian patriots, the 'children of light,' must do battle with the satanic 'forces of darkness.' Others believe 'one-world' conspirators will attack American patriots on that date.

This has not been lost on those who battle right-wing terror. Early next year, the FBI will launch a nationwide assessment of the threat of domestic terrorism on and around Jan. 1, 2000. 'I worry that every day something could happen somewhere,' Robert Blitzer, head of the FBI's domestic terrorism unit, told the *Los Angeles Times* recently.

'The odds are that something will happen.'

Hard-line revolutionaries like Wickstrom are not the only ones to tie apocalyptic visions to the Y2K problem. Pat Robertson's relatively mainstream Christian Broadcasting Network (CBN), for instance, offers news stories describing the computer bug and its possible ramifications such as 'The Year 2000, A Date With Disaster' and 'Countdown to Chaos: Prophecy for 2000.' Robertson markets a CBN video, 'Preparing for the Millennium: A CBN News Special Report,' that includes a synopsis of 'the Y2K computer crisis' with his futuristic novel, *The End of an Age*, which describes a 'possible scenario of a future biblical Armageddon' triggered by a meteor's crash.

The audience for such ideas is not even limited to evangelical Christians. A large number of new religious books have crossed over strongly into the secular market.

Left Behind, a recent series of four apocalyptic novels co-authored by an evangelical Christian minister and a former journalist, has sold almost three million copies. The series made 'publishing history in September when all four of the books ascended to the top four slots on *Publishers Weekly* magazine's lists of bestsellers,' according to a report in *The New York Times*. The book's authors say every major prophecy of the biblical Book of Revelations has been fulfiled, and they expect the Y2K bug could set off the crisis.

Y2K and the Antichrist

'It could very well trigger a financial meltdown, co-author Tim LaHaye writes on his publisher's Web site, which attracts 80,000 electronic visits a day, 'leading to an international depression, which would make it possible for the antichrist or his emissaries to establish a one-world currency or a one-world economic system, which will dominate the world commercially until it is destroyed.'

The series has spun off a companion children's book series, a music CD, T-shirts and caps. More books and a movie also are in the works, the *Times* reported. And now, Tennessee trade magazine publisher Tim Wilson has launched a new periodical, *Y2K News Magazine*, that includes tips on defending property from would-be attackers.

Reaction to the Y2K problem on the extreme fringes of the right has varied widely, usually depending on the religious or ideological bent of each group. Probably the most consistent theme has been a survivalist one, with ideologues warning that people must prepare for the worst. And entrepreneurs around the country have leaped to take advantage of these fears, offering for sale everything from dried foods to underground bunkers.

At the Preparedness Expo '98 held in Atlanta last June, for instance, at least a dozen speakers offered bleak assessments of the coming crisis. For those who took the bait, there was a plethora of products available: water purifiers, hundreds of types of storable foods from 'enzyme-rich vegetable juice extracts' to 'gourmet' dehydrated fruits, seeds, herbal medicines, 'Cozy Cruiser' trailers and all manner of books on survival skills.

Such merchants aren't the only ones pandering to millennial fear.

Land, Gold and Medical School

In Idaho, so-called 'Patriot' James 'Bo' Gritz hawks remote lots of land that he describes as 'an ark in the time of Noah,' along with a huge range of survivalist products and training. . . . In Montana, Militia of Montana leader John Trochmann has a catalog of holocaust-survival items. In states around the country, far right 'investment counselors' sell strategies to protect one's money as civilization collapses. And on the Internet, two self-described 'Christian Patriots' signing themselves Michael Johnson and Paul Byus offer 'foolproof' gold certificates to a mining claim in Oregon.

'We (also) have set up schools to cover kindergarten, 1st thru 12th grades, adult school, community college, 4 yr college, university, and even the medical school I told you about 6 months ago,' one of the Internet salesmen claims. 'Bring your kids and entire family to participate in our secure decentralized Patriot community. . . .'

Other reactions on the extreme right run the gamut, from seeing the crisis as an opportunity for global conspirators to seize dictatorial powers, to viewing it as an opening for revolution or a fulfilment of biblical prophecy. Recent examples:

• *The New American*, an organ of the ultraconservative John Birch Society, speculates that the Y2K bug could be America's Reichstag fire, a reference to the 1933 arson attack on Germany's Parliament building that was used by Hitler as an excuse to enact police state laws. '(C)ould the Millennium Bug provide an ambitious President with an opportunity to seize dictatorial powers?' the magazine asks. 'Such a notion seems plausible. . . .'

• Norm Olson, a Michigan militia leader, is busy doing 'wolfpack' training for the apocalypse, reports *Media Bypass*, a magazine popular among Patriots. 'Survival is the key. As with most other people, we will rely on our self-supporting "covenant community," said Olson, who believes constitutional rights probably will be suspended before the real crisis hits. 'It will be the worst time for humanity since the Noahic flood.'

• In his *Anti Shyster* magazine, Patriot editor Alfred Adask speaks of entire cities running out of food and of the possibility of 'millions of American fatalities.' 'If the Y2K information I've seen is accurate, we are facing a problem of Biblical proportions,' he says. 'Potentially, Y2K . . . (is) a dagger pointed at the heart of Western Civilization.'

• Bo Gritz's *Center for Action* newsletter, describing Y2K as 'a pandemic electronic virus more deadly than AIDS,' predicts 'worldwide chaos' and then goes on to offer lots for sale at Gritz's 'Almost Heaven' community. 'If Y2K has the predicted effect . . . we can expect to see, out of the ashes of decimated fiat systems and economic chaos, the rise of a 'MONEY MESSIAH,' who will offer a miraculous fix to a bleeding, begging world,' Gritz adds. He also predicts imposition of a worldwide 'electronic currency.'

• Writing in *The Jubilee*, the leading periodical of the racist and anti-Semitic Christian Identity religion, correspondent Chris Temple says that 'the net result of the Year 2000 problem as I have described it will be POSITIVE! Internationalism and capitalism will be dealt severe blows; efforts to recapture local control . . . will spread.'

• In his *Patriot Report*, Identity proselytizer George Eaton concludes: 'We need to act as if our lives depend upon our decisions, because they do. What can we do? Continue to work and save up money for survival items. A person can never be over-prepared.'

• In a July Internet posting on a Klan news page, a contributor described as a computer programmer demands that the federal government 'surrender' in return for programmers' assistance in fixing the Y2K bug. The posting speaks of 'the thousands (probably millions) joining us in our rural retreats. We've got the bibles, the beans, the bandages, the bullets – and the brains. . . . You will reap what you have sewn (sic). . . . Some cities will indeed end in flames – flames that will light a path to our posterity's freedom.'

From Fallout Shelters to Y2K

Interestingly, one of the most salient commentators on the Y2K problem – a man often quoted in the mainstream press – has been Gary North. North is a hardline opponent of abortion and a theocratic thinker who advocates imposing biblical law on the United States. In his books, he has written of the possibility of a 'political and military' confrontation 'in the philosophical war against political pluralism.' Although he is widely described as a Y2K 'expert,' he is also something of a professional doomsayer.

In 1986, long before the Y2K problem came to public attention, North co-authored a book on how to survive nuclear Armageddon. Called *Fighting Chance: Ten Feet to Survival*, it features a shovel – for digging fallout shelters – on its cover.

North's huge Y2K Web site has made him into a guru to many extremists. The neo-Nazi Aryan Nations is one of many groups that link their Web sites to that of North.

'These are people who are super-sensitive to anything that suggests the collapse of social institutions,'

Michael Barkun, a Syracuse University expert on millennialism, said of Y2K fearmongers. 'Since nuclear war really is no longer out there as a terribly likely way for civilization to end, they've got to find something else. Y2K is convenient.'

Many experts, including Barkun and the FBI's Blitzer, agree that extremists' fears and hopes surrounding Y2K have increased the danger of domestic terrorism. 'It adds to apocalyptic fears,' says Chip Berlet, who studies the far right for Cambridge-based Political Research Associates. 'Therefore, it adds to the potential for violence.'

James Wickstrom may best illustrate that potential.

At the meeting he co-hosted with Identity leader August Kreis in Ulysses, Pa., he warned his audience – several clad in Aryan Nations uniforms – that authorities would use the crisis to confiscate weapons, conduct forced marches of Americans into concentration camps and eliminate private medical facilities. Already, he warned, national food reserves have been deliberately reduced from 230 million to 2 million tons. Two-thirds of godly white racists, he predicted, will die in the war that comes in 2000

The enemy, said Wickstrom, must be 'exterminated.' He must be 'shot.' He must be 'hanged.' 'The battle is upon us,' Wickstrom bellowed. 'Battle!'

From the Southern Poverty Law Center *Intelligence Report* (Fall, 1998 /# 92).

FIGHTING TERRORISM

Leading FBI Official Discusses Domestic Terrorism

Robert Blitzer is the FBI's point man on handling the threat posed by domestic extremist movements. As the chief of domestic terrorism and counterterrorism planning, he oversees FBI units dealing with analysis of the terrorist threat, criminal and intelligence investigations, weapons of mass destruction, domestic preparedness and other matters. In an interview with the *Intelligence Report*, Blitzer discussed extremist views of the year 2000 and the Y2K computer bug, weapons of mass destruction, and the state of the antigovernment and white supremacist movements.

Intelligence Report
We've seen a great deal of talk in American extremist movements, parts of which are deeply affected by millennial beliefs, about the coming of the year 2000. Is the FBI noticing the same thing?

Blitzer
My analytical people are seeing snippets of this out there, both on the Net and to a lesser degree in our investigative activity. Many of these groups have apocalyptic visions. Sometimes that's connected to the millennium and sometimes it's not. The millennium is certainly an event that a lot of extremists are focusing on. There probably is some sense that something will happen. We're not seeing anything in the cases that we've been working pointing to any particular planned violent action around that time. But a lot of the groups are very security-conscious and operate in a clandestine fashion, so we won't always know when something is about to happen.

IR
How would you assess the potential threat?

Blitzer

I think it's going to continue the way it has over the last couple of years with little eruptions happening here and there around the nation. We've had cases, for instance, like the Klan case outside Fort Worth, Texas, where they were going to blow up a (gas) tank farm. There was the group in Illinois connected to the Aryan Nations that was planning some terrorist operations. We had the Phineas Priests up in the Pacific Northwest, robbing money from banks and blowing up facilities as diversions. That's the kind of pattern that I've seen over the last three years, and I don't see that changing.

IR

There's also been a lot of talk in the movement about the so-called 'Y2K' computer problem. How does that fit into the picture?

Blitzer

I think it's just another manifestation of their paranoia. It's like everything else that we've seen in the past – black helicopters, those kinds of things. It's another element of that paranoia about the government taking over and becoming totalitarian. This is just a newer thing for them to pound on.

IR

You recently discussed conducting a national assessment of dangers surrounding the year 2000. What are you planning?

Blitzer

I was speaking not so much of a formal assessment as an informal polling of all FBI field officers prior to the year 2000. We want to see what they're hearing through their contacts just to get a sense, a national sense, of what's going on.

IR

You recently told Congress that the number of investigations into the use of chemical, biological, radiological and nuclear materials had risen to 86 this year over 68 in 1997. How serious is that threat?

Blitzer

My sense is that the threat is low in the arena of weapons of mass destruction. We're seeing lone individuals engaging in either hoaxes or actual cases. These are the people I'm most afraid of, the people capable of doing something like another Oklahoma City bomb. It doesn't take but one or two people to put a major bomb like that together. The ability of law enforcement to discover and prevent that kind of an act, absent help from someone who knows what they're up to, is very slim.

We've had guys playing with (the deadly toxin) ricin and we've had some anthrax threat cases. There's also concern that some state sponsor who has the scientific know-how could decide to hurt a lot of people using some kind of biological or chemical device. I think everyone feels that's out in the future. There's no indication that this is going to happen anytime soon, but that being said, the intelligence game is not perfect.

The biological and chemical know-how to make these things is out there, but the technical capability to execute an attack is a different thing. If you're handling that stuff you really have to have training. If you're doing biologicals, in particular, it can be very scary – you better really know what you're doing. A chemical (attack), on the other hand, is not as hard. But it still is not that easy, technically, to disperse the stuff.

IR

Some politicians have complained that the country isn't preparing quickly enough for such a threat. How well prepared are we?

Blitzer

We're making progress, but I think there's still a long way to go. I think the attorney general and others at senior levels are committed to trying to improve things.

IR

There seems to have been a remarkable rise in the number of domestic terrorism conspiracies in the three-and-a-half years since the Oklahoma City bombing. How many such cases is the FBI working presently?

Blitzer

It seems to hover right around 1,000 (compared to few than 100 before the Oklahoma City attack). There are a lot of bombing cases around the United States that come under the domestic terrorism mantle. I'm always running a half a dozen to a dozen domestic terrorism intelligence cases – a very small number. The vast majority of my cases are investigating crimes that have already occurred and that have been linked in one way or another to a domestic terrorism group.

There are really two things going on here. Because we've had additional resources (with the hiring of several hundred new agents), we've been able to do a better job in preventing or at least identifying criminal activity. When you've got people out there working it, you're developing additional investigations that may have gone unnoticed in past years.

IR

Almost all the major terrorist conspiracies have been stopped by law enforcement before people were killed or buildings blown up. To what do you attribute these successes?

Blitzer

Frankly, I thing the reason is that we've had such good interaction in our task forces between state and local police, the bureau and other federal law enforcement agencies such as Secret Service and ATF. That synergy has been there. We've done a lot of training with the states and locals through a couple of programs we've had.

Also, everyone in this nation, including the law enforcement family, was very deeply touched by Oklahoma City, and so police nowadays are much more vigilant when they see things happen. A lot of these cases have come to us through other law enforcement agencies and through people (inside the movement) who just don't want to be involved in something like that. In the Fort Worth case, one of the guys just couldn't do it – he didn't want to kill a lot of people. In another Texas case, there were two guys who were going to go down to Fort Hood (a large Army base in Killeen) and do some assassinations. That came to us from an undercover operation being run by state police.

So I'm knocking on wood here, but we've got a good run. Still, you just don't know what else is out there. You can't be everywhere. It's a big country with a lot of people.

IR

We've notices that the so-called 'Patriot' movement seems to have shrunk in size but at the same time become more hard-line. Would you agree?

Blitzer

I think it has really flattened out. There was a big surge (in numbers) after the Persian Gulf conflict and even prior to the Oklahoma City bombing. After Oklahoma, a lot of people seemed to sit back and say. 'Is this really what we want?' It's one thing to defend your country – and a lot of these militia groups believe they are defending their country – but it's another to be tainted by the murder of your own citizens.

So there is a smaller number of groups. But I do think that what is left is more serious people, more serious than those who we saw in the early '90s out there training in the woods. They are much more concerned about security and being penetrated by law enforcement. They're just more careful.

IR

How would you categorize the kinds of threats the FBI is seeing now on the domestic terrorism front?

Blitzer

They really cut across a lot of different areas. You have people who have personal beefs with other people. I've seen them go off on divorce matters. There are people who are mentally unstable. You have people who have a grudge against the government for many reasons – and it doesn't have to be the federal government. We also get a lot of hoaxes. But you have to treat each one seriously. The one you don't focus on could be the one to get you.

MILITIA TEXTS

WHY NOW? THE NEED FOR MILITIAS

This selection of militia texts begins with a lament for the state of the nation first published in the newspaper *Common Sense* by 'a group of concerned citizens' in 1994. America is depicted as a country in serious decline, as a place in which the government is 'commencing an assault on every Constitutional liberty', in which dissenters are 'ruthlessly persecuted', and where plans are afoot for the disarming of American citizens so as to make them easier to control. A similarly unfavourable assessment of American life is to be found in a poem taken from the April 1995 issue of the *Kentucky Riflemen News*. 'A Visitor from the Past' also evidences the militias' conviction that they are protecting the 'legacy' of the American founding and their sense that this legacy (discussed in detail in a subsequent section) has been betrayed in recent years. We conclude with an 'updated' version of the Declaration of Independence presented to Congress by the Militia of Montana in 1995.

From *Common Sense* 'Liberty or Death: Don't Tread On Me' (1994).

EDITORIAL: DON'T TREAD ON ME

In America today, we are confronted with a Federal Government that, at the same time it is spending itself into a hole from which it cannot return, is commencing an assault on every Constitutional liberty enumerated in the Bill of Rights.

This same Government persecutes those who want to practice their religious beliefs in peace, to the extent of gassing them, and then incinerating them, while recommending to state and Federal prosecutors leniency for violent criminals, and requiring early release from prison for rapists and murderers, on grounds of overcrowding.

This same Government packs the prisons with drug addicts, who, if anything, deserve to be treated in a hospital, like alcoholics, and with people who have fallen foul of various obscure Government regulations.

Today, the dollar has fallen to a new low against the Japanese Yen. This is happening because foreign investors will not buy US Government debt, be it Treasury Bonds, T-Bills, or Treasury Notes. They will not buy our debt instruments because they sense that the risk of default is too great.

Indeed, at a debt level of $4.7 trillion, rising $400 billion each year, it won't be long before we get into a debt crisis, and be forced to default on interest payment on these debt obligations. When this happens, interest rates will skyrocket as the value of those bonds hits bottom. We will be forced to print money, so that the dollar will no longer be a store of value.

It isn't that Japan's economy is all that strong, either; it's that our

320

Government debt strangles our economy, tearing the lifeblood of investment dollars away from our domestic industry.

When this happens, lots of people will lose their jobs, since the companies they work for no longer have access to capital to run their operations. The people who lose their jobs will be unable to pay their mortgages, and the banks will be forced either to make massive foreclosures, throwing these people out into the street, or to go into bankruptcy themselves.

At this point, it is possible that the Government, which is the source of the policies which caused these problems in the first place, will declare a State of Emergency. If this happens, we will see the Executive Orders about which we have heard so much recently, put into action.

In this case, the Federal Emergency Management Agency will take over almost every aspect of each American's life, from regulating how much food a family can have, to regulating their travel, to confiscating their weapons.

We already see an ominous trend in this direction in legislation currently in Congress. Numerous Gun Control bills, designed to strip the people of all kinds of guns, from bolt-action hunting rifles, to pistols and revolvers, to semi-automatic rifles, to 'assault weapons,' have been enacted, or are in the process of being made law. Registration of all weapons, components, and ammunition will be required if Brady II passes.

One of the bills before Congress right now is a bill that would prohibit the assembly in any given place of more than four civilians who are armed. The 'Anti-Militia' Act is a heinous violation of essential Constitutional rights, and could only come from a Government that wanted to create an absolute totalitarian police state, a Government that feels a threat from people going out hunting.

This trend exists not only for our Second Amendment rights, but for other rights as well. Take, for example, the Fourth Amendment. This is a guarantee against unreasonable and unwarranted searches and seizures.

It also applies to wiretapping and electronic surveillance, and spying by Federal Agencies on computer networks. One of the big initiatives of the Clinton Administration is the Clipper Chip, which, along with the National Information Infrastructure, the Data Superhighway, would allow Government agencies to freely spy on private communications of all sorts.

A new spy satellite has been launched that allows broad spectrum intercepts of essentially all conversations and messages from and to people in the US and foreign countries. Coupled with Artificial Intelligence software, to pick out key words and phrases, it allows intelligence agencies like the CIA, the FBI, and the NSA to make a narrow choice of which data will be closely analysed, and which people will be watched.

Moreover, there is an initiative from the US Postal Service to create a 'smart card' that each American citizen would be forced to carry, in order to interact with the Government. This card would be a national driver's license, the access card to the National Health Care System, the access card to file tax returns, to collect Social Security, Veterans, and AFDC benefits, and so on. It would serve as an internal passport, and would be required as identification.

There are rumors that the United States will soon adopt a 'cashless' economy, both to ease collection of taxes, and to destroy the 'underground economy'. This move would not be surprising after a monetary crisis of the sort mentioned above, and the technology is in place to make the transition easily.

Go to the grocery store sometime. At the checkout, there is a machine you can use to pay for your groceries with your bank debit card. These machines are popping up all over.

It would be a quick transition to require all people to carry a US Card, instead of a bank card; just say that after a two-week period is finished, all cash transactions are illegal, and those found with any form of cash would be arrested, and the cash confiscated.

Allow people to go to their bank, and convert all their cash to a balance on their US Card, before the time

limit is up, and most of the people would gladly comply, especially when they were told they no longer had to file [Tax] Form 1040.

These measures allow for unrestricted spying on the part of the Government into every minor aspect of each of our private lives. The US Card will track what we buy, what we sell, our income, where we go and how we travel.

The Mentor satellite and Clipper Chip will track and record our conversations. The only thing left private will be our unexpressed thoughts.

All of this comes from a Government that is spending itself into a hole at the rate of $1.1 billion a day, a Government that does not trust its citizens with guns or ammunition, a Government that is so afraid of its citizens that it ruthlessly persecutes dissenters, be they abortion protesters or jury rights advocates, growers of herbal medicine or pastors of unregistered churches, and lets vicious rapists and murderers go free to rob and kill again.

What can we do, in the face of this Government, at once both tyrannical and lawless? Can we restrain its actions? Should we attempt direct military action, against the strongest Army in the world? Or should we meekly submit, in the words of Samuel Adams, 'to bend down and lick the hand which feeds us'?

We must resist, if we are to stay loyal to the spirit of the Founding Fathers of this Nation and to the

Declaration of Independence and the Constitution which they created, to guarantee to us our God-given natural rights, which no man or Government may deny us.

It is true that the Government is strong, but remember that the Continental Army, at its largest, consisted only of 20,000 men, out of a total population of 2.5 million people. In 1778, this Army consisted of 5,000 men, less than 2/10ths of a percent of the total population.

The lesson to be learned here is that you can make a difference. People who get up, and take action, smart, disciplined, prudent action, will see results, and good results at that.

How do we resist, if we are to live in a cashless society? We create a cashless society of our own. We look to our family, our friends, and our communities, either in our churches or in our neighborhoods. We find out what skills each of us has, and then we work together to trade those skills, without using cash, of the US Card.

We create barter networks, and communications networks to facilitate this trade. We find out how to do encryption, using PGP, which is the way that NSA uses to encrypt messages it wants to stay private. Those in the country grow food, and those in small towns trade their services for food and farm products.

Christians who expect not to take 'the Mark of the Beast' should note: Either learn to live together in community, relying on your brethren in Christ, or be isolated, and die cut off.

For those wealthy Christians who expect to somehow 'preserve their wealth' by putting their money in gold and silver, while the less fortunate members of their churches and communities go without food, shelter, or the other necessities of life, Beware! Your gold and silver will not survive the Day of Wrath. You can't take it with you, so share it and help your less fortunate brethren.

Others who are equally concerned should note that the Government is quite willing to take on people who bunker themselves into fortresses, be it the Branch Davidians in Waco, Texas, or the Church Universal and Triumphant in Montana. The Government wins, too.

For loners like Randy Weaver, the same result holds. Lone wolves will be hunted down, and will be made examples of in the controlled media, in order to keep the sheep in line.

The mistake that both the Branch Davidians and C.U.T. made was that they made no secret of their stockpiles of weapons. Discreet and prudent people will not suffer as soon as those who make a big production out of their resistance to the System; if you don't stick out, you won't be pounded down.

We must begin to form our networks as soon as possible. Existing networks should be interlinked. It isn't necessary to know last names, or where people live, or meet in a network member's house.

People should be careful in what information they let go outside of their group, especially as regards political actions, tactics, strategies, and logistics. Exercise prudence and caution, and you will not regret it.

In conclusion, now that we are well aware of the problem, we must now form communities and networks to begin to resist and fight for our essential liberties.

We need to work in the legislative arena, to get Tenth Amendment resolutions passed in our States, as has been done in Colorado, Hawaii, and Missouri.

We need to set up our own cashless societies, our barter networks, and unhook from the grid, to become self sufficient, away from the power company, the gas company, and the water company.

Finally, we need to re-create the Ready Militia, the originally-intended duty corresponding to our natural right to keep and bear arms as enumerated in the Second Amendment.

From the *Kentucky Riflemen News*, 'A Visitor from the Past' (April 1995).

A VISITOR FROM THE PAST

I had a dream the other night I did not understand
A figure walking through the mist with a flintlock in his hand.
His clothes were torn and dirty, as he stood there by my bed.
He took off his three-cornered hat, and speaking low he said:
'We fought a revolution to secure our liberty.
We wrote the Constitution as a shield from tyranny.
For future generations this legacy we gave.
In this, the land of the free and home of the brave.'

'The freedom we secured for you we hoped you'd always keep
but tyrants labored endlessly, while your parents were asleep.
Your freedom gone, your courage lost, you're no more than a slave.
In this, the land of the free and home of the brave.'

'You buy permits to travel, and permits to own a gun,
permits to start a business or to build a place for one.
On land you believe you own, you pay a yearly rent.
Although you have no voice in choosing how the money's spent.'

'Your children must attend a school that doesn't educate.
Your Christian values can't be taught according to the state.
You read about the current news in a regulated press.
You pay a tax you do not owe to please the IRS.'

'Your money is no longer made of silver or gold.
You trade your wealth for paper so you can be controlled.
You pay for crimes that make our nation turn from God in shame.
You've taken Satan's number, as you've traded in your name.'

'You've given government control to those who do you harm
so they can padlock churches and steal the family farm
and keep our Country deep in debt, put men of God in jail,

harass your fellow countrymen, while corrupted courts prevail.'

'Your public servants don't uphold the solemn oaths they've sworn.
Your daughters visit doctors so their children won't be born.
Your leaders ship artillery and guns to foreign shores
and send your sons and DAUGHTERS to slaughter – fighting other
peoples' wars.'

'Can you regain the freedom for which we fought and died?
Don't you have the courage to stand up to them with pride?
Are there no more values for which you'll fight to save?
Do you wish your children to live fearful and enslaved?'

'Sons of the Republic, arise and take a stand.
Defend the Constitution the supreme law of the land! Preserve our great
Republic and each God-given Right
and pray to God to keep the torch of freedom burning bright.'

As I awoke he vanished in the mist from which he came. His words were
true, we are not free, we have ourselves to blame. For even as tyrants
trample each God-given Right, we only watch and tremble too afraid to
stand and fight.

What would be your answer if he called out from the grave?
Is this still the land of the free and home of the brave?

ANONYMOUS

Reprinted from the hearing before Subcommittee on Terrorism, Technology and Government Information of the Committee on the Judiciary of the United States Senate examining 'The Militia Movement in the United States' (June 15, 1995).

THE MILITIA OF MONTANA – 'THE DECLARATION OF INDEPENDENCE'

When in the Course of human events, it becomes necessary for one people to dissolve the political bands which have connected them with another, and to assume among the powers of the earth, the separate and equal station to which the Laws of Nature and of Nature's God entitles them, a decent respect to the opinions of mankind requires that they should declare the causes which impel them to the separation.

We hold these truths to be self-evident, that all men are created equal, that they are endowed by their Creator with certain unalienable Rights, that among these are Life, Liberty and the pursuit of Happiness. That to secure these rights, Governments are instituted among Men, deriving their just powers from the consent of the governed. That whenever any Form of Government becomes destructive of these ends, it is the Right of the People to alter or to abolish it, and to institute new Government, laying its foundation on such principles and organizing its powers in such form, as to them shall seem most likely to effect their Safety and Happiness. Prudence, indeed will dictate that Governments long established should not be changed for light and transient causes; and accordingly all experience hath shown, that mankind are more disposed to suffer, while evils are sufferable, than to right themselves by abolishing the forms to which they are accustomed. But when a long train of abuses and usurpations, pursuing invariably the same Object evinces a design to reduce them under absolute Despotism, it is their right, it is their duty to throw off such Government, and to provide new Guards for their future security. Such has been the patient sufferance of these Colonies; and such is now the necessity which constrains them to alter their Former Systems of Government. The history of the present King of Great Britain is a history of repeated injuries and usurpations, all having in direct object the establishment of an absolute Tyranny over these States. To prove this, let Facts be submitted to a candid world.

He has refused his Assent to Laws, the most wholesome and necessary for the public good. *[1995 – By increasing Police Powers, militarizing local Police; never carrying out Honest Inquests on Government Corruption.]*

He has forbidden his Governors to pass Laws of immediate and pressing importance, unless suspended in their operation till his Assent should be obtained; and when so suspended, he has utterly neglected to attend to them. *[1995 – Vetos and Presidential Orders.]*

He has refused to pass other Laws for the accommodation of large districts of people, unless those people would relinquish the right of Representation in the Legislature; a right inestimable to them and formidable to tyrants only. *[1995 – Federal Mandates and Controls through Financial and Political blackmail.]*

He has called together legislative bodies at places unusual, uncomfortable, and distant from the depository of their public Records, for the sole purpose of fatiguing them into compliance with his measures. *[1995 – Requiring States to alter Laws to conform into the Unconstitutional GATT and NAFTA Treaties.]*

He has dissolved Representatives Houses repeatedly, for opposing with manly firmness his invasion on the rights of the people. *[1995 – Passing laws Infringing on Several of the People's Rights guaranteed to Them under the Constitution; Presidential Executive Orders that side-step Representative Government.]*

He has refused for a long time, after such dissolutions, to cause others to be elected, whereby the Legislative powers, incapable of Annihilation, have returned to the People at large for their exercise; the state remaining in the meantime exposed to all dangers of invasion from without, and convulsions within. *[1995 – Interrupting final Judgements and Settlements against Government, bankrupting private Litigants.]*

He has endeavored to prevent the population of the States; for that purpose obstructing the Laws for Naturalization of Foreigners, refusing to pass others to encourage their migrations hither, and raising the conditions of new Appropriations of Lands. *[1995 – Pretending acceptance of World cooperation while Restricting immigrants; selective acceptance of immigrants to fit the personal needs of Those in Power.]*

He has obstructed the Administration of Justice, by refusing his Assent to Laws for establishing Judiciary Powers.

He has made Judges dependent on his Will alone, for the tenure of their offices, and the amount and payment of their salaries. *[1995 – Congressional and Presidential Acts of Immunity and Obligations of Judges to Power; covertly through selective Appointments.]*

He has erected a multitude of New Offices, and sent hither swarms of

Officers to harass our people, and eat out their substance. *[1995 – Establishing Federal Armies of Abuse under dozens of Enforcement Agencies. Such as the ATF, DEA, BLM, IRS, MJTF, FINCEN, USFS to name a few.]*

He has kept among us, in times of peace, Standing Armies without the consent of our legislature. *[1995 – Expanding United Nations Forces with training bases; Foreign equipment storage; Permanent Foreign military bases; Foreign, including Russian cooperative training.]*

He has affected to render the Military independent of and superior to the Civil power. *[1995 – Presidential Decision Directive 25; classified.]*

He has combined with others to subject us to a jurisdiction foreign to our constitution, and unacknowledged by or laws; giving his Assent to their Acts of pretended Legislation *[1995 – The GATT trade Agreements. Designed for years to side-step our Sovereignty.]*

For Quartering large bodies of armed troops among us. *[1995 – Foreign materials and Equipment: Honest Representatives being lied to by the Executive Branch and U.N. Executives with regard to this equipment.]*

For protecting them, by a mock trial, from punishment for any Murders which they should commit on the Inhabitants of these States. *[1995 – Iran-Contra cover-up; Drugs, Murders; 1980 October Surprise Cover-up; White Water Cover-up; Inslaw theft Cover-up; Noreiga Connections to Government Cover-up; Murder of Panamanian Citizens; WACO Cover-up.]*

For cutting off our Trade with all parts of the world. *[1995 – Aligning with Nations into a World Government. Disalignment from those that would NOT become a 'New World Slave State.']*

For imposing Taxes on us without our Consent. *[1995 – Executive Orders giving Tax Dollars (Billions) away with no representation. Mexican bailout and the war in Iraq.]*

For depriving us in many cases of the benefits of Trial by Jury. *[1995 – Every Illegal IRS seizure for 20 years.]*

For Transporting us beyond Seas to be tried for pretended offenses.

For abolishing the free System of English Laws in a neighboring Province, establishing therein an Arbitrary government, and enlarging its Boundaries so as to render it at once an example and fit instrument for introducing the same absolute rule into these Colonies. *[1995 – Arbitrary false Confiscation of Property by IRS and Land Management placing the Confiscated Property into a United Nations Biosphere Park or selling Property for financial expansion of the Enforcing Agency.]*

For taking away our Charters, abolishing our most valuable Laws, and altering fundamentally their Forms of our Government.

For suspending our own Legislatures, and declaring themselves invested with power to legislate for us in all cases whatsoever. *[1995 – Placing any questionable cases under Federal Mandates and Controlled Jurisdictions.]*

He has abdicated Government here, by declaring us out of his Protection and waging War against us. *[1995 – WACO, Weaver, New Orleans, Chicago: All areas of Federal Force abuses.]*

He has plundered our seas, ravaged our Coasts, burnt our towns, and destroyed the lives of our people. *[1995 – WACO.]*

He is at this time transporting large Armies of foreign Mercenaries to complete the works of death, desolation and tyranny, already begun with circumstances of Cruelty and perfidy scarcely paralleled in the most barbarous ages, and totally unworthy of the Head of a civilized nation. *[1995 – The out of Control expansion of Police at all levels, while Crime declines three years in a row. The Creation of 'Ethnic' forces, hiring Foreign Enforcement, for Prison Guards, the passage of a Bill for 2500 'hit men' for Janet Reno's Office.]*

He has constrained our fellow Citizens taken Captive on the high Seas, to bear Arms against their country, to become the executioners of their friends and Brethren, or to fall themselves by their Hands. *[1995 – Training Gang members or young Law breakers into a 'youth marine corps' as 'brown shirts' for future Action against Private Citizens.]*

He has excited domestic insurrections amongst us, and has endeavored to bring on the inhabitants of our frontiers, the merciless Indian Savages, whose known rule of warfare, is an undistinguished destruction of all ages, sexes and conditions. *[1995 – Covert Instigators and Provocateurs in Los Angeles Riots (Creation of Crisis); Assisting in International chaos.]*

In every stage of these Oppressions We have Petitioned for Redress in the most humble terms. Our repeated Petitions have been answered only by repeated injury. A Prince, whose character is thus marked by every act which may define a Tyrant, is unfit to be the ruler of a free people. *[1995 – All Requests for Redress are Denied, except at the Whim or Pleasure of the Oppressive State.]*

Nor have We been wanting in attention to our British brethren. We have warned them from time to time of attempts by their legislature to extend an unwarrantable jurisdiction over us. We have reminded them of the circumstances of our emigration and settlement here. We have appealed to their justice and magnanimity, and we have conjured them by the ties of our common kindred to disavow these usurpations, which would inevitably interrupt our connections and correspondence. They too have been deaf to the voice of Justice and to consanguinity. We must, therefore, acquiesce in the necessity, which denounces our Separation, and hold them, as we hold the rest of mankind, Enemies in War, in Peace Friends.

We, therefore, the Representatives of the United States of America, in General Congress, Assembled, appealing to the Supreme Judge of the world for the rectitude of our intentions, do, in the Name, and by Authority of the good People of these Colonies, solemnly publish and declare, That these United Colonies are, and of Right ought to be Free and Independent States; that they are Absolved from all Allegiance to the British Crown, and that all political connection between them and the State of Great Britain, is and ought to be totally dissolved; and that as Free and Independent States, they have full Power to levy War, conclude Peace, contract Alliance, establish Commerce, and to do all other Acts and Things which Independent States may of right do. And for the support of this Declaration, with a firm reliance on the protection of Divine Providence, we mutually pledge to each other our Lives, our Fortunes, and our sacred Honor.

RECRUITMENT, ORGANIZATION AND STRUCTURE: HOW TO FORM A MILITIA

Issues of recruitment, organization and structure are addressed in this section of militia texts, which opens with a selection of militia flyers. These are followed by advice from the White Mountain Militia and the Virginia Citizens Militia on how to start a militia group, and a membership application form for the Kansas Second Amendment Militia. The range of organizational strategies available to militia members are then considered, beginning with a copy of the Missouri 51st Militia's By-Laws describing the 'Purpose', 'Mission' and 'Goals' of the group, as well as detailing its 'Membership' and 'Organizational Structure', its 'Uniform and Equipment' requirements, and its 'Code of Conduct'. Suggestions from the Militia of Montana on setting up a 'cell system' to provide for 'security from infiltration and subterfuge', together with advice for keeping militia members 'out of trouble' follow. The section closes with a copy of *The Patriot's Creed*.

Flyers announcing militia events. Florida State Militia, Washington State Militia, the American Underground, Kentucky Riflemen Militia.

Colonel Nguyen Ngoc Loan, South Vietnam's police chief summarily executes a Vietcong *suspect* in Saigon. A filmed version of the startling event was shown on international television.

Don't let this happen to you!

Attend the ...

Florida state militia

Information Fair and Campout

September 16, 17 & 18, 1994

Events

Turkey Shoot (Rifle, Pistol & Shotgun)
Hog Roast & B.B.Q. - Featured Speaking

Classes

Firearms Safety - Chemical Defense
Residential Fortification - Firearms Maintenance
Cover & Concealment - Still & Moving Targets
Communications - Counterintelligence
Surveilance Communications
Decoy Construction - Propaganda

Bobby Lee
"The Mouth of the South"
Talk show host and producer
of *The Magical Money Machine, New World Order* and *Murder By Injection* featuring Eustace Mullins.

Pre-registration required for all campers, guests and vendors.
Mail your pre-registration slip back immediately for confirmation.
All book, videotape, equipment and provision vendors
must make reservations in advance!
For more information call:
Robert Pummer (407)287-6012 - Fax (407)287-5970

Directions will be mailed after your registration is received!

Yes, I want to attend ...

Include $20 dollars per campsite and $5 dollars per person in your party

Your name _____

Address _____

City_____, State_____PZ_____

Phone Number_____Fax_____

1. How many persons will there be in your party? ___
2. Will you need a hook-up for a R.V.? ___
3. List below the three classes you will be most interested in: 1._____ 2._____ 3._____

This is the event you've been looking for!

Make checks, money orders, etc., payable to Robert Pummer, Information Officer
5033 Front Avenue, Stuart, Florida 34997 - (407)287-6012 - Fax (407) 287-5970

334

ALPHA-1

Washington State Militia P.O. Box 714 Deming Wa. 98244 592-2668

THE WASHINGTON STATE MILITIA IS PROUD TO ANNOUNCE

A PUBLIC MEETING

To be held at the Fife Best Western Inn on March 10, 1996 from 2 P.M. to 7 P.M.

John Trochmann of the Militia of Montana will be speaking on enemies foreign and domestic and how to survive the coming one world government

Fred Fisher assistant director of the Washington State Militia will be speaking on the United Nations friend or foe.

John Pitner will be M\C and will speak about recent and past allegations that the militias are anti semitic and tied to white supremacists groups.

We are also pleased to have Karl Klang who will be entertaining us with some of his great music

If you have any questions please call W.S.M at 360~592~2077 or you may call the Fife Best Western Inn at 206~922~0080.

Suggested donation is $5.00 but none will be turned away for lack of money. this information is just too important to put a price tag on

ALL ARE WELCOME!!

pass this flyer to others

Directions: North or south bound on I.5 Exit 137 Two miles North of Tacoma Dome

335

Militia News

The Kentucky Rifleman Militia

Kevin is forming a militia in the Louisville and surrounding areas to uphold & protect the Bill of Rights & the Constitution of the United States of America.

The Kentucky Rifleman Militia encourages any and all correspondence with other local militia groups in all states, for information, equipment and readiness preparedness.

The Kentucky Rifleman Militia
P.O. Box 605
Brooks, Kentucky 40109-0605
Phone # (502) 957-5765
Fax # (502) 634-3199

The Texas Constitutional Militia's

goal is "To return both the Texas and United States governments to constitutional republics." They are a publicly and democratically formed group of law-abiding, concerned citizens.

Mr. Bill Utterback
Texas Constitutional Militia
Southern Region
5525 Blanco Road, Suite 112
San Antonio, Texas 78216
(210) 342-4867

Kansas Second Amendment Militia

is a regionally based, grass-roots organization which is determined to:

1) Counter the designs of pernicious legislators
2) Confront the media's twisted portrayals of gun rights issues
3) Politicize and activate gun owners in defense of their constitutional rights
4) Acquaint the public with the true nature of the Second Amendment
5) Network with other pro-gun, pro-constitution groups and coordinate national strategies
6) Train women and men in basic handgun defense
7) Sponsor and support pro-gun, pro-constitution legislation
8) Actively support pro-2nd Amendment activist candidates for NRA board of directors
9) Make Politicians Aware that gun-owners are awakening from their accustomed apathy and will *tolerate no erosion of their freedoms!!*

KANSAS SECOND
AMENDMENT MILITIA
P O Box 544
Spring Hill, Kansas 66083
(913) 592-3266

The Kansas Second Ammendments Statement of Purpose: Dedicated to the restoration of the right to keep and bear arms, individual and state sovereignty, and the rule of law.

CALIFORNIA MILITIA STARTS PETITION TO REMOVE ALL FOREIGN TROOPS FROM U.S.

A petition to disarm and remove foreign troops from American soil has been started by Mike Howse of Fort Bragg, CA.:

"We the people of the United States of America, concerned for the security and sovereignty of the United States, herein, hereby, petition the government for the issuance of a mandate, ordering the immediate disarmament, removal and debarment of the United Nations troops, and all their equipment, and all other foreign troops and equipment from United States soil.

We the people, armed and ready, are the security of this Nation; and by our hand, we reject every aspect of being subject to any foreign jurisdiction, and the fact that foreign troops are too readily available to a foreign power, or an unjust federal government, to deprive us of our lives, our liberties, and our properties."

Patriots applaud this effort to keep America independent. Although many patriots doubt a petition will do any good, or if it is wise to place your name and address on a petition that the federal government could record, the Fort Bragg Militiamen are good patriots doing what they feel is best to defend America from all enemies, foreign and domestic.

For information about this petition, write:

Unorganized Militia of California
Fort Bragg Unit
18603 N. Hwy 1, Ste 377
Fort Bragg, California 95437

Information concerning Fort Bragg Unit from: Patriot Report
P.O. Box 437
Uniontown, AR 72955

Please enclose a self addressed, stamped envelope.

"Let us fall into the hands of the Lord and not into the hands of men, For equal to his majesty is the mercy that he shows." The Holy Bible

US CONSTITUTION RESTORATION RALLY

FEATURING:

MARK KOERNKE

(AKA: MARK OF MICHIGAN) HE IS THE
SPEAKER ON THE FOLLOWING TAPES:
AMERICAN IN PERIL
A CALL TO ARMS
EQUIP FOR THE NEW WORLD ORDER

A MEETING FOR ALL THOSE WHO
WANT TO CONTINUE TO ENJOY
THE RIGHT TO BEAR ARMS

SAT. MAY 13, 1995
1 P.M. & 7 P.M. EST.
61 LOUISE STREET
JEFFERSONVILLE, IN
ADMISSION:
$5.00 IN ADVANCE
$7.00 AT THE DOOR
(812)-282-3781

N. Scott Stevens, the White Mountain Militia, Lebanon, New Hampshire, 'Suggestions for Budding Patriots, Constitutionalists and Militia participants' (February 1995).

WHITE MOUNTAIN MILITIA INFORMATION SERVICE

So many people have written for information in the past several weeks, it is truly amazing. I offer these suggestions for budding patriots, Constitutionalists and Militia participants:

1. Understand and obey the law regarding militia and weapons. Do not allow yourself to become or be characterized as a 'private army' . . .

2. Organize locally and contact individuals (such as myself) that are spokespeople to get connected with other towns. Keep operations compartmentalized, town by town. Remain as independent as possible, but network with others for support, advice and information.

3. Acquire storage food and other resource materials immediately. Make shortwave and other communications equipment a priority. Subscribe to Liberty News, an excellent publication out of Northfield, Vermont. If there is no crisis, these resources will still be of value. Tools, food, ammunition, gold, silver, communications equipment, and of course, truth, will always be useful. Paper money, if our information is correct, can become worthless almost overnight.

4. Work with local law enforcement, paramedical teams and volunteer fire departments. Make a serious effort to enlighten local politicians to the eminent dangers [sic] with which we are concerned. Remind them that a sense of community will offer security in the event of any crisis, natural or manmade.

5. Use your knowledge and skill to build support for one another, then select a spokesperson to work with other towns and the press. Choose only the most articulate and well informed individuals for such roles. We must build public support across the political spectrum if we are to be successful.

Promote a credible political agenda starting with the repeal of War and Emergency Powers. Pick someone who is influencing and moderate. No camos for this job !!

6. Some of us must be in the publics eye [sic] if we are to grow and promote the message of individual Liberty. This is NOT without risk so anyone in this position should have several contingency plans for the security and safety of themselves and families. It is hoped that outspoken patriots will be sheltered by those who have remained better hidden, in the event of a crisis or political repression.

THE MISSION OF WHITE MOUNTAIN

To provide accurate information and help establish a compartmentalized unorganized militia force that will serve locally in the event of a crisis. To promote a spirit of cooperation and sense of community that will support the ideals of individual liberty for all People. Trusting in divine providence, to reestablish the principles expressed in the United States and New Hampshire Constitutions as the inspired Law of the Land. United in the spirit of truth and liberty we strive to convey these gifts and the land that they secure to future generations without mortgage or encumbrance.

JOIN US IN THIS HISTORIC MISSION!

Donald R. Doyle, the Virginia Citizens Militia, 'Starting A Militia Group'. Pamphlet (n.d.).

STARTING A MILITIA GROUP

**THE MOST IMPORTANT THING OF ALL IS TO
GET YOUR HEART RIGHT WITH THE LORD ! ! !
JUDGEMENT DAY WILL COME ! ! ! ! ! !
READ THE COMPACT AND TAKE THE <u>OATH</u>**

HERE'S WHAT YOU NEED TO GET A GROUP STARTED. WE WILL ASSIST YOU IN ANY WAY POSSIBLE PLEASE *DON'T HESITATE TO ASK THE INFO OFFICER FOR HELP.*

THE INFORMATION OFFICER *DOES NOT WANT OR NEED* TO KNOW HOW MANY PEOPLE ARE IN YOUR GROUP. WE JUST NEED 1 PERSON TO CONTACT FOR SENDING NEWSLETTERS/ INFORMATION TO YOUR GROUP, THAT'S ALL !!!!!

1) THIS IS **SERIOUS** STUFF FOLKS, WERE NOT PLAYING HALLOWEEN G.I. JOE. THE MILITIA IS A MILITARY ORGANIZATION AND **WILL BE RUN ACCORDINGLY**. IF YOU CAN'T MAKE THE COMMITMENT SAY SO *NOW* !!!!

2) **READ *ALL* OF THE MATERIAL WE GIVE YOU, IT'S FOR A REASON !!!! YOUR LIFE / FELLOW MILITIA MEMBERS LIVES MAY HANG IN THE BALANCE.**

3) VOTE FOR YOUR GROUP / CELL OFFICERS AS IN COLONIAL TIMES BY THEIR A) MILITARY BACKGROUND B) EDUCATIONAL BACKGROUND C) WORK-SCHEDULE D) **FREE TIME TO DEVOTE TO THE MILITIA** UNIT LEADERS SHOULD HOLD **NO MORE** THAN THE RANK OF 1st LT. AND THE ASST. CAN BE A 2nd LT. UNIT LEADERS WITH A STRONG SOLID MILITARY BACKGROUND WILL GET A HIGHER RANK.

4) *ALL* VCM MEMBERS PERSONAL CONDUCT *WILL* BE ABOVE REPROACH AT ALL TIMES. WE WILL NOT TOLERATE INFIDELITY,

SUBSTANCE ABUSE, OR ANY IMMORAL BEHAVIOR ON THE PART OF OUR MEMBERS. ANY MEMBER WHO WOULD BE INVOLVED IN / CONDONE / LISTEN TO AND NOT REPORT TO THEIR SUPERIOR OFFICER, A FELLOW MEMBER MAKING / PLANNING BOMBS OR CONVERTING A SEMI-AUTO RIFLE ILLEGALLY TO A FULL AUTO RIFLE *WILL BE DISCHARGED AND TURNED INTO THE PROPER LAW ENFORCEMENT AGENCY.* IMMEDIATELY

5) THE VCM IS A D-E-F-E-N-S-I-V-E ORGANIZATION ALWAYS !!!!!

6) **NO ONE** IS TO SPEAK TO THE MEDIA AT ANYTIME *EXCEPT FOR THE* **SPOKESMAN & INFORMATION OFFICERS.**

7) KEEP YOUR GROUP / CELL TO UNDER 15 PEOPLE IF AT ALL POSSIBLE.

8) LEADERS, YOUR GROUPS SUCCESS / FAILURE DEPENDS ON YOU. SET A GOOD EXAMPLE AND KEEP THINGS MOVING ALONG. GROUP OFFICERS SHOULD MEET AT LEAST *ONCE A MONTH BEFORE THE GROUPS MONTHLY MEETING.*

9) MONEY $$$$ PASS THE HAT AT **EACH MEETING**. THERE IS A $10 **INITIATION FEE** ON EACH NEW MEMBER. PLEASE REMEMBER ALL THE MATERIAL YOU GOT FROM HQ COST $$$ ALONG WITH ALL THE INFO. KITS AND GENERAL MAIL THAT CONSTANTLY GOES OUT EVERY DAY AND THE WEB SITE AND NEWSLETTER ETC. SEND A POSTAL MONEY ORDER EACH MONTH MADE OUT TO *DONALD R. DOYLE* AND THEN MAIL IT TO:
VCM BOX 11851 ROANOKE, VA. 24022
TO BE MAILED **NLT THE 25th OF EACH MONTH**

10) ABSENCES: THE ONLY EXCUSE IS WORK, ILLNESS, OR SERIOUS FAMILY PROBLEMS. YOU **WILL CALL YOUR GROUPS SECRETARY 1 HOUR PRIOR TO THE MEETING TO NOTIFY. THE 2nd UNEXCUSED ABSENCE IS DISCHARGE**. IF WE CAN'T TRUST YOU TO CALL IN, HOW CAN WE TRUST YOU WITH SERIOUS MILITIA DUTIES ????????

11) PLEASE **WATCH WHAT YOU SAY** ALWAYS ASSUME YOU'RE BEING RECORDED.

12) UNIFORM – SEE THE COMPACT YOU CAN GET YOUR INSIGNIAS THRU:

CUSTOM EMBROIDERY 7215 BONNY OAKS DR. CHATTANOOGA, TN 37421

SEND A SASE FOR A PRICE LIST

EACH FATIGUE SHIRT / FIELD JACKET YOU'LL NEED:
1 CIVILIAN MILITIA ROCKER;1 O.D. AMERICAN FLAG
1 **VIRGINIA** NAME TAPE; 1 YOUR **LAST NAME** TAPE
1 LIBERTY OR DEATH DON'T TREAD ON ME PATCH

YOU MAY WANT TO GO IN WITH US AT INFO. HQ SINCE WE GET A PRICE BREAK WITH BULK ORDERS.

*PRAY WE DON'T HAVE TO USE IT BUT ALWAYS KEEP YOUR RIFLE/SHOTGUN, AMMO, AND GEAR CLOSE BY AND **READY TO GO!!!!***

YOU'RE IN THE MILITIA NOW!!!!!

The Kansas Second Amendment Militia, Membership Application Form (1995).

MEMBERSHIP APPLICATION

KANSAS SECOND AMENDMENT MILITIA

"I ask sir, what is the militia? It is the whole people... To disarm the people is the best and most effectual way to enslave them." - **George Mason (1788)**

KSAM is a regionally based, grass-roots organization which is determined to:

1) **Counter** the designs of pernicious legislators
2) **Confront** the media's twisted portrayals of gun rights issues
3) **Politicize** and activate gun owners in defense of their constitutional rights
4) **Acquaint** the public with the true nature of the Second Amendment
5) **Network** with other pro-gun, pro-constitution groups and coordinate national strategies
6) **Train** women and men in basic handgun defense
7) **Sponsor** and support pro-gun, pro-constitution legislation
8) **Actively** support pro-2nd Amendment activist candidates for NRA board of directors
9) **Make Politicians Aware** that gun-owners are awakening from their accustomed apathy and

WILL TOLERATE *NO* EROSION OF THEIR FREEDOMS!!

KANSAS SECOND AMENDMENT MILITIA
P O Box 544
Spring Hill, Kansas 66083
(913) 592-3266

Date: (mm/dd/yy)_____ ____ _____

Name_____

Address:_____

City:_____ State:_____ Zip:_____ County:_____

Occupation:_____

Home Phone: (_____) _____-_____ Bus. Phone (_____) _____-_____

Y/N (yes/no): NRA Member _____ Registered Voter _____ G.O.A. Member _____

Federal Congressional District: _____ State Congressional District: _____

State Senatorial District: _____ Ward/Precinct: _____

Access to: (check each) ____ Computer w/LQ Printer ___ Fax ___ Modem ___ Photocopier

Referred by: _____

Circle Membership Type:	**ANNUAL $25.00** (Voting Rights/Bi-Monthly Newsletter)	**ASSOCIATE/SPOUSE $10.00** (Non-Voting)

The Missouri 51st Militia By-Laws (1999).

MISSOURI 51ST BY-LAWS

1. PURPOSE: To explain the mission, goals and organizational structure of the **Missouri 51st Militia.**[1]

(A well-regulated militia being necessary to the security of
a free State, the right of the people to keep and bear arms
shall not be infringed.)
2nd Amendment Bill of Rights

(Right to keep and bear arms-exception – That the right of
every citizen to keep and bear arms in defense of his home,
person and property, or when lawfully summoned in aid of the
civil power, shall not be questioned; but this shall not justify
the wearing of concealed weapons.)
Section 23, Article 1 of the Missouri Constitution

2. STATEMENT of ETHICS: Under no circumstances will the **Missouri 51st Militia** tolerate criminal behavior or racism. We will not support any specific political party or candidate, nor will we espouse any particular religious ideology or doctrine.

3. MISSION: To support the Missouri Militia. To defend the Constitution of the State of **Missouri** and the **Constitution of the United States of America**. To uphold and to defend the **Bill of Rights**, seen as unalienable, given by GOD to free men that they may remain free. To support County Sheriffs Dept. To insure that all citizens regardless of race, color, religion, sex, physical characteristics, or national origin shall have the right and opportunity to due process of law as established and guaranteed by the Great Document which guided this Great Nation.

4. GOALS: It will be the goal of the **Missouri 51st Militia** to:
  1) PRESENT itself to the citizens of this region as well-regulated, well-

trained, well-equipped, and knowledgeable militia units consisting of ordinary citizens rather than professionals.

2) ASSIST citizens in the event of national disaster, civil defense, and in the defense of self and state.

3) ESTABLISH a cohesive command structure able to instruct and to task as needs arise.

4) TRAIN its membership in many disciplines necessary to the function of the militia as a whole, and as members individually.

5) EDUCATE its members in areas of history, law, and principle from knowledge imparted from this country's historical record and from the Bible, which has been the greatest single guiding influence for all nations desiring to be free.

6) INFORM its members of local, national, and global events which would imperil the Constitution and impact the direction of the country.

7) ENCOURAGE its members to stand against tyranny, which threaten to undermine our form of government and these United States of America.

8) UPHOLD the pure constitutional rule of law whereby all citizens have the right to a trial by a jury of their peers in a court of law.

9) SEEK the protection, wisdom, and leadership of Almighty God as we submit to Him to do His will in protecting the liberty and freedom He has given to all Americans.

5a. ORGANIZATIONAL STRUCTURE: In order to achieve the goals listed above, a Command Staff has been created. Subordinate to the Command Staff will be other support elements. Each element will be made up of subordinate units necessary to perform the mission of the Brigade as a whole.

The Command staff is made up of commissioned officers selected and appointed by the existing staff. The **Commander** will hold the rank of **Colonel. X.O.. Communication, Public Relations, Special Ops** will have the rank of **Major. Company officers and the Chaplin** will hold the rank of **Captain.** Subordinate staff unit officers will hold the rank of **Lieutenant.** Squad leaders (if not the officer in charge) will be chosen by the staff unit officer in charge and assigned the rank of **Sergeant.** Squad members will be chosen likewise and assigned the rank of **Corporal** and **Private** based upon experience.

5b. Authority: Officers and Noncommissioned Officers elected and appointed to command and support positions are given their authority by you. As a member, you are expected to support and follow the orders and directives of the Chain of Command. Trust and teamwork are the cornerstones of our organization. If you feel compelled to disobey or openly reject the Chain of Command, you should immediately withdraw from the militia, without prejudice. Provision is made to remove members who discredit the militia through a hearing (Court Martial) by the Chain of Command and, upon appeal, a two-thirds vote of the members in good standing.

6. Uniforms and Equipment: As a member of the **Missouri 51st Militia**, you are encouraged to procure and maintain items of uniform and equipment. When in uniform, you represent the **51st.** Therefore your uniform will be clean, buttons buttoned, shirts tucked in, patches sewn on properly. Proper impression is very important to the public. The primary weapon of a **51st** member will be the rifle. It will be required of all militia members not otherwise opposed for conscience sake, to have his own rifle, ammunition, and knapsack. Militia members are required to remain proficient in the maintenance and safe operation of the rifle and to have a minimum of 200 rounds of ammunition and 75 rounds per sidearm available at all times. The militia member's knapsack shall consist of necessary items to be determined, based on the member's assignment. The knapsack, thus outfitted, will be kept available at all times for rapid deployment by the militia member. If you are restricted to limited funds, set your priority on proper uniforms and attire rather than exotic military hardware. A professional image is more creditable than a lot of neat toys. Militia members **WILL** be expected to obey all Constitutional state and local firearms laws.

Militia members are normally expected to carry military style firearms. Only in self defense will a militia member discharge his weapon. As with members of organized military units within **Missouri**, militia members are expected to abide by all hunting rules and regulations pertaining to the use of firearms for that purpose.

All militia members will be required to take the oath and sign it, to uphold the **Constitution of the United States** and to protect it from all enemies.

While it is intended that the militia intrudes as little as possible in the private lives of its members, it is also clear that individual members are volunteers and must be ready to meet periodically and to deploy as the need arises. It will be the objective of the staff to infringe as little as possible on the time of militia members, recognizing their responsibilities to their families and jobs.

Militia members are highly encouraged to live exemplary lives. Blatant violation of the law places the legitimacy of the **Missouri 51st Militia** at risk. Just one member can jeopardize the civilian militia by illegal acts when those wishing to discredit us look for such opportunity. Therefore, in order to protect the body as a whole, militia members will be subject to a court-martial made up of the Command Staff convened to hear the facts of the case before it. Members may stand trial for such acts that would discredit the **Missouri 51st Militia** or place the Brigade at risk. The accused will stand in his or her own defense. No charge will be brought to court martial unless supported by at least two witnesses. The maximum penalty for any offense will be permanent dismissal from the militia. After counsel the convened Command Staff will vote on action. Any militia members may voluntarily withdraw from the militia at any time without prejudice for conscience sake. In such case, all issued equipment must be returned. It shall also be the right of each militia member to appeal to authority within the direct chain of command regarding grievances. In every case however, the militia member shall follow the order or directive first and make his appeal afterward.

7. ASSEMBLY MEETINGS: Periodic musters and assemblies are necessary and shall be called to achieve the overall goals of the militia unit. Members must discipline themselves to set aside time each month, for assembly. Militia members will be notified of actual assembly times and places.

All militia members will be required to provide information about themselves in order to best utilize their experience and background. Information provided will be kept confidential and will be used only for the functioning of the Brigade.

Under no circumstances are militia members to discredit the **Missouri 51st Militia** by pressuring citizens to join or to contribute material or financial support. All material and financial contributions will be accepted with the clear understanding that the unalienable rights of all will be protected without qualification.

8. MEMBERSHIP: Membership in the Missouri 51st Militia shall be open to any citizen over the age of 17 regardless of sex, race, religion, physical characteristic or national origin. Membership is voluntary, and will last until the member withdraws or is dismissed by proper authority.

Types of Membership:

a) Member – An active participant in the 51st activities, abiding by the rules and regulations of the 51st, and having completed the 90 day probationary period, providing information required by the Command Staff, signed and taken the oath.

b) Supporter – An active supporter, who, due to his or her profession or employment, must remain anonymous. A supporter does not take the oath, has no voting rights or say in the running of the 51st.

Withdraw / Dismissal – A member may voluntarily withdraw his or her membership in the militia at any time by notifying the Commanding Officer, in writing, of his or her decision to withdraw. Following the 90 day probationary period, a member may be removed from membership only after a formal hearing by the Chain of Command. Two thirds vote from the Chain of Command will be required.

9. OATH OF THE MILITIA MEMBER

For Noncommissioned Members:

'I, (Name), do solemnly swear that I will support and defend the Constitution of the United States against all enemies, both foreign and domestic; that I will bear true faith and allegiance to the same; and that I will obey the lawful orders of those appointed over me, for conscience sake;
So Help Me God.'

For Commissioned Officers

'I, (Name), having been appointed an officer in the Missouri 51st Militia, in the grade of (grade), do solemnly swear that I will support the Constitution of the United States against all enemies, both foreign and domestic; that I will bear true faith and allegiance to the same; that I will take this obligation freely, without any mental reservation or purpose of evasion; and that I will willing and faithfully discharge the duties of the office upon which I am about to enter;
So Help Me God.'

10. CODE OF CONDUCT FOR MEMBERS OF THE MILITIA

1) I am an American serving with the unorganized civilian militia which guards my homeland, our **Constitution**, and our way of life. I am prepared to give my life in their defense.
2) I will never surrender of my own free will. If in command, I will never

surrender the members of my command while they have the means to resist.

3) If I am captured I will continue to resist by all means possible. I will make every effort to escape and aid others to escape. I will accept neither parole nor special favors from the enemy.

4) If I become a prisoner of war, I will keep faith with my fellow prisoners. I will give no information or take part in any action which might be harmful to my comrades. If I am senior, I will take command. If not, I will obey the lawful orders of those appointed over me and will back them up in every way.

5) When questioned, should I become a prisoner of war, **I am bound to give only name, rank, and date of birth**. I will evade answering further questions to the utmost of my ability. I will make no oral or written statements disloyal to my beloved homeland and its citizens or harmful to their continued struggle for liberty and freedom as prescribed in the **Constitution of the United States**.

6) In all cases, I will endeavor to instruct and to inform members of organized militia units, seeking to persuade them to join the **Patriot** struggle: urging them for justice and conscience sake to return **America to the Constitutional Republic** our forefathers envisioned.

7) I will never forget that I am an American, a citizen of the greatest nation on earth, fighting for freedom, responsible for my actions, and dedicated to the principles which made my country free. I will place my trust in **Almighty God, the United States of America**, and the goodness of her people.

*

Missouri 51st Militia
Membership Oath

I_____do solemnly swear that I will support and defend the Constitution of the United States against all enemies, both foreign and domestic; that I will bear true faith and allegiance to the same; and that I will obey the lawful orders of those appointed over me, for conscience sake; So help me God.
Signature:

Address:_____

Phone #:_____

Witnessed by;   1._____
                2._____

Date:_____

Note

1.   These kinds of 'By-Laws' are commonly found within the militia movement. The 'blueprint' for them appears to have been provided by the Michigan Militia Corps.

From the Militia of Montana, *Information and Networking Manual* (1994).

NETWORKING: THE NUTS & BOLTS

On page [352] there are two diagrams on how to set up your cells.[1] The bottom diagram can also be used for other purposes. Diagram number one is how to set up your cell system. This is based on a seven man cell format. Some like five or even three man cells. Starting out you build your first cell until it reaches a total of seven. One of you will be chosen the leader of this cell (remember we are all volunteers – watch for egos). When one of the members of your cell recruits a new member, bringing your number to eight, three of your eight will break off to form a new cell. The other four, which includes the leader, will stay behind in the old cell. Both of these cells will now grow to seven again. The process of building and splitting will continue. Always have one of your members stay in contact with the cell from which the three originated from [sic]. This way there will always be contact.

After three tiers of cells have been built those in the fourth tier will not know who is in the originating tier. This will allow security from infiltration and subterfuge. If one cell messes up, the network as a whole will not fall.

Diagram number two not only shows how cells can maintain contact, but also stimulates the creative process for setting up camps, etc. away from your home base. The circle with the x through it is home. Set up base camps or safe-houses around your home with ample supplies. Make sure your camps are a safe distance from water supplies or any other area that would be suspect for such activities.

These camps should be well stocked with supplies. Remember, keep your food and clothing away from any metal. Keep your caches small and spread out. Your camps should, at a minimum, have enough supplies for all of your cell and their families. Have out-post camps that will accommodate just a few from your cell.

Note

1. The Manual also contains advice for establishing a 'Militia' or a 'Militia Support Group' based on a 'military styled format' similar to that employed by the Missouri 51st Militia but it advises that the 'cell format should be used' in whatever 'organizational structure' is chosen.

NETWORKING
THE NUTS & BOLTS

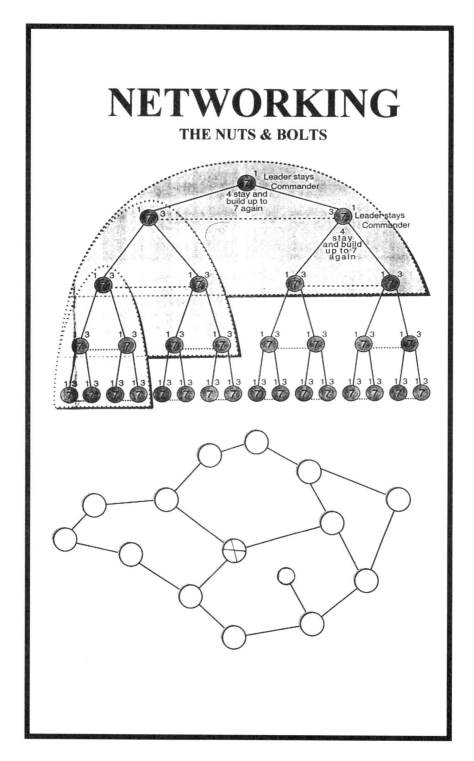

From the Militia of Montana, *Information and Networking Manual* **(1994).**

NETWORKING

What follows are suggestions to help keep us out of trouble, discovered the hard way by people who continue to pay the price.

1) Beware of all strangers. Historically, resistance to tyrants has taken the form of small autonomous groups (cells) whose members know and trust one another from long experience.

2) Beware of the man who is 'too perfect.' He says all of the right things, needs little persuasion, plus, he supplies a substantial amount of money.

3) Beware of handling someone else's firearms, or, you may find your fingerprints showing up at a crime scene.

4) Be double aware of a stranger who proposes illegal activities. You will soon find him testifying against you in federal court.

5) Beware of those who draw checks from the enemy. They are very likely to have divided loyalties.

6) Avoid drunks, drug users and any one of unstable character. Always choose quality over quantity.

7) Beware of someone whose intellect, education and background appear different from those with whom he attempts to associate. Most people inter-relate with others of similar interests and background.

8) Do a little investigation. To be sure, the federals can create good cover. But they seldom bother because up to now resistance groups have almost never checked their associate's backgrounds.

9) Recognize the ruthlessness of the tyrants and act accordingly. A government which will mass murder innocent families, including women

and children, is not going to play 'fair' with you.

10) Beware of signing up for any militia organization or you could find yourself taking orders from F.E.M.A. as much of California and 23 other states are now finding out.

11) Recognize the media tactics. Do not react to buzz words: Religious Separatists; White Supremacists; Tax Protesters; Cultists; Bigots; Nazis and other words which the masses are conditioned to hate. After the media has demonized the target, as in Weaver and Waco, the government is free to murder as it chooses.

We must create our own means of informing the masses to cause them to be sympathetic to our cause (learn to fish in friendly waters). We must be committed to spreading the truth, the whole truth and nothing but the truth. Endeavor always to send messages which will ring true in the ears of our countrymen. There is an enormous amount of moral and ideological high ground which has been abandoned by our foes. Claim it and use it.

As our cause continues to rapidly grow in numbers and knowledge, it has not been without pain. We must all bear in mind that we are volunteers from all walks of life. Each of us must guard against ego eruptions. To be a good leader, you must first be willing to be a servant. Study the book *The Art Of War* over and over again.[1] You must earn respect – don't demand it.

Keep it simple – building from the bottom up – private cells and public meetings. Have you ever tried to build a house starting with the shingles first? The militia is as strong as the preparedness of each individual family. If you can't eat it, wear it or shoot it, do you really need it? What good are your guns and bullets if your stomach is empty and your feet are bloody or frozen?

Note

1. *The Art of War* by Sun Tzu is one of the books sold by the Militia of Montana. It is described as a book 'known by heart by every great general, every great executive and politicians since ancient times' and as a 'must for all who are in, or would like to be in, a leadership position'.

From the Virginia Citizens Militia, Information Packet (1999).

The Patriot's Creed

I recognize the United States of America as a Soverign, Constitutional Republic.

I recognize God creates all men equal, blesses us with unalienable rights and those rights are guaranteed by the Constitution. I understand no man made law can take away rights granted to me at birth.

I recognize the founding of America as a Christian Nation and the word of God as the cornerstone of our Republic.

I pledge my life, liberty and all I may ever posess in the defense of my country against all enemies, foreign or domestic.

I recognize "eternal vigilance" is necessary to make or keep my country free.

I recognize the need to promote the ideas, the philosiphy, the way of life and the fundamental values upon which my country was built.

I reconize the need to be involved in government and in the process of establishing justice, providing for the common defense and securing the blessings of liberty for all Americans.

I recognize the hardships I may face in taking this course, but I take it freely, without reservation. I shall never give up on the United States of America.

'MILITIA IS NOT AN UGLY WORD': RESPONDING TO THE CRITICS

In the three articles reproduced here we find the militias responding to what they see as an attempt by the 'mainstream media', the federal government and monitoring agencies such as the Anti-Defamation League and the Southern Poverty Law Center to 'demonize' militia members by depicting them as 'racists', 'gun nuts', 'uninformed rednecks' and 'religious fanatics'. In the first extract, from the April 1995 issue of the *Aid & Abet Newsletter*, Jack McLamb urges America's police officers and soldiers 'not to be fooled' into seeing the militia groups as 'the "BAD GUYS"' but rather to go and attend militia meetings for themselves. This is followed by 'A Heartfelt Invitation to Black Americans' made by J. J. Johnson of the Ohio Unorganized Militia in the November 1995 issue of *Media Bypass* Magazine. The section ends with an article from the Missouri 51st's newsletter, *Necessary Force*, in which Don Kilbane objects to the attempts of the '"politically correct" crowd' to manipulate language in an attempt 'to defeat us'.

From Police Against The New World Order, *Aid & Abet Police Newsletter: Constitutional Issues For Lawmen* (Vol. 2. No. 8, April 1995).

Volume 2   **Constitutional Issues For Lawmen**   **Number 8**

Published for members of Law Enforcement, Military, National and Coast Guard. Publisher\Exec, Editor: Police Officer Jack McLamb, Ret., Editor: Police Officer A. Rick Dalton, Writers: National Guardsman Fred Willoughby, Mr. Louis E. Stradling, Marketing: Peter Giordano

NOW IS THE TIME FOR MILITIAS

by
Officer Jack McLamb, Ret.

THE MILITIA'S LEGAL FUNCTION IS TO STOP TYRANNY IN GOVERNMENT. But 'WHAT and 'WHO' is the MILITIA?

What we know for sure is that we soldiers and police officers are being told by the despots in our government and in their media, that any who are involved in, or promote the MILITIA, are the BAD GUYS. This always make the wise leery. . .

[T]he American people's militia is a LAWFUL and important part of the people's defense of the Republic. It is one of the important 'checks and balances' within our Country. And we as Officers of the Law, have sworn to protect the Constitution and the people's **rights**. The militia is one of those rights. And our duty is to assist, if we can, as they command these necessary forces for good. We can help them as they seek good militia leaders. They will need intelligent, reasonable, and God-Fearing, leaders of the caliber of our Forefathers. Leaders who are not 'Hot-Heads,' but understand that every non-violent effort must be attempted in saving our great REPUBLIC for our posterity, **before** righteously taking action explained by Jefferson thusly, 'The tree of liberty must be watered from time to time with the blood of Tyrants and Patriots.' The mere formation of militias may prevent the necessity of their use.

America's Socialist/Globalist leaders in the Democratic and Republican parties fear the People's MILITIA, and **must** get their Enforcers (police officers and soldiers) to CRUSH THEM. But, HOW can they get us to crush those in our society who are on the side of freedom and liberty? Actually, it's very simple. It's done by **deceiving us**, the police and military. By making us believe they are BAD GUYS, 'criminals,' just like at the Weaver cabin and at Waco.

DEMONIZE THEM – There is an old communist tactic that goes like this **'Call (label) your enemy, what you are.'**! The Globalists are worried that the American people (the militia) are awakening and may try to stop their plans for a U.N. controlled, Socialist America. In an attempt to shut down the militias, they are using Psycho Politics techniques – misleading smear tactics, mis-labeling and name-calling in their controlled media, government bulletins, intelligence reports, to turn the uninformed police, military and public against some of our nation's best citizens. These are some of the negative misleading labels (names) they are giving any who are attempting to stop their tyrannical activities: 'Racists,' 'Militants,' 'Homophobes,' 'White Supremacists,' 'Anti-Semites,' 'Neo-Nazis,' 'Gun-Nuts,' 'Radicals,' 'Right-Wing Extremists,' 'Tax-Protesters,' 'Religious Extremists' or 'Cults,' etc.

These elitists are also successfully taking such good names as 'Christian,' 'Patriot,' 'Conservative,' 'Militia,' 'Constitutionalist,' 'White,' 'Freemen,' 'Posse Comitatus,' and making us believe **anyone** using these names are criminals or EVIL in some fashion. The truth is they are worried that every cop or soldier, if we took the time to actually know these folks that are being thusly smeared and branded with these negative labels, would support most of them in their stand against the anti-American gangsters presently in control of our beloved Republic. Why would we like and understand them? Because these good people are just like you and me. They are **our kind of Americans**, those who will fight tyranny to the death, i.e. . . . . 'against every form of tyranny over the mind of man' (as President Thomas Jefferson said). But alas, you and I are supposed to believe they are criminals, **evil**, out trying to destroy our nation. We are to believe that the Militia is our ENEMY. The very opposite is true.

This mis-labeling is actually a 'blessing in disguise.' When you hear these government/media smear tactics, let it serve as your 'key' to do your own checking, BEFORE blindly following orders to 'start shooting,' or participate in a **'dynamic entry'** into their home, business, 'COMPOUND,' the government/media name for the Waco church, or 'FORTIFIED BUNKER' as the government/media called the Weaver family's 1/2 inch plywood-covered, mountain cabin.

REAL BAD GUYS – In addition to our hate-promoting Socialist leaders and their media, there are some other **real** hate groups out there, however, most are well infiltrated, controlled and led by these same Socialist leaders. Why? because DIVISIVENESS has always been part of the enemy's plan. Remember **DIVIDE AND CONQUER?** The most important thing is to remember WHY these traitors in our government want to deceive us about militias. THE ANSWER . . . They need us, their ENFORCERS, to CRUSH any opposition to their anti-God, unAmerican plans. This old cop asks you to check these government/media labeled so-called 'hate groups' out! You will find that about 95% of the groups listed as the 'BAD GUYS,' are actually just like you – the GOOD GUYS. Most militia meetings are public, so go see for yourself.

Do not be fooled like others of our police and military peers have been and allow yourself to be sent against our BEST Americans. Sheriff Richard Mack said it this way: **'The precious rights secured in the U.S. Constitution have been entrusted to police for safekeeping. . . .Law officers are required by the Constitution to take an oath of office, and no authority exists to break that oath – NOT EVEN AN EXCUSE LIKE FOLLOWING ORDERS OF A SUPERIOR.'**[1]

LASTLY, Globalists, hear these words well: Throughout our Constitutional history in America, no lawman nor soldier has feared good countrymen bearing arms, just the opposite. It is only when a government begins to enslave the people that the 'leaders' rightly fear guns in the hands of the citizens. 70,000,000 plus, GOOD Americans (militia) own guns. And most, including, many of us in uniform, will not die keeping them, but alas, will see that those who would try to take them, **DIE IN THE TRYING**. It is our fervent prayer that all you anti-America globalists truly understand this.

Note

1. This is a quotation from Sheriff Mack's book *From My Cold Fingers: Why America Needs Guns* which McLamb had referred to in a section of the article not reproduced here. Mack is a former Sheriff of Graham County in Arizona, and a prominent figure in Patriot and militia circles. His book is currently out of print.

J. J. Johnson, 'A Heartfelt Invitation to Black Americans'. First published in *Media Bypass* (November 1995).

A HEARTFELT INVITATION TO BLACK AMERICANS

I think it's about time to take a closer look at those 'racist, anti-Semitic' militia groups, you know the ones, those hate groups that exclude membership based on race and ethnic origin.

One should wonder why the National Association for the Advancement of Colored People, the Anti-Defamation League, Southern Poverty Law Center or other 'civil rights organizations' have failed to bring even one civil suit against the militia. Plenty of suits have been brought against the Ku Klux Klan. Answer: No evidence!

The 'angry white male' label has been gratuitously assigned to us by the mainstream press; the same press that has painted black males as illiterates, drug addicts and gang members; the same press that has depicted black women as welfare mothers, prostitutes and junkies; the same press that keeps our focus on such grave national issues as Rodney King and O. J. Simpson; the same controlled press that is desperately trying to convince minorities and ethnic groups to fear and despise the militia.

I have never witnessed nor even heard of anyone being excluded from the militia based solely on their racial or ethnic ancestry. I have challenged the media to provide me proof of even one such incident. None have come forward.

So, if all these claims of racism and anti-Semitism are just so much media hype, exactly what is the militia's agenda and why should minorities and ethnic groups consider joining their ranks?

The militia is dedicated to protecting and defending the God-given rights and liberties of all Americans, which are guaranteed by the Constitution and enumerated in the Bill of Rights. This is the heart and soul of the militia and is also the reason I refer to it as 'The Civil Rights Movement of the '90s.' The very rights and liberties that our parents fought for and some even died for in the 1960s are currently being held in utter contempt by our elected officials, not only as they apply to black Americans but to all Americans.

The militia vehemently opposes the militarization of our law enforcement personnel, those 'peace officers' who can be found clad in their black Ninja suits while they storm inner-city neighborhoods, indiscriminately shooting and beating residents while fighting their 'War on Drugs.'

We are fighting to keep the manufacturing industry alive in America. Self-serving politicians have exported far too many of the industries that once employed and sustained many inner-city residents, and afforded them the opportunity to realize 'The American Dream.'

We demand a judicial system free from corruption and bias, a monetary system backed by gold and the abolishment of the Federal Reserve Bank, which is leading all Americans down the path of slavery.

We refuse to relinquish our God-given right to freely possess personal firearms. Countless studies have shown that the most effective deterrent to crime is a well-armed community. Make no mistake about it – Americans of African descent are being physically, morally, socially, and economically disarmed at this very moment. If allowed to continue, our social level, along with that of most other Americans, will be reduced to pre-Civil War status. Remember – if our ancestors would have been armed, they would not have been slaves!

And yes, we stand firmly against the United Nations and its desire to create a 'New World Order,' which promises to take care of the dark-skinned peoples of the world, because we're too uncivilized to take care of ourselves! The same U.N. which treats Africa like a 'Continental Step-child' while it wrings its hands in pretended dismay over the outbreak of viruses that coincidentally appeared shortly after the World Health Organization immunized the African populace against smallpox.

We use the First Amendment as a first strike weapon and therefore, arming you with knowledge is a primary goal of the militia, just as it was with Fredrick Douglass [sic] and Booker T. Washington. We have organized ourselves to loudly protest threats to our liberty, as did Cryspus Attucks – a Black American who was one of the first to give his life in the War for Independence (1776). And yes, we are prepared to stand down excessive force, just like Lemuel Haynes – a black colonial militiaman from Boston.

It was the militia who stood against the illegal searches and seizures in the urban neighborhoods of Chicago, Boston, Kansas City, Shreveport and other American cities. It was the militia who demanded congressional hearings into the atrocities committed by the federal government at Waco, Texas that culminated in the gruesome deaths of some 80 Christians, many of whom were black Americans. It was the militia who exposed a campout where federal, state and local law enforcement agents passed out 'Federal Nigger Hunting Licenses' and denied entry to their black co-workers while the Black Congressional Caucus and other 'civil rights groups' remained noticeably silent. And it was the militia who welcomed the inclusion of this angry black American male, who neither has nor needs a 'Federal Hunting License'!

The KKK and the Aryan Nation neither invite nor desire the presence of non-whites at their meetings. The militia does. The government controlled, mainstream press has deliberately created the fear and apprehension that keeps us apart. They fully understand and have implemented the undeniable truth found in the historic words of Benjamin Franklin: 'Gentlemen, if we do not hang together, we will most assuredly hang separately.' The militia does not hyphenate its membership. We are all Americans first.

And finally, if you wonder why you haven't seen more blacks in the militia, it is because you have yet to accept our repeated invitations. There is a welcome mat waiting for you. Join us.

*

J. J. Johnson is a proud American servant in the Ohio Unorganized Militia. Johnson hosts a weekly shortwave radio program and is organizing a nationwide underground network of pirate FM radio stations that would broadcast in the inner cities of America.

Dan Kilbane, 'View from the Foxhole'. First published by the Missouri 51st Militia, *Necessary Force* (June 1997).

Necessary Force

Language is our greatest tool. So the way to defeat us might be to put words into the language that make us appear to be evil. The 'politically correct' crowd has manipulated the people with words that show how prejudiced they are.

'Angry white males, uneducated and uninformed rednecks, right-wing gun nuts, the unwashed,' and last, but not least, 'religious fanatics.' All of these terms have been used to describe the militia.

Day after day, the news media describe everyone who is right-wing or conservative as a potential militia member with delusions of the Nazi party. They paint us with their own form of hatred, and then turn around and say that we hate them for their beliefs.

Even freedom of speech on talk radio has been condemned as 'hate talk.' In the sixties, there were people who made speeches at universities and colleges around the country, promoting antiwar sentiments and rebellion. Those same people are now saying that the rest of America should bow their knees and obey the heinous laws that come from Washington. The only word I have for such people is 'hypocrites.'

Clinton shows how Christian he is by going to church and 'schmoozing' with the church leaders. And yet, he allows partial birth abortion to remain legal. How hypocritical can you get?

The news media use every chance to discredit any public official who has 'ties' to the patriot movement or militia. The dividing line has become so wide that there may not be any way to close the rift without civil strife.

If I could speak to Mr. Clinton, I would ask him if he has lost his mind. We are on the brink of civil war, and he is leading the way. I would ask, 'Do you really want a New World Order? Don't you know what will happen if you pass an absolute gun control law?'

He would probably laugh in my face as he counts his profits from his various endeavors, and makes reservations for his retirement in the Bahamas with several attractive women (not including Hillary, of course).

THE AMERICAN FOUNDING

The militia movement's understanding of the political principles upon which America was founded are presented in this section. We begin with an article from the January 1995 issue of the Ohio Unorganized Militia's newsletter *E Pluribus Unum* in which Helen Johnson argues that America was originally intended to be a republic and that the 'move from Republic to Democracy' which has occurred since the late 1920s has been the result of a deliberate 'propaganda campaign' on the part of the nation's élites. Clark Simmons of the Missouri 51st Militia next explains 'The Importance of Our Constitution' in an article taken from the June 1997 issue of *Necessary Force*. For Simmons the Constitution was intended to establish a political system in which 'almost all political power was vested in the several states', and the 'corruption of the Constitution in recent years has cost the United States both power and prosperity'. The section ends with Jon Roland's essay 'The Social Contract and Constitutional Republics'. Providing a more detailed exposition of the nation's founding principles than is to be found in the previous pieces, Roland also offers a philosophical framework within which to see militia membership as a duty of citizenship under the social contract.

Helen Johnson, 'America . . . Representative Republic or Democracy?' From the Ohio Unorganized Militia, *E Pluribus Unum* (Vol. II, No. I, January 1995).

E Pluribus Unum

P. O. Box 44404
Columbus, Ohio 43204-4404
Voice Mail (614) 627-1065 Fax (614) 272-8866
Email 74634.33@compuserve.com
Cost to Print & Mail $ 1.50

Volume II Number I   *Champions of Liberty - Arming You With Knowledge*   January - 1995

The word *Democracy* is not found in the *Declaration of Independence, The Bill of Rights, The U.S. Constitution,* or *any* state's Constitution. Our Founding Fathers created a Representative Republic. They well understood the nature of these two distinctly different types of government and meticulously worked to create for themselves and their posterity a form of government that they hoped would forever prevent the tyranny of democracy.

Tyranny of democracy? The Constitution of the United States of America is to be interpreted by the intent of it's [sic] writers, at the time it was written. As per James Madison, primary author and supreme expert on the Constitution: **'Do not separate text from historical background. If you do, you will have perverted and subverted the Constitution, which can only end in a distorted, bastardized form of illegitimate government.'**[1] Based upon that, let's see what the Founding Fathers had to say about democracies.

'The evils we experience flow from the excess of democracy. The people do not want (for) virtue; but are the dupes of pretended patriots.' – Eldridge Gerry [sic]

'It has been observed that a pure democracy if it were practicable would be the most perfect government. Experience has proved that no more position is more false than this. The ancient democracies in which the people themselves deliberated never possessed one good feature of government. Their very character was tyranny; their figure deformity.' – Alexander Hamilton

'We are a Republican Government. Real liberty is never found in despotism or in the extremes of Democracy.'

'Remember, Democracy never lasts long. It soon wastes, exhausts and murders itself!' – Samuel Adams

'. . . democracies have ever been spectacles of turbulence and contention;

have ever been found incompatible with personal security, or the rights of property; and have in general been as short in their lives as they have been violent in their deaths.' – James Madison

Getting a bit more current with the debate:

The 1928 U.S. Army Training Manual defined democracy as: 'A government of the masses. Authority derived through mass meeting or any form of "direct" expression. Results in mobocracy. Attitude toward property is communistic – negating property rights. Attitude toward law is that the will of the majority shall regulate, whether it be based upon deliberation or governed by passion, prejudice, and impulse, without restraint or regard to consequences. Results in demagogism, license, agitation, discontent, anarchy.'

In 1928, our nation was still defined as a Representative Republic and the original repugnance to a democracy was still espoused. Look however, at the 1952 edition of this same Army manual:

'Meaning of democracy. Because the United States is a democracy, the majority of the people decide how the government will be organized and run – and that includes the Army, Navy, and Air Force. The people do this by electing representatives, and these men and women then carry out the wishes of the people.'

Something *significantly changed* in our national mindset by 1952. What was once despised as tyrannical government was now embraced as our own. Make no mistake, this move from Republic to Democracy did not occur without a *massive* propaganda campaign. A campaign launched in our public schools – already tainted by the Communist influence of UNESCO – and reinforced in Army training manuals. Democratic tenets, preached from pulpits in churches that had incorporated themselves as entities of the state in exchange for favorable tax treatment. Embodied in political campaign platforms and hailed by newscasters . . . Democracy has become the standard-bearer of a 'free people.'

To paraphrase Hitler . . . *The bigger the lie, the more likely the people are to believe it.* So, when next you hear Mr. Clinton boast of his efforts to spread democracy throughout the world remember the warnings of our Founding Fathers. . . . Democracy equals Tyranny! Yes, Mr. Clinton, as with many before him, have hidden the **BIG LIE** in plain sight. The lie that has enabled our treasonous politicians to adopt *'a bastardized form of illegitimate government.'*

We Patriots are long overdue for a propaganda campaign of our own; a campaign to Restore the Republic. God's-speed, my friends . . . our Constitution hangs in the balance!

Note

1. This purported quotation from James Madison can also be found in The Militia of Montana's *Information and Networking Manual* (reproduced in this volume at pages 380–381) providing an example of the 'sharing' of material which goes on within the militia movement.

Clark Simmons, 'The Importance of Our Constitution'. First published by the Missouri 51st Militia, *Necessary Force* (June 1997).

Necessary Force

The Constitution of the United States recognizes the preexistence of individual rights. It does not presume to grant any individual rights.

In order to prevent future tyranny by the government of the United States, almost all political power was vested in the several states. The federal government was designed to defend the nation, to deal with foreign affairs, to act as arbitrator between the several states and to maintain an infrastructure.

This also prevents tyranny by the state governments. If a state enacts laws that are too restrictive, the people have the option of picking up and going to a state that is more to their liking, lock, stock and barrel.

Under the Constitution of the United States, this nation became the most powerful and prosperous in history. The corruption of the Constitution in recent years has cost the United States both power and prosperity.

In looking at the constitutions of other nations, I find that the framers of those constitutions reserved the power to restrict individual rights for various reasons, usually for 'security of the state.'

A couple of years ago I was talking politics with a friend, a Cuban expatriate who was a Brigade veteran at the Bay of Pigs. I remarked about how lucky we are to have freedom. His reply went something like this, 'No, we are the lucky ones. When Cuba fell to the Communists, we had a place to go. Where will you go when the United States is no longer free?'

It was then that I began to realize that the United States is the last hope of freedom anywhere in the world. It is imperative that we return to adherence to the Constitution. Failure to do so will result in the supersession of it by the United Nations Charter, or by a constitution that is compatible with that charter. The United Nations Charter is a poor compromise in protection of individual rights

It is for these reasons, then, that those of us who have studied this issue are adamant in our demands to return to adherence to the Constitution of the United States – because it works for us!

Jon Roland, the Texas Constitutional Militia, 'The Social Contract and Constitutional Republics' (1994).

THE SOCIAL CONTRACT AND CONSTITUTIONAL REPUBLICS

Between 1787 and 1791 the Framers of the U.S. Constitution established a system of government upon principles that had been discussed and partially implemented in many countries over the course of several centuries, but never before in such a pure and complete design, which we call a constitutional republic. Since then, the design has often been imitated, but important principles have often been ignored in those imitations, with the result that their governments fall short of being true republics or truly constitutional. Although these principles are discussed in civics books, the treatment of them there is often less than satisfactory. This essay will attempt to remedy some of the deficiencies of those treatments.

The Social Contract and Government

The fundamental basis for government and law in this system is the concept of the social contract, according to which human beings begin as individuals in a state of nature, and create a society by establishing a contract whereby they agree to live together in harmony for their mutual benefit, after which they are said to live in a state of society. This contract involves the retaining of certain natural rights, an acceptance of restrictions of certain liberties, the assumption of certain duties, and the pooling of certain powers to be exercised collectively.

Such pooled powers are generally exercised by delegating them to some members of the society to act as agents for the members of the society as a whole, and to do so within a framework of structure and procedures that is a government. No such government may exercise any powers not thus delegated to it, or do so in a way that is not consistent with established structures or procedures defined by a basic law which is called the constitution.

While it is possible in principle for such a constitution to consist entirely of a body of unwritten practices, traditions, court decisions, and long-established statutes, in practice no such basic order can be considered secure against confusion or corruption if it is not primarily based on a written document, which prescribes the structure, procedures, and delegated powers of government, and the retained rights of the people, and which is strictly interpreted according to the original intent of the framers.

Although in principle the procedures may allow for the direct adoption of legislation by vote of the people, this is both impractical and potentially dangerous, especially to the rights of minorities, so that it is generally best that most legislation require approval at some point in the legislative process by a body of elected representatives rather than by direct popular vote, and that any such legislation be subject to judicial review, whereby legislation not consistent with the constitution can be voided. Such a form of government is called a republic, as distinct from a democracy, in which all legislation is adopted solely by direct popular vote. And if it operates under a well-designed constitution, it is a constitutional republic.

Origins of the Social Contract

Critics of social contract theory argue that almost all persons grow up within an existing society, and therefore never have the choice of whether to enter into a social contract. Not having a choice, they say, makes any such contract void.

The original proponents of the social contract theory, John Locke, David Hume, and Jean-Jacques Rousseau, answered these critics, but not in a way that is entirely satisfactory. To understand how the social contract comes about, we need to look at the kinds of contract that prevail during each stage in the development of a human being in society.

Each of us begins life under the terms of a special kind of social contract called a filial contract, between a child and his parents, and by extension to his siblings. That contract is established at the moment of bonding between parents and child following birth, and the terms of the contract are that the child will provide the parents certain pleasures that come with parenthood, particularly the satisfaction of helping to form a happy and admirable adult, and support for the parents in their later years, and in turn receives their love, support, guidance, and protection during childhood.

Although a filial contract can exist in a family that is isolated from any larger society, when the parents join a society, they pool their rights and duties as parents with other members of that society, and thereby become agents of the larger society in the raising of their own children, and accountable to that larger society for doing so properly.

As a child grows, it encounters other members of the larger society, usually beginning with other children. Whenever any two or more individuals meet with the understanding and expectation that they will live together in harmony and not fight with one another using any available means, they are establishing a social contract among themselves. In most cases they will be contracting with persons who have already established such a contract with still other persons, so that the terms of the contract are not only to live in harmony with those in direct contact, but also with all those with whom each of the parties is already engaged in a social contract, and by extension, to all others that those are in a social contract with, and so on. In other words, the social contract is transitive: if a is in a social contract with b, and b with c, then a is in a social contract with c. In this way each of us is bound under a social contract with all the other members of the society, most of whom we have never met.

As a person makes the transition from childhood to adulthood, his obligations change to match his abilities, and the filial contract gives way to the larger social contract and obligations to larger communities at the local, provincial, national, and global levels.

Of course, the social contracts of several societies may not extend to one another, giving rise to tribes or nations, whose members are bound by social contract within their membership, but are in a state of nature with respect to one another. If that state of nature involves active conflict, whether at the individual, tribal, or national level, it is said to be a state of war.

Breaches of the Social Contract

Although the situation of there never having been a social contract is a fairly simple one, the situation of either deceiving another into thinking there is a social contract between them, or of entering into a social contract and then violating its terms, can be much more complicated, and much of law and government is concerned with dealing with such situations.

In his treatment of the subject, Locke tended to emphasize those violations of the social contract that are so serious that the social contract is entirely broken and the parties enter a state of war in which anything is permitted, including killing the violator. Today we would tend to place violations on a scale of seriousness, only the most extreme of which would permit killing. Some would even go so far as to exclude killing for any transgression, no matter how serious, but that extreme view is both unacceptable to most normal persons and subversive of the social contract itself, which ultimately depends not on mutual understanding and good will, but on a balanced distribution of physical power and the willingness to use it. Sustaining the social contract therefore depends in large part on so ordering the constitution and laws as to avoid unbalanced or excessive concentrations of power whether in the public or the private sector.

Checks and Balances

The framers of the U.S. Constitution addressed the problem of avoiding unbalanced or excessive concentrations of power in government by adopting a constitution in which legislative, executive, and judicial powers are largely divided among separate branches, with each having some power to check the abuses of the others. Legislative powers were further divided between two legislative bodies. Some powers were delegated to the central national government, which others were reserved to the component states or the people.

Around the end of the 19th century, however, it became increasingly apparent that excessive and unbalanced concentrations of power in the private sector could subvert the system of checks and balances in government, and the first anti-trust laws were passed to try to provide a check on those undue influences. Unfortunately, such legislation has not been entirely effective, and we now face a situation in which to an intolerable degree the real powers of government are being exercised not by constitutional bodies but by secret cabals based in the private sector but extending throughout government, cabals which are increasingly coherent and increasingly abusive of the rights of the people, including the right to have government be accountable to them and not to a power elite.

The continued constitutional development of this society will therefore require the development of a new, more sophisticated system of checks and balances that extends throughout the private sector as well as the public and does not entirely rely on market forces.

Much of the abuse that has developed arises from the assumption by the national or central government of powers not delegated to it under the Constitution, and the erosion of the powers of the States with respect to that central government. Some of those powers are arguably best exercised by the central government, but without constitutional authority even the exercise of reasonable powers becomes an abuse and leads to an escalating cycle of abuses as more and more people resist such intrusions, creating a crisis of legitimacy not only for those unconstitutional activities but for the constitutional ones as well. If government is to be brought into compliance with the Constitution, then there will have to be a carefully planned program of repealing or overturning unconstitutional legislation and official acts, combined with a number of amendments that will provide the needed authority for legislation and acts which are best exercised by the central government, and the re-enactment of legislation based on such amendments. That will leave a difficult problem of dealing with all those actions conducted without constitutional authority before the amendments are adopted. Making the amendments retroactive is not permissible under constitutional principles, which exclude not only *ex post facto* laws but *ex post facto* amendments as well.

Of Rights Natural and Constitutional

Under the theory of the social contract, those rights which the individual brings with him upon entering the social contract are natural, and those which arise out of the social contract are contractual. Those contractual rights arising out of the constitution are constitutional rights. However, natural rights are also constitutional rights.

The fundamental natural rights are life, liberty, and property. However, it is necessary to be somewhat more specific as to what these rights include. Therefore, constitution framers usually expand them into such rights as the right of speech and publication, the right to assemble peaceably, the right to keep and bear arms, the right to travel over public roadways, and so forth. The exercise of such natural rights may be restricted to the extent that they come into conflict with the exercise of the natural rights of other members of society, but only to the minimum degree needed to resolve such conflict.

Such natural rights are inalienable, meaning that a person cannot delegate them or give them away, even if he wants to do so. That means that no constitutional provision which delegated to government at any level the power to take away such rights would be valid, even if adopted as an amendment through a proper amendment process. Such rights apply to all levels of government, federal, state, or local. Their enumeration in the constitution does not establish them, it only recognizes them. Although they are restrictions on the power of government, the repeal of the provisions recognizing them would not remove the restrictions or allow the delegation of any power to deny them. The people do not have that power, and therefore cannot delegate it to government.

Yet constitutions recognize the power to deprive persons of their rights under due process of law. Strictly speaking, a person may not be deprived of such rights in the sense of taking them away. Natural rights are never lost. Their exercise can, however, be restricted or, to use the proper legal term, disabled. While some might question the practical distinction between losing a right and having it disabled, that distinction is important. A right which is disabled under due process may also be re-enabled by the removal of that disability, and the disability is removed if the social contract is broken and persons return to the state of nature.

Due process is not defined in the written U.S. Constitution, which points out the fact that the constitution consists not only of the written document itself, but the body of court precedents, legal definitions and traditions, and prevailing civic processes as of the date the written document was ratified, which is called pre-ratification Common Law. It also includes the commentaries and records of the debates of the framers and ratifiers insofar as they provide guidance on how to interpret the provisions of the written document. The constitution is further expanded to include the body of court precedents since ratification which interpret its provisions, called post-ratification Common Law, but only insofar as those court precedents are consistent with the written document, pre-ratification Common Law, and the original intent of its framers and ratifiers.

Certain rights, therefore, such as the rights of due process and the right to vote, are contractual. They have no meaning in a state of nature, only within the context of a civil society. And they are defined within Common Law rather than in the written Constitution.

Due process requires, among other things, that any disablement of a right be done only by a court of competent jurisdiction in response to a petition to do so, and after arguments and evidence are heard from all sides to support or refute the granting of such petition. The only rights which may be disabled by statute and without a specific court proceeding are the rights of majority, or adulthood. Common Law recognizes that persons are born with disabilities of minority, and constitutions and laws typically define some age at which those disabilities are removed, such as age 18 in the United States for purposes of voting, although it may allow for such disabilities to be removed earlier, or retained past the usual age of majority, upon petition to do so.

Due process therefore requires that each and every right which is to be disabled be argued separately on its merits, and the ruling or sentence of the court explicitly disable each such right.

This requirement therefore comes into conflict with legislation which prescribes the disablement of certain rights for persons convicted of certain types of crimes, such as the right to vote or to keep and bear arms, without that disablement being made an explicit part of the sentence or the sentencing hearing. Such legislation must be considered unconstitutional, for even though there may be due process in the case which results in the explicit disablement of the rights to certain liberties or properties, those disablements are openly stated and argued, and the statutory inclusion of other disablements that are not made explicit or separately argued is a denial of due process.

Duties under the Social Contract

While a constitution prescribes the legal rights of individuals and the powers of government, the social contract also includes certain duties which members assume upon entry. Those duties include the duty to avoid infringing on the rights of other members, to obey just laws, to comply with and help enforce just contracts, to serve on juries, and to defend the community.

It is important to recognize that although individuals have a right of self-defense in the state of nature, when they enter into society under the social contract, the pooling of that right transforms it into a duty to defend the community, and therefore to risk or sacrifice one's life, liberty, or property if such defense should require it. The right of self-defense is no longer supreme, although it survives the transition to society as a duty to defend oneself as part of the community. Pacifism in the face of mortal danger to oneself or others is therefore not consistent with the social contract, and persons who insist on that position must be considered not to be members of society or entitled to its benefits, and if they live in the same country, have the status of resident aliens.

This duty implies not only individual action to defend the community, but the duty to do so in concert with others as an organized and trained militia. Since public officials may themselves pose a threat to the community, such militias may be subject to call-up by officials, but may not be subject to their control except insofar as they are acting in accordance with the constitution and laws pursuant thereto, and in defense of the community. Since any official designated to call up the militia may be an enemy of the constitution and laws, and may fail to issue a call-up when appropriate, militias must remain able to be called up by any credible person and independent of official control.

Another important duty is jury duty. Since officials may be corrupt or abusive of their power, grand jurors have the duty not only to bring an indictment upon evidence presented to it by a prosecutor, but to conduct their own investigations and if necessary, to appoint their own prosecutors to conduct a trial on the evidence. Petit jurors have the duty to not only follow the instructions of the judge to bring a verdict on the 'facts' in a case, but to rule on all issues before the court, overriding the judge if necessary. No matter how despicable an accused defendant might be or how heinous his acts, they have the duty to find that accused not guilty if the court lacks jurisdiction, if the rights of the accused were seriously violated in the course of the investigation or trial, or if the law under which the accused is charged is misapplied to the case or is unconstitutional; and to find the law unconstitutional if it is in violation of the constitutional rights of the accused, if it is not based on any power delegated to the government, if it is unequally enforced, or if it is so vague that honest persons could disagree on how to obey or enforce it. Since most jury instructions now discourage petit juries from exercising that duty, almost all convictions brought by such juries in which there was an issue in law must be considered invalid, due to jury tampering by the court.

Governmental Powers and Duties

Some critics of social contract theory argue that there are some powers of government that are not derived from powers of the people or delegated to the government by them. However, a careful analysis will show that all powers exercised by government derive either from the people as a whole, or from some subset of the people, or from one person, and that only the first are legitimate. The power to tax? Persons in the state of nature have the power to tax themselves, although they would not ordinarily think of it that way.

Most written constitutions prescribe the powers delegated to government, but are not always explicit about the duties. It is implied that the government has the duty to exercise its powers wisely and pursuant to the purposes of the social contract. But some persons argue that the power to act is also the power not to act. Could the government choose not to exercise its power to conduct elections, or to defend the country, or to maintain a sound currency, or to organize and train the militias of each state? No. Except in case of emergency, and only for the duration of the emergency, government must exercise the powers delegated to it according to their purposes to the best of its ability. That is its duty. Just as it is the duty of every member of society to exercise his or her powers in service of the community.

References:

Ernest Barker, ed., *Social Contract*, Oxford U. Press, London, 1960. Contains the essays: John Locke, *An Essay Concerning the True Original, Extent, and End of Civil Government*; David Hume, Of the Original Contract; Jean-Jacques Rousseau, *The Social Contract*.

James Madison, *Notes of Debates in the Federal Convention*. The definitive record of the proceedings of the Constitutional Convention of 1787.

James Madison, Alexander Hamilton, John Jay, *The Federalist*. Bernard Schwartz, *The Roots of the Bill of Rights*, Chelsea House, New York, 1980.

Leonard W. Levy, *Original Intent and the Framers' Constitution*, 1988, Macmillan, New York. Scholar examines 'original intent' doctrine and its alternatives.

Stephen P. Halbrook, *That Every Man Be Armed*, 1984, Independent Institute, 134 98th Av, Oakland, CA 94603.

Clarence Streit, *Atlantic Union Now*, 1962, Freedom & Union Press, Washington DC.

THE SECOND AMENDMENT

T he militias' interpretation of the Second Amendment is central to their ideological beliefs. This is illustrated in this selection of essays and articles which begins with an extract from the Militia of Montana's *Information and Networking Manual* explaining the 'true purpose' of the Second Amendment and examining the 'history' of the militia from 'Caesar's invasion of Britain in 54 B.C.' to the experiences of Yugoslavia during the 1990s. It is followed by Rick Hawkin's article 'The Truth about the Second Amendment' taken from the August 1997 issue of the Missouri 51st Militia's newsletter *Necessary Force*. Finally, Norman Olson, Commander of the Northern Michigan Regional Militia, asks, 'Is the Citizen Militia Lawful?' Olson argues that the Second Amendment merely recognizes 'the existing natural right' which all people have 'to defend and protect themselves', and as such militias should be seen as 'historic lawful entities predating all federal and state constitutions'.

From the Militia of Montana, *Information and Networking Manual* (1994).

THE MILITIA

A well regulated Militia, being necessary to the security of a free State, the right of the people to keep and bear Arms, shall not be infringed.

The Second Amendment

The following accounts regarding 'Militias' will explain why our founding fathers included the militia in the 2nd Amendment when they had already provided provisions for the militia in the first and second Articles of the Constitution, and reflects the urgent requirement for a 'militia' today.

History of the Militia

The history of the militia goes back almost to the beginning of time. I will cover just a few examples as to how the militia was used.

54 B.C.: Caesar's invasion of Britain

On this day Caesar landed at Britain with 23,000 troops, with some 800 support vessels. The total number of full time military facing them was numbered at about 500 in all between the 'four Kings of Kent.'

A man by the name of Cassivellaunus was made the commander-in-chief of the forces of Britain. Cassivellaunus knew that he wouldn't stand a chance against Caesar's 23,000 troops. It was time to call out the militia. Cassivellaunus martialed [sic] the individual forces of the land owners, freemen and men at arms. Thenceforth, they set out on a campaign of harassment against Caesar.

To make a long story short, on the 13th of August after, in Caesar's words, 'in extracting tribute and prisoners for the Brits' embarked and left Britain for evermore, having the coveted British Isles for the glory of Rome.

The fact is, the militia defended Britain and forced Caesar and his army to leave.

*

'A man's home is his castle'
The Magna Charta

On the 19th of June, 1215, the barons of King John appeared

378

before him, bearing arms, compelling him under force, to sign what is called the Magna Charta (Magna Carta). This Great Charter was a pact between the crown and the citizen's of England, declaring the rights and liberties of the citizen's, which included the right to 'keep and bare arms'[sic]. The arms spoken of were not specified, but were implied to be the articles of war that were necessary to go into battle. Thus, for the Knights and Nobles, this likewise meant castles with moats, ramparts, drawbridges, etc., and all of the other paraphernalia of a castle and needs to secure it. Thus comes the comment, '*a man's home is his castle,*' meaning that a man had a right to fortify his home against any who may assault it, and likewise, have right to defend it in like manner.

The right to keep and bear arms and defending his home '*like a castle,*' was passed down from generation to generation.

The Militia and the Founding of America

Our founding fathers were schooled in these lessons of history, in fact most of them were quite fluent in Latin, Greek, and many of them in Hebrew. They read and knew of the Gaelic Campaigns of Caesar, The Greek City States, and many other books written about the military history of each of the nations and why they either excelled as a nation, or failed as a society.

Our founding fathers were wise to the ways of the world in Europe, Asia, and in the Spanish possessions in Central and South America. They knew that without the militia they would never succeed – and so history has proven.

The true purpose of the 2nd Amendment

There was much discussion during the constitutional convention as to how the states would secure their sovereignty and liberties from a national government. They were afraid that sooner or later there would come a time that this nation might be attacked or that the government would turn into a monarchy. They established the three branches of government, with the separation of powers. To further ensure that this nation could not be subverted from within, they protected the right of the militia of the several states to keep and bear arms through the Second Amendment.

The majority of Americans today, believe the reason that our fore fathers wanted the people to have the right to keep and bear arms was for the purpose of self-defense against criminals, hunting, etc. This is **NOT** the primary reason for the enactment of the 2nd Amendment. Let's let Thomas Jefferson explain it for us:

379

The strongest reason for the people to retain the right to keep and bear arms is, as a last resort, to protect themselves against tyranny in government.

Thomas Jefferson

Thomas Jefferson also understood that those who would attempt to take away the liberty of the citizens of this nation must first disarm them. He knew what their argument for infringing on the Second Amendment would be and what their argument would be for abusing it. We are all familiar with the anti-gun advocates argument, that if we take away the guns of the people, we will lower the crime rate. But this argument was dealt with by Thomas Jefferson when he copied in his Commonplace Book, the words of the Italian philosopher Cesare Beccaria in 1775:[1]

False is the idea of utility . . . that would take fire from men because it burns, and water because one may drown in it; that has no remedy for evils except destruction (of liberty). The laws that forbid the carrying of arms are laws of such nature. They disarm only those who are neither inclined nor determined to commit crimes, such laws serve rather to encourage than to prevent homicides, for an unarmed man may be attacked with greater confidence than an armed man.

Our founding fathers were very familiar with the words of Beccaria, and they no doubt knew this quote by Lord George Littleton:

To argue against any breach of liberty from the ill use that may be made of it, is to argue against liberty itself, since all is capable of being abused.

Most of our founding fathers served in the militia, including George Washington, who commanded the Virginia Militia during the French-Indian War. They all had a vision and intimate knowledge of the militia as being the source for the protection of the rights of the people, local government rights and the Constitution. They had fought the French Regular Army and alongside their brothers the British Army, as militia. During the Revolution, they had fought, some as militia and others as regular troops of the Army of the United States of America, alongside the French Army, against both Tory Militia, Regular British and German troops.

They also knew that if in the future our constitution was not interpreted according to the history in which it was drafted, we would not have a proper understanding of the original intent of our founding fathers, or in the words of James Madison, primary author and supreme expert on the Constitution:

Do not separate text from historical background. If you do, you will have perverted and sub-verted the Constitution, which can only end in a distorted, bastardized form of illegitimate government.

The Militia in Foreign Nations

The militia is not new or unique to America. There are many nations who have had both good and bad experiences with the militia.

In current Croatia, Bosnia Herzegovina, and Yugoslavia, we have seen that it has been by and through the militia that Croatia gained its independence, Bosnia would have been overrun by the regular forces of Yugoslavia without a militia, and Yugoslavia would be under attack from a foreign nation if it were not for a nearly one million man armed militia.

In Iraq, there exist two separate militia forces, one in the north, and one in the south. Currently the United States, and United Nations, are in the process of helping those militia maintain peace and security from their own country and President from attacking them. If it were not for the militia of the Kurds and Suni Muslims in Iraq, it is a documented fact that the nation in which they live would be practicing [sic] a genocidal war upon them. The militia of the Kurds and Suni is the only thing that stands between

them and death.

In Greece, Rome and Israel, a militia was used for many years. However, as these nations passed into time and history, they all went away from the concept of a militia as the security backbone, to a standing army, and finally to either a king or emperor who had total and complete control over the military just as the National Guard Act does currently in the United States. The result is obvious, Greece, Rome and Israel all passed into oblivion.

*

Militias that have been Disbanded

What has happened in nations where the militia once existed and then was disbanded? We do not hear of little East Timor, who, by the power of a militia overthrew a central government oppressive to the right of the people, and was backed by the foreign nation of Indonesia. When they won the war, the militia was disbanded, and weapons collected. In three months, Indonesia attacked, with the aid of the United States, and captured and annexed East Timor, as a nation it no longer exists. **ENOUGH SAID!**

Is this a unique example? No. The loss of the militia organization to the civilian populace has always been followed by a change in government. We can look at the examples of Poland, after World

War II, and the extensive role that the militia, called partisans, played in the freeing of that nation from the grasp of Hitler's Germany, and after the war the government ended the militia, and began regulations on the kind of arms the citizens could possess. The result was that two years later, a backroom revolution brought Poland into the family of Communist nations. Nor is Poland an isolated example. Czechoslovakia followed the experience, as did Hungary, Romania, and Yugoslavia, who had the largest militia armies at the close of the war.

In the cases of the Communist takeovers, the governments themselves precipitated the crises to subvert the people and eliminate the militia within each nation. It was not that the people themselves could not own a weapon[;] even up until its formal demise you could own a shot gun or hunting rifle in the Soviet Union. Italy, Germany, all of the Communist nations have gun control laws that allow the citizen to keep arms. What all of those nations have eliminated was the ability to be organized and bare the arms [sic]. In each and every one of the Communist nations there was a backroom takeover of the central governments, the elimination of organizations and leadership that would have allowed for a militia or any kind of training and preparation was eliminated prior to the political haggling that brought down the free government to be replaced with the socialist government [sic].

Militia Versus Arms

Many feel that it is too much to have a militia, that we need to just settle for the possession of arms. Or that a militia is too militaristic sounding, and out of date. Has it been out of date for Bosnia, Croatia, the Kurds, Suni? A gun and a few hundred rounds of ammunition? This is not the concept of the Founding Fathers and the purpose and level of preparation of the militia. The militia, under the Second Amendment is to be able to bare arms [sic], meaning to use them in a military confrontation. Not just pack them around the house, yard or forest. To stand on the Second Amendment means that you are willing, able, and have desires of belonging to a militia, to whom the right of keeping and bearing arms is guaranteed. The security of a free state is not found in the citizens having guns in the closet. It is found in the citizenry being trained, prepared, organized, equipped and led properly so that if the government uses its force against the citizens, the people can respond with a superior amount of arms, and appropriately defend their rights.

The framers had learned that the regular Army would not protect the rights of the people when the bureaucracy or a tyrant went mad with power. It was not the Army, or the bureaucratic officials, members of parliament or Governors who made up the Revolutionary militia, Continental Congress, or Committees of Correspondence that started the war to protect the rights of man. It was John Q. Public – the common man. Thus, the right of the people to keep and bear arms is the essential element of a well regulated militia, which is the right of a free state for its defense and security.

Our government by passing these Crime Bills and the Brady Bill have shown us that they are attempting to disarm the militias of the several states. With the National Guard belonging to the Armed forces of the United States the several states will have lost their power to protect and defend the citizens and property of their state.

It is not enough to have a gun, it takes knowing how to us it, when, and who you can trust and rely upon.

The lessons of history should not be lost on us. History if not studied is bound to be repeated. It's up to us to know and appreciate what our founding fathers gave us, and how hard they had to study to give it to us.

If the army has control of the militia, then the militia will be obedient to the command of the army, which is in the command of the government. If the militia is independent and viable, then only laws which are right and just will come forth from the government, keeping the populace supportive and loyal to the government. To balance the military power of the nation, with the might of the militia, will put at odds any scheme by government officials to use the force of the government against the people. Therefore, when the codes and statutes are unjust for the majority of the people, the people will rightly revolt, and the government will have to acquiesce without a shot being fired, because the militia stands vigilant in carrying out the will of the people in defense of rights, liberty and freedom.

The purpose of government is in the protection of the rights of the people. When it does not accomplish this, the militia is the crusader who steps forward, and upon it rests the mantle of defense of the rights of the people.

The United States of America, formerly a Republic, now hangs in the balance. We can leave our fate in the hands of corrupted, self-serving, foreign mercenaries, trust our fate to their decisions, which are fostered by agencies of our government and private corporations in its employ, denying us the freedom to 'keep and bare arms,' which is 'necessary to the security of a free State,' or we can return to the original intent of our founding fathers (who bled and died for this country), in the defense of our God given unalienable rights, protected by the Constitution, and guaranteed to us as citizens, by the Second Amendment.

Put simply, one cannot believe in the Right to keep and bear arms without believing in the '**Militia**.'

Captain, what do you think, I asked, of the part your soldiers play?
The Captain answered, I do not think, I do not, think, I obey!
Do you think you should shoot a patriot down and help a tyrannt [sic] slay?
The Captain answered, I do not think, I do not think, I obey!
Do you think your conscience was meant to die and your brains to rot away?
The Captain answered, I do not think, I do not think, I obey!
Then if this is your soldiers code, I cried, you're a mean unmanly crew, and for all of your feathers and guilt and braid, I'm more of a man than you. For whatever my lot on earth may be and whether swim or sink, I can say with pride – I do not obey – I do not obey – I think.

Author unknown

**JOIN THE ARMY AND
SERVE THE UN or
JOIN THE MILITIA AND
SERVE AMERICA.**

**YOUR CHOICE: FREEDOM
OR SLAVERY**

**JOIN OR FORM YOUR
LOCAL MILITIA TODAY!!**

'The security of a state wholly depends upon the good graces of the citizens upon whose backs it rests. When the individual citizen no longer takes an active part in the defense of his nation, that nation is soon to fall.'

Note

1. This quotation is from Beccaria's *On Crime and Punishment*, first published in 1764. The reference to its use by Thomas Jefferson in his Commonplace Book is probably taken from Stephen Halbrook's *That Every Man Be Armed: The Evolution of a Constitutional Right* (Alburqurque, University of New Mexico Press, 1984), 34–35. Indeed, this appears to have been the source for much of the material included in the essay.

Rick Hawkins, 'The Truth about the Second Amendment'. First published by the Missouri 51st Militia, *Necessary Force* (August 1997).

I don't know how many times I've heard some liberal puke arrogantly proclaiming that 'You can't hunt deer with an AK47.' Then some well-meaning patriot type tries to explain how an AK47 is really just a 30-30, and it's really not that powerful, blah, blah, blah! **WRONG ANSWER!**

The correct response would be to say, as politely as possible, without slapping the fool, 'You know the Second Amendment has nothing to do with hunting deer, or hunting anything else, for that matter.'

You are not guaranteed the right to hunt, or even the right to self-defense. You are guaranteed the **RIGHT** to serve in the militia and to do so, you must have a weapon of minimum military specifications.

The founding fathers knew that any form of government, no matter how well conceived, could become corrupt, and that standing armies could become the pawns of that corrupt government. An armed citizenry was the best and only way to ensure that the people could maintain the ability to retake the government if it should become necessary.

Any other response to the misguided liberal is futile, as well as incorrect. You have to stay with what the Constitution says, and what it means. Remind them that it is a Bill of Rights, not a Bill of Needs and Wants.

Another argument that angers me is the 'collective rights' argument, which claims that the 'right of the people' referred to in the Second Amendment is actually the right of the state.

If the other articles of the Bill of Rights guarantee the individual rights of each person, how can the Second Amendment be the only one which does not?

Remember, you will encounter two types of people out there. The first type includes the ones who don't understand, simply because they don't understand. Explain it to them.

The second type is those who don't understand because they don't want to. Don't waste your time with them. It's not worth the aggravation.

Norman Olson, Northern Michigan Regional Militia, 'Is The Citizen Militia Lawful?' (1999).

IS THE CITIZEN MILITIA LAWFUL?

Is the citizen militia legitimate and lawful? Our Governor, the Lawmakers, and others say no. You've heard their lies. Now here are the facts: The Second Amendment to the U.S. Constitution recognizes the inherent right of states to form militia units. That amendment reads: 'A well-regulated militia, being necessary to the security of a free State, the right of the people to keep and bear arms shall not be infringed.'

Not only does the Constitution allow the formation of a Federal Army, it specifically recognizes state militias, and confirms that the citizen and his personal armaments are the foundation of the citizen militia. The arming of the militia is not left to the state but to the citizen. Should the state choose to arm its citizen militia, it is free to do so under the United States Constitution (bearing in mind that the Constitution is not a document limiting the citizen, but rather one that establishes and limits the power of government). Should the state fail to arm its citizen militia, the right of the people to keep and bear arms becomes the source of the guarantee that the state will not be found defenseless in the presence of a threat to its security. It makes no sense whatsoever to look to the Constitution of the United States or that of any state for permission to form a citizen militia.

Logic demands that the power to grant permission is also the power to deny permission. Brought to its logical conclusion in this case, a state may deny the citizen the right to form a militia. If this were to happen, the state would assert itself as the principle of the contract making the people the agents. Liberty then would be dependent on the state's grant of liberty. Such a concept is foreign to American thought. While the Second Amendment to the U.S. Constitution acknowledges the existence of state militias and recognizes their necessity for the security of a free state and while it also recognizes that the right of the people to keep and bear arms shall not be infringed, the Second Amendment is not the source of the right to form a militia nor to keep and bear arms. Those rights existed in the states prior to the formation of the federal union. In fact, the right to form militias and to keep and bear arms existed from antiquity. The enumeration of those rights in the Constitution only underscores their natural occurrence and importance. The Tenth Amendment to the U.S.

Constitution reads: 'The Powers not delegated to the United States by the Constitution, nor prohibited by it to the States, are reserved to the States respectively, or to the people.'

Ultimate power over the militia is not delegated to the United States by the Constitution nor to the states, but resides with the people. Consequently, the power of the militia remains in the hands of the people. Again, the fundamental function of the militia in society remains with the people. Therefore, the Second Amendment recognizes that the militia's existence and the security of the state rests ultimately in the people who volunteer their persons to constitute the militia and their arms to supply its firepower. The primary defense of the state rests with the citizen militia bearing its own arms. Fundamentally, it is not the state that defends the people, but the people who defend the state. The secondary defense of the state consists in the statutory organization known as the National Guard. Whereas the National Guard is solely the creation of statutory law, the militia derives its existence from the inherent inalienable rights of man which existed before the Constitution and whose importance are [sic] such that they merited specific recognition in that document. While the National Guard came into existence as a result of legislative activity, the militia existed before there was a nation or a constitutional form of government. The militia consisting of people owning and bearing personal weapons is the very authority out of which the United States Constitution grew. This point must be emphasized. Neither the citizen's militia nor the citizen's private arsenal can be an appropriate subject for federal legislation or regulation. It was the armed militia of the American colonies whose own efforts ultimately led to the establishment of the United States of America! While some say that the right to keep and bear arms is granted to Americans by the Constitution, just the opposite is true. The federal government itself is the child of the armed citizen. We the people are the parent of the child we call government. The increasing amount of federal encroachment into the territory of the Second Amendment in particular and the Bill of Rights in general indicates the need for parental corrective action. In short, the federal government needs a good spanking to make it behave.

One other important point needs to be made. Since the Constitution is the limiting document upon the government, the government cannot become greater than the granting power, that is the servant cannot become greater than his master. Therefore, should the Chief Executive or other branch of government, or all branches together act to suspend the Constitution under a rule of martial law, all power granted to government would be canceled and defer back to the granting power, the people. Martial law shall not be possible in this country as long as the people recognize the Bill of Rights as inalienable. The present actions of this country's government have been to convince

Americans that the Bill of Rights controls the people. The Bill of Rights has nothing to do with control of the people, nor control of the government established by the people. The Bill of Rights stands as immutable and unaffected by any change determined upon the Constitution by government.

In Michigan, the militia is the subject of Article III, Sec. 4. 'The militia shall be organized, equipped and disciplined as provided by law. 'The law alluded to speaks of militias of the state, to be equipped, supported and controlled by the Governor. A thoughtful consideration of this arrangement leads immediately to the question of 'Who really governs the militia?' Article 1, Sec. 1 of Michigan's Constitution says, 'All political power is inherent in the people. Government is instituted for their equal benefit, security and protection.' Once again we see the inherent right of citizen militias vested in the people. The organizing and support of a state sponsored militia of the state is a power granted to the Governor. This fact is further supported by Art. 1, Sec. 7, 'The military shall in all cases and at all times be in strict subordination to the civil power.' But which military? It cannot be the citizen militia since the agent of a contract can hold, but cannot control the principle [sic]. Therefore, the military spoken of is the military force permitted to be formed by the state, which is the National Guard. Neither can it be the citizen militia because, like the Federal Constitution, the Constitution of Michigan is the child of vested power reserved to the people forever. There is no possible way that the Governor of this State or the Chief Executive of the United States, or any legislative body can 'outlaw' the citizen's militia for to do so would rob inherent power from the people and thereby transform the limited Constitutional Republic to a government controlled state. If that were to happen, our entire form of government would cease.

How then can the citizen militia be controlled? In simplest terms, it cannot be. It is the natural occurrence of the people who gather to defend against a perceived threat. Historically, citizen militias emerge when a clear and present danger exists, threatening the well-being of the people. It would stand to reason that power granted to the Governor to form a militia for the security of the people is intended to reduce the need for the citizen militia. Simply, if the National Guard did it's job in securing the state, the citizen militia would not emerge. That it has emerged so dramatically seems to indicate that the people do not feel secure. Nor can the people be given promises of security. Well-being is not measured by promise, but by experience. Surely our experience has been that security is lacking, hence the emergence of the citizen militia. When safety and security are reestablished in Michigan, the citizen militia will return to its natural place, resident within the body of the people, only to emerge again when security is threatened. Security is the common desire of all mankind. We can no more control the militia than we can change the nature of men. For their safety and security, people everywhere will form militia if and when necessary.

By now it should be clear that the militia predates state and federal constitutions. Its right to exist among the citizenry cannot be subjected to legal challenge. The only effective challenge to citizen militias would be political engineering. One may envision an effort to amend both the state and federal constitution specifically abolishing the right for citizens to form militia units. Should such a venture be dared, the natural need of the citizens militia would increase, actually drawing more free people to it. By now also, one should draw the conclusion that the militia is inherent to all social, interactive people concerned about the well-being of fellow citizens. This conclusion is that which is so clearly stated in the Bill of Rights. No man-made law can abolish the citizen militia since such a law would be in fact an unlawful act designed to dissolve power vested in the people. Such an effort would reveal an intent of any tyrant to transform limited government created by the people into a government limiting the people. Most tyrants know that such a move must be well timed. It is no wonder then, that power-hungry central government and groomed courts view the Second Amendment as applying only to organized militias, i.e. armies of the individual states, that is, the National Guard.

To summarize: Citizen militias in Michigan are historic lawful entities predating all federal and state constitutions. Such militias are 'grandfathered' into the very system of government they created as clearly revealed in both the Constitution of the United States and that of Michigan. These constitutions grant no right to form militias, but merely recognize the existing natural right of all people to defend and protect themselves. The governments created out of well armed and free people are to be constantly obedient to the people. Any attempt to take the means of freedom from the people is an act of rebellion against the people. Currently in Michigan, the citizen militia is subject only to the historic role of American militias as defined in *Black's Law Dictionary*: 'Militia: The body of citizens in a state, enrolled for discipline as a military force, but not engaged in actual service except in emergencies, as distinguished from regular troops or a standing army.' In order to conform to this definition, and to remain able to oppose a rebellious and disobedient government, the citizen militia must not be connected in any way with that government lest the body politic lose its fearful countenance as the only sure threat to a government bent on converting free people into slaves.

GUN OWNERSHIP AND
THE DISARMING OF AMERICA

The practical and symbolic significance of gun ownership to militia members is explored in this section. Challenging the 'constant' Hollywood image of the gunowner as 'a "lone nut" . . . spraying gunfire in every direction' and the 'romantic image' of the gunowner as a self-sufficient 'individualist', we begin with a call from the newspaper *Common Sense* in 1994 for gun owners to join together in militias to work for 'the restoration of our essential liberties'. Jim McKinzey then employs the example of America's revolutionary forefathers as a means of inspiring readers of *Necessary Force* to resist any further attempts at gun control following the passage of the Brady Bill. The necessity for gunowners to stand up against gun control legislation is also demonstrated in the nightmarish scenario envisioned in 'Bolshevik America, 1984 + 13?' taken from the *Kentucky Riflemen News* of January 1995. This is followed by some practical advice for gunowners from Howard Fezell on 'What to do if the Police Come to Confiscate Your Militia Weapons' reproduced from the May 1998 issue of the *New Jersey Militia Newsletter*. Persuading police officers to resist any attempt to 'get the guns away from your fellow

Americans' is the task Jack McLamb sets himself in the extract from *Operation Vampire Killer 2000* which concludes this section. For McLamb, the disarming of American citizens is part of a plan by the agents of the New World Order to create a '"utopian" Socialist Society' in America and police officers have a crucial role to play in preventing its success.

From *Common Sense* 'Join Or Die' (1994).

EDITORIAL: JOIN OR DIE

'Gentlemen, Gentlemen, we must all hang together, or we most assuredly shall hang separately.'
– Dr Benjamin Franklin, at the First Continental Congress.

The motto on the cover says it all: 'Join or Die.' Individual gunowners cannot hope to hunker down in their basements, sitting around on boxes of ammunition and dried food, and hope to weather the coming storm. Nor can they make a defiant last stand like 'Rambo,' fighting until their guns are at last pried from their cold, dead fingers, unless they wish to become anonymous martyrs to a lost cause.

We must have a clear vision of what the future holds, and of what we are fighting for. A journey is always easier if we hold in our mind's eye what awaits us at journey's end. Pessimism, uncertainty and worry are banished, by taking action, by making decisions and working together with our fellow countrymen and women to carry them through to their final resolution.

Too many gunowners and others concerned with the speedy erosion of our Constitutional liberties have no faith that there will be a victorious conclusion to the work of restoration. Too many people have bumper stickers which say things like 'They'll get my guns when they pry them from my cold dead fingers,' and too many people believe that they will end up this way! Prophecies like this are often self-fulfilling; people who believe that they are doomed for failure are often accident-prone and tend to make unconscious mistakes which bring about their premature demise.

Many gunowners watch TV and accept the steady stream of lies and myths which comes out as factual objective truth. This is not their fault, other than that they are addicted to a source of propaganda paid for by those who would see the Constitution destroyed. The people who pay for the TV shows dictate the content. 'He who pays the piper, calls the tune' is especially true in the case of TV. The constant image of the gunowner as a 'lone nut,' suspicious of all, spraying gunfire in every direction, and creating untold havoc, is a creation of Hollywood and the television studios, designed to isolate him or her from the rest of the population. From television we get the images which create pessimism amongst those who watch and uncritically absorb.

On top of the propaganda from TV and the mass media, there is the romantic image of the gunowner as individualist, self-sufficient and not dependent on anyone else for anything. People believe this to the point where it is impossible for them to work together with others to form an effective force, so that the 'unorganized militia' is in actuality the disorganized mob, easily split and easily dispersed by our foes.

We fight for the restoration of Constitutional government in these several United States, for the dismantling of the unelected bureaucracy, for essential liberties as enumerated in the Bill of Rights, and for our lives, property, and sacred honor.

To make this fight effective, so that we may secure the ends for which we contend, we must learn to work with others. There is a lot of loose talk going around about forming 'militias,' and of various people going off to arrest Congress in Washington, DC, and so on.[1] A militia is *not* a group of people who go off half-cocked and expose themselves to certain arrest or death, nor is it a bunch of guys who go out shooting once or twice a month, and then party.

A militia is a well-disciplined, well-practiced, well-regulated group of individuals who have taken the considerable time and trouble to learn military discipline, common tasks, history, strategy, small unit tactics, and marksmanship, who have taken the trouble and effort to get into a state of physical fitness and conditioning appropriate to the tasks at hand; and who have gone to the expense of acquiring special skills and equipment, to do everything from running a secure radio communications network, to learning herbal medicine and first aid, to running a intelligence-gathering network, to assess the capabilities and intentions of the opposition. A bunch of ill-disciplined, poorly trained, physically unfit individuals pose

[sic] no threat to any opposition which has a minimum of determination; a militia as described above can pose a formidable threat.

The government, in the recent past, has shown a certain determination to stop, at the very earliest stages, formation of such militias as mentioned above. People who wish to form militias must do so quietly and unobtrusively. Military history and strategy may be studied in discussion groups; many people have an interest in such things, and there are lots of bookstores which carry excellent study materials. Small unit tactics can be taught while playing paintball, or by simply taking walks in the woods or countryside.

Marksmanship is a natural interest for gunowners, and many common tasks can be taught as needed, as well as militia discipline. Perhaps one reason HCI wants to ban re-enactments is that they provide training in common tasks, marksmanship and military discipline, as well as small-unit tactics, history, and strategy.

Finally, there are many people who, enjoy amateur radio, and who are active participants in the local Red Cross, as well as people interested in alternative kinds of medicine. The government is a long way away from banning most of these activities, so interested people should be inventive and find ways to take advantage of the opportunities and profit from them.

The present series of events, beginning with the passage of the Brady Bill and culminating, so far, in the passage of the Assault Weapons Ban has shown us that time is short. It is time to put individual differences aside, and join together as one. We must indeed hang together, one for all and all for one, for the long haul, no matter how tiring or difficult it may be, or we shall most certainly hang separately, as the provisions of the various Crime Bills dictate. If we keep our attention steady on our goal, the restoration of our essential liberties and Constitutional government, with God's help we shall prevail.

Note

1. Linda Thompson's call on behalf of the Unorganized Militia of the United States of America to march on Washington, 'arrest' Congress and place it on trial for treason was planned for September 19 1994. It was widely criticized by some sections of the militia movement and in the end Thompson called the march off.

James A. McKinzey, 'HQ Bunker'. First published by the Missouri 51st Militia, *Necessary Force* (January 1997).

Force

As we get closer to the twenty-first century, and further from the birth of our country, with the passage of time we tend to forget all the sacrifices made by the tens of thousands who died giving us this country, and who have died keeping it for us.

Our forefathers took on the most powerful nation of that time with the support of only about 4% of the people in the American colonies. Those men did this for a lot of reasons, but the primary trigger for the Revolution was the same then as it is today: you don't mess with a free man's right to keep and bear arms. This was true when the Redcoats marched on Concord to take the powder and shot from the colonists on April 19, 1775. The Redcoats were met by only 70 farmers (MILITIA) at 4:00 am. By the next evening, the number of militia had increased to about 20,000 men.

History can and does repeat itself. Bills like the Assault Weapons Ban and the Brady Act have pushed too many of us back into a corner, where there is no more room to back up. Brady II, the expansion of the Brady Act, will if it passes be the bell to come out swinging. When you can't go right, left or back, the only way left is to bow down and let the heavy foot of tyranny squash you, or come out fighting. What choice will you make?

As long as 'we the people' are armed, the possibility of our liberties being taken away is slim. The question now becomes, 'Are we the people, being at the door of the twenty-first century, ready to let the responsibility of protecting ourselves and our families fall into the hands of government?' Brady II is going to do just that. I have found that I cannot count on anyone to take care of me and mine but me, nor would I have it any other way. I will insist on doing it for as long as my Maker wills it.

Coming for my guns, powder or shot will get the same response from me as it did from our forefathers. I will look at it the same way as if someone was coming to molest my kids, or rape my wife. This will be one case where Newton's law of motion will not apply. The reaction to Brady II will be far greater than the action.

You don't mess with a free man's right to keep and bear arms.

At this time I don't know when Brady II will come up in the 105th Congress. I do know that Mr. and Mrs. Clinton and Sarah Brady have already stated in many speeches that it will come up. If we are to defeat it, it will take eternal vigilance. If the saying is true that 'Success is not measured by what you have accomplished, but by the distance you traveled to get there' then we have many miles to go before we sleep.

Please, do not go willfully into the night, without the ability to resist the dangers found there. **LIVE FREE OR DIE!**

Reproduced from the *Kentucky Riflemen News* (Vol. 1, No. 1, 1995).

From the *Kentucky Riflemen News*, 'Bolshevik America, 1984+13?' (Vol. 1, No. 1, 1995).

BOLSHEVIK AMERICA, 1984 + 13?

First, black-masked, armor-vested, machine-gun toting Federal Police came for 'assault rifles' (as previously featured on Television). But, since I did not own one, I did nothing when they came to take my neighbor's 'assault rifle.' After all, who needs such a gun for hunting?

Then they came for 'sniper rifles' – all center fire rifles with scopes or mounts for telescopic sights. I didn't object because the news media said these guns were made to kill people at long range.

Then they came for handguns. But, unlike many of my neighbors, I did not possess a handgun. The government said these are weapons used in crime. So, I did nothing and continued to trust in the police to protect me.

I did not approve of hunting; so, I thought it was wonderful when the police swarmed through the county (with a list of all hunting license holders in their hands) and confiscated all shotguns and hunting rifles.

Next, came the United Nations Peace-Keeping Force. They searched each house in my community and confiscated all other firearms (along with shortwave radios, computers, typewriters, and copying machines). At last, I thought, all the weapons and all the mischief making tools of extremists and trouble-makers have been confiscated. Now, we will have peace, serenity, and security.

Then, they rounded up all the children and placed them in government 'education centers.' But, my children were grown. So, I did not concern myself with the matter.

Then they came for the Christians. On television they were called the Religious Right and Cultists, and we had been convinced how dangerous these extremists were.

Then they arrested all those people who had expressed fondness for the discarded U.S. Constitution. They were known as patriots and revolutionaries. But, I was not worried. I trusted religious and political affairs to preachers, judges, experts, authorities, and politicians who I knew would properly define religious practice and freedom of speech.

Finally, they came for me because I own property and have been successful. The State Consumer Committee charges that I own too much and have used too many resources. Now, I cannot resist because all the people who might have came to my aid are disarmed, in prison, or dead. The country is under martial law, and only the Federal Police and the U.N. Peace-Keeping Forces have weapons.

Slowly starving in a bleak concentration camp, I am finally reflecting on my non-resistance to creeping tyranny. I now realize what my indolence has brought upon us. Now, I can see that the excessive attention given to the Lorena Bobbit trial, the O. J. Simpson saga, the Tonya Harding caper, endless sporting events, and daily soap operas and sitcoms were all media-generated circuses to undermine our values and divert our attention away from the treachery and treason that was taking place in our government.

However, in all honesty, I really knew that things were not right. It was just much easier to ignore it and hope it would go away. So, I remained cowardly silent when I should have resisted with every means at my disposal. I should have encouraged my family, friends and neighbors to do the same. In those days, we owned millions of firearms which we could have used to protect our God-given rights to life, liberty, and property.

Because we did nothing, we are now slaves – owned by the World State. Our very lives are constantly at the mercy of heavily-armed goons. My life, the lives of my loved ones, and the lives of my countrymen are ruined; and I have permitted the destruction of the future of my children and grandchildren. By allowing our thoughts and actions to be guided by the government and media manipulators, we Americans have lost everything that our God and our Western Heritage have given us.

If only I had it to do again. I would do it differently. I would remember what Churchill said: 'If you will not fight for the right when you can easily win without bloodshed, if you will not fight when your victory will be sure and not so costly, you may come to the moment when you will have to fight with all the odds against you and only a precarious chance for survival. There may be a worse case. You may have to fight when there is no chance of victory, because it is better to perish than to live as slaves.'

Howard J. Fezell, 'What to Do if the Police Come to Confiscate your Militia Weapons'. First published in the *New Jersey Militia Newsletter* (Vol. 3, No. 11, May 1998).

WHAT TO DO IF THE POLICE COME TO CONFISCATE YOUR MILITIA WEAPONS

As California and New Jersey have enacted bans on the sale and unlicensed possession of militia-style semi-automatic rifles, every Marylander who professes loyalty to the Constitution should consider what action he or she should take in the event that Congress, or our own General Assembly, were to follow suit. The points addressed in this article are premised on three assumptions.

1. Either Congress, or our General Assembly, has enacted legislation prohibiting or severely restricting the possession of weapons protected by the Second Amendment (e.g., military pattern semi-automatic rifles).

2. The reader has already decided to uphold the Constitution and not turn over his or her 'prohibited' firearms under any circumstances, nor to register such weapons in order to facilitate their future confiscation. The reader has also failed to respond to government directives to dispose of or surrender such firearms.

3. The reader has secured all 'prohibited' firearms away from his or her principal residence so as to prevent their unconstitutional seizure by the authorities.

What do you do when the police show up on your doorstep demanding the surrender of your militia weapons? In responding, bear in mind that you have two important rights guaranteed by the Fourth and Fifth Amendments to the United States Constitution.

The Fourth Amendment protects you against unreasonable searches and seizures. If the police want to search your home without your consent, they need a warrant. Warrants may only be issued upon a showing of probable cause, supported by an affidavit. The facts contained in the affidavit must do more than support a mere suspicion. The test is whether the information in the affidavit would justify a person of prudence and caution in believing that an offense is being committed, e.g., that 'prohibited' weapons can be found on your premises. The requirement of probable cause for the issuance of warrants is one of your most precious constitutional protections.

NEVER GIVE THE AUTHORITIES YOUR CONSENT TO SEARCH YOUR HOUSE, YOUR CAR, YOUR PLACE OF BUSINESS, OR ANY OTHER PREMISES UNDER YOUR CONTROL.

Consent dispenses with the necessity of probable cause. While lacking probable cause, if the police conduct a search with your consent and seize evidence or use it against you in court, your lawyer will not be able to suppress it on the basis that the search was warrantless.

The Fifth Amendment protects you against giving evidence against yourself. i.e. your right to remain silent. Just as you cannot be compelled to testify against yourself in a criminal trial, neither can you be compelled to answer a policeman's questions about that AR-15 you bought a couple of years ago and never surrendered. Don't be bashful about invoking this right. It is always better to remain silent and appear guilty than to open your mouth and prove it.

At the outset of any contact with the police, ask them if they have a warrant to search your premises, or a warrant for your arrest. Without one or the other, don't let them inside your front door. If they have neither, politely request that they leave and gently close the door. (Ed: Or better yet, talk to them through a window or closed door. In New Jersey police

have barged through a cracked door.) If you have an attorney, keep one of his or her cards in your wallet. Give it to the officer in charge and request that all inquiries be made through your counsel. Remember, the police wouldn't be at your doorstep if you were not the target of a criminal investigation. You have no obligation whatsoever to cooperate with people who intend to unlawfully confiscate your property and put you in jail. They can't arrest you for keeping your mouth shut and going about your business.

The police may still persist in trying to question you, or ask your consent to 'take a look around.' Again, if you have an attorney, give the officer in charge one of his cards and request that all inquiries be make through your counsel. Above all, remember that you have the right to break off this conversation. Do so immediately.

In some instances where the police lack a search warrant, they will tell you that it's a simple matter for them to obtain one and they 'just want to save everybody a lot of time.' This is hogwash. Politely tell them to get one, and close the door. If they suggest that it will 'go a lot easier on you' should you give them your consent to search, tell them to call your lawyer, and close the door.

In the event that police do in fact have a warrant either to arrest you or to search your premises, do not offer any resistance. You will have other battles to fight (presumably with the weapons you have hidden) and you want to be alive and kicking when the time comes. You are a member of the militia and we don't want to lose you or your weapon. You also don't want to do anything to endanger your family or deprive them of a home. Don't be foolish and engage the authorities in a fire fight that you have no chance of winning.

On the other hand, you are not obliged to do anything to make the officers' job easier, such as giving them the combination to your gun safe. You have the right to remain silent and should take advantage of it. That may cause the authorities to forcibly open your safe, with resulting damage. But let them work at their task. After all, it's a search warrant.

Politely request to see a copy of any warrants, and above all, remain silent. Anything you say can be used against you in court. Tell the officers that you do not want to say anything or answer any questions – and that you want to talk to an attorney immediately. If you already have a lawyer, request permission to telephone him or her. If you have been taken into custody, the police are obliged to cease and desist from interrogation once you have asserted your right to remain silent and request the assistance of legal counsel.

Your spouse and your children will be natural targets of interrogation for the authorities. Do they know where the firearms are hidden? Although Maryland law generally prohibits your spouse from testifying against you in a criminal trial, that will be of no help if he or she breaks down under questioning and the authorities know where to retrieve your guns. Never forget that your objective is to safeguard your weapons and ammunition for the defense of the Constitution against all enemies, foreign and domestic.

If you or a family member is subpoenaed to testify before a Grand Jury or a judicial or government body, get an attorney immediately. Legal counsel can be very helpful, either in trying to quash the subpoena or helping to invoke one's rights against self-incrimination.

Never, under any circumstances, should you lie to the authorities. Simply exercise your right to remain silent. Don't try to show them phony bills of sale that can easily be checked out and used to impeach your credibility in court should you decide to testify. Above all, don't file a false

police report that your guns were lost or stolen. Making a false report to a police officer that results in an investigation being undertaken is a criminal offense in Maryland. Remember, you are not a criminal. Your ultimate goal is to defend the Constitution.

Likewise, don't fall for any of the authorities' lies. Police love to play 'Mutt & Jeff' (also know as Good Cop/Bad Cop). One officer comes across as a real hardcase, telling you about all the jail time you're looking at. After a few minutes of this, his partner takes you aside, offers you a cigarette, and in a friendly tone tells you that he 'only want to help you.' He only wants to help you confess. Tell Mr. Nice Guy you want to talk to a lawyer. Another police tactic is to tell you that a friend of yours has confessed and given them a statement implicating you for all kinds of things. They're just trying to rattle your cage and make you blurt something out. Keep your mouth shut and let your attorney handle the police. If they really have such a statement, your counsel will be able to discover it.

If the authorities have a warrant to search your home, they might imply (sometimes none too subtly) that if you do not come across with what they're looking for they'll tear the place apart. Don't give in. Just keep your mouth shut. If you hand over your 'prohibited' weapons, you've just given them all the evidence they need to put you in prison. Even if you fall for this scare tactic, the police may still trash your house. Although this is the rare exception, not the rule, such conduct is not unheard of.

In the event you are on the receiving end of a search warrant, do not be pressured into signing any inventories of property seized without first consulting with an attorney. There might be something on that list that is prohibited

according to some obscure regulation that you've never heard of. Also be sure that you or some family member receives an itemized list of any property seized. Under Maryland law the police are obliged to sign one and leave it at the premises from which the property is taken. If it is subsequently determined that the authorities took anything that was not within the scope of their warrant, your attorney should motion the court for its prompt return.

Hopefully, you will never have to avail yourself of the advice set forth above. Remember, the battle to defend our liberties has already begun – and you are one of the Constitution's foot soldiers.

'The spirit of resistance to government is so valuable in certain occasions, that I wish it to be keep alive. It will be often exercised wrong, but better so than not to be exercised at all. I like a little rebellion now and then. It is like a storm in the atmosphere.'

– *Thomas Jefferson*, letter to Abigail Adams, 1787

From Police Against the New World Order, *Operation Vampire Killer 2000* (1992).

AMERICANS WON'T NEED GUNS IN 'UTOPIA'

Police Officers must remember what the renowned H. L. Mencken said,

'To die for an idea; it is unquestionably noble. But how much nobler it would be if men died for ideas that were true.'

Officers are told the reason the guns have to be removed from the American People is to stop crime and the killing of the innocent. This is a fabrication. Truthfully, the only reason the guns must be removed is to stop any chance of our countrymen raising up and throwing off the 'wonderful' programs that their 'philanthropic' government leaders have planned for them.

It is time to seriously consider what each of us will do when these Global elitists in our government instruct OFFICERS and NATIONAL GUARDSMEN to go forth and take the guns away from the armed, good people of your city or town . . . 'FOR THEIR OWN GOOD'. Most Officers know the day will come when they will have to make that very hard decision on this gun removal issue. The **evidence** is all around us that this day is near.

Consider the Imperialist NWO position. For the World Elite to truly enjoy their 'utopian' Socialist Society, the subject masses must not have a means to protect themselves against **more** 'voluntary compliance'. When one grasps this logical position, there is no longer any question about it: THE GUNS WILL HAVE TO GO.

If there are any Officers who still doubt this, we are about to prove this planned scenario to you. Keep in mind that the second part of the three-part plan of the NWO Regional Government program (which precedes the One World Government) is that Canada, USA, Mexico and South and Central America are to be combined into one Region. Hence, the North American Free Trade Agreement (NAFTA) is on a FAST-TRACK with the backing of our notorious NWO President, NWO Congressmen, Senators and Governors. The other 2 parts presently in the works are: First part – the uniting of the European Nations (Common Market), and # 3 – the uniting of the Asian nations. These make up the 'TRI' [3] parts of the Tri-lateral One World Government . . .

Realizing that the plan is to merge us Americans, Latin Americans, and Canadians, into , one Region, you already know whose gun policies we are to adopt. (Mexico has the same very limited gun rights as Canada and Australia.)

DON'T WORRY. BE HAPPY, OFFICER!

Officers should not worry. There is a 'good' plan to get the guns away from your fellow Americans. Should Officers be concerned – just because **this 'good' plan** calls for **them** to go get 200,000,000 firearms (BATF figures are very low) away from 250,000,000 very 'peaceful and cooperative' citizens? **What do you think?**

SOME 'AN EASY MARK'

Some guns will be easily removed. Many unsuspecting (and very naive) Americans will turn in their 'liberty teeth' (means of personal protection) when told to do so. Every officer knows such people in the community, i.e. those 'good' citizens who are too scared to oppose **anything** their government tells them to do.

Yes, even if they know it's wrong, they will go along or just keep their mouths shut. Every captive nation has a large percentage of such people. These are the 'production units' (PU's) that will fit very well into the New World Order. They are ready-made slaves.

As strange as it may seem, many of these 'sheep' still believe that they can trust and believe in our government to **SAVE THEM** from anarchy. This is amusing to some of our government officials and Police Officers. It amazes them that these people are so unaware of what is happening and continue trusting the same government that has **planned** and **promoted** the anarchy in the streets in the first place – precisely to scare them into submission. (See Aid & Abet, Police Newsletter 2-2.)

L.A. RIOTS – AN ORCHESTRATION

A prime example was the recent L.A. riots. The beating of King was not part of the plan, but it offered a grand opportunity to accomplish three important things for the Globalists.

1) Get rid of Chief Gates, who for years had stood in the way of Socialist-NWO gang member, Tom Bradley and others involved in trying to get the L.A. Police Dept. into the coming national police force. (See soon to be released book, THE CENTRALIZATION OF U.S. POLICE POWERS, available from U.S. Federal Law Research Center, P.O. Box 8712, Phx. A.Z. 85066.)

2) Further convince the People that their only salvation from crime and evil in society will be found in the 'protection' provided by a global government.

3) A grand opportunity for Globalists George, Pete and Tom to practice FEMA-style Martial Law. It matters little that some among the masses have to die. Remember, the new government philosophy is the same as that of the Communist, **'THE END DOES INDEED JUSTIFY THE MEANS.'**

Once again, the masses were to think that **everything** was out of control. It was not (the riots were planned). But it **was** a good enough reason that in a matter of hours, 2,000 U.S. Marines were on the streets of an American city. This was a very important test. A most severe breach of Constitutional law was brought to bear; and more importantly, **the People said nothing**. The masses complained only that the government should have acted sooner and in greater strength. For, when there is anarchy in the streets the 'sheep' do not care who saves them. This planned Martial Law scenario actually worked out better than the NWO social planners ever expected. . . .

Officers should keep in mind that some of the guns are not going to be easily removed. For the guns are not going to be easily removed. For instance, those owned by true patriots – those freedom-loving Americans who know, without a doubt, what's coming next **if** they give up their guns. It should not be a surprise to Police Officers that many good Americans will not walk meekly into NEW WORLD ORDER slavery. And there are few Officers who would want it any other way.

So the question each Officer individually must face is a very difficult but realistic one: 'Which way will your own gun face when the orders are issued?' Will you protect the people you have sworn to protect? Or, will you do what other patriotic officers from other countries have done to their countrymen, **'obediently just follow orders'?**

PATRIOTIC AMERICANS WILL FIGHT TO THE DEATH

Police officers would do well not to see the above title as only part of the script out of an old John Wayne movie.

We should consider, with utmost seriousness, that if good Americans (including internal protectors) allow this plan of the Globalists to get this far, it can be expected that casualties among Police Officers, National guardsmen, and armed 'criminal' patriotic citizens **will be very high** before the gun removal process can be successfully completed. (If indeed **can** be completed.) But, with Police Officers and Guardsmen serving as the 'cannon fodder' to enforce the Globalist plan, these deaths will be merely 'acceptable losses' to those giving the orders and looking down from their **safe** and **secure** Ivory Towers.

It is therefore entirely relevant that our brothers and sisters decide very soon which side they will serve in the setting up of this 'Utopian' Global Society. They must not be fooled by government officials that tell them that all men and women with American blood running through their veins will walk gently into lifelong servitude.

It cannot be contradicted that a great many out there on the other end of those half-billion 'Liberty Teeth' (guns) still underscore the statement of J.J. Rousseau:

> **'I prefer liberty with danger to peace with slavery.'**

INTELLIGENT Americans read and study history. On the other hand, the vast majority of government 'leaders', 'educators' and media persons apparently don't! Concerning the 2nd Amendment, for example, they try to tell us that the Founding Fathers meant for only the Organized Militia (National Guard) to have weapons. Please read the quotes given below and decide: Could these countrymen have spoken any more plainly?

> **'NO FREE MAN SHALL EVER BE DE-BARRED THE USE OF ARMS. THE STRONGEST REASON FOR THE PEOPLE TO RETAIN THEIR RIGHT TO KEEP AND BEAR ARMS IS AS A LAST RESORT TO PROTECT THEMSELVES AGAINST TYRANNY IN GOVERNMENT.' – THOMAS JEFFERSON**

> **'THE SAID CONSTITUTION SHALL NEVER BE CONSTRUED TO AUTHORIZE CONGRESS TO PREVENT THE PEOPLE OF THE UNITED STATES WHO ARE PEACEABLE CITIZENS FROM KEEPING THEIR OWN**

ARMS.' – SAM ADAMS

'THE GREAT OBJECT IS THAT EVERY MAN BE ARMED. EVERYONE WHO IS ABLE MAY HAVE A GUN.' – PATRICK HENRY

'AMERICANS NEED NEVER FEAR THEIR GOVERNMENT BECAUSE OF THE ADVANTAGE OF BEING ARMED, WHICH THE AMERICANS POSSESS OVER THE PEOPLE OF ALMOST EVERY OTHER NATION.' – JAMES MADISON

Well now, those statements are really ambiguous aren't they?! Don't you wish our Founders would have stated clearly what was on their minds?

Why are our school children lied to by Establishment educators about this? You know the answer, don't you? Good NWO slaves will not need guns. And that is exactly what our children will have to look forward to if American Police Officers and National Guardsmen don't say 'NO' TO THE NEW WORLD ORDER.

POLICING THE MILITIA MOVEMENT:
IS 'BIG BROTHER' WATCHING?

The militia movement's concerns over the apparent militarization of American law enforcement and their fears of 'infiltration', 'informers' and 'government surveillance' are presented here. For Bill Bingham, in an article from the April 1997 issue of *Necessary Force*, events such as the death of 'tax protester' Gordan Kahl in 1983 and the 'sieges' of Ruby Ridge and Waco point to a deliberate campaign of 'state sponsored terrorism' on the part of law enforcement agencies against 'dissenters'. Writing in *The Resister,* Steven Barry next reports on the FBI's attempts to place an informant in the Special Forces Underground. For Barry, this is indicative of the 'KGB-style' tactics which have been applied to policing in America in recent years. An article from the *New Jersey Militia Newsletter* follows, as Carl Alexander provides an account of the arrest and imprisonment of John Pitner (founder of the now defunct Washington State Militia) in which an FBI informant is said to have played a key role. The section concludes with an essay by James Barber in which he objects to the Clinton Administration's attempt to use the 'phony militia threat' to enact new anti-terrorist legislation. Such legislation, Barber argues, will precipitate the destruction of the Bill of Rights and bring about 'The End of Constitutional America'.

Bill Bingham, 'What would you call it?' First published by the Missouri 51st Militia, *Necessary Force* (April 1997).

Necessary Force

In 1983, Gordon Kahl, a tax protester from Medina, North Dakota, was ambushed by federal marshals outside of town. Kahl fled to Arkansas, where he was finally cornered. He burned to death in a house into which federal agents had injected chemicals. John Duncan, an attorney and author, claims that Gordon Kahl was summarily executed by the agents.

On Oct. 2, 1992, a multi-level law enforcement group raided Donald P. Scott's ranch in Ventura County, California, searching for drugs. They kicked in the door and killed Scott when he appeared with a weapon in his hand. Oops! No drugs were found.

On August 25, 1992, again in California, Donald Carlson's door was kicked in by Drug Enforcement Administration (DEA) agents just after midnight. Carlson dialed 911 and then reached for his gun. He was riddled by DEA bullets. He managed to survive after spending seven months in intensive care. Oops, again! No drugs were found.

In the summer of 1996, the home of Terry Taylor of Fort Davis, Texas, was raided by U.S. Fish and Wildlife officers. Terry is an entomologist who imports and exports dead insects to universities, scientists and collectors. While Terry and his wife were attending a funeral, their house was raided and cleaned out by the officers. The Taylors were forced to go to court to get their own property back, and that cost them dearly. As of this writing, no charges have been filed against them.

In 1994, Red Beckman and his family had an IRS lien filed against them. They were thrown off their property, and their house was bulldozed. Reportedly, their land was seized. It is not known if the IRS lien was valid.

Again in 1994, the home of Monique Montgomery of Missouri was raided by agents of the Bureau of Alcohol, Tobacco and Firearms at 4:00 a.m. When she reached for a gun, she died with four bullets in her body. Nothing illegal was found.

At Ruby Ridge, Idaho, in August, 1992, Randy Weaver's 14-year-old son, his wife, Vicki, and his dog were all killed by federal marshals and agents of the Federal Bureau of Investigation. One federal marshal was killed. Although Randy Weaver and his friend, Kevin Harris, were acquitted of murder, no one was ever tried for the murder of Weaver's wife and son. Five U.S. marshals were given commendations for their conduct at Ruby Ridge.

And then, of course, there was Waco, Texas, where the Branch Davidians were under siege by BATF and FBI agents from Feb. 28, 1993 until the holocaust which occurred on April 19, 1993. Eighty-some people died because a tax of $200 might not have been paid on an

automatic weapon which may or may not have existed.

And then there was the World Trade Center bombing in New York City, and the bombing of the Murrah Federal Building in Oklahoma City in 1995. In the case of the World Trade Center, trial testimony was given that the FBI was aware of the plot to bomb the building. There appears to be some indication that federal agencies were aware in advance of the Oklahoma City bombing as well. But the bombs went off anyway, and hundreds died.

The result of the Oklahoma City bombing was that our 'coward-in-chief' got his un-Constitutional antiterrorism bill passed by Congress. Congress has been busy passing un-Constitutional laws, while the Senate has been quite consistent in ratifying treaties and other international agreements which in many cases violate our Constitutional rights.

The Department of Interior is grabbing land via the Bureau of Land Management, the Parks Department and the Environmental Protection Agency. At the same time, the government has been 'federalizing' the various police agencies of the states, counties and cities.

Now I don't know what you would call all of this governmental activity, but I would call it a very well-planned operation. I would also call it **STATE-SPONSORED TERRORISM!**[1]

Government is like fire: a dangerous servant and a fearful master.

– Attributed to George Washington

Note

1. Many of the incidents in Bingham's article are discussed in James Bovard's *Lost Rights:The Destruction of American Liberty* (New York, St. Martin's Griffin, 1995) and David Kopel and Paul Blackman's *No More Wacos: What's Wrong With Federal Law Enforcement and How to Fix it* (Amherst, Prometheus Books, 1997).

Steven Michael Barry, 'Ministerstvo Gosudarstvennoe Bezospasnosti'. First published in *The Resister* (Vol. IV, No. 2, 1997).

MINISTERSTVO GOSUDARSTVENNOE BEZOSPASNOSTI

Since the 'fall' of the Soviet Union, the FBI has been sending personnel to the MGB and KGB as 'liaison' officers to 'share crime fighting' techniques. The MGB has a motto: 'Give us the man. We'll find the crime.' Apparently, the FBI thinks that's a pretty spiffy motto. You can almost imagine 'comfortably merged' FBI agents returning to America and saying to themselves, 'No reason that can't work here!' Apparent also is that our 'comfortably merged' FBI learned a few techniques from their Communist buddies about harassing and intimidating American anti-Communist dissidents. And so the Tetrick saga continues to unfold; this time on *The Resister.*

Early on the morning of 24 February 1998, Special Agents William P. Flynn and William Bradbury, Jr., from the Jacksonville, North Carolina, FBI office (910-577-0334), paid a visit to former Sergeant First Class Bruce Nelson (late of 7th SFG(A)), who is a distributor for *The Resister.*

Without going into the specifics of agents Flynn and Bradbury's *stated* reason for visiting Mr. Nelson, they told Mr. Nelson that it would be 'beneficial' for him to become an informant within *The Resister* and Special Forces Underground. The specific information they said they were after was the 'cell structure' of SFU, and how far throughout the military it spreads. Mr. Nelson declined the FBI's generous offer and told agents Flynn and Bradbury that if they have any questions about *The Resister* or SFU they should simply 'go to Barry's house and knock on the door.' They said, 'We can't do that'; then politely informed Mr. Nelson that they would call first if they were going to arrest him.

By the way; 'We can't do that,' means: 'No crime has been committed – unless you help us manufacture one.' In other words, 'Give us the man. We'll find the crime.'

My guess is that they're fishing for a 'conspiracy' indictment. That's such a broad charge that anybody 'snared in the net' is then a potential informer who can help spread the 'conspiracy' wider and thus expand the scope and reach of the link-diagram. Note that fully one-third of East Germans were *Stasi* informants. Please also note that advocating a restoration of limited constitutional republican government is now an 'anti-government conspiracy.' Just like their MGB mentors, the FBI now believes its own propaganda.

After Action Review

The infamous 'They' always try to come first thing in the morning. What they'll do is place surveillance on your home in order to determine what time you get up. When they come-a-calling they'll try to time their visit for *just before* you normally wake up. That way, when they cringe behind their badge, they catch you groggy and not thinking clearly. It can be pretty intimidating if you're not used to it. Not that that technique is uniquely Soviet. All internal security *apparatchik* basically think alike.

The reason they say things like 'if we arrest you' is to keep your anxiety level running out of control. The first time it happens to you the *only* thing you can think about is the possibility of being arrested. You get a persistent sick feeling in the pit of your stomach that nags on you until you get to the point where you either call them back and agree to be a snitch, or sit around making yourself more sick wondering if you're going to be arrested. And if they do arrest you, by then you're

such an emotional wreck, that turning snitch – which is all they really want in the first place, I mean, link diagrams would be mighty sparse indeed without informants – is a weight suddenly lifted from your shoulders. You *feel* good about it! Which is why they 'sweat' you. They *need* you to feel good about ratting on your friends. That emotional breaking point is what I refer to as 'getting religion.' Right, S.A. Flynn, S.A. Bradbury?

So, what's a citizen to do? First, NEVER invite 'them' (or allow them to invite themselves) into your home. 'I have nothing to hide' is not an excuse for being stupid. Second, ask only two questions: 'Am I under arrest?' If the answer is 'no,' then the second question is, 'Then, I'm free to leave?' followed by – without waiting for the answer or looking over your shoulder – leaving (or, if 'they' are on your doorstep, no second question is required; just shut the door in their face). From that point forward, the operative principle is KYMS. (Keep Your Mouth Shut.)

Counsel has sent agents Flynn and Bradbury a letter stating that if they have any questions about *The Resister* or Special Forces Underground all they need do is ask. Which is what honorable *men* would have done in the first place. But, with a 'female' as Attorney General of the United States, and a weasel as FBI director, what can you expect from their agents?

Welcome to the Union of Soviet Socialist America.

Carl Alexander, 'In the Belly of the Beast'. First published in the *New Jersey Militia Newsletter* (Vol.3, No. 10, April 1998).

IN THE BELLY OF THE BEAST

Trying to sell your house is dangerous business these days. Ask John Pitner, the founder of the Washington State Militia – he listed his family home in Deming, WA for sale, back in the summer of 1996. After showing the home to some prospective buyers, six days later he wound up being arrested and jailed. The 'buyers' turned out to be FBI agents, casing the premises – without a warrant

Pitner remains in federal custody to this day, held at the new SEATAC Federal Detention Center in Seattle, WA, but he's not serving out a prison sentence. Though convicted of a federal firearms violation in March 1997, on the sole testimony of a paid undercover informant he has never been sentenced for that, or any other crime.

In the words of a smiling FBI agent, on the day of Pitner's arrest, 'Well, Mr. Pitner . . . it looks like we don't have anything on you but we're going to keep you in jail for a couple of years anyway.' In five more months, that general threat will have become an absolute reality.

Pitner's nightmare began on July 27, 1996, when he was arrested for conspiracy to construct explosive devices, and possession of illegal firearms. Eleven other persons, including three more members of the Bellingham militia unit, as well as several members of a Freeman group from Tacoma, were also arrested and charged in the case.

Pitner, who had resigned his position as WSM Director in May, 1996, having suffered a stroke three months earlier, adamantly maintains he is innocent of all charges. There is substantial reason to believe he is telling the truth.

The government's star witness against Pitner was a paid undercover informant named Ed Mauerer. Mauerer, a convicted felon, volunteered to infiltrate the militia group for the FBI. The FBI arranged for Mauerer's release from his cell in the Whatcom County Jail where he was serving time for writing bad checks to cover numerous unpaid debts, and began paying him over $2,000 per month to infiltrate and spy on WSM activities.

Over the next year, Mauerer provided his FBI handlers with a variety of information concerning the militia and Freeman groups – that they were stockpiling dynamite, hand grenades and automatic weapons (purportedly stored in Pitner's garage), training to kill FBI agents, planning to assassinate David Rockefeller when he came to visit Olympic National Park, and that they had possession of night-vision devices stolen from nearby Ft. Lewis, WA. As a result of these reports, the FBI initiated a full field investigation of the WSM and inserted an undercover FBI agent into the Tacoma Freeman group.

At that juncture, evidently to ensure the safety of their undercover operative, the FBI decided to administer a polygraph examination to Mauerer, primarily to find out whether he had told anyone of his role in the on-going operation – but he was also asked to corroborate his earlier reports concerning WSM activities.

Mauerer could not pass the lie-detector test. On three separate occasions, he failed, and it was not until he had admitted to lying about his earlier reports – and more specifically, about John Pitner's involvement in any illegal activities – that he was able to pass a subsequent test. Despite this, the FBI proceeded with their investigation and placed their undercover agent in position. Pitner's arrest, and those of the others, were the eventual result.

During the subsequent trial. Federal Judge John C. Coughenour suppressed the information concerning Mauerer's failure to pass those polygraph examinations, and the defense was not allowed to present that evidence to the jury. Mauerer then took the stand for the prosecution, and testified under oath repeating the same charges against Pitner that he could not sustain under polygraph examination.

The jury ultimately deadlocked on the conspiracy charges against the defendants – but Pitner was convicted on a single charge of possessing and transferring an illegal weapon, solely on the testimony of informant Mauerer, who had 'brokered' the sale. The WSM member who actually owned the weapon (a Korean-war vintage UZI machine-gun brought home from that war by his father) later pleaded guilty to the sale and submitted a sworn affidavit to the court that Pitner was not in any way involved. Judge Coughenour accepted his guilty plea, sentenced him for the crime, and dismissed the affidavit on Pitner's behalf as inappropriate.

Since that time, John Pitner has remained incarcerated while the government decides whether to seek a re-trial on conspiracy charges against him and the other defendants. Under the rules for prisoners who are held at FDC SEATAC without formal sentence, he is not allowed any visitors except for immediate family, and is only entitled to medical treatment for serious emergencies. He cannot access the prison law library to assist in his appeal.

As Samuel Johnson, the noted English author, once observed. 'The power of punishment is to silence, not to refute.' Like so many others who have raised their voices against the encroachment of Tyranny, John Pitner is a modern-day example of the aptness of that quote.

Cards and letters of encouragement can be sent to: John Pitner, 426151-086/4BO9, c/o FDC SEATAC, P.O. Box 68976, Seattle, WA 98168.[1]

Note

1. An account of the activities of John Pitner and the Washington State Militia can be found in David Neiwert's *In God's Country: The Patriot Movement in the Pacific Northwest* (Pullman, Washington State University Press, 1999). Pitner is currently incarcerated in the King County Detention Center in Kent, Washington, following his conviction for various weapons offences. He is attempting to block his retrial on any of the conspiracy charges he faced. After two years his case remains backlogged in the Court of Appeal. (Correspondence between editor and Neiwert).

James S. Barber, the Ohio Unorganized Militia, 'The End of Constitutional Militia' (April, 1996).

THE END OF CONSTITUTIONAL AMERICA

The latest act of alleged 'Domestic Terrorism,' a suspiciously convenient pipe bomb attack at the International Olympics in Atlanta, is even more ominous and terrifying than the death and injury it produced.

For weeks prior to the start of the '96 Olympics, rumors of terrorist attacks at this prestigious international event were rampant in the media. So much of this wishful thinking was displayed by federal law enforcement agents and operatives, they found it necessary to plant pipe bombs they themselves helped construct, on some uncooperative Georgia Militia member's property, a few weeks before the games were to begin. Subsequently, CBS NEWS proceeded to erroneously trumpet an alleged conspiracy to pipe bomb the Olympics by the Georgia militiamen caught in this now infamous ATF sting.[1]

Moreover, media and the Clintonistas in the Congress used this 'Militia threat' to produce the usual hysterics that they were so fond of after Oklahoma City and even after the TWA flight, so curiously unresolved regarding its cause, to date. Militia madness it seems, is the *cause célèbre* for all manner of conspiracy theories by administration propagandists, to overthrow the government and to whip up public hysteria regarding 'Terrorism.'

The Clinton administration predictably responded to this phony militia threat, by dispatching close to thirty thousand, federal state and local, anti-terrorist paramilitary and active duty military troops to safeguard the Olympics.

Imagine our surprise, when a pipe bomb attack did indeed occur barely a week into this international event, killing one woman and wounding over one hundred innocent victims. Ironically, imagine their (Clinton, Schumer's, et.al.) surprise, when they could not blame the militia terrorists they have created in their own minds for the deed. The prime suspect is an AT&T security guard and five year sheriff's deputy veteran hired for

418

Olympic security. Some have gone so far as to rumor the bombing an 'inside job conspiracy' by the feds themselves. Allegedly, a number of the extensive military security forces involved were told to expect a terrorist attack during the Olympic festivities. One wonders if they were surprised?[2]

Can this bombing be just one more example of the extreme lengths proponents of the 'Global Community' will perpetrate in order to destroy the Constitution of the United States? Is this one of the methods to transform America into the socialist democracy that can be harmonized with the other interdependent serfdoms of the 'New World Economic Order?'

The pattern seems quite predictable. No sooner were the victims hospitalized, than Clinton and his bunch of congressional toadies were calling for more sweeping anti-terrorist legislation to further empower federal law enforcement and the attendant destruction of the Bill of Rights.

As with the vaunted 'War on Drugs,' a war that has used all manner of deceit, corruption and death to erode our treasured unalienable rights, so too has the new horseman of the apocalypse, terrorism, been fully exploited by the Clinton, Bush and congressional conspirators, to destroy the Bill of Rights and by default, the entire Constitution. Only then can a new form of globalist monarchy be imposed upon us and reduce once proud Americans to the status of serfs in a country devoid of liberties, national heritage and pride.

As early as 1974, Richard N. Gardiner, currently Clinton's Ambassador to Spain, professed in *Foreign Affairs*, the Council on Foreign Relation's publication of world domination thusly,

'As in the case of the U.S. Constitution, we are more likely to make progress by pressing the existing instrument to the outer limits of its potentialities through creative use . . . [T]he house of World Order will have to be built from the bottom up rather than the top down . . . an end run around sovereignty, eroding it piece by piece, will accomplish much more than the old-fashioned frontal assault.'

'Creative use' in this context is analogous to the undermining of the very document that distinguishes America from socialist democracies that resulted from monarchs relinquishing some, but not all of their power and influence over their subjects, as exists today in Europe and other parts of the world.

In order to 'harmonize' the United States with the other components of the global community, this Constitutional, Republican form of government must be remade in the image of other socialist democracies. Since the Founding Fathers were adamant in preventing this degradation of a form of government that stood head and shoulders above the European monarchies, our Constitution contained many safeguards in order to prevent what unfortunately is being perpetrated on America today. It remains the major stumbling block of those that would return America to a colonial possession of our masters. When these monarchs of the New World Order reach the 'outer limits of its potentialities, by creative use,' the United States Constitution will be, and make no mistake, invalidated, by force if necessary, and replaced with a more compliant form of government that suits the needs of the global community of nations. The Constitution, and America as we knew her, will cease to exist.

I need not detail the numerous affronts committed against the Constitution and the millions of Americans that realize the consequences of the slippery slope we have began to descend.

In the event that those who mistakenly rely on the upcoming elections to save our republic from this fate, consider the recent article that appeared in 'Foreign Affairs' magazine by conservative republican talking heads, William Kristol and Robert Kagan. 'Toward a neo-Reaganite Foreign Policy' describes a 'benevolent global hegemony,' where the U.S. president ascends to the throne of president of the world. In Kristol and Kagan's opinion, having won the cold war, America deserves to run the world. An idea that both Clinton and Dole must be convinced its time has come [sic]. Throw in for good measure, Gingrich and the rest of our esteemed global congressional proponents, and voila, instant New World Order.

Now it is becoming tougher to tell who, Republicans or Democrats, aspire to this global monarchy. However, the major problem they have encountered is how to square this leap to a brave new world with the Constitution of the United States. The truth is it won't square, and since Richard Gardiner's blatant proclamation in the 1974 Foreign Affairs article, i.e. 'pressing the existing instrument to its outer limits' has been more or less accomplished, the next phase is an obvious invalidation of 'the instrument.'

There exists now over 900,000 reserve and national guard personnel and another few hundred thousand federal, state and local paramilitary trained and equipped law enforcement agents in the United States. With the complicity of our congressional friends, that have lavishly funded these organizations through defense authorizations, and we now have the 'internal security forces' necessary to crush any domestic objections to becoming citizen serfs in the 'New World Order.' Hitler accomplished the 'SS' controlled, Reserve Police Battalions that terrorized Germans in more or less the same way. Nationalizing the civilian police forces through legislation like the 1933 Nazi 'Law to relieve the distress of the people and the Reich' and Clinton's Crime Bill and Anti-Terrorist Act(s), in this Congress, accomplishes the goal of the formation of the 'Directorate of

National Police Forces.'

Rather than the proclamations about protecting the public from crime and/or terrorism by executive branch spokesmen, it is rather obvious that such paramilitary forces like 'Hostage Rescue Teams' and other components of the national police forces, exist to protect our 'protectors' in government and no one else.

People like Pat Buchanan and other adherents of strict constructionalist interpretations of the U.S. Constitution are labelled 'extremists' in their own nation. The apologists and proponents of a 'living document,' regarding the Constitution, would in the past, have been pilloried as traitorous collaborators with a foreign power. Not so today, as now treason is regarded as enlightened interpretation of a rather archaic and outmoded document and form of government, Constitutional Republicanism.

The lines of confrontation are clearly drawn. The rules of engagement are being established. History will record the final outcome of the battle for the fate of the world, either as a global plantation or freedom and liberty, which was the goal of the Founding Fathers.

Notes

1. Twelve members (ten men and two women) of the Arizona based Viper Militia were arrested on July 1 1996. Following their arrest President Clinton congratulated the law enforcement agencies for having averted 'a terrible terrorist attack' on government buildings in Phoenix. However, none of the twelve were subsequently charged with conspiracy to destroy government buildings. Instead they were charged with a number of lesser, although still serious, conspiracy, weapons and explosive offences including 'conspiracy to unlawfully manufacture, receive, and possess destructive devices made with ammonium nitrate' and 'conspiracy to furnish instructions in the use of explosive devices and other techniques in the furtherance of civil disorder.' On these lesser offences all but one of the Militia members were convicted, but a feeling remained in some quarters that the government had overstated the extent of the threat posed by them. Indeed, prior to their trial District Court Judge Earl Carroll released six of the defendants on bail because he did not think they posed a threat to their communities. There were also allegations that an undercover BATF Agent and a paid informant had penetrated the Viper Militia, and that they had tried to encourage its members to engage in criminal activities. See, for example, the *Associated Press Wire Service Report*, 'Viper Militia: What Exactly is the Government's Case?' (July 23, 1996).

2. On the bombing of the Atlanta Olympics see, for example, 'Terror at the Olympics,' *U.S.News and World Report* (August 5, 1996), 24–27. The anti-abortion activist Eric Rudolph was subsequently charged with the bombing.

CONSPIRACIES AND THE
NEW WORLD ORDER

This selection of photographs, flyers, pamphlets and articles illustrate the range of fears about the New World Order which exist within the militia movement: fears of 'unmarked black helicopters' and 'foreign troops training in the United States', fears of 'Big Brother police' and the building of detention camps to house 'Radical Christians and Kooky Patriots' and behind these, fears of the Illuminati, Freemasonry, the Bildeburgers, the 'World Money Powers', and the United Nations. Taken from a variety of militia publications including *The Kentucky Rifleman News*, *The Freedom Networker*, the Militia of Montana's manual *Enemies: Domestic and Foreign*, and the Police Against the New World Order's *Operation Vampire Killer 2000*, these documents also provide an opportunity to assess the 'evidence' on which the militias' fears are based.

From the *Kentucky Riflemen News,* 'Will Americans Allow The Imposition Of A National Police State As Part Of The U.N. New World Order?' (Vol. 1, No. 1, 1995).

A NATIONAL POLICE STATE AS PART OF THE U.N. NEW WORLD ORDER?

Has the New World Order already been established while Americans slept? Is it already directing the Clinton Administration and much of the United States government?

Have we already become an occupied nation?

Thousands of sightings of unmarked black helicopters have been documented across the nation. Whose are they? What does their presence mean?

Why are thousands of foreign troops training in the United States?

Why are U.S. troops being sent to serve in United Nations operations around the world?

Why are Americans being conditioned to serve in a U.N. army under foreign commanders?

Why are thousands of Soviet trucks, tanks, chemical warfare vehicles, and armored personnel carriers being shipped into the U.S.?

Why are closed American military bases being converted to U.N. bases here in the U.S.?

Why are numerous civilian detention centers being established in the U.S.?

Why do the media and certain government agencies try to create the idea that patriots, Christians, home schoolers, pro-life groups, petitioners for prayer in school, gun owners and Second Amendment organizations, constitutionalists and states rights advocates, opponents of the New World Order, and similar groups – are 'extremists,' 'cultists,' 'radicals' and a threat to 'peace and security'?

Is the outlawing of 'assault rifles' and other significant weapons, and the intended disarming of the American people, a necessary step – so that Americans cannot oppose our merger into the New World Order?

Why is the U.S. military being trained for police enforcement and civilian control, in direct violation of the Constitution and U.S. law?

Why is illegal and unconstitutional search and seizure being made 'lawful' by the Congress and the courts?

Why are local law enforcement personnel being 'federalized'?

Why are SWAT teams needed by the Post Office, Park Service, Forest Service, Fish and Game Commission, and nearly every state and federal agency?

What is the MJTF (Multi-Jurisdictional Task Force)? Is it to control and enslave the American people?

Are these things real or only paranoid delusions of the Patriotic Right?

Are Americans willing to consider the facts and accept the truth?

Why, for 50 years, have all our presidents, whether Democrat or Republican, worked to strengthen the United Nations Organization and numerous international agencies while weakening our national sovereignty and giving away our national resources?

What will the New World Order mean to citizens of the United States?

Are Americans simply too stupid, lazy and pre-occupied with nonsense to observe important events and recognize their ominous danger?

Are the American people too brainwashed by the controlled media to even care?

Will the uninformed and unconcerned care when they are done away with as part of the program Global 2000 (the U.S. approved NWO program to reduce the world population from nearly 6 billion people to only 2 billion)?

Do the liberals and the wimps realize that they will be liquidated just like the patriots, only more easily?

When millions of Americans are taken away to be gassed or have a bullet put in the back of their heads, will they still believe that all of the information and warnings provided by constitutional, Christian, patriotic organizations such as APRA were only the imagination of those dedicated Americans who for decades had been fighting for the freedom and independence of the United States and the liberties of American people?

> *'And they did not understand until the flood came and swept them away.'*
>
> **(Matthew 24:39)**

Time is running out!

From Police Against the New World Order, *Operation Vampire Killer 2000* **(1992).**

THE NEW AGE/NEW WORLD GOVERNMENT PLAN

Many of our nation's INTERNAL PROTECTORS know of the well-laid plan which will culminate before the year 2000, to usher the United States, along with the rest of the nations of the world, into a 'utopian' global community allegedly under the control of a 'philanthropic' United Nations. A great many of our fellow Officers and National Guardsmen are taking a stand against this plan because they realize that their fellow Americans were never allowed to know of this plan nor given the opportunity to vote on such a change in their government. In addition, the officers are concerned patriots and realize that this plan of world domination is injurious in the extreme, and a total fraud perpetrated against the people of the world!

This publication outlines **the plan** of these American Internal Protectors which they believe will stop this diabolical agenda.

THE NEW ORDER

Allegedly this new order is being set up to save **THE PEOPLE OF THE WORLD** from a whole variety of 'imminent' life and world-threatening disasters. Of those sworn protectors of the people that are aware of this global scheme, few realize that the actual behind-the-scenes plan is for an oligarchy of the world's richest families to place 1/2 the masses of the earth in servitude under their complete control, administered from behind the false front of the United Nations. To facilitate management capabilities, the plan calls for the elimination of the other 2.5 billion people through war, disease, abortion and famine by the year 2000. As we can plainly see, their plan for 'Population Control' (reduction) is well established and under way.

Our OPERATION VAMPIRE KILLER 2000 plan involves the awakening (education) of our fellow officers to the extreme need for them to take an immediate and active roll in assisting their fellow Americans in stopping this plan for world dominion, using every lawful means available. . . .

It is felt that this name [Operation Vampire Killer 2000] reflects the actual program in which officers are involved, designed to stop or 'kill off' the ongoing, elitist, covert operation which has been installed in the American system with great stealth and cunning. They, the Globalists, have stated that the date of termination of the American way of life is the year 2000. Therefore it is fitting that our date to terminate, at the very least; their **plan**, is also the year 2000.

LET IT BE WELL UNDERSTOOD, WE PROTECTORS OF THE AMERICAN PEOPLE HAVE NOT ASKED FOR THIS BATTLE. IT IS OUR NATION'S ENEMIES WHO HAVE BROUGHT THIS FIGHT TO THE VERY DOOR OF EVERY GOOD AMERICAN.

BE IT RESOLVED:

• Our **prayer** and **promise** is to do all within our power, as faithful countrymen, to overthrow this evil, treasonous plan in a completely non-violent, lawful manner.
• Our sworn **duty** is to protect the people of this nation and its constitutional, republican form of government from any enemy that would come against it.

• Our **pledge** is that WE **WILL**, BY EVERY MEANS GIVEN UNTO US, UPHOLD OUR OATHS AND FULFIL OUR SWORN DUTY TO OUR COUNTRYMEN.

PUTTING THE STAKE THROUGH DRACULA'S HEART

WHAT CAN WE DO, WHAT SHOULD WE DO? The Globalists' agenda is a diabolical program which, through **patient gradualism**, is slowly draining the moral, economic and political **life blood** from the United States and the hard working American people.

We in America, Officers and private citizens alike, are fortunate that at this moment in our history we can still LAWFULLY **EXTERMINATE** these parasitic Global Blood Suckers by placing numerous 'STAKES' made of **words, paper, pen, and hard work** through their hardened hearts.

*

TRAITORS' GRAND FINALES (Martial Law the Goal)

PLAN A

RACE WARS: We will see the fanning of the flames of their planned

RACE WAR program in the months ahead as government, through some of their covert national organizations, promotes 'whites hating people of color' and vice-versa. Aided by their controlled media, and NWO government-paid agitators/'leaders' on both sides, the goal is to frighten Americans, of all colors, into accepting Martial Law.

These elitists actually have no love for 'minorities' or 'commoners' of any race. Those who have studied these Imperialists will notice that there is continual intermarriage among these super-rich Internationalists' families. NEVER do they participate in the mixing of blood other than BLUE BLOOD.

The race-mixing program was created for their 'subjects' – i.e. the world's common people of all races. Some of these Internationalists have stated over the years, '. . . when all other humans are of one color, (brown), then they will be more easily managed.'

KEEP THE RACES FROM JOINING TOGETHER!

Racial strife is one of their most important NWO tools and they mean to keep it going. It has worked well for promoting the globalist cause in the recent past. **HATE** must be kept flowing to prevent the various races in America from finding out the truth. If they find out who is destroying their freedoms and economic future, they might find some way to work **together** to overthrow their **COMMON ENEMY**.

WHO ARE THE AGENT-PROVOCATEURS?

Our problem is in **identifying** these NWO lackeys (agent/provocateurs). Incoming intelligence over the years has informed us that these provocateurs are of all racial mixes. Yes, whites, blacks, hispanic etc. are involved in promoting planned racial hate incidents and tensions to assist in causing the masses to accept Martial Law and serve the NWO gang. Although these employee/provocateurs have been promised a position of power in this 'utopian' Socialist society, it is a shame that they are not smart enough to  know that they are to be 'eliminated' when their usefulness has run out. (As has been the practice of every Marxist/Socialist conquering army after taking power.)

There is sound logic in this 'execution of your agent/provocateurs,' after you're in power.

The logic is: If these agents will spy and turn against their **own people** then there is no way you can trust them to not turn on you.' VERY TRUE! The other shame is that **no tears** will be shed for these traitors to their own people.

PLAN B

The globalists, along with their controlled media, are well along in the promotion of their **PLAN B** program. Here it is: With the threat of nuclear war supposedly subsiding, the American people 'must have' a new Boogie Man!

ECOLOGICAL COLLAPSE: This phase involves the fraud of the **'imminent ecological collapse of the world.' This phase** is being promoted by those who were not able to completely destroy America with Marxism. These NWO Marxists have therefore started, or taken over, the various GREEN (environmentalist) parties.

Many of these environmentalists are rightfully labeled the 'WATERMELONS of the world'. That is to say, **green** on the outside, but **RED** (Marxist) on the inside. Many wonderful, good, well-intentioned Americans are being duped into assisting with this fraud. Sadly, some are our families and friends.

PLAN C

VISITORS FROM AFAR: This phase makes certain that few Americans escape the NWO program. How? By creating TOTAL PANIC. This is accomplished with 3 choices being offered to the gullible. The Globalists have 'suddenly' brought to light their long planned and well established 'UFO-Little-Devils-from-Outer-Space' CON, to strike utter fear in the hearts of all the people of the earth.

• The first choice: The subtle message to us, 'the masses' is that, if we don't go willingly and gently into global government, we will be 'eaten,' 'raped,' or become the experimental guinea pigs of some far-out evil 'SPACE CADETS.' And of course, you can't ask for assistance and protection from your own country's government because as we all have been told, **'no individual nation could possibly stand a chance in**

defense against this obviously "Superior" Race from space.' AH, but isn't it wonderful that 'salvation' is only a **one-world government** away?!?
• A second twist to this planned scenario is: These 'cute little space things' are our BOSOM BUDDIES; they bring tidings of good will, and come 'conveniently' to SAVE our world from the brink of total destruction! 'Isn't that precious?!'

In other words, this particular plan is to convince gullible Americans that anyone or anything (but that Jesus Christ 'guy'), WILL SAVE OUR WORLD!

Quite 'coincidentally,' these same 'funny little fellows' are also here to set up a UTOPIAN GLOBAL SOCIETY! Surprised?

• And the newest twist to the CON (to grab **religious** Americans that did not fall for the first two) is **that Christ Himself has sent these wonderful little 'UFO things,' in HIS place, to save us**. (Suggesting, we suppose, that Jesus Christ got busy and had to 'delegate.' And as soon as these 'wonderful' Space 'Disciples of Christ' get us all together in a New World Society, He (Christ) will be along to take over. Think of them as God's Secret Service advance team!) **Believe it or not**.

Is there something there? . . .'**OUT THERE**'? Absolutely! But, are **THEY** truly coming from 'out-there'? We are not to be told at this time, the truth about what these entities are, or who has **absolute** control over them. If we were told the truth we would never fall for their New World Order UFO Con.

It is sad to see coming true what the Scriptures foretold, namely, that some of the most spiritual and intelligent people in our world are being completely deceived by our government and 'spiritually enlightened' con men . . . (and women).

As foretold, it's happening before our eyes. **SHAME!**

In all seriousness, for anyone that does not believe that the UFO scare is a contrived fraud, it should be agreed that the wise position to take is on the side of caution. Consider it **possible** that those who promote the NWO plan are presently involved in a 'trial run' of all three of the above-described UFO scenarios. Such plans are being promoted by the Globalists, among those whom they consider to be the 'Wacko,' 'Radical,' 'Extremist,' Nationalist, Pro-American organizations, in order to test which scenario is more **acceptable**. For example, pick any one of the three scenarios below:

(1) The evil little devils from outer space, who will dissect, destroy, or devour us all.

(2) The sweet, funny, little COSMIC critters who, like our government, are only 'HERE TO HELP YOU'!

And lastly, for the gullible religious masses:

(3) The Space 'Disciples of God' bringing salvation to earthlings.

Indeed the Globalists care not which we choose. For they **all** lead to their NEW WORLD ORDER. Tell our brothers and sisters to just – Think about it!

(Some of the above information has come from those on the 'inside' and some from 'outside' of our government. It's nice to have our own agents inside their anti-American, anti-God cliques. What is that French word – TOUCHÉ'?)

*

ENEMY'S WORST NIGHTMARE

Pushing hard for their vision of a collectivist, 'utopian' New World Order, the behind-the-scenes controllers of Clinton, Bush and Perot undoubtedly have as their worst nightmare the prospect that you, their ENFORCERS, might awaken and return to the side of the People. Their plan cannot succeed unless you will **act without thinking**, not understanding how they will manipulate and **use** you to implement their plan for world conquest. Think about it: Whatever would they do if you, because of your strong patriotism, decide to **do nothing more** than uphold your oath of service and protection to the **People** of America and **JUST SAY 'NO'?** What **could** they do?

GREAT POWER IN YOUR HANDS

Have you ever desired great power? Dear Officer, Guardsman, Soldier, you already have **GREAT POWER!!** The secret enemies now in control of America know of your great power, even if you don't. That is why they will do anything to stop you from learning about your power. They cannot allow you to be awakened, because they know that if **you**, our nation's INTERNAL PROTECTORS, turn from being Enforcers of the SYSTEM, and return to being PROTECTORS of the PEOPLE, **there is no way they can pull off their coup**.

'MAKE YOURSELVES SHEEP AND THE WOLVES WILL EAT YOU'

This admonition is one given by our good brother and Right Honorable Top Cop, Professor James Jarrett of Phoenix. May it serve to lead us into the last main point we wish to leave with you – something we hope you will remember **above all else**.

As stated earlier, these treacherous Internationalists absolutely cannot accomplish their goals without the nation's Enforcers aiding & abetting their treasonous, unconstitutional mandates. But, they know also that for the most part if they can label certain patriotic Americans as 'criminals,' most of our fellow Police Officers will respond accordingly and treat them as such.  This is presently occurring in many areas. IRS Director, Donald Alexander, admitted to Congress 20 years ago, '**We now have so many regulations that everyone is guilty of some violation.**' Imagine what it's like today.

Another such attempt, is not only to label as 'criminals' those who refuse to relinquish or register weapons of personal defense, but also all those Americans who wish to exercise their Constitutionally-guaranteed right to dissent or speak out. Such as we officers have done in this publication and we do regularly through the *AID & ABET Police Newsletter*.

Keep in mind the following:

THERE IS NO WAY WE CAN LOSE IN THIS STRUGGLE TO SAVE OUR GREAT REPUBLIC, IF WE AMERICAN 'INTERNAL PROTECTORS' WILL DO WHAT WE **MUST** DO, AND THAT IS TO **UPHOLD OUR OATH OF OFFICE TO PROTECT OUR PEOPLE FROM ALL ENEMIES**.

It does sound simple, does it not?

SOMETIMES 'DISORDER' IS GOOD

As Protectors of the People, let us involve ourselves now and for the future in bringing **DISorder** to the 'New World Order' by committing ourselves this day alongside Thomas Jefferson to this wonderful pledge:

> **'I have sworn upon the altar of Almighty God eternal hostility against every form of tyranny over the mind of man.'**

For those of our brothers and sisters who have children, this very evening quietly steal in and look down into the small faces of your posterity and ask yourselves this question: Can there be a greater work than to save our nation for these little ones? Working together with our fellow countrymen, we can place the final **stake** through the heart of this Parasitic Beast that has gripped our once vibrant nation by the throat. In so doing, we will secure for ourselves, our children and grandchildren, a grand and

From the *Freedom Networker*, 'Chinese Police to be hired for America' (Vol. 1. No. 5, November 1994).

CHINESE POLICE TO BE HIRED FOR AMERICA

Among the world's top police forces are British trained police. The Royal Hong Kong police force is British trained and even has a few Brits in charge. Among these police are the Gurkhas of Nepal who are known as being among the most deadly fighters in the world.

The United States has agreed to hire the entire Royal Hong Kong police force to the extent that it can! These are all English-speaking police. But there's a catch: All these police are really working for INTERPOL (International Police) which has its primary base in England. If you refer to an updated Title 22, USC 263 (a) you'll find that federal enforcement agencies, FBI, DEA, ATF, etc. operate under the direction of INTERPOL, a British controlled organization.

Hong Kong is being turned over to the Chinese mainland in 1997. Under the new Crime Bill that was rammed through the Congress and Senate in August before the recess, nine billion dollars will be appropriated to hire 100,000 federal police who will be distributed throughout America in contrary [sic] of state sovereignty.

This is much like Texas sending police to Oklahoma without Oklahoma's having anything to say in the matter.

These are really Big Brother police. Scanners for New World Order microchipped (called transponders) identification cards are being erected on church steeples and high points. More to the point, video cameras are being installed on lamp posts and other vantage points all over the country.

Indeed, the New World Order is installing Big Brother more thoroughly than George Orwell described in his book, *1984*. Why not? We've made a lot of progress since 1984 haven't we?

You can look forward to highly armed police and control personnel under the New World Order that will treat you with hostility, that is, if we don't get active and take our country back pronto.

From the *Freedom Networker*, 'Federal Government Hiring 3,000 Detention Camp Guards!' (Vol. 1. No. 5, November 1994).

FEDERAL GOVERNMENT HIRING 3,000 DETENTION CAMP GUARDS!

Radical Christians and Kooky Patriots to be 'Detained.'

As broadcast on the Chuck Harder radio talk program, a patriot from Nebraska stated that he answered an ad to become a prison guard for the federal government.

The federal interviewer asked him questions on a person-to-person basis about his disposition. When the patriot inquired about what was expected of him, the interviewer freely responded that they were hiring 3,000 prison guards to administer a 40,000 prisoner detention camp facility. The interviewer, when asked who would be the detainees in this facility responded by saying those who are opposing the federal government under the Christian banner and patriots who are inciting others to oppose the federal government are going to be detained.

I regret that we have only this sketchy report at this time. Hopefully, we'll have full details later.

I can surmise that the guards to be hired will be only the executors of detention policies and be in direct contact with the 'detainees.' From reports, I know that these facilities have guard towers and sophisticated electronic detection equipment. I think that these 'guards' will not be armed. I surmise that well-armed 'UN' troops (really New World Order troops) will be on hand as a threat to those who contemplate escaping.

From the *Freedom Networker*, 'Trained as Traitors, Liars and Slavemasters!' (Vol. 1. No. 5, November 1994).

TRAINED AS TRAITORS, LIARS AND SLAVEMASTERS!

Did you know there are more than a million among us who are trained as traitors to the American constitutional way of life? Who are slated to be our slavemasters under the New World Order?

Who are trained to treat us as cattle unfit for self-determination and self-rule?

Who are trained to believe in their inherent superiority. Who fancy themselves as destined to rule and enslave us? Who are already in almost all positions of power in this country?

Who are these million plus would be New World Order slavemasters?

Let's not beat around the bush. They are members of secret societies called Skull and Bones, Freemasons (only the highest degree of Freemasonry also called Illuminized Freemasons are privy to the plot) and their many spinoffs and controllers like the Knights Templar, the Knights of Malta, Order of the Eastern Star (female counterparts), the Council of Foreign Relations, the Trilateral Commission, the Bilderbergers (who are mostly British and American and really run the show with prominent Jews as fronts in many areas, especially banking) and yet numerous other tightly controlled groups, foundations, institutes and closed organizations.

The subject for this discussion are the Freemasons, the single largest block and who touch our lives rather closely though we may be unaware of it. They're trained, mind you, to fabricate lies with a sense of self-righteousness and a straight face! They are modern Benedict Arnolds for, just as Benedict Arnold sold out his American compatriots to his British masters, these modern traitors have been trained by their mostly British and American super rich masters to abrogate every virtue with which humans are naturally endowed.[1]

While many of our country's founders were Freemasons, they were not quite the breed as are modern Freemasons. They were pre-Illuminati Freemasons. From the beginning of Illuminism, Freemasons were indoctrinated with notions of superiority and a one world government, a tyranny that would be presided over by the Freemasons in alliance with the super rich who are even more secretive yet. . . .

One of the symbols that tells us just how much the New World Order and the Freemasons already run the show is their *Great Seal* on the dollar bill showing the tip of a pyramid having an eye overlooking all. Its inscription is 'Novus Ordo Seclorum' meaning the New World Order. This might be said to be subliminal advertising to implant their Great Seal for conditioning us for things to come. Remember, they had to be in control of the U.S. Treasury and Mint to have the dollar bill redesigned and printed with this on it!

The Freemasons and other secret orders are already in control in America! They pretty much hold all the political positions of significance from the county level up through state and federal government. They are not only widespread in government at all levels, but in law enforcement, banking, the legal fraternity, all courts in the land, and touches [sic] our lives in yet other control positions.

Freemasons put up most of the candidates for both the Republican and Democratic parties. In short they and the New World Order win

no matter which 'faction' wins or loses.

How do you uproot this unholy arrangement operating under the guise of a democratically elected government? (As one reader always says: 'Don't just tell me about it. Get me out of the misery. What is the solution? How do we get ourselves out of this mess?')

You and your neighbors can begin your campaigns NOW to expose the Freemasons and their wicked schemes to enslave us all. They hate nothing more than exposure! Secret societies want to stay secret!

The new issues are: 'Are you a Freemason?' Don't expect an honest yes answer for they have been trained to lie. Freemasons are usually well known to be that by neighbors. They often boast about it. Discreet inquiries usually reveal this vital data about those who put themselves up or who are put up for local positions at the township, city and county levels.

The township, city and county levels is where we must take control! The big fish die when taken out of the ocean and subjected to a lot of little ponds. We must do this and soon! Remember, there is little time. The year 2000 is supposed to see the New World Order in place.

Again, the big issues in all elections are: Are any of the candidate Freemasons? Freemasons must be automatically exposed.

438

Their membership in a secret society alone is grounds for voting for a nonFreemason. They take an oath of office which they intend to violate at every turn. They keep ONLY their secret oaths to the brotherhood of Freemasons.

Freemasonry is a gigantic conspiracy against all of us! Of its nearly four million members, more than one million are 'illuminized' and in on the conspiracy to do what is outlined herein.

Freemasons are often ingratiating, gladhanders. But some have been notable scoundrels. Notable among them was Jacques De Molay who was burned at the stake for his efforts to undermine the French government and the Catholic Church. He was a notorious homosexual and had a marked taste for young boys. This is worth mentioning because Jacques is today a martyr among Freemasons and there is an order of Jacques De Molay! The most honored person in this order in America is President Bill Clinton! He is a Freemason and belongs to several secret societies.

Another scoundrel of the first order was J. Edgar Hoover. He was a 33rd degree Freemason. He was a noted homosexual and a transvestite. He refused to go after organized crime with the FBI inasmuch as Mayer Lansky and other Mafia participants had the goods on him. He did not want to be exposed.

J. Edgar Hoover loaded the FBI with Freemasons and Mormons who were founded along Masonic lines. Educate, educate, educate! You're due to be a slave! Get your neighbors and friends together for entertaining and informative discussions and video viewings about the ways to recapture America for ourselves.

Goethe has aptly said: 'None are more hopelessly enslaved than those who falsely believe they are free.' Of course, it bears observing that anyone who would enslave another is also a slave!

Note

1. Benedict Arnold was an American General who spied for the British during the Revolutionary War. His name is now synonymous in America with being a traitor.

From the Militia of Montana, *Taking Aim*, 'German Troops Training in New Mexico' (Vol. 4, No. 1 April, 1997).

GERMAN TROOPS TRAINING IN NEW MEXICO

Trainloads of German military equipment will soon be rolling through Texas on its way to the White Sands Missile Base in New Mexico for future training exercises.

91 shipping containers and 159 trucks and trailers full of equipment were off loaded from the Germania at the Port of Beaumont over the weekend of March 22-23. The Terrier also began unloading 692 trucks and trailers.

2,700 German Air Force, Amy and Navy Troops will be congregating in New Mexico with their equipment, mainly ground-to-air missile systems, for a training exercise called 'Operation Roving Sands.'

The German Air Force already leases space from Holloman, AFB near Alamagorda, NM for training purposes.

Reproduced from the Militia of Montana's *Enemies: Foreign and Domestic*.

From The Militia of Montana's, *Enemies: Foreign and Domestic* (1995).

PHOTOGRAPHIC EVIDENCE

In the USA now Soviet Flat Bed KAM AZ 5320

From Soviet green to UN white.

Here Now – Urban Assault

Here Now – US built 113s – Armored Personnel

Russian Tanks in West Texas, June 12 1994

Right here in the USSA

The New Jersey Militia, 'United Nations – Friend or Foe'. Pamphlet (n.d.).

UNITED NATIONS – FRIEND OR FOE?

The United Nations is praised by the media, the public school system, and the Federal Government as 'the last, best hope of mankind,' an institution that will bestow upon humanity 'freedom from war.'[i] But a look beneath the surface reveals something entirely different – a tyrannical, grasping and anti-human creature that seeks to largely depopulate the earth and permit the survivors to live only in restricted areas. Strong words perhaps. Let's examine the charges one by one – then you decide.

Tyrannical? The UN's Covenant on Human Rights is merely a list of privileges. Art. 13 permits freedom of religion 'subject to limitations prescribed by law.' Art. 14 grants the privilege to impart ideas 'subject to certain penalties, liabilities and restrictions.' Thus the concept of rights is foreign to the UN, which was deliberately designed so as to concentrate all power in an omnipotent government 'for the good of humanity.' Unfortunately unchecked power has been shown to result in fatal consequences, in accordance with the 'Power Principle: power kills and absolute power kills absolutely.'[ii]

Grasping? The UN has already laid claim to 43.6 million acres in the U.S. under the Biosphere Reserve Program. It has also designated the Wildlands Project as the model for 'biological diversity.'[iii] That project, promoted by a board member of the Sierra Club, is working to return 'at least 50 percent' of America to 'core wilderness areas' where human activity is barred.[1] Core wilderness areas are to be connected by miles-wide corridors surrounded by 'buffer zones' in which limited human activity may be permitted. In both the core areas and buffer zones 'the collective needs of non-human species must take precedence over the needs and desires of humans.' Thus human habitat will be mainly confined to 25 percent of the land. For now the UN is content with the other 75 percent.

Anti-human? In 1947 Julian Huxley, the first Director-General of the UN Educational, Scientific and Cultural Organization, wrote, 'Thus even though . . . any radical eugenic policy will be for many years politically and psychologically impossible, it will be important for UNESCO to see that

444

. . . the public mind is informed of the issues at stake so that much that now is unthinkable may at least become thinkable.'[iv] – In other words the 'educational' arm of UNESCO must condition the public to accept the idea that life and death decisions should be made by the UN.

In a 1994 UNESCO publication Jacques Cousteau stated: 'It's terrible to have to say this. World population must be stabilized and to do that we must eliminate 350,000 people per day. This is so horrible to contemplate that we shouldn't even say it.'[v] – Thus authoritarian people hiding behind an environmental mask wish to reduce the population by 125,000,000 per year. To put this in perspective governments in this century have murdered 169 million people,[vi] exclusive of battle dead, or 1.7 million per year on average. The UN's 'scientific' arm is promoting the elimination of sixty-five times that number for an indefinite period! Will our families be among them?

An indication of the UN's pitilessness was its 1990-96 ban on Iraqi oil sales. Denied the money with which to purchase food and medicine an estimated 30,000 Iraqi children died per month. Not quite Cousteau's 350,000 a day, but a start.

Who will protect the people from this monstrosity?

The Federal government? You decide: the Department of the Interior, USAID, the IMF and World Bank (both US-funded) all work hand in glove with the UN; the State Department alone has transferred $95.3 billion to that body, as of 1993. – The armed forces, won't they protect the people? No, for they are to be disarmed and replaced by a UN Peace Force (standing army),[vii] in fact U.S. soldiers are taking orders today from a Finnish UN general in Macedonia. – The National Guard? Totally federalized, it has been used against the people, as at Kent State where guardsmen killed four students.[2] – The police? Federal police have remorselessly killed scores of peaceable Americans; local police can be federalized, as were the Texas Rangers during the Waco incident.

If the government, the armed forces, the National Guard and the police either will not or cannot protect the people, who will?

"We Defend Their Freedom"

Don't Let That Shadow Touch Them
Defend the Militia!

New Jersey Militia Notes

(i). Department of State Publication 7277, Freedom from War: The United States Program for General and Complete Disarmament in a Peaceful World, 1961.
(ii). R.J. Rummel, Death by Government, xvi.
(iii). UN Environmental Programme, Global Biodiversity Assessment, Sect. 10.4.
(iv). William F. Jasper, Global Tyranny . . . Step by Step, 16 5.
(v). UNESCO Courier, Nov. 1994, 13 A.
(vi). R.J. Rummel, Death by Government, 4.
(vii). Freedom from War, 10.

Editor's Notes

1. The Sierra Club is an environmental campaign group.
2. During a demonstration against the Vietnam War at Kent State University in Ohio in May 1970, National Guard troops opened fire killing four and wounding eleven students. See, for example, William J. Chafe, *Unfinished Journey: America Since World War II* (New York, Oxford University Press, 1995), 406–7.

PREPARING FOR Y2K – THE STATE OF THE NATION REASSESSED

This final selection of militia texts begins with another lament for America in the form of Carolyn Hart's poem for the Missouri 51st Militia, 'I Can Feel My Country Dying'. Two views on the impeachment trial of President Clinton are then presented. In the first, the New Jersey Militia awards the President the 'Pettifogger of the Year Award', and in the second Kay Sheil reflects on what the outcome of the trial says about Americans' values and the example it sets for her granddaughter's generation. Donald Doyle, spokesman for the Virginia Citizens Militia, next offers his views on American involvement in Kosovo. We conclude with the militias concerns about the year 2000. A press release from the Northern Michigan Regional Militia announces the 'regathering' of militia units to combat the expected 'chaos' of Y2K; Norman Olson then speculates on just how bad things might be in his essay 'Militias and Y2K'; and finally the Virginia Citizens Militia offer some practical suggestions on preparing for the Millennium.

Carolyn D. Hart, the Missouri 51st Militia, 'I Can Feel My Country Dying'. Pamphlet (1999).

I CAN FEEL MY COUNTRY DYING!

I can feel my country dying.
I feel its death throes every day.
Our liberty is fading
As freedom slowly loses its way.

I can feel my country dying
As its young are sent to war
By a cowardly one-worlder
Who refused to go before.

I can feel my country dying
As its Bill of Rights is torn apart
By greedy politicians
With power-hungry hearts.

I can feel my country dying.
Can you not feel it, too?
Can you feel the pain and terror
As the tyrant comes to view?

Thank God, there are those who see it clear,
Who know the time is nigh
When they must rise above their fear
And reclaim what will not die.

The militia have seen the death throes.
They have come together as one
To defend our precious heritage
And to do what must be done.

The militia will fight to restore liberty.
It will live to bring it back.

The militia will not hesitate
To take up from others the slack.

The militia will defeat the tyranny.
It will bring freedom back to this land.
For they know it is better to lose one's life
Than to live without making a stand.

From the *New Jersey Militia Newsletter*, 'Pettifogger of the Year Award' (Vol. 3, No. 5, November 1998).

PETTIFOGGER OF THE YEAR AWARD

A Pettifogger is someone who **'engages in legal trickery, argues about unimportant details,'** particularly **'a petty, quibbling, unscrupulous lawyer,'** according to the dictionary. President Clinton expounded on 'unimportant details' with great clarity of mind before the Grand Jury, but couldn't remember much on the important issues.

After listening to Clinton's 'legal definition' of sex with Monica Lewinsky before Starr's Grand Jury, we are forced to concede that Clinton wins the Pettifogger of the Year Award. Clinton's skill in the art of pettifoggery is truly remarkable. As one viewer of *The O'Reilly Factor* on the Fox News Network quipped: **'Damn it! All these years I thought I was having great sex only – to find out I wasn't having sex at all!'**

Clinton's lack of memory, if real, borders on Alzheimer's. Here's a breakdown of his answers before Starr's Grand Jury:

'I don't remember' (54 times)
'I don't recall' (15 times)
'I didn't remember' (8 times)
'I have no recollection' (4 times)
'I just don't remember' (4 times)
'I couldn't remember'(3 times)
'I don't have any memory' (3 times)
'I've tried to remember' (2 times)
'I don't necessarily remember' (2 times)
'I have no specific memory' (2 times)
'I honestly don't remember' (2 times)
'I don't have an independent memory' (1 time)
'I certainly don't remember' (1 time)
'My memory is not clear'(1 time)
'I may have been confused in my memory'(1 time)
'I just don't recall' (1 time)
'I don't have the memory that you assume that I should' (1 time)
'I literally don't remember' (1 time)
'I can't possibly remember' (1 time)
'I honestly tried to remember' (1 time)

Note: You'd have to go to a rest home to get similar responses as these.

The Quote of the Year goes to Rep. Dick Armey. When asked if he would resign if he were in President Clinton's place, he said: 'If I were in the President's place I would not get a chance to resign. I would be lying in a pool of my own blood hearing Mrs. Armey standing over me saying, "How do I reload this damn thing?"'

Kay Sheil, 'Out of the Mouths of Babes'. First published by the Missouri 51st Militia, *Necessary Force* (March 1999).

Necessary Force

So! The 'trial of the century' is a done deal and Bill Clinton is still in the White House. Now the media, with the aid of their political experts and consultants, are excitedly stripping the last of the meat and picking the bones of the carcasses to 'fairly and without any bias' tell us who were the winners and the losers. Of course, anyone who reads this publication already knows who lost. It's US, THE AMERICAN PEOPLE, WE ARE THE LOSERS! When equal justice for all was not applied equally, we all became losers.

I believe the pollsters were accurate when they reported that the majority of Americans think Clinton is doing a good job as president and tying his popularity to the economy. This underlines the sad fact that too many Americans believe the President runs this country like a CEO runs a major corporation. It is disheartening to realize that most of them don't understand that it's us, all of us, the plain old everyday Americans, who are responsible for creating our so-called booming economy.

How sad for America when there are so many who think that this is the best that it can ever be in our country. How horrible for America when so many say they have no respect for or trust in Bill Clinton and that they believe all the charges brought by the House of Representatives are true. Even so, they say, they are willing to put Bill Clinton above the law and have him remain in office to keep the economy booming because they falsely believe that their future has to be controlled by the person in the White House. How sorrowful for us, for all Americans and people everywhere who are devoted to the concept of equal justice for all. How sad when so many Americans are willing to settle for so little when they could have it all: individual freedom and liberty, equal justice for all and a booming economy to boot.

All this brings me to a conversation I had a short time ago with my 17-year-old granddaughter, Brandi. Among other things, we talked about the President's behavior. Brandi was showing me an assignment she was required to do for one of her classes a few weeks ago. She was to decide on which side of the impeachment issue she stood and then write a thesis using quotes from recent publications to support her thesis. I asked her what her friends and classmates were saying about the scandal. Brandi said, 'Some of the kids thought what the President did was okay and thought he was being unfairly punished, but most of us think he is a sleazy jerk. My friends and I think he is an embarrassment and should be removed from office.'

Since Brandi will be eligible to vote in 2000, I asked her if she and her friends were planning to vote. She said she would vote and some of her friends would be voting. Brandi said the problem would be voting for the candidate 'they had the least dislike for.' When I asked why they would choose a candidate in that way, she said, 'Well, we really don't think there is much of a difference between the Republicans and Democrats because neither party seems really interested in changing things to make our lives better and return our freedoms.' Brandi went on to say, 'I and a lot of my friends are libertarians but we don't think a libertarian will ever be elected as President because the Republicans and Democrats have total control of the media because of how much money it takes to be elected. They can raise and spend so much money they just buy what they want.'

Brandi said that her generation, the one following Generation X, is being called the 'NEXT' generation. She and other members of her generation resent being the ones who will be responsible for paying off all the debt incurred by previous generations. Brandi wants to know, 'Just how are people my age supposed to be able to pay off those debts, provide social security for the baby boomers and have anything left for ourselves?' Brandi says the NEXT generation is growing weary of big government and she hears a lot of talk about anarchy from people her age. 'A lot of kids are saying, why don't we just do away with the government.'

Brandi and others her age think government has failed to deliver and has become a parasite on their futures. I think they're all too right. The possibility that members of the NEXT Generation will be called upon to have to literally wage war to regain their lost liberties looms over their future. I can only hope we, the older generations, can educate, nourish and protect the NEXT generation until they are ready for the task. I pray they will be loyal patriots committed to the ideals upon which our country was founded.

From the Virginia Citizens Militia, *Southern Ranger*, 'Kosovo' (April-May, 1999).

KOSOVO

AS A PATRIOT AND MILITIA MEMBER I WAS OPPOSED TO U.S. FORCES BEING INVOLVED IN THE BALKANS. NO DECLARATION OF WAR HAS BEEN DECLARED (AS USUAL) AND THE BALKANS ARE NOT A THREAT TO OUR NATIONAL SECURITY. THE WORLD IS NOT, AND WILL NOT BE, A PERFECT PLACE. AMERICA IS NOT THE POLICEMAN OF THE WORLD !!!

AS A CHRISTIAN I'M DEEPLY CONCERNED ABOUT THE SUFFERING OF THE CIVILIANS OF THE KOSOVO REGION. AN ELDERLY BRITISH WOMAN TOLD ME WHO, AS A CHILD, SPENT 1940 IN THE LONDON SUBWAYS DURING THE BLITZ PRAYING FOR HER OLDER BROTHER WHO WAS AN R.A.F. PILOT OVER HEAD *'HERE WE GO AGAIN WITH ANOTHER HITLER THE SERBS HAVE GOT TO BE STOPPED !!'* WELL THE SERBS ARE A THIRD STRING BUNCH OF NAZI WANNABEES. I WORK WITH REFUGEE RELIEF OUT OF ROANOKE AND I'VE WORKED WITH FAMILIES FROM BOSNIA AND CROATIA AND I'VE HEARD SOME TRULY HORRIBLE STORIES FIRST HAND ABOUT THE SERBS.

THE EUROPEANS ARE A JOKE, THIS IS IN THEIR OWN BACKYARD BUT THE U.S. (AS USUAL) HAS TO LEAD THE CHARGE. THE PROBLEM IS WE DON'T HAVE THE CAVALRY THAT WE HAD IN 1990 DURING THE BUILD-UP STAGE OF OPERATION DESERT SHIELD. THANKS TO MASSIVE MILITARY BUDGET CUTTING FROM THE CLINTON ADMINISTRATION THROUGHOUT THE 90'S WE CAN'T HAVE A GROUND WAR EVEN IF WE WANTED ONE. OUR SUPPLY OF CONVENTIONALLY ARMED CRUISE MISSILES IS DOWN TO BELOW 100 AND IS NOT BEING REPLACED. WHAT DO YOU BET THAT STEALTH FIGHTER WRECKAGE IS BEING ANALYZED RIGHT NOW IN MOSCOW ?? WE ALSO HAVE 3 ARMY GUYS AS P.O.W.S WHO ARE BEING BEAT-UP ON A DAILY BASIS I'M SURE. I WONDER IF THEY WERE ARMED WHEN SURROUNDED BY THAT SERB PATROL ?? PLEASE KEEP THEM IN YOUR PRAYERS AND THEIR FAMILIES.

CLINTON LOVES THIS I'M SURE SINCE IT PUTS CHINAGATE,

FILEGATE, ETC. ON THE BACKPAGES OF THE NEWSPAPERS. AL GORE SAID IT WAS TERRIBLE OVER THERE FOR POLICE IN BLACK UNIFORMS TO FORCE PEOPLE OUT OF THEIR HOMES AT GUNPOINT. AT FIRST I THOUGHT HE WAS TALKING ABOUT RUBY RIDGE THEN HE SAID THE SERBS, MAYBE THE SERBS GOT THEIR TRAINING FROM THE B.A.T.F. AMERICA'S VERY OWN GESTAPO.

AMERICA IS SOMEWHAT TO BLAME FOR THIS MESS BY IMPOSING AN ARMS EMBARGO ON THE WEAKER NEIGHBORS OF SERBIA SO I FEEL WE SHOULD GET INVOLVED. I THINK THE BEST THING THAT COULD HAPPEN IS FOR THE USAF/NATO TO COMPLETELY LEVEL 2 OR 3 OF THEIR BIG CITIES FORCING THEM TO BACK OUT OF KOSOVO.

WHAT I'M AFRAID WILL HAPPEN IS THAT SINCE WE DON'T HAVE THE CAVALRY TO DO THE GROUND WAR, THAT MEANS SOME MORE BOMBING AND THEN. . . 'AN AGREEMENT WILL BE REACHED,' THE FINAL CASUALTIES WILL BE NATIONAL SOVEREIGNTY, OUR HONOR, SOME AMERICAN LIVES, AND OF COURSE THE TAXPAYER WILL FOOT THE BILL.

THIS ALL GOES BACK TO PRIVATE OWNERSHIP OF GUNS. THE JEWS WERE ROUNDED-UP BECAUSE THEY DIDN'T OWN GUNS TO DEFEND THEMSELVES AGAINST THE NAZIS AND NOW IT'S THE PEOPLE OF KOSOVO'S TURN, WILL PEOPLE EVER LEARN ????

Norman Olson, Northern Michigan Regional Militia, Press Release (May 3, 1999).

PREPARE TO RESIST MARTIAL LAW

PRESS RELEASE – FOR IMMEDIATE RELEASE

Recall of Militias Signal Final Preparations to Resist Martial Law. Wolverine, MI (May 3) – Spurred by increasing threats of unbridled executive power by President Clinton and rumblings within Washington that Y2K could trigger chaos leading to martial law, commanders of militia units around America are regathering this summer and refitting for a showdown.

In Georgia, the Confederacy of Patriot States will hold an assembly on May 8th near Conyers, GA. The council is made up of militia leadership from units from the Southeastern States' Alliance. In Northern Michigan, Norman Olson, Commander of the Northern Michigan Regional Militia has issued a recall of militia for Armed Forces Day, May 15, 1999.

In a press release from his office in Alanson, Commander Olson states that the objective of the recall will be: 1. To recall and reassemble the militia in order to make it visible and distinctive once again; 2. To discuss probable actions of state and federal authorities resulting from Y2K and the associated financial collapse leading invariably to martial law and to discuss the militia's response to a declaration of martial law; 3. To determine what members need in the way of support equipment, arms, ammo, etc., and to seek ways of outfitting units quickly; 4. To discuss general strategies to help insure mutual support, maintain essential communication, and to keep vital transportation open; and, 5. To enlist new members.

Driving the increase of militia activity are the threats of the federal government's attempt to quell a domestic crisis by unleashing the US military against civilian targets. Around the country over the past year, citizens have been awakened in the night by sounds of explosions and gunfire only to find out that US military units were training in actual civilian neighborhoods. Recently, Defense Secretary William S. Cohen signed off on a plan to create a Joint Task Force for Civil Support, whose commander (soon to be chosen) would develop ways for the US military to aid federal agencies in 'time of domestic crisis.' Olson and other militia commanders see this rising military activity, and the blending of US military and federal agency assets, as an indicator that martial law has been planned.

'With the declaration of martial law will come a severe loss of individual rights. We expect restrictions of travel, speech, and association under the guise of attempting to restore law and order,' Olson explained. 'We anticipate confiscation of privately owned supplies and the arrest and prosecution of anyone not complying with federal martial law. But we will not, must not, submit to martial law. We are Americans! We've dealt with hardship and danger from the day the Pilgrims walked off the Mayflower. We are not going to submit to tyrants! We expect to have a difficult time and we will probably suffer through hardship, but we must remain free Americans suffering together. Resistance may mean open armed conflict, but so be it!'

Olson states however that preparation to resist martial law is not a call to start shooting or to retreat to the wilderness. 'The meltdown of our society is beginning despite a mood that all is well. We are not advocating offensive armed insurrection, but we are calling for coordinated and measured civil disobedience if the Bill of Rights is ignored in a time of civil unrest. We are putting the federal government on notice that our state and counties are sovereign and as far as Michigan is concerned, we will resist all efforts to crush us under the boot of federal martial law jurisdiction. I've put the Governor on notice of our intent and have asked for his help when the chaos begins. Either he includes the militia or he rejects our help. Either way, we are planning to take our stand on the side of liberty.'

The recall assembly of the Northern Michigan Regional Militia will take place at Fort Wolverine in Wolverine, Michigan. Invitations have been sent to all militia units within Michigan to attend.

The media has not been invited and will not be allowed entry into Fort Wolverine during this time.

END PRESS RELEASE

Norman Olson, Northern Michigan Regional Militia, 'The Militia and Y2K' (1999).

THE MILITIA AND Y2K

The militia was born out of fear – fear of the government. The same 'rebirth' is taking place because of fear – fear of the digital disaster facing the world. In less than 370 days a disaster of unparalleled proportions will strike the world. While some poo-poo the magnitude of the impact, experts themselves are growing concerned, some frightened, at the affect of the millennium bug.

Forecasters who seem to know speak in apocalyptic terms while politicians smile at the camera and reassure the constituents, saying 'we (the government) are ready.' One can only imagine why they omit a comment on the private sector. Private sector people are less optimistic, and most assuredly, they need to be.

Simply stated, the Y2K may be the greatest single disaster to hit the world since the Biblical flood of Noah. And it's the 'may be' that causes all the trouble.

As I see it, the greatest obstacles to preparing for Y2K are, 1. Reality, 2, Reference, and 3. Sufficient Fear. For many, just getting a mental grasp on what Y2K means is an impossibility. Many people have lived so long with their hat in their hand waiting for the government to provide their needs (and most of their wants), that their mental function is impaired. They reason, 'if there is a problem, trust the government to fix it. After all, they've fed, clothed, educated, housed, and entertained us our whole life, why should we worry?' This portion of the teeming mass of humanity is utterly lost and cannot be helped.

The second obstacle to Americans grows out of a lack of 'reference.' There are those who know in some measure that there is a problem ahead, but since they have no REFERENCE they cannot grasp the serious nature of the calamity. Recently the British House of Commons announced to the people of England that the Y2K millennium bug would cause significant disruptions. The Parliament told the people to prepare. The difference between telling Americans to prepare and telling Brits to prepare is different by virtue of what they suffered from 1940-1945. When Brits prepare, THEY PREPARE! Why? Because they have reference to a time when they once before prepared for disaster.

The third obstacle is 'sufficient fear.' If one is aware that peril lurks ahead, one must make provisions to face it. The level of provision is dependent on 'sufficient fear.' Unfortunately, only a small portion of people have sufficient fear to start preparing.

And herein lies the secret to survival. One must ACT on ones fear for survival to work.

The militia was born in a time when the fear of the government brought people with sufficient fear together to form a defensive group ABLE to repel the threat. As Y2K approaches, people are again coming together in groups to discuss the means and ways of surviving a 'worse case scenario.' Talk to them about the millions who still doubt that Y2K is dangerous and they'll ignore you. They no longer want to argue about the issue. They have moved from doubters to people who are sufficiently afraid to frightened people who are really doing something.

The militia will serve a vital part in survival. As we move into 1999, we can expect the silent federal government to speak about Y2K. When it does, it will announce to the millions that a calamity of unimaginable proportions may be on our doorstep. The federal government will impose Executive Order 12919 to protect the country from itself. It will issue restrictions on buying gasoline, food stuffs, and dozens of other needful things. As people begin to feel the first pangs of fear, the government will step in to assuage those fears by announcing that FEMA and the Red Cross have everything under control and if people will just do as the government directs them, everything will be well.

Mistake!

Everything will not be well. The militia will not bow to martial law. Neither will many materialistic Americans be bound by a national martial law, especially if it restricts their ability to gorge themselves with food, fuel, and other material luxuries. Austerity isn't something that Americans will cotton to, certainly not after the DOW has rocketed to 9000 while gas has plummeted to 85 cents a gallon. So whether for a sense of patriotism and constitutionalistic ideal or for a sense of gluttonous excess, Americans will be unable and unwilling to 'tighten their belt' or give in to government agents dictating how, when, and how much one can buy.

War will break out. The haves will fight to keep what they have ferreted away. The government will fight against patriots who will not abide by martial law. The cities will turn into war zones with robbery and tribal warfare on virtually every block. Law and order will collapse as police will refuse to enter the cities. The law of the jungle will prevail. Frightened masses will move from the cities to the county only to be met by frightened people who will shoot to protect what they have. The government will collapse. The nations of the world will begin fighting and a global war will begin.

Speculation? Of course. But could it be possible that such a course of events will take place? Don't say 'no' so quickly. Nations such as France are dependent on nuclear power for nearly 80% of their power generation. The nuclear power plants will not be able to survive Y2K. What then? Add to that the other nations of Europe that are dependent on deep sea oil. The oil rigs, refineries, and transportation systems will fail. Hungry and frightened people will fight to stay alive.

While back in the US of A . . . The militia will call together communities to build defenses. Work will be delegated and assigned. People coming to the communities will be required to work. Soldiers of the government determined to take what we have will be met with armed force.

Virginia Citizens Militia, Y2K Policy Statement, (March 6, 1999).

Y2K POLICY STATEMENT

THERE IS A LOT OF CONFLICTING IDEAS ABOUT HOW BAD THE COMPUTER PROBLEM WILL BE. THE VCM SUGGESTS YOU *HOPE FOR THE BEST AND PREPARE FOR THE WORST*. THE 2 BIGGEST CONCERNS ARE THE UTILITIES AND THE FEDERAL GOVERNMENT.

AMERICAN ELECTRIC POWER CLAIMS IT WILL BE Y2K READY BY JUNE OF 1999 AND WILL HAVE ALL ITS SUB-STATIONS MANNED ON NEW YEARS EVE TO FLICK OVER THE RESET BUTTONS IN CASE OF SHUT-DOWNS. WELL MAYBE THEY WILL BE READY AND MAYBE NOT. WE DO LIVE IN A WORLD THAT ALMOST ENTIRELY RUNS OFF OF ELECTRICITY. ENERGY SECRETARY BILL RICHARDSON HAS ALREADY STATED THAT SOME POWER GRIDS WILL GO DOWN.

SOCIAL SECURITY ADMITTED LAST WEEK THAT IT WILL **NOT** BE Y2K READY COME JANUARY. WHEN YOU THINK ABOUT WELFARE CHECKS,FOOD STAMPS, MILITARY CHECKS, RETIREMENT CHECKS, ETC. JUST A SMALL AMOUNT OF THIS NOT BEING PAID OUT COULD CAUSE BIG PROBLEMS.

THE MAIN CONCERN OF THE VIRGINIA CITIZENS MILITIA IS RIOTS/LOOTING BREAKING OUT BECAUSE OF THIS AND **THE FEDERAL GOVT. TAKING ADVANTAGE OF IT BY DECLARING MARSHALL LAW !!!! [sic]**

DECLARING MARSHALL LAW BASICALLY DOES AWAY **WITH ALL OF OUR CONSTITUTIONAL RIGHTS AND TURNS AMERICA INTO A POLICE STATE !!!** POLITICIANS IN CANADA AND ENGLAND ARE NOW PUBLICLY DISCUSSING MARSHALL LAW.

ALL NATIONAL GUARD UNITS ACROSS AMERICA WILL GO ON ALERT IN MAY IN PREPARATION FOR THE BIG ALERT IN DECEMBER. GUARD UNITS WILL RECEIVE 2 MONTHS PAY IN DECEMBER, SO THEY WON'T FORGET TO SHOW UP FOR DUTY IN JANUARY.

AT A GOVERNORS' CONFERENCE IN WILLIAMSBURG RECENTLY GOV. JIM GILMORE STATED 'ALL ANTI-TERRORISM ACTIVITIES MUST STAY WITHIN CONSTITUTIONAL SAFEGUARDS. THE RIGHTS OF THE INDIVIDUAL MUST BE PROTECTED, *THANK YOU GOV. GILMORE ! ! !*

READ UP ON Y2K ALL THAT YOU CAN AND I STRONGLY RECOMMEND YOU START WITH THE APRIL 99 EDITION OF AMERICAN SURVIVAL GUIDE.

*

VIRGINIA CITIZEN'S MILITIA
RECOMMENDED <u>MINIMUM</u> REQUIREMENTS FOR Y2K

REMEMBER THE STORY OF THE ANT AND THE GRASSHOPPER. THE ANT WORKED HARD ALL SUMMER PUTTING AWAY FOOD FOR THE WINTER WHILE THE GRASSHOPPER SPENT THE SUMMER PLAYING ? WHEN WINTER CAME AND FOOD WAS SCARCE THE GRASSHOPPER WENT TO THE ANT AND ASKED FOR FOOD BUT THE ANT SAID 'YOU PLAYED WHILE I WORKED AND I DON'T HAVE ENOUGH FOOD FOR TWO MOUTHS.' THEN HE CLOSED THE DOOR ! ! !

1) DON'T BUY ANY SO-CALLED Y2K PREPAREDNESS BOOKS OR VIDEO'S. STEER CLEAR OF THOSE TRYING TO MAKE A BUCK OFF OF Y2K. YOU'LL NEED THE MONEY FOR OTHER THINGS.

2) START PUTTING BACK CANNED FOOD LIKE YOU NORMALLY BUY WHEN GROCERY SHOPPING. GET 3 CASES EACH WEEK IN ADDITION TO YOUR REGULAR GROCERIES. STAY AWAY FROM THE EXOTIC FREEZE DRIED 10 YEAR SHELF LIFE STUFF.

3) WHEN YOU FINISH WITH A GALLON MILK JUG WASH IT OUT WITH HOT SOAPY WATER,LET IT AIR DRY,THEN FILL IT UP WITH TAP WATER. PUT A DROP OF NON-SCENTED BLEACH INSIDE OF EACH JUG.

4) GET STOCKED UP ON ANY SERIOUS PRESCRIPTION MEDICATIONS YOU AND YOUR FAMILY MAY BE TAKING (3 MONTHS WORTH).

5) GET AN ALTERNATE HEAT & COOKING SOURCE FOR YOUR

HOME. A PROPANE HEATER IS MY CHOICE ESPECIALLY IF YOU ALREADY HAVE A GAS GRILL. A WOOD STOVE IS ONLY GOOD IF YOU HAVE A HEALTHY SUPPLY OF WOOD. STAY AWAY FROM KEROSENE HEATERS. THEY STINK AND YOU CAN'T LEAVE THEM RUNNING WHILE YOU'RE ASLEEP.

6) HAVE A FIREARM FOR ALL THE RESPONSIBLE' ADULT MEMBERS OF YOUR HOUSEHOLD. IF YOU DON'T HAVE ONE THEN GET ONE AND ALSO GET SOME HOME FIREARM DEFENSE TRAINING FROM YOUR LOCAL GUN STORE/CLUB. I RECOMMEND A LADYSMITH 38-357 FOR THE WOMEN.

7) HAVE A FEW 'Y2K DRILLS' IN YOUR HOME. THROW THE CIRCUIT BREAKER IN YOUR HOUSE AND GO WITHOUT POWER FOR 12 HOURS THEN NEXT TIME DO IT FOR 24 HOURS THEN DO IT FOR A WHOLE WEEKEND. THIS WILL GIVE YOU A TASTE OF WHAT IT WILL BE LIKE. THIS IS ESPECIALLY GOOD FOR GETTING YOUR CHILDREN USED TO NOT HAVING POWER. CARRY A PAD AND PENCIL WITH YOU TO MAKE NOTES ABOUT WHAT YOU DISCOVER YOU'LL NEED LIKE: CANDLES, FLASHLIGHTS AND LOTS OF BATTERIES, LAMPS, ETC.

8) GET WITH YOUR FAMILY/FRIENDS, AND START PREPARING **NOW** ! ! !

FOLKS THIS IS A SIMPLE YET INEXPENSIVE WAY TO DEAL WITH Y2K. **REMEMBER IT'S YOUR RESPONSIBILITY TO TAKE CARE OF YOUR FAMILY NOT THE GOVERNMENT'S.** *BE AN ANT NOT A GRASSHOPPER !!!!*

BIBLIOGRAPHY

Abanes, Richard, *American Militias: Rebellion, Racism and Religion* (Downers Grove, Illinois, InterVarsity Press, 1996).

Aho, James A., *This Thing of Darkness: A Sociology of the Enemy* (Seattle, University of Washington Press, 1994).
___, *The Politics of Righteousness: Idaho Christian Patriotism* (Seattle, University of Washington Press, 1990).

The American Jewish Committee, *Militias: A Growing Danger* (1995).

The Anti-Defamation League:
___, *Armed and Dangerous: Militias Take Aim at the Federal Government* (1994).
___, *Beyond The Bombing: The Militia Menace Grows* (1995).
___, *Special Report: Paranoia As Patriotism – Far-Right Influences on the Militia Movement* (1996).
___, *Vigilante Justice: Militias and 'Common Law Courts' Wage War Against the Government* (1997).

Barnett, Randy E. 'Guns, Militia, and Oklahoma City,' *Tennessee Law Review* (Vol. 62, No. 3, Spring 1995), 443–459.

Bell, Daniel (ed.), *The Radical Right* (New York, Doubleday & Co., 1963).

Bennett, David, *The Party of Fear: The American Far Right from Nativism to the Militia Movement* (New York, Vintage Books, 1995).

Bock, Alan W., *Ambush At Ruby Ridge: How Government Agents Set Randy Weaver Up and Took His Family Down* (Irvine Press, Dickens Press, 1995).

Bovard, James, *Lost Rights: The Destruction of American Liberty* (New York, St Martin's Press, 1994).

Braun, Aurel (ed.), *The Extreme Right: Freedom and Security At Risk* (Boulder, Colorado, Westview Press, 1997),
___, Michi Ebta, 'Right-Wing Extremism: In Search of a Definition,' 12–35.
___, Stephen Scheinberg, 'Right-Wing Extremism in the United States,' 55–83.

Burkun, Michael, *Religion and the Racist Right: The Origins of the Christian Identity Movement* (Chapel Hill, The University of North Carolina Press, 1994).
___, 'Religion, Militias and Oklahoma City: The Mind of Conspiratorialists,' *Terrorism and Political Violence* (Vol. 8, No. 1, Spring 1996), 50–64.

Chafe, William H., *The Unfinished Journey: America Since World War II* (New York, Oxford University Press, 1995).

The Coalition of Human Dignity, 'The American Militia Movement,' (1995).

Coates, James, *Armed and Dangerous: The Rise of the Survivalist Right* (New York, Hill and Wang, 1987, 1995).

Cooper, Marc, 'Montana's Mother of All Militias,' *The Nation*, (May 22, 1995), 714–721.

Corcoran, James, *Bitter Harvest: The Birth of Paramilitary Terrorism in the Heartland* (New York, Penguin, 1990, 1995).

Crawford, Alan, *Thunder On The Right: The New Right and the Politics of Resentment* (New York, Pantheon Books, 1980).

Cress, Lawrence Delbert, *Citizens in Arms* (Chapel Hill, University of North Carolina Press, 1982).
___, 'An Armed Community: The Origins and Meaning of the Right to Bear Arms,' *The Journal of American History* (Vol. 71, June 1984, No.1), 22–42.

Dees, Morris and James Corcoran, *Gathering Storm: America's Militia Threat* (New York, Harper Perennial, 1996).

Denning, Brannon P. and Glenn Harlan Reynolds, 'It Takes A Militia: A Communitarian Case For Compulsory Arms Bearing,' *William & Mary Bill of Rights Journal* (Vol. 5, Issue 1, Winter 1996), 185–214.

Dionne, E.J. Jr., *Why Americans Hate Politics* (New York, Simon & Shuster, 1991.)

Dobratz, Betty A. and Stephanie L. Shanks-Meile, *White Power, White Pride: The White Separatist Movement in the United States* (New York, Twayne Publishers, 1997).

Doskoch, Peter, 'The Mind of the Militias,' *Psychology Today* (July/August, 1995), 12–70.

Dowlut, Robert, 'Federal and State Constitutional Guarantees To Arms,' *University of Dayton Law Review* (Vol. 15, Fall 1989, No.1), 59–89.

Durham, Martin, 'Preparing for Armageddon: Citizen Militias, the Patriot Movement and the Oklahoma City Bombing,' *Terrorism and Political Violence* (Vol. 8, No. 1, Spring 1996), 65–79.

Dyer, Joel, *Harvest of Rage: Why Oklahoma City is Only the Beginning* (Boulder, Colorado, Westview Press, 1997).

Ehrman, Keith A. and Dennis A. Hennigan, 'The Second Amendment in the Twentieth Century: Have You Seen Your Militia Lately?' *University of Dayton*

Law Review (Vol. 15, No. 1, Fall 1989), 5–57.

Gavin Esler, *The United States of Anger: The People and the American Dream* (London, Penguin, 1998).

Finch, Phillip, *God, Guts, and Guns: A Close Look at the Radical Right* (New York, Seaview/Putnam, 1983).

Flynn, Kevin and Gary Gerhardt, *The Silent Brotherhood* (New York, The Free Press, 1988).

George, John and Laird Wilcox, *American Extremists: Militias, Supremacists, Klansmen, Communists and Others* (Amherst, New York, Prometheus Books, 1996).

Gibson, James William, *Warrior Dreams: Violence and Manhood in Post Vietnam America* (New York, Hill & Wang, 1994).

Glastris, Paul, 'Patriot Games,' *The Washington Monthly* (June 1995), 23–26.

Greider, William, *Who Will Tell The People: The Betrayal of American Democracy* (New York, Simon & Schuster, 1992).

Hainsworth, Peter (ed.), *The Extreme Right in Europe and the USA* (London, Pinter, 1993).

Halbrook, Stephen, *That Every Man Be Armed: The Evolution of a Constitutional Right* (University of New Mexico Press, Albuquerque, 1984).

Halpern, Thomas and Brian Levin, *The Limits of Dissent: The Constitutional Status of Armed Civilian Militias* (Amherst, Massachusetts, Aletheia Press, 1996).

Hancock, Peter, McVeigh's Lawyer Insists Others Unknown Were Involved In OKC Bombing,' The Kansas *Pitch Weekly* (December 24–30, 1998), 8–9.

Hart, Gary, *The Minutemen: Restoring An Army of the People* (New York, The Free Press, 1998).

Himmelstein, Jerome. L., *To The Right: The Transformation of American Conservatism* (Berkeley, University of California Press, 1990).

Hirsh, Alan, 'The Militia Clauses of the Constitution and the National Guard,' *Cincinnati Law Review* (Vol. 56, Part 3, 1988), 919-969.

Hoffman, Bruce, *Inside Terrorism* (London, Indigo, 1999).

Hofstadter, Richard, *The Paranoid Style in American Politics and Other Essays* (London, Jonathan Cape, 1966).

Horwitz, Tony, 'Run, Rudolph, Run,' *The New Yorker* (March 15, 1999) 46–52.

Jasper, William, 'The Rise of Citizen Militias,' *The New American* (February 6, 1995), 4–29.

Johnson, George, *Architects of Fear: Conspiracy Theories and Paranoia in American Politics* (Los Angeles, Jeremy P. Tarcher Inc., 1983).

Jones, Stephen and Peter Israel, *Others Unknown: The Oklahoma City Bombing Case and Conspiracy* (New York, PublicAffairs, 1998).

Keith, Jim, *Black Helicopters Over America: Strikeforce for the New World Order* (Lilburn, Georgia, IllumiNet Press, 1994).
___, *Okbomb! Conspiracy and Cover-up* (Lilburn, Georgia, IllumiNet Press, 1996).

Kelly, Michael, 'The Road To Paranoia,' *The New Yorker* (June 19, 1995) 60–75.

Kopel, David and Paul H. Blackman, *No More Wacos: What's Wrong With Federal Law Enforcement and How to Fix it* (Amherst, Prometheus Books, 1997).
___,'Clinton's Terrifying Response To Terror,' *The American Enterprise* (Vol. 6, July/August, 1995), 70–73.

Levinson, Sanford, 'The Embarrassing Second Amendment,' *The Yale Law Journal* (Vol. 99, 1989–90), 637–659.

Lewis, James R. (ed.), *From The Ashes: Making Sense of Waco* (Lanham, Maryland, Rowman & Littlefield, 1994).

Lipset, Seymour Martin and Earl Raab, *The Politics of Unreason: Right-Wing Extremism in America, 1790–1970* (London, Heinemann, 1971).
___, *American Exceptionalism: A Double-Edged Sword* (New York, W.W Norton & Co., 1996).

Madison, James, Alexander Hamilton and John Jay, *The Federalist Papers* (London, Penguin, 1987).

Mahon, John K., *History of the Militia and the National Guard* (New York, Macmillan, 1983).

Malcolm, Joyce Lee, *To Keep and Bear Arms: The Origins of an Anglo-American Right* (Cambridge, Harvard University Press, 1994).

Mariani, Mack, 'The Michigan Militia: Political Engagement or Political Alienation,' *Terrorism and Political Violence* (Vol. 2, No. 4, Winter, 1998), 122–148.

Merkl, Peter H. and Leonard Weiberg (eds.) T*he Revival of Right-Wing Extremism in the Nineties* (London, Frank Cass & Co. Ltd, 1997).
___, Leonard Weinberg, 'The American Radical right in Comparative Perspective,' 231–253.

The Montana Human Rights Network:
___, *A Season of Discontent: Militias, Constitutionalists and the Far Right in Montana* (1994).
___, *What To Do When The Militia Comes To Town* (1995).

Neiwert, David, *In God's Country: The Patriot Movement in the Pacific Northwest* (Pullman, Washington State University Press, 1999).

Newman, Stephen, *Liberalism At Wit's End: The Libertarian Revolt Against the Modern State* (London, Cornell, University Press, 1984).

Newsweek, 'Terror In America' (May 1, 1995), 14–30.

La Pierre, *Wayne, Guns, Crime, and Freedom* (Regnery Publishing, Inc., Washington, D.C., 1994).

Pipes, Daniel, *Conspiracy: How the Paranoid Style Flourishes and Where it Comes From* (New York, The Free Press, 1997).

Plotke, David, 'Against Government: The Contract with America,' *Dissent* (Summer, 1995), 350.

Pratt, Larry (ed), *Safeguarding Liberty: The Constitution and Citizen Militias* (Franklin, Tennessee, Legacy Communications, 1995).

Reavis, Dick J., *The Ashes of Waco: An Investigation* (New York, Simon & Schuster, 1995).

Reynolds, Glenn 'Upin Arms about a Revolting Movement,' the *Chicago Tribune* (January 30, 1995), 11
___, 'A Critical Guide To The Second Amendment,' *Tennessee Law Review* (Vol. 62, No. 3, Spring 1995), 461–512.

Ridgeway, James and Leonard Zeskind, 'Revolution U.S.A,' *Village Voice* (May 2, 1995), 23–26
___, *Blood in the Face: The Ku Klux Klan, Aryan Nations, Nazi Skinheads, and the Rise of a New White Culture* (New York, Thunder's Mouth Press, 1990).

Robins, Robert S. and Jerrold M. Post, *Political Paranoia: The Psychopolitics of Hatred* (New Haven, Yale University Press, 1997).

Rodgers, Daniel T., 'Republicanism: The Career of a Concept,' *The Journal of American History* (Vol. 79 No. 1 June 1992), 11-38.

Rose, Tricia, *Black Noise: Rap Music and Black Culture in Contemporary America* (London, Wesleyan University Press, 1994).

Sargent, Lyman Tower, *Extremism in America: A Reader* (New York, New York University Press, 1995).

Sherry, Michael, *In the Shadow of War: The United States Since the 1930s* (New Haven, Yale University Press, 1995).

Shy, John, *A People Numerous and Armed* (New York, Oxford University Press, 1976).

The Southern Poverty Law Center:
___, *Intelligence Report* (December 1994/ #76).
___, *Intelligence Report* (June 1995/ #78).
___, *False Patriots: The Threat of Anti-Government Extremists* (1996).
___, *Intelligence Report* (Winter 1997/ #85).
___, *Intelligence Report* (Spring 1997/ #86).
___, *Intelligence Report* (Fall 1998/ #92).

Spitzer, Robert J., *The Politics of Gun Control* (New York, Chatham House Publishers, 2nd edition, 1998).

Steinfels, Peter, *The Neo-Conservatives: The Men Who Are Changing America's Politics* (New York, Simon & Schuster, 1979).

Stern, Kenneth S., *A Force Upon the Plain: The American Militia Movement and the Politics of Hate* (Norman, University of Oklahoma Press, 1997).

Tanner, Mack 'Extreme Prejudice: How the Media Misrepresent the Militia Movement,' *Reason* (July, 1995), 42–50.

Tarbor, James and Eugene Gallacher, *Why Waco?: Cults and the Battle for Religious Freedom in America* (Berkley, University of California Press, 1995).

Time:
___, 'The Face of Terror (May 1, 1995), 24–57.
___, 'Enemies of the State,' (May 8, 1995) 22–31.
___, 'The Atlanta Massacre,' (August 9, 1999), 20–32.

U.S.News & World Report:
___, 'The Rise of Citizen Militias,' (August 15, 1994), 34–35.
___, 'An Epidemic of Fear and Loathing,' (May 8, 1995), 37–44.
___, 'Mainstreaming the Militia,' (April 21, 1997), 24–37.
___, 'The Secret FBI-Militia Alliance,' (May 12, 1997), 40–41.

Vankin, Jonathan, *Conspiracies, Cover-ups and Crimes* (Lilburn, Georgia, IllumiNet Press, 1996).

Weaver, Randy et al, *The Federal Siege At Ruby Ridge: In Our Own Words* (Mass Market Paperback, 1998).

Weinberg, Leonard 'On Responding to Right-Wing Terrorism,' *Terrorism and Political Violence* (Vol. 8, No. 1, Spring 1996), 80–92.

Wilcox, Laird, *Guide To The American Right* (Kansas, 21st ed, 1996).
___, *The Watchdogs: A Close Look at the Anti-Racist 'Watchdog' Groups* (1998).

Williams, David, C., 'Civic Republicanism And The Citizen Militia,' *The Yale Law Journal* (Vol. 101, 1991–1992), 551–615.

Wills, Garry, 'The New Revolutionaries,' *The New York Review of Books* (August 10, 1995), 50–55.

Wright, Stuart A. (ed.), *Armageddon In Waco: Critical Perspectives on the Branch Davidian Conflict* (Chicago, University of Chicago Press, 1995).

CONTACT ADDRESSES

A: MAINSTREAM CONTACTS

Editor's note: The following addresses are intended only to provide a starting point for those readers who wish to pursue further any of the issues raised in this book.

1) Monitoring Agencies

The American Jewish Committee: The Jacob Blaustein Building, 165 East 56 Street, New York, New York, 10022–2746 (www.ajc.org).
The Anti-Defamation League: 823 United Nations Plaza, New York, New York, 10017 (www.adl.org).
The Coalition for Human Dignity: PO Box 21266, Seattle, Washington, 98111 (chdpdx@aol.com).
The Militia Watchdog: www.militia-watchdog.org.
The Montana Human Rights Network: PO Box 1222, Helena, Montana, 59624 (mhrn@initco.net).
The Southern Poverty Law Center: 400 Washington Avenue, Montgomery, Alabama, 36104 (www.splcenter.org).

2) Newspapers and News Journals

The *Chicago Tribune*: 435 N. Michigan Avenue, Chicago, Illinois, 60611 (www.chicago.tribune.com).
The *Detroit Metro Times*: 733 St. Antoine, Detroit, Michigan, 48226 (www.metrotimes.com).
The Kansas *Pitch Weekly*: 3535 Broadway, Suite 400, Kansas City, Missouri 64111 (www.pitch.com).
The New York Times: 229 W. 43rd Street, 9th Floor, New York, New York, 10036 (www.nytimes.com).
U.S.News & World Report: 2400 N. Street, N.W. Washington DC 200037–1196 (www.usnews.com).
The Washington Monthly: 1611 Connecticut Avenue N.W., Washington DC, 20009 (www.washingtonmonthly.com).

3) Other Contacts

The American Civil Liberties Union: 125 Broad Street, 18th Floor, New York, New York, 10004–2400 (www.aclu.org).
The Cato Institute: 1000 Massachusetts Avenue, N.W. Washington DC, 20001–5403 (www.cato.org).
The National Rifle Association: (www.nra.org).
Laird Wilcox: Editorial Research Service, PO Box 2047, Olathe, Kansas, 66051.

4) Militias and Related Groups

*Editor's Note: These are the contacts for the militias and other related groups which have featured or have been referred to in this volume. Many other militia organizations exist and can be contacted through the 'links' pages of the websites noted below. See also the 'links' section of the Militia Watchdog's website 'www.militia-watchdog.org'. The mark * below indicates that the group is no longer believed to be in existence.*

The *Common Sense* newspaper: 7335 Ward Parkway, Kansas City, Missouri.*

Florida State Militia: 5033 Front Avenue, Stuart, Florida, 34997.

Gun Owners of America: 8001 Forbes Place, Suite 102, Springfield, Virginia, 22152 (www.gunowners.org).

Jews for the Preservation of Firearms Ownership: 2872 South Wentworth Avenue, Milwaukee, Wisconsin, 53207 (www.jpfo.org).

The Kansas Second Amendment Militia: PO Box 544, Spring Hill, Kansas, 66083.*

The Kentucky Riflemen Militia: PO Box 605, Brooks, Kentucky, 40109–0605.*

Media Bypass Magazine: PO Box 5326, Evansville, Indiana, 47716.

The Militia of Montana: PO Box 1486, Noxon, Montana, 59853 (www.montana.com/militiaofmontana/).

The Missouri 51st Militia: PO Box 182, Grain Valley, Missouri, 64029 (www.tfs.net/~sbarnett/51stweb.htm).

The New Jersey Militia: PO Box 10176, Trenton, New Jersey, 08650 (www.exit109.com/~njm/index.htm).

The Ohio Unorganized Militia: PO Box 44404, Columbus Ohio, 43204-4404.*

The Texas Constitutional Militia: 6900 San Pedro # 147–230, San Antonio, Texas, 78216 (www.constitution.org/mil/tx/mil_ustx.htm).

Unorganized Militia of California: Fort Bragg Unit, 18603 N. Hwy 1, Ste 377, Fort Bragg California 95437.*

Police Against the New World Order: HC 11, Box 357, Kamlah, Idaho, 83536.

Special Forces Underground: PO Box 47095, Kansas City, Missouri, 64188.

The Virginia Citizens Militia: PO Box 11851, Roanoke, Virginia, 24022 (www.city-online.com/cops/vcmilitia).

The Washington State Militia: PO Box 714, Deming, Washington, 98244.*

The White Mountain Militia: PO Box 1858, Lebanon, New Hampshire, 03766.*

INDEX